A·N·N·U·A·L EDITIONS

Educational Psychology

Sixteenth Edition

01/02

EDITORS

Kathleen M. Cauley
Virginia Commonwealth University

Kathleen M. Cauley received her Ph.D. in educational studies/human development from the University of Delaware in 1985. Her research interests center on applying cognitive developmental research to school learning. Currently, she is studying children's mathematical understanding.

Fredric Linder
Virginia Commonwealth University

Fredric Linder received an A.B. in American civilization from the University of Miami, Florida, an M.A. in psychology from the New School for Social Research, and a Ph.D. in educational psychology from the State University of New York at Buffalo. His research focuses on the values and cognitive learning styles of students.

James H. McMillan
Virginia Commonwealth University

James H. McMillan received his bachelor's degree from Albion College in 1970, an M.A. from Michigan State University in 1972, and a Ph.D. from Northwestern University in 1976. He has reviewed and written extensively in educational psychology.

McGraw-Hill/Dushkin
530 Old Whitfield Street, Guilford, Connecticut 06437

Visit us on the Internet
http://www.dushkin.com

Credits

1. Perspectives on Teaching
Unit photo—© 2001 by Cleo Freelance Photography.
2. Development
Unit photo—McGraw-Hill/Dushkin photo.
3. Exceptional and Culturally Diverse Children
Unit photo—© 2001 by PhotoDisc, Inc.
4. Learning and Instruction
Unit photo—McGraw-Hill/Dushkin photo.
5. Motivation and Classroom Management
Unit photo—© 2001 by Cleo Freelance Photography.
6. Assessment
Unit photo—© 2001 by Cleo Freelance Photography.

Copyright

Cataloging in Publication Data
Main entry under title: Annual Editions: Educational Psychology. 2001/2002.
1. Educational psychology—Periodicals. 2. Teaching—Periodicals. I. Cauley, Kathleen M., *comp.*; Linder, Fredric, *comp.*; McMillan, James H., *comp.* II. Title: Educational psychology.
ISBN 0–07–243336–1   370.15′05   82–640517   ISSN 0731–1141

© 2001 by McGraw-Hill/Dushkin, Guilford, CT 06437, A Division of The McGraw-Hill Companies.

Sixteenth Edition

Cover image © 2001 by PhotoDisc, Inc.

Printed in the United States of America   1234567890BAHBAH54321   Printed on Recycled Paper

Members of the Advisory Board are instrumental in the final selection of articles for each edition of ANNUAL EDITIONS. Their review of articles for content, level, currentness, and appropriateness provides critical direction to the editor and staff. We think that you will find their careful consideration well reflected in this volume.

Editors/Advisory Board

Staff

To the Reader

In publishing ANNUAL EDITIONS we recognize the enormous role played by the magazines, newspapers, and journals of the public press in providing current, first-rate educational information in a broad spectrum of interest areas. Many of these articles are appropriate for students, researchers, and professionals seeking accurate, current material to help bridge the gap between principles and theories and the real world. These articles, however, become more useful for study when those of lasting value are carefully collected, organized, indexed, and reproduced in a low-cost format, which provides easy and permanent access when the material is needed. That is the role played by ANNUAL EDITIONS.

Educational psychology is an interdisciplinary subject that includes human development, learning, intelligence, motivation, assessment, instructional strategies, and classroom management. The articles in this volume give special attention to the application of this knowledge to teaching.

Annual Editions: Educational Psychology 01/02 is divided into six units, and an overview precedes each unit, which explains how the unit articles are related to the broader issues within educational psychology.

The first unit, *Perspectives on Teaching,* presents issues that are central to the teaching role. The articles' authors provide perspectives on being an effective teacher and the issues facing teachers in the twenty-first century.

The second unit, entitled *Development,* is concerned with child and adolescent development. It covers the biological, cognitive, social, and emotional processes of development. The essays in this unit examine the issues of parenting, moral development, the social forces affecting children and adolescents, as well as the personal and social skills needed to cope with school learning and developmental tasks.

The third unit, regarding exceptional and culturally diverse students, focuses on the learning disabled, the gifted, and multicultural education. Diverse students require an individualized approach to education. The articles in this unit review the characteristics of these children and suggest programs and strategies to meet their needs.

In the fourth unit, *Learning and Instruction,* articles about theories of learning and instructional strategies are presented. The different views of learning, such as information processing, behaviorism, and constructivist learning, represent the accumulation of years of research on the way humans change in thinking or behavior due to experience. The principles generated by each approach have important implications for teaching. These implications are addressed in a section on instructional strategies, covering such topics as instructional methods, authentic instruction, and learning styles.

The topic of motivation is perhaps one of the most important aspects of school learning. Effective teachers need to motivate their students both

to learn and to behave responsibly. How to manage children and what forms of discipline to use are issues that concern parents as well as teachers and administrators. The articles in the fifth unit, *Motivation and Classroom Management,* present a variety of perspectives on motivating students and discuss approaches to managing student behavior.

The articles in the sixth unit review assessment approaches that can be used to diagnose learning and improve instruction. The focus is on how alternative assessments, such as performance assessments and portfolios, can be integrated with instruction to enhance student learning. Approaches to grading are also reviewed.

A feature that has been added to this edition are selected *World Wide Web* sites, which can be used to further explore the articles' topics. These sites are cross-referenced by number in the *topic guide.*

This sixteenth edition of *Annual Editions: Educational Psychology* has been revised in order to present articles that are current and useful. Your responses to the selection and organization of materials are appreciated. Please complete and return the postage-paid *article rating form* on the last page of the book.

Kathleen M. Cauley
Editor

Fredric Linder
Editor

James H. McMillan
Editor

Contents

UNIT 1

Perspectives on Teaching

Four selections discuss the importance of research and the value of scientific inquiry to the teaching process.

UNIT 2

Development

Six articles examine how social interaction in the classroom influences child and adolescent development.

The concepts in bold italics are developed in the article. For further expansion please refer to the Topic Guide and the Index.

UNIT 3

Exceptional and Culturally Diverse Children

Eight articles look at the problems and positive effects of educational programs for learning disabled, gifted, and culturally diverse children.

The concepts in bold italics are developed in the article. For further expansion please refer to the Topic Guide and the Index.

UNIT 4

Learning and Instruction

Twelve selections explore the
important types of
student/teacher interaction.

The concepts in bold italics are developed in the article. For further expansion please refer to the Topic Guide and the Index.

vii

The concepts in bold italics are developed in the article. For further expansion please refer to the Topic Guide and the Index.

UNIT 5

Motivation and Classroom Management

Eight selections discuss student
control and motivation
in the classroom.

The concepts in bold italics are developed in the article. For further expansion please refer to the Topic Guide and the Index.

ix

The concepts in bold italics are developed in the article. For further expansion please refer to the Topic Guide and the Index.

UNIT 6

Assessment

Four articles discuss the implications
of educational measurement for the
classroom decision-making process
and for the teaching profession.

The concepts in bold italics are developed in the article. For further expansion please refer to the Topic Guide and the Index.

This topic guide suggests how the selections and World Wide Web sites found in the next section of this book relate to topics of traditional concern to educational psychology students and professionals. It is useful for locating interrelated articles and Web sites for reading and research. The guide is arranged alphabetically according to topic.

The relevant Web sites, which are numbered and annotated on pages 4 and 5, are easily identified by the Web icon (◉) under the topic articles. By linking the articles and the Web sites by topic, this ANNUAL EDITIONS reader becomes a powerful learning and research tool.

TOPIC AREA	TREATED IN	TOPIC AREA	TREATED IN
Alternative Assessment	40. Teaching About Performance Assessment 41. Lessons Learned About Student Portfolios ◉ **29, 30, 31**	**Constructivism**	24. Constructivist Theory in the Classroom: Internalizing Concepts Through Inquiry Learning 25. Challenges of Sustaining a Constructivist Classroom
Behaviorism	23. Caution—Praise Can Be Dangerous ◉ **1, 11, 13, 14**	**Diffentiated Instruction**	26. Mapping a Route Toward Differentiated Instruction 27. Reconcilable Differences? ◉ **6, 9, 13**
Brain-Based Education	19. Brain Basics: Cognitive Psychology and Its Implications for Education 20. In Search of . . . Brain-Based Education 21. Educators Need to Know About the Human Brain ◉ **2, 3, 8, 9, 23, 24**	**Disabilities**	11. Does My Child Need Ritalin? 12. Good Questions to Ask: When a Child With a Developmental Delay Joins Your Class ◉ **15, 20, 28**
Character Education	20. In Search of . . . Brain-Based Education 26. Keeping in Character: A Time-Tested Solution ◉ **2, 3, 8, 9, 11**	**Discipline**	38. Salinas, California: Peace Breaks Out ◉ **26, 27, 28**
Child/ Adolescent Development	5. What Do We Know From Brain Research? 6. Play an Endangered Species 7. Re-Evaluating Significance of Baby's Bond With Mother 8. Self-Esteem and Beyond 9. How Well Do You Know Your Kid? 10. Truth About High School ◉ **11, 12, 13, 14**	**Diverse Students**	15. Goals and Track Record of Multicultural Education 16. Celebrate Diversity 17. Cultural and Language Diversity in the Middle Grades 18. Voices and Voces ◉ **15, 16, 17, 18, 19, 21**
Classroom Management	34. Moving Beyond Management as Sheer Compliance: Helping Students to Develop Goal Coordination Strategies 35. Teaching Students to Regulate Their Own Behavior 36. Using Classroom Rules to Construct Behavior 37. How to Defuse Confrontations ◉ **26, 27, 28**	**Early Childhood**	5. What Do We Know From Brain Research? 6. Play an Endangered Species 13. Meeting the Needs of Gifted Learners in the Early Childhood Classroom ◉ **1, 13, 14**
		Educational Issues	3. Schools and Curricula for the 21st Century: Predictions, Visions, and Anticipations 4. Standards Juggernaut 22. Ability and Expertise ◉ **9**
Cognitive Development	5. What Do We Know From Brain Research? 6. Play an Endangered Species ◉ **13, 14**	**Effective Teaching**	1. Year That I Really Learned How to Teach 2. Reflection Is at the Heart of Practice ◉ **24, 25**
Cognitive Learning	19. Brain Basics: Cognitive Psychology and Its Implications for Education 20. In Search of . . . Brain-Based Education ◉ **22, 23, 24, 25**	**Emotional Development**	7. Re-Evaluating Significance of Baby's Bond With Mother
		Family Structure	7. Re-Evaluating Significance of Baby's Bond With Mother 9. How Well Do You Know Your Kid? ◉ **1, 13, 14**

● AE: Educational Psychology

The following World Wide Web sites have been carefully researched and selected to support the articles found in this reader. The sites are cross-referenced by number and the Web icon (●) in the topic guide. In addition, it is possible to link directly to these Web sites through our DUSHKIN ONLINE support site at *http://www.dushkin.com/online/*.

The following sites were available at the time of publication. Visit our Web site—we update DUSHKIN ONLINE regularly to reflect any changes.

General Sources

1. American Psychological Association
http://www.apa.org/psychnet/
By exploring the APA's "PsychNET," you will be able to find links to an abundance of articles and other resources that are useful in the field of educational psychology.

2. Educational Resources Information Center
http://www.accesseric.org:81
This invaluable site provides links to all ERIC sites: clearinghouses, support components, and publishers of ERIC materials. Search the ERIC database for what is new.

3. National Education Association
http://www.nea.org
Something—and often quite a lot—about virtually every education-related topic can be accessed at or through this site of the 2.3-million-strong National Education Association.

4. National Parent Information Network/ERIC
http://npin.org
This is a clearinghouse of information on elementary and early childhood education as well as urban education. Browse through its links for information for parents.

5. U.S. Department of Education
http://www.ed.gov/pubs/TeachersGuide/
Government goals, projects, and grants are listed here, plus many links to teacher services and resources.

Perspectives on Teaching

6. The Center for School Reform
http://www.educenter.org
This is the home page of the Center for School Reform, self-described as a "not-for-profit, non-partisan research organization" focusing on K–12 education reform strategies. Click on its links about school privatization.

7. Classroom Connect
http://www.classroom.net
This is a major Web site for K–12 teachers and students, with links to schools, teachers, and resources online. It includes discussion of the use of technology in the classroom.

8. Education World
http://www.education-world.com
Education World provides a database of literally thousands of sites that can be searched by grade level, plus education news, lesson plans, and professional-development resources.

9. Goals 2000: A Progress Report
http://www.ed.gov/pubs/goals/progrpt/index.html
Open this site to survey a progress report by the U.S. Department of Education on the Goals 2000 reform initiative. It provides a sense of the goals that educators are reaching for as they look toward the future.

10. Teacher Talk Forum
http://education.indiana.edu/cas/tt/tthmpg.html
Visit this site for access to a variety of articles discussing life in the classroom. Clicking on the various links will lead you to electronic lesson plans, covering a variety of topic areas, from Indiana University's Center for Adolescent Studies.

Development

11. Association for Moral Education
http://www.wittenberg.edu/ame/
AME is dedicated to fostering communication, cooperation, training, curriculum development, and research that links moral theory with educational practices. From here it is possible to connect to several sites on moral development.

12. Child Welfare League of America
http://www.cwla.org
The CWLA is the United States' oldest and largest organization devoted entirely to the well-being of vulnerable children and their families. This site provides links to information about issues related to morality and values in education.

13. Guidelines for Developmentally Appropriate Early Childhood Practice
http://www.newhorizons.org/naeyc.html
Here is a 23-page excerpt from a report, edited by Sue Bredekamp, that covers every aspect of appropriate programs that serve children from birth through age 8, published on the Web by the National Association for the Education of Young Children.

14. The National Academy for Child Development
http://www.nacd.org
This international organization is dedicated to helping children and adults reach their full potential. Its home page presents links to various programs, research, and resources into such topics as ADD/ADHD.

Exceptional and Culturally Diverse Children

15. The Council for Exceptional Children
http://www.cec.sped.org/index.html
This page will give you access to information on identifying and teaching gifted children, attention-deficit disorders, and other topics in gifted education.

16. Global SchoolNet Foundation
http://www.gsn.org
Access this site for multicultural education information. The site includes news for teachers, students, and parents, as well as chat rooms, links to educational resources, programs, and contests and competitions.

17. International Project: Multicultural Pavilion
http://curry.edschool.virginia.edu/curry/centers/multicultural/papers.html
Here is a forum for sharing of stories and resources and for learning from the stories and resources of others, in the form of articles on the Internet that cover every possible ra-

cial, gender, and multicultural issue that could arise in the field of multicultural education.

18. Let 1000 Flowers Bloom/Kristen Nicholson-Nelson
http://teacher.scholastic.com/professional/assessment/100flowers.htm
Open this page for Kristen Nicholson-Nelson's discussion of ways in which teachers can help to nurture children's multiple intelligences. She provides a useful bibliography and resources.

19. Multicultural Publishing and Education Catalog
http://www.mpec.org
This is the home page of the MPEC, a networking and support organization for independent publishers, authors, educators, and librarians fostering authentic multicultural books and materials. It has excellent links to a vast array of resources related to multicultural education.

20. National Attention Deficit Disorder Association
http://www.add.org
This site, some of which is under construction, will lead you to information about ADD/ADHD. It has links to self-help and support groups, outlines behaviors and diagnostics, answers FAQs, and suggests books and other resources.

21. National MultiCultural Institute (NMCI)
http://www.nmci.org
NMCI is one of the major organizations in the field of diversity training. At this Web site, NMCI offers conference data, resource materials, diversity training and consulting service information, and links to other related sites.

Learning and Instruction

22. Education Week on the Web
http://www.edweek.org
At this page you can open archives, read special reports, keep up on current events, and access a variety of articles in educational psychology. A great deal of material is helpful in learning and instruction.

23. Online Internet Institute
http://www.oii.org
A collaborative project among Internet-using educators, proponents of systemic reform, content-area experts, and teachers who desire professional growth, this site provides a learning environment for integrating the Internet into educators' individual teaching styles.

24. Teachers Helping Teachers
http://www.pacificnet.net/~mandel/
This site provides basic teaching tips, new teaching-methodology ideas, and forums for teachers to share their experiences. It features educational resources on the Web, with new ones added each week.

25. The Teachers' Network
http://www.teachnet.org
Bulletin boards, classroom projects, online forums, and Web mentors are featured on this site, as well as the book *Teachers' Guide to Cyberspace* and an online, 4-week course on how to use the Internet.

Motivation and Classroom Management

26. Canada's Schoolnet Staff Room
http://www.schoolnet.ca/home/e/
Here is a resource and link site for anyone involved in education, including special-needs educators, teachers, parents, volunteers, and administrators.

27. Early Intervention Solutions
http://www.earlyintervention.com
EIS presents this site to address concerns about children's stress and reinforcement. It suggests ways to deal with negative behaviors that may result from stress and anxiety among children.

28. National Institute on the Education of At-Risk Students
http://www.ed.gov/offices/OERI/At-Risk/
The At-Risk Institute supports a range of research and development activities designed to improve the education of students at risk of educational failure due to limited English proficiency, race, geographic location, or economic disadvantage. Access its work and links at this site.

Assessment

29. Awesome Library for Teachers
http://www.neat-schoolhouse.org/teacher.html
Open this page for links and access to teacher information on everything from assessments to child development topics.

30. Phi Delta Kappa International
http://www.pdkintl.org
This important organization publishes articles about all facets of education. You can check out the online archive of the journal, *Phi Delta Kappan*, which has resources such as articles having to do with assessment.

31. Washington (State) Center for the Improvement of Student Learning
http://www.K12.wa.us/reform/
This Washington State site is designed to provide access to information about the state's new academic standards, assessments, and accountability system. Many resources and Web links are included.

We highly recommend that you review our Web site for expanded information and our other product lines. We are continually updating and adding links to our Web site in order to offer you the most usable and useful information that will support and expand the value of your Annual Editions. You can reach us at: *http://www.dushkin.com/annualeditions/*.

www.dushkin.com/online/

Unit Selections

1. **The Year That I Really Learned How to Teach,** Ranae Hagen Stetson
2. **Reflection Is at the Heart of Practice,** Simon Hole and Grace Hall McEntee
3. **Schools and Curricula for the 21st Century: Predictions, Visions, and Anticipations,** Weldon F. Zenger and Sharon K. Zenger
4. **The Standards Juggernaut,** Marion Brady

Key Points to Consider

❖ Describe several characteristics of effective teachers.

❖ How does reflection improve teaching?

❖ As we move into the twenty-first century, what new expectations should be placed on teachers and schools? What expectations will fade?

 **Links** **www.dushkin.com/online/**

6. **The Center for School Reform**
   http://www.educenter.org
7. **Classroom Connect**
   http://www.classroom.net
8. **Education World**
   http://www.education-world.com
9. **Goals 2000: A Progress Report**
   http://www.ed.gov/pubs/goals/progrpt/index.html
10. **Teacher Talk Forum**
    http://education.indiana.edu/cas/tt/tthmpg.html

These sites are annotated on pages 4 and 5.

The teaching-learning process in school is enormously complex. Many factors influence pupil learning—such as family background, developmental level, prior knowledge, motivation, and, of course, effective teachers. Educational psychology investigates these factors to better understand and explain student learning. We begin our exploration of the teaching-learning process by considering the characteristics of effective teaching.

In the first article, Ranae Hagan Stetson describes her experiences as a professor who returns to a first grade classroom to try out her ideas about student-centered instruction. Next, Simon Hole and Grace Hall McEntee describe one characteristic of effective teaching—reflection. They describe two protocols that teachers can follow to make reflection more useful.

Finally, we look toward the future and the educational issues that may ultimately change the teacher's role. The third article, "Schools and Curricula for the 21st Century: Predictions, Visions, and Anticipations," maintains that educational technology will dominate thinking about education. The authors discuss ways in which technology will change curriculum, teaching strategies, and schools in general. The fourth article, "The Standards Juggernaut," suggests that schools ought to be forward looking institutions. The author asks us to think more carefully about the goals of education and what should be in the curriculum to prepare students for the future.

Educational psychology is a resource for teachers that emphasizes disciplined inquiry, a systematic and objective analysis of information, and a scientific attitude toward decision making. The field provides information for decisions that are based on quantitative and qualitative studies of learning and teaching rather than on intuition, tradition, authority, or subjective feelings. It is our hope that this aspect of educational psychology is communicated throughout these readings, and that, as a student, you will adopt the analytic, probing attitude that is part of the discipline.

While educational psychologists have helped to establish a knowledge base about teaching and learning, the unpredictable, spontaneous, evolving nature of teaching suggests that the best they will ever do is to provide concepts and skills that teachers can adapt for use in their classrooms. The issues raised in these articles about effective teaching, and the issues facing teachers in the twenty-first century, help us understand the teaching role and its demands. As you read articles in other chapters, consider the demands they place on the teaching role as well.

The Year That I Really Learned How to Teach

Ranae Hagen Stetson

Ten years ago, I left my teaching position at the University of Nevada, Las Vegas, and returned to a 1st grade classroom in the Clark County School District. It was time for me to either "walk the talk" about child-centered, integrated-literacy instruction or never again preach to my university students how to do something I had never tried doing myself.

"No big deal," I told myself. "After all, I'm an experienced K–1 classroom teacher, almost finished with my doctorate in education, and armed with a thorough understanding of the research base supporting integrated-literacy instruction."

Reality Bites

As Nevada state law requires, I received a textbook for every child in every subject—306 textbooks in all! Somehow I was supposed to shovel this mountain of information into the minds of my 6-year-olds in the next nine months. How could we possibly get through these books and still study mammals, space, earthquakes, or the dozens of other topics that 1st graders are interested in learning? As I was repeatedly reminded throughout that year, the year-end tests would be on mandated curriculum, not on all that "other stuff"—the topics that interested the children.

The temperature was already close to 100 degrees when the children arrived. Each class had its number and a corresponding line painted on the

playground where teachers were to pick up their students. Decked out in my new red suit and high heels, I welcomed what seemed an endless line of excited and nervous faces. Suddenly, one child leaped out of line, wrapped both of his arms around my thighs, and began sobbing hysterically. After determining that he was neither bleeding nor near death, I asked him what was wrong. My heart broke as he shrieked between sobs that he *could not read.*

I thought of all the textbooks in my classroom and knew that I wouldn't be passing them out after all. Then I did a really stupid thing— I bent down to look into his eyes and told him not to worry. By the end of the day, I promised, he would be able to read. My distraught student, Trevor, clung to me as I finished making my way down the line. I berated myself: How could I have just made that promise to a child about whom I knew absolutely nothing? Frantic, I mentally reviewed my academic plans for the day.

No books changed hands that day as we popped popcorn and used our observations to write a language-experience story. We ate popcorn. We sang popcorn songs. We smelled popcorn before, during, and after popping. We measured equal portions of popcorn to eat. We created popcorn art. By the end of the day, we had read our popcorn story at least 15 times, and Trevor could read it all by himself. Whether or not he memorized the story didn't matter in the least to Trevor—or to me—because now he believed that he could read.

> Child-centered instruction does work. And best of all, the children are worth the effort it takes to make it happen.

Lessons Learned

The year was both the hardest and the most rewarding that I have ever had professionally. My class did study mammals, space, earthquakes, jungles, marine biology, and dozens of other topics. I began to understand more about how important the job of a classroom teacher really was. Classroom teachers are sometimes the only buffer between the children and the regulations that can hamper the learning process that they are supposed to help. Daily, I agonized whether I was doing the right thing by teaching the topics that the children were interested in studying. I was questioned by some of the more traditional teachers—the 2nd grade teachers in particular wanted to make sure that I covered volume 1 of the textbooks so that the children would be ready for volume 2 in 2nd grade.

I had unbelievable parental support, however. Parents loved the books that their children were creating, the stories that they were writing, and the knowledge of current topics that their children were developing. For example, we studied why the columns on the two-tier freeways in California collapsed in perfect symmetry with one another during a major earthquake. We looked at both sides of the tuna fish boycott that resulted in the dolphin-safe labels on the tuna cans. And when one of my students brought in a piece of the Berlin Wall, we studied that as well.

We never did make it all the way through volume 1 of the handwriting, the spelling, or the language-arts textbooks, but somehow my class's average on the year-end test was in the 90th percentile.

I now teach at a private, urban university in Texas. I am often deluged with the "Yes, buts" from my graduate and undergraduate students questioning the feasibility of implementing child-centered, integrated instructional practices. I happily play the videotapes of my 1st grade classes as I explain how I bucked the system. It can be done, I tell them. You will survive. Child-centered instruction does work. And best of all, the children are worth the effort it takes to make it happen.

Ranae Hagen Stetson is Associate Professor of early childhood education for the School of Education, Texas Christian University, TCU Box 297900, Ft. Worth, TX 76129.

Simon Hole and Grace Hall McEntee

Reflection Is at the Heart of Practice

The ordinary experiences of our teaching days are the essence of our practice. Using a guide to reflect on these experiences—either individually or with colleagues—is an entry to improving our teaching.

The life force of teaching practice is thinking and wondering. We carry home those moments of the day that touch us, and we question decisions made. During these times of reflection, we realize when something needs to change.

A protocol, or guide, enables teachers to refine the process of reflection, alone or with colleagues. The Guided Reflection Protocol is useful for teachers who choose to reflect alone. The Critical Incidents Protocol, which we developed through our work with the Annenberg Institute for School Reform at Brown University, is used for shared reflection. The steps for each protocol are similar; both include writing.

Guided Reflection Protocol

The first step in guided reflection is to collect possible episodes for reflection. In his book *Critical Incidents in Teaching: Developing Professional Judgement* (1993), David Tripp encourages us to think about ordinary events, which often have much to tell us about the underlying trends, motives, and structures of our practice. Simon's story, "The Geese and the

> **Guided reflection is a way to find the meaning within the mundane.**

Blinds," exemplifies this use of an ordinary event.

Step One: What Happened?

Wednesday, September 24, 9:30 a.m. I stand to one side of the classroom, taking the morning attendance. One student glances out the window and sees a dozen Canada geese grazing on the playground. Hopping from his seat, he calls out as he heads to the window for a better view. Within moments, six students cluster around the window. Others start from their seats to join them. I call for attention and ask them to return to their desks. When none of the students respond, I walk to the window and lower the blinds.

Answering the question What happened? is more difficult than it sounds. We all have a tendency to jump into an interpretive or a judgmental mode, but it is important to begin by simply telling the story. Writing down what happened—without analysis or judgment—aids in creating a brief narrative. Only then are we ready to move to the second step.

Step Two: Why Did It Happen?

Attempting to understand why an event happened the way it did is the

> **We all have a tendency to jump into an interpretive or a judgmental mode, but it is important to begin by simply telling the story.**

From *Educational Leadership,* May 1999, pp. 34-37.

beginning of reflection. We must search the context within which the event occurred for explanations. Simon reflects:

> It's not hard to imagine why the students reacted to the geese as they did. As 9-year-olds, they are incredibly curious about their world. Explaining my reaction is more difficult. Even as I was lowering the blinds, I was kicking myself. Here was a natural opportunity to explore the students' interests. Had I stood at the window with them for five minutes, asking questions to see what they knew about geese, or even just listening to them, I'd been telling a story about seizing the moment or taking advantage of a learning opportunity. I knew that even as I lowered the blinds. So, why?

Searching deeper, we may find that a specific event serves as an example of a more general category of events. We need to consider the underlying structures within the school that may be a part of the event and examine deeply held values. As we search, we often find more questions than answers.

> Two key things stand out concerning that morning. First, the schedule. On Wednesdays, students leave the room at 10:00 a.m. and do not return until 15 minutes before lunch. I would be out of the classroom all afternoon attending a meeting, and so this half hour was all the time I would have with my students.
>
> Second, this is the most challenging class I've had in 22 years of teaching. The first three weeks of school had been a constant struggle as I tried strategy after strategy to hold their attention long enough to have a discussion, give directions, or conduct a lesson. The hectic schedule and the need to prepare the class for a substitute added to the difficulty I've had "controlling" the class, so I closed the blinds.

There's something satisfying about answering the question Why did it happen? Reflection often stops here. If the goal is to become a reflective practitioner, however, we need to look more deeply. The search for meaning is step three.

Step Three: What Might It Mean?

Assigning meaning to the ordinary episodes that make up our days can feel like overkill. Is there really meaning behind all those events? Wouldn't it be more productive to wait for something extraordinary to happen, an event marked with a sign: "Pay attention! Something important is happening." Guided reflection is a way to find the meaning within the mundane. Split-second decision making is a crucial aspect of teaching. Given the daily madness of life in a classroom, considering all the options and consequences is difficult. Often, it is only through reflection that we even recognize that we had a choice, that we could have done something differently.

> Like a football quarterback, I often make bad decisions because of pressure. Unlike a quarterback, I don't have an offensive line to blame for letting the pressure get to me. While it would be nice to believe that I could somehow make the pressure go away, the fact is that it will always be with me. Being a teacher means learning to live within that pressure, learning from the decisions I make and learning to make better decisions.

Our growing awareness of how all events carry some meaning is not a new concept. In *Experience and Education* (1938), John Dewey wrote about experience and its relationship to learning and teaching: "Every experience affects for better or worse the attitudes which help decide the quality of further experiences" (p. 37). He believed that teachers must be aware of the "possibilities inherent in ordinary experience" (p. 89), that the "business of the educator [is] to see in what direction an experience is heading" (p. 38). Rediscovering this concept through the examination of ordinary events creates a fresh awareness of its meaning.

The search for meaning is an integral part of being human. But understanding by itself doesn't create changes in classroom practice. The last phase of guided reflection is more action oriented and involves holding our practice to the light of those new understandings.

Step Four: What Are the Implications for My Practice?

Simon continues:

> My reaction to the pressure this year has been to resort to methods of control. I seem to be forever pulling down the blinds. I'm thinking about how I might better deal with the pressure.
>
> But there is something else that needs attention. Where is the pressure coming from? I'm sensing from administration and parents that they feel I should be doing things differently. I've gotten subtle and overt messages that I need to pay more attention to "covering" the curriculum, that I should be finding a more equal balance between process and product.
>
> Maybe they're right. What I've been doing hasn't exactly been a spectacular success. But I think that what is causing the lowering of the

---

Guided Reflection Protocol (For Individual Reflection)

1. *Collect stories.* Some educators find that keeping a set of index cards or a steno book close at hand provides a way to jot down stories as they occur. Others prefer to wait until the end of the day and write in a journal.

2. *What happened?* Choose a story that strikes you as particularly interesting. Write it succinctly.

3. *Why did it happen?* Fill in enough of the context to give the story meaning. Answer the question in a way that makes sense to you.

4. *What might it mean?* Recognizing that there is no one answer is an important step. Explore possible meanings rather than determine the meaning.

5. *What are the implications for practice?* Consider how your practice might change given any new understandings that have emerged from the earlier steps.

blinds stems from my not trusting enough in the process. Controlling the class in a fairly traditional sense isn't going to work in the long run. Establishing a process that allows the class to control itself will help keep the blinds up.

Cultivating deep reflection through the use of a guiding protocol is an entry into rethinking and changing practice. Alone, each of us can proceed step-by-step through the examination of a particular event. Through the process, we gain new insights into the implications of ordinary events, as Simon did when he analyzed "The Geese and the Blinds."

Whereas Guided Reflection is for use by individuals, the Critical Incidents Protocol is used with colleagues. The goal is the same: to get to the heart of our practice, the place that pumps the lifeblood into our teaching, where we reflect, gain insight, and change what we do with our students. In addition, the Critical Incidents Protocol encourages the establishment of collegial relationships.

Critical Incidents Protocol

Schools are social places. Although too often educators think and act alone, in most schools colleagues do share daily events. Stories told in teachers' lounges are a potential source of rich insight into issues of teaching and learning and can open doors to professional dialogue.

Telling stories has the potential for changing individual practice and the culture of our schools. The Critical Incidents Protocol allows practitioners to share stories in a way that is useful to their own thinking and to that of the group.

Three to five colleagues meet for the purpose of exploring a "critical incident." For 10 minutes, all write a brief account of an incident. Participants should know that the sharing of their writing will be for the purpose of getting feedback on what happened rather than on the quality of the writing itself.

Next, the group decides which story to use with the protocol. The presenter for the session then reads the story while the group listens carefully to understand the incident and the context. Colleagues ask clarifying questions about what happened or why the incident occurred, then they discuss what the incident might mean in terms of the presenter's practice. During this time, the presenter listens and takes notes. The presenter then responds, and the participants discuss the implications for their own practice. To conclude, one member leads a conversation about what happened during the session, how well the process worked, and how the group might change the process.

The sharing of individual stories raises issues in the fresh air of collegial support. If open dialogue is not already part of a school's culture, however, colleagues may feel insecure about beginning. To gain confidence, they may choose to run through the protocol first with a story that is not theirs. For this purpose, Grace offers a story about an incident in the writing lab from her practice as a high school English teacher.

Step One: What Happened?

We went into the computer lab to work on essay drafts. TJ, Neptune, Ronny, and Mick sat as a foursome. Their sitting together had not worked last time. On their single printer an obscene message had appeared. All four had denied writing it.

The next day Ronny, Neptune, and Mick had already sat together. Just as TJ was about to take his seat, I asked him if he would mind sitting over at the next bay of computers. He exploded. "You think I'm the cause of the problem, don't you?"

Actually I did think he might be, but I wasn't at all certain. "No," I said, "but I do want you to sit over here for today." He got red in the face, plunked down in the chair near the three other boys, and refused to move.

I motioned for him to come with me. Out in the hall, I said to him quietly, "The bottom line is that all

---

> **Telling stories has the potential for changing individual practice and the culture of our schools.**

Critical Incidents Protocol (For Shared Reflection)

1. *Write stories.* Each group member writes briefly in response to the question: What happened? (10 minutes)

2. *Choose a story.* The group decides which story to use. (5 minutes)

3. *What happened?* The presenter reads the written account of what happened and sets it within the context of professional goals. (10 minutes)

4. *Why did it happen?* Colleagues ask clarifying questions. (5 minutes)

5. *What might it mean?* The group raises questions about the incident in the context of the presenter's work. They discuss it as professional, caring colleagues while the presenter listens. (15 minutes)

6. *What are the implications for practice?* The presenter responds, then the group engages in conversation about the implications for the presenter's practice and for the participants' own practice. A useful question at this stage might be, What new insights occurred? (15 minutes)

7. *Debrief the process.* The group talks about what just happened. How did the process work? (10 minutes)

of you need to get your work done." Out of control, body shaking, TJ angrily spewed out, "You always pick on me. Those guys.... You...." I could hardly hear his words, so fascinated was I with his intense emotion and his whole-body animation.

Contrary to my ordinary response to students who yell, I felt perfectly calm. I knew I needed to wait. Out of the corner of my eye, I saw two male teachers rise out of their chairs in the hallway about 25 feet away. They obviously thought that I, a woman of small stature, needed protection. But I did not look at them. I looked at TJ and waited.

When he had expended his wrathful energy, I said softly, "You know, TJ, you are a natural-born leader." I waited. Breathed in and out. "You did not choose to be a leader; it was thrust upon you. But there you are. People follow you. So you have a tremendous responsibility, to lead in a positive and productive way. Do you understand what I am saying?"

Like an exhalation after a long in-breath, his body visibly relaxed. He looked down at me and nodded his head. Then he held out his hand to me and said, "I'm sorry."

Back in the room, he picked up his stuff and, without a word, moved to the next bay of computers.

Step Two: Using the Critical Incidents Protocol

At first you'll think that you need more information than this, but we think that you have enough here. One member of the group will take the role of Grace. Your "Grace" can answer clarifying questions about what happened or why it happened in whatever way he or she sees fit. Work through the protocol to figure out what the incident might mean in terms of "Grace's" practice. Finally, discuss what implications the incident in the writing lab might have for her practice and for your own as reflective educators. Then, try an event of your own.

We think that you will find that whether the group uses your story or someone else's, building reflective practice together is a sure way to get to the heart of teaching and learning.

References

Dewey, J. (1938). *Experience and education.* New York: Macmillan.

Tripp, D. (1993). *Critical incidents in teaching: Developing professional judgement.* New York: Routledge.

Simon Hole is a 4th grade teacher at Narragansett Elementary School in Narragansett, Rhode Island. He may be reached at 36 White Oak Dr., Wyoming, RI 02898 (e-mail: ropajavi@aol.com). **Grace Hall McEntee** is cofounder of Educators Writing for Change. She may be reached at Box 301, Prudence Island, RI 02872 (e-mail: Gmcente@aol.com).

REFORM FOR THE NEXT CENTURY

Schools and Curricula for the 21st Century: Predictions, Visions, and Anticipations

By Weldon F. Zenger and Sharon K. Zenger

If the research on education for the 21st century were to be summed up in three words, they would be technology, technology, and technology. Almost without exception, information regarding education in the 21st century directly or indirectly involves technology in some way. How might technology affect education and schools in the next century?

Society is becoming more and more involved in thinking about and planning for tomorrow's world. Technology will be a determining factor in how and what the teacher will use for instruction (Berliner, 1992). Classroom management must change so technology can be used. Sandra Welch, Executive Vice President at PBS (Baker, 1993), envisions schoolchildren having a device the size of a tape recorder that serves as a source of knowledge from all over the world. Sharon Bell, director of technology for New Orleans Public Schools (Baker, 1993), sees children with hand-held pads containing one million times more power than any computer today. This power pad would recognize handwriting and voice, and would type, register, respond, and store this information.

Literacy skills needed for the 21st century include accessing, thinking, and communication (Hill, 1992). According to the U.S. National Commission on Libraries and Information Science, "Our nation's schools must recognize information literacy as an essential

> **Literacy skills needed for the 21st century include accessing, thinking, and communication.**

skill and strive to develop an information literate society" (1989, p. xiii). For students to be information literate, "they must know how to find, analyze, synthesize, evaluate, and communicate information and ideas" (p. xiii). The Commission maintains that information processing will be a determining factor in an individual's ability to succeed and will be the focus of education in the 21st century.

Future curricula must be developed around major or universal themes such as change and adaptability, global interdependence, cultural diversity, quality of life, increasing technology, self-actualization, lifelong learning, and world economic systems in balance with the national environment (Wilson et al., 1991). State-of-the-art communication systems, technology, and transportation have all fostered the globalization of business (Carlock, 1991). Education must provide students with an international perspective.

Awareness of the global economy and the basics of international business is the first step in preparing students to compete in the business world of the future (McCaslin, 1992). In the future, global education will include the study of the environment, migratory pollution, national security, nuclear war, economics, world population, and food distribution (Smith, 1990). Our youth need to be educated about these concerns. Legislation is already being passed in many states to develop and improve global knowledge in schools. All subjects can, and should, be taught from a global perspective. Many topics will be controversial.

By the year 2010, every job will require some skill in information-processing technology.

More emphasis must be placed on the education of the poor and minorities. All schools should expect the same high standards. Schools will use more apprenticeships and internships, especially for at-risk students. Increased learner diversity, including the increase in the number of older Americans, will increase the use of instructional assistive technologies (Hofmeister, Menlove, and Thorkildsen, 1992). With the increase in learner diversity and increased availability of videos, open and closed captioning in video courseware may be the most important trend in schools for the 21st century. An increase in the number of hearing impaired students in public and higher education, an increase in learners of English as a second language at all levels, and an increase in lifelong learning will all be a part of this demand for more assistive technology instruction.

By the year 2010, every job will require some skill in information-processing technology (Cetron, 1989). Many public schools will be open 24 hours a day, retraining adults and renting out computer systems after the school day ends. Vocational education will become as crucial as traditional education. School days and years will lengthen. Class sizes will be cut from an average of 17 to 10. Students will be promoted by performance, not on the time spent in class. Teachers will also be recruited from business and industry. Computer-aided learning programs will be replacing books. Schools will work more with business and industry.

The biggest challenge is funding. In places like Independence, Mo.—the first 21st Century School site—parent fees nearly cover operating expenses. Parental involvement in school affairs is undoubtedly going to increase in schools of the future (Murphy, 1991). School councils will consist of parents with varying political, social, cultural, and economic values that will require school leaders to become more politically astute if they are to survive.

Schools and Curricula in the 21st Century

Curriculum planners in the 21st century will have knowledge of real-world requirements and will be able to set guidelines for the skills needed for elementary, middle, and high school students (Cetron, 1985). Instead of talking about which grade they are in, students will talk in terms of outcomes, topics, issues, job experiences, projects, or community applications with which they are working.

As has been noted, technology dominates the ideas and predictions for the 21st century schools. Interwoven with technology are information, communication, and globalism. The parents, home, community, and businesses will play a larger role in schools of the future. Some very thought-provoking, challenging, and perhaps alarming predictions for schools of the next century follow, some of which have already come to fruition.

Lewis (1991) gives us a taste of what we might see in the 21st century schools:

- Computers may be integrated into the desktop of students and teachers.
- Students and teachers will travel from class to class with their own personal computer. In a few years, battery-powered notebook computers that can be plugged into a school's network will be available.
- Video wallpaper where images surround students may be a part of the classroom.

Berliner (1992) has very insightful projections for schools of the future. They include:

- Notebook or backpack computers assigned to all students in the place of textbooks will be possible.
- Textbooks will be on disks with interactive elements and dynamic rather than static graphics, and will allow erasing and rerecording.

15

- Sophisticated calculators with animated graphics will be used for mathematical work and problem solving.
- Communications from home to school will easily be carried out through local communication networks.
- Teachers will be seen as managers of information and complex environments rather than authoritative sources of information.
- Teachers will become more collegial and informal due to the individual use of technology and will be viewed more as facilitators or coaches, leading to higher levels of productivity for both students and teachers.
- New technology will make more individual and group projects possible, promoting a multidimensional classroom approach.
- Project methods of intrinsic interests to students will be used to teach critical thinking skills.

The parents, home, community, and businesses will play a larger role in schools of the future.

Reigeluth (1992) offers the emerging features of an information-age educational system compared to the current industrial-aged system:

- Continuous progress as opposed to grade levels
- Outcomes-based learning as opposed to covering the content
- Individualized testing as opposed to norm-referenced testing
- Performance-based assessment as opposed to nonauthentic assessment
- Personal learning plans as opposed to group-based content delivery
- Cooperative learning as opposed to adversarial learning
- Learning centers as opposed to adversarial learning
- Teachers as coach or facilitator of learning as opposed to teacher as dispenser of knowledge
- Thinking, problem-solving skills, and meaning-making as opposed to memorization of meaningless facts
- Communication skills as opposed to isolated reading, writing skills
- Advanced technologies as tools as opposed to books as tools (p. 12).

Reigeluth (1992) also offers the following features for an information-age educational system based on changes in the family:

- A "teacher" is responsible for a child for a period of about 4 years.
- That teacher is responsible for educating the whole child.
- Each school has no more than 10 teachers, to create a smaller caring environment (schools-within-schools).
- Each student develops a quarterly contract with the teacher and parents (p. 12).

Reigeluth (1992) also indicated the need for a new paradigm in education based on massive changes in the conditions and educational needs of an emerging information society. Reigeluth and Garfinkle (1992) present a more detailed image of the features that appear to be emerging from those new conditions and educational needs of the information society. They call that image "LearningSphere 2000." The purpose of LearningSphere 2000 is to present one possible image of a different paradigm for education.

Reigeluth and Garfinkle caution that the features in this new paradigm are illustrative rather than prescriptive and are to stimulate thinking rather than to present a solution. Not all aspects of the paradigm should be considered as necessary or even advisable for any given community. Some of the features of the LearningSphere 2000 paradigm are:

- Mastery of tasks before progression
- Tasks completed in a variety of ways within and outside the school
- Teacher as facilitator and instructional manager
- Teacher as guide for a student for 3–5 years
- Clusters of guides (4–10 per cluster) functioning somewhat independent of the school district
- Parents requesting the guides for their student
- Learning centers providing instruction in areas of focus whether in a traditional discipline area or a cross-discipline thematic area such as pollution
- Learning contracts developed for each student, each period with input from the guide, parents, and student
- Five levels of development, starting with birth. The earliest level (birth to age 3) will take place at home or in a "home room" daycare situation provided by the school
- Students' progress assessed across the disciplines through real-world projects as well as separately in the academic disciplines
- Technology such as multimedia, hypermedia, electronic networks, and computer-based simulations used at all levels

- Social services provided through the schools, including child care services, health care and family services, as well as parenting education
- Peer tutoring, parents, and senior citizens as well as other volunteers used to reduce the labor costs of education.

Edward Hammond (1997), president of Fort Hays State University and a visionary committed to computerization and information technology, agrees there is a need for a new paradigm in education based on massive changes in the information society. As the information age reaches maturity and the bioengineering age develops, he contends that the ability to learn will become the driving force to success. Lines between grades and levels of education will disappear and as the electronic learning environments develop, a whole new array of educational providers will enter the scene.

Bauer (1991) seems to sum it up with some predictions for the curriculum of the 1990s and beyond, including the following elements:

... the emerging new format of education for the 21st century is struggling to be born in 19th-century buildings.

Halsted (1992) is concerned that the emerging new format of education for the 21st century is struggling to be born in 19th-century buildings. Drawing from the major concerns of educators and architects who met for the purpose of identifying school designs for the future, Halsted suggests that schools should be hospitable environments and welcoming places for no more than 400–500 students, and where:

- Classrooms will be like studios.
- Each student will have his or her own workstation and research space.
- There will need to be an array of spaces of various sizes, including:

  ✓ Central gathering places for the school community

  ✓ Work spaces for cooperative learning by groups of different sizes

  ✓ Quiet, private areas for one-on-one sessions with a teacher, mentor, or fellow student

  ✓ Nooks where students can think and work independently

- The microcomputer will be used as a standard tool for learning.
- Software will become easier to learn and all students will know word processing, database, spreadsheet, and desktop publishing software.
- Advanced typewriting will be replaced with advanced word processing applications.
- Records management will be absorbed into database applications.
- Desktop publishing will move from word processing into document processing.
- Office administration will rely on integrated computer skills.
- Secretaries will be known as support staff, with an increase in administrative duties and salaries.
- The three R's will be replaced with the four C's: comprehension, critical thinking, communication, and coping.
- Blackboards will be obsolete; modular seating, personal computers, and encyclopedias stored on disks will be common.
- Voice activated keyboards will be used.
- There will be a greater emphasis on visual education.
- The new computers will be able to read handwriting with almost human accuracy and convert handwritten notes into typewritten form and store the information in the computer's memory.
- Adaptability will be the survival skill. As job requirements change and electronics affect technological skills, adaptability will be the key to success (p. 21).

  ✓ Offices for teachers where they can work as true professionals, do individual testing and counseling, organize individualized study programs for their students, and do their own research, with telephone and voice mail access to parents and teacher colleagues.

- There will be a need to incorporate the wide range of existing and anticipated educational technology, making it accessible to all.
- There should be a full range of social services in or near the school: preschool education, daycare, parent education, health, mental health, employment, recreational, substance abuse, and family counseling.
- Above all, the new schools should be institutions where all feel welcome and have a sense of belonging in spaces that flow from social and public areas to smaller work areas, to private spaces that encourage contemplation (p. 47).

Infotech-Based Education in the 21st Century

In an article entitled "Cyberspaced out by 2025?" Cornish (1996) gives us one of the most recent and complete anticipations of how technology could shape education in the future. He is careful to point out these are possible future developments and *not* predictions.

- Infotech will allow children to start formal education in their cribs. Interactive instruction can begin in infancy, especially as equipment is adapted to cradle, crib, and playpen. Playing electronic games should stimulate early development of mental faculties. Some youngsters will teach themselves to read before age 3.
- The education experience will be dramatically enhanced by multimedia, computer stimulation, virtual reality, etc. Interactive programs will offer virtual-reality experiences of stirring events.
- There will be a boom in packaged educational products. Highly engaging and effective products should become increasingly available at reasonable cost. Parents and teachers must see that children use these "automated tutors" properly. These products should greatly benefit children taught at home by parents.
- The stupendous increase in knowledge in libraries and databases will pose the question: What do youngsters really need to learn? Youths can study only the tiniest bit of the knowledge base at our disposal. Deciding wisely what they should learn becomes essential for students' long-term success. Society must make hard choices about what children must know and what is merely useful or interesting.
- Teachers will be better able to handle classes of students with widely different abilities and interests. Educational infotech should permit most students to learn mainly on their own. Computerized multimedia courses reduce the need for constant instruction by a human teacher. However, youngsters will still need guidance to stay focused on what they need to learn.
- Handicapped people will be special beneficiaries of infotech-based education. The homebound can take courses from teachers all over the world in any subject. The blind, deaf, and paralyzed will have equipment that largely offsets their handicaps.
- Infotech will enable students to get personal help with homework without parents. Homework hotlines are multiplying. New teleconferencing systems will enable youngsters to work easily with distant teachers. And a student who wants a general review of any standard school topic should be able to summon up a computer tutor for a quick briefing.
- Incredible information resources will be available for students doing papers. One problem is the temptation to copy from electronic source material rather than writing one's own thoughts.
- Global universities will emerge, connecting students, lecturers, and researchers in many nations via computer networks, satellite television, etc. Students may be required to spend little or no time at a university campus.
- Future infotech alone will not ensure good education: Teachers will continue to be needed. The many exciting technologies will not necessarily be used effectively and may even be abused. Most students have difficulty staying on task without a human teacher. So the future teacher's main task may be to provide one-on-one guidance, supervision, and intimate discussion.
- Teachers will resist infotech in education when it threatens jobs or privileges but may accept it when it frees them for more interesting tasks.
- Infotech will allow students to take courses at their own pace and get credit whenever material is mastered. College students in a hurry could whip through a course, while others, with less time, might spend several years. Increased efficiency in pumping information into students' minds through infotech should also permit students to spend more time in other important developmental activities.
- Education may become compulsory for adults as well as children. As more adults waste their lives because they lack skills for good jobs, interpersonal relationships, and global citizenship, society will reassess letting people escape badly needed training simply because they are no longer youngsters (pp. 5–7).

A Word of Caution

All these predictions, projections, visions, and anticipations of education for the 21st century could lead one to believe that technology will solve all the problems of education. Many of the authors cited by these writers warned against doing this. Postman (1994) goes so far as to say technology is part of the problem, not the solution. He contends that the great problems of education are social and moral and have nothing to do with dazzling new technologies. He believes our children, like the rest of us, now suffer from information glut, not information scarcity.

McCluskey (1994) agrees technology will not solve the problems facing education. He does not dispute that technology has an important and vital role in education of the future. In fact, he reminds us that it does, but it may also produce unanticipated and perhaps unpleasant consequences. Further, he contends that if more and more advanced technology is introduced into the educational scheme without a concomitant emphasis on knowledge acquisition, it will allow some students to operate at lower levels of thinking. Students who possess knowledge will tend to use technology as a tool, and those who do not will use it as a crutch.

Sequencing Content into the School Curriculum

In further search of how technology and other predictions for education may affect education in the future, these writers are extending their research with a study of placement, scope, and sequencing content into the infotech school curricula of the 21st century. To do this, in addition to reviewing the literature and curriculum planning books, the following are being contacted: All 50 state chief school officers, national councils and committees of education, major textbook publishers, major universities and educational leaders who can be identified.

The early response from chief school officers has been excellent. Some designs appear to be taking shape, especially at the state level, pertaining to what is guiding and may guide the scope and sequencing of school curricula in the new millennium.

Almost all states responding to a written survey report that curriculum development, especially scope and sequencing of content to specific grade levels, is left up to local school systems. Most of them did indicate, however, that they develop standards, benchmarks, frameworks, goals, or essential learning outcomes to assist and provide guidance for local systems to follow as they develop curricula. Most of these broad standards are not grade-level specific. In developing these state-level standards, the following were listed as sources and guidelines: National and international standards, other state standards, standards from the National Assessment of Educational Progress, New Standards Project, national councils and commissions of education in specific subject areas, existing research, professional judgment, current practice, and teacher expertise. The processes for developing these standards were described by some states responding, in which case many educators from all levels were involved as well as some outside the field of education.

To this point in the current study, the only response indicating that specific criteria have been established to scope and sequence content is by the National Council for the Social Studies. Through a series of task force studies, 24 criteria and six scope and sequence models have been developed that can be used by local school districts to guide scope and sequencing social studies subject content to grade levels. Responses from state chief school officers indicate that placing and sequencing content to grade levels is left to the local districts.

A review of curriculum planning and development books has identified criteria that could be used, but what actually is being used by local districts is not clear. The primary purpose in further researching this area is to identify criteria that have been used to place, scope and sequence subject matter content to specific grade levels in the past, are being used in the present, and project that which will be appropriate for use in the infotech schools of the future. *Any suggestions or ideas for helping to locate this information will be welcomed by these writers.*

Authors' Note: The original idea and much of the impetus for this research was the brainchild of Charles Leftwich, Dean of the College of Education at Fort Hays State University. An earlier version of this article including a section on higher education was published in the "Record," a publication of the Kansas Association for Supervision and Curriculum Development.

References

Baker, D. E. "Technovisions." *America's Agenda* 1(1993): 34–35.

Bauer, D. E. "Predicting the Next Ten Years." *Business Education Forum*, April 1991.

Berliner, D. C. "Redesigning Classroom Activities for the Future." *Educational Technology*, October 1992.

Carlock, L. L. "Internationalizing the Business Education Curriculum." *National Business Education Yearbook* 29(1991): 1–7.

Cetron, M. "Long-Term Trends Affecting Undergraduate Education into the Twenty-First Century." Paper presented at the National Educational Conference, Kansas City, Mo., September 1988.

_____. "Preparing Education for the Year 2000." *The Education Digest*, April 1989.

_____. *Schools of the Future: How American Business and Education Can Cooperate To Save Our Schools.* New York: McGraw-Hill, 1985.

Cornish, E. "Cyberspaced Out by 2025?" *The Education Digest*, April 1996.

Halsted, H. "Designing Facilities for a New Generation of Schools." *Educational Technology*, October 1992.

Hammond, E. Interviewed by authors January 8, 1997, Hays, Kans.

Hill, M. "The New Literacy." *Electronic Learning*, September 1992.

Hofmeister, A. M.; Menlove, M.; and Thorkildsen, R. "Learner Diversity and Instructional Video: Implications for Developers." *Educational Technology*, July 1992.

Lewis, P. H. "The Technology of Tomorrow: Here's a Taste of What You Can Expect in 21st Century Schools." *Principal* 71(1991): 6–7.

McCaslin, J. "Preparing for Success in the World Economy: A Governmental perspective." *The Balance Sheet*, January/February 1992.

McCluskey, L. "Gresham's Law, Technology, and Education." *Phi Delta Kappan*. 7(1994): 550–52.

Murphy, P. J. "Collaborative School Management: Implications for School Leaders," *NASSP Bulletin*, October 1991.

Postman, N. "Technology as Dazzling Distraction." *The Education Digest*,. April 1994.

Reigeluth, C. M. "The Imperative for Systemic Change." *Educational Technology*, November 1992.

Reigeluth, C. M. and Garfinkle, R. J. "envisioning a New System of Education." *Educational Technology,MD* November 1992.

Smith, A. F. "First Steps and Future Trends." *Momentum*,. February 1990.

U.S. National Commission on Libraries and Information Science. *Information Literacy and Education for the 21st Century: Toward an Agenda for Action.* Chicago, ILL.: American Association of School Librarians. ERIC Document No. ED 330 343, 1989.

Wilson, C., and Others. *A Vision of a Preferred Curriculum for the 21st Century: Action Research in School Administration.* Rochester, Mich.: Oakland University, Schools of Education and Human Services. ERIC Document No. 344 275, 1991.

Weldon F. Zenger is professor emeritus of education and President's Distinguished Scholar at Fort Hays State University (1993), Hays, Kans., as well as adjunct professor emeritus of education at Kansas State University, Manhattan, conducting research; Sharon K. Zenger is professor emeritus of education at Tabor College, Hillsboro, Kans. The authors may be reached at 2504 Meadowood Drive, Manhattan, Kans. 66502.

The Standards Juggernaut

It is hard to resist the notion that what is important is whatever we and our peers happen to know. But if we buy that simplistic idea, the clones we create will be poorly prepared to cope with changing reality, Mr. Brady points out.

BY MARION BRADY

WHAT should the young be taught? No question we can ask ourselves is more important. Nothing less than the survival of humankind hinges on our choice of answers.

Perhaps surprisingly, the question rarely generates "deep" debate. Of course, there have been long-running arguments about creationism versus evolution, phonics versus whole language, the acceptability of certain novels for classroom use, and whether or not some textbooks encourage socialist or other "anti-American" perspectives.

But these are arguments over details. There has been very little dialogue focusing on fundamental curricular issues—little debate about the ultimate goals of education, little debate about what new knowledge belongs in the curriculum, little debate about what old content can be abandoned, little debate about whether or not the traditional disciplines are the best organizers of knowledge, and little debate about the appropriateness of the arbitrary boundaries that separate fields of study.

We have had no comprehensive national conversation about these questions. Hands are wrung about almost everything else connected with the schools—discipline, standardized test scores, teacher qualifications, funding, vouchers, charters, and so on—but the most important questions about schooling are not being answered. Indeed, they are not even being asked.

There is almost no dialogue about fundamental curricular issues because it seems to be widely assumed that there are no serious problems with the traditional curriculum. What should the young be taught? Without hesitation, policy makers and politicians answer, "They should be taught what those of us who are educated know." This is the philosophical underpinning of the latest educational fad: the standards movement.

Enter, center stage, the people Susan Ohanian has called the "Standardistos." No need, in the Standardisto view, to identify and clarify an overarching reason to educate. No need to decide what new knowledge belongs in the curriculum. No need to agree on what old knowledge to discard to make room for the new. No need to weigh the merit of alternative ways of organizing knowledge. No need to introduce students to the integrated, mutually supportive nature of all knowledge. From the Standardisto perspective, all that

is necessary is to determine what most "well-educated" people know, organize it, distribute it to the schools, and demand that teachers teach it and students learn it. In the name of reform, the Standardistos are freezing in bureaucratic place the worst aspects of traditional education.

The standards movement has a lot going for it. Its promoters are true believers who have ready access to the media because they are considered authorities. The movement has massive political and corporate backing. Educators who oppose the movement are not well organized. It enjoys an inspired label—who can reasonably oppose the setting of standards? Perhaps most important, it meshes well with simplistic, popular views of what educating is all about.

Every day, across America, committees are at work embedding and reinforcing the standards fad. Sadly, because the consequences of their actions will take so long to manifest themselves, the causal link between what they are doing and its ultimately calamitous consequences may not become apparent in time to do anything about it. The perspectives of the Standardistos demand much closer scrutiny than they are getting.

Your Facts or Mine?

It hardly needs to be said that we are experiencing an information explosion that is unprecedented in human history. We can teach only the tiniest fraction of all there is to know, and that fraction grows smaller by the hour.

To the question "What should the young be taught?" the Standardisto answer is the one noted above: that body of general knowledge that those of us who are educated already know. That generations should share a large body of general knowledge makes good sense. Every society needs a "language of allusion" in order to function. Such statements as "The Monroe Doctrine is still a sensitive issue for many Latin Americans" or "He has the patience of Job" have meaning only if the speaker and the listener share some level of understanding of the Monroe Doctrine and of the Biblical story of Job's troubles.

A shared language of allusion provides a significant means of holding a society together. However, it is a mistake to assume that whatever members of the dominant elite know should determine what is taught to the young. The importance of a fact has nothing whatsoever to do with either the status of the people who know it or their number. What counts, finally, is societal survival, from which it follows that *the relative importance of a bit of knowledge depends on the long-term effects of its being generally known.* That is a very different criterion.

A fact-based curriculum that teaches students about ancient Rome's battles with Carthage but fails to explore the differing value systems that underlie most conflict is missing a significant learning opportunity. A curriculum that requires students to learn the names of major rivers or mountain ranges but leaves them unaware of the implications of a gradual drop in the level of their region's water table tacitly invites eventual disaster.

Determining the probable or possible long-term consequences of knowing or not knowing something is, of course, no easy task. The process requires looking at the world as a system, and traditional schooling does not encourage that. Ordinary experience may tell us, say, that medical research increases life expectancy; that increased life expectancy expands the total population; that increased population expands the demand for food, water, and living space; and that those needs are on a collision course that could have disastrous consequences.

But what ordinary experience tells us is not addressed by the traditional curriculum that the Standardistos are so eager to reinforce. Tracing even a simple causal sequence like the one above touches on physiology, technology, geography, economics, and sociology. In our schools, such subjects are taught, if at all, at different levels and at different times, as if they had little or nothing to do with one another. Standards are written for disciplines. It is a rare standards document that tries to promote the exploration of relationships *between* or *beyond* the familiar disciplines.

It is hard to resist the notion that what is important is whatever we and our peers happen to know. But if we buy that simplistic idea, the clones we create will be poorly prepared to cope with changing reality.

Depth or Breadth?

Two theories about how students learn best have long been in competition. One of them is summarized by the old saying "Throw enough mud on the wall, and some of it is bound to stick." This view acknowledges that not everything taught is learned, but it suggests that there is nevertheless merit in bombarding students with information because at least some of it will be remembered.

The second theory is summarized in the statement "Less is more." Early in the 20th century, mathematician, teacher, and philosopher Alfred North Whitehead maintained that dumping vast amounts of information on students was counterproductive. He argued that humans are simply not mentally equipped to handle a great deal of random, "inert knowledge." The young, Whitehead said, need to study in great depth a relatively few really powerful ideas, ideas that encompass and explain major aspects of human experience.

For example, Whitehead probably would have approved studying the concept of polarization. This process, by means of which minor differences between humans become major ones, touches almost every dimension of life. Polarization gradually turns complex, "gray" issues into ever simpler "black and white" ones, attaches to those issues ever greater significance, and loads them with ever more emotion until effective communication becomes impossible, and conflict becomes all but inevitable. A shared, thorough understanding of the process of polarization sheds light on the dynamics of friendship, marriage, neighborhood incidents, labor/management relationships, barroom brawls, religious schisms, international relations, and much more.

There are concepts even broader than polarization, concepts that cut across all fields of knowledge and disclose their inherent interrelations. For example, concepts such as "pattern," "structure," "relationship," and "system" are central to all disciplines, including those not yet developed. By focusing on these kinds of large-scale mental organizers, students will be equipped to expand existing fields of study and to explore intellectual territory of which we currently have little or no knowledge.

Such organizers are essential. Give adults the exams they took a few years earlier in high school or college, and their poor performance will prove that facts that are not made part of an often-used larger scheme of meaning are soon forgotten. The Standardistos pay lip service to the necessity for both breadth and depth, but nowhere in evidence in their efforts are "big" ideas that organize the myriad facts they demand that students remember. Indeed, most are convinced that the young cannot handle big ideas, that facts must come first, and that, given enough facts, some master pattern will eventually emerge to bind them together in a way that makes useful sense.

Here or There?

Effective teachers of the young are much concerned with what, in educational jargon, is called "developmentally appropriate material." Certain sequences are taken for granted. The simple is taught before the complex, the tangible before the intangible, the concrete before the abstract.

Most Standardistos have little use for such ideas. E. D. Hirsch, Jr., surely a closet Standardisto, asks, "What, exactly, does 'developmentally appropriate' mean?...Must children in the second grade have their horizons bounded by the local mall, as opposed to...learning about China and India, ancient Greece, and the Civil War?"[1]

The question, of course, is whether reach equals grasp. Learning about China, India, and ancient Greece involves learning about extremely complex cultural systems that are shaped by deep-seated assumptions about life, death, the individual, significant others, nature, causation, the good life, the supernatural, and much more. The assumptions that undergird these cultural systems manifest themselves in myriad social institutions and physical productions and arrangements. There is no doubt some merit in teaching second-graders how to locate China and India on a globe, but it is surely naive to think that an ability to recall rehearsed answers to a few carefully chosen and phrased questions about those countries is of value.

What's more, the local shopping mall to which Hirsch gives such short shrift deserves more respect than most Standardistos give it. To those who have not thought much about the matter, it might seem too mundane to merit the attention of second-graders. But choose any field of study—physics, language, economics, art, sociology, even history—and any randomly selected mall will provide enough raw study material to keep a team of graduate students occupied indefinitely. It is only the extreme familiarity of shopping malls that keeps their inherent complexity below our threshold of awareness.

The same could be said for the study of a student's school. There is no concept appropriate for the general education curriculum that does not manifest itself in some teachable way within the physical boundaries of a school.

To the casual observer, attempting to teach the young about China or India might seem to indicate more respect for the intellectual capabilities of the young than does a focus on the mall or other topics drawn from student experience. In fact, just the opposite is the case. Because they know little or nothing about things remote in time and space other than what they are told, second-graders have few options other than to parrot such information back. But make their own experience a legitimate focus of study, and their insights and critical powers can begin to be displayed, sometimes in startlingly impressive ways that demand genuine respect.

I do not mean to suggest that schoolwork should be confined to the study of immediate reality. Even the very young have imaginations that can transport them almost anywhere. But surely, given the difficulties inherent in dealing in a systematic way with the complex, the abstract, and the remote, immediate reality is the place to begin to build the descriptive and analytical conceptual models that will eventually take students to wider experience. Standardistos, unaccustomed to the instructional use of what students know rather than what they themselves know, rarely write standards that exploit the teaching power of a student's own experience.

There is yet another reason for focusing primary attention on the student's "here and now" rather than on preprocessed, canned information. Back in the 1960s, the education establishment's thinking about thought became somewhat more sophisticated. "Thinking" began to be seen as actively engaging in a wide range of mental processes. Recalling was just one of those processes. Categorizing, translating, hypothesizing, valuing, generalizing, and synthesizing were others. Even the very young, it became apparent, use a great many thought processes in the course of ordinary experience.

When teaching is seen primarily as telling by means of teacher talk or textbook reading, the mental processes available to students dwindle down to just one: recall. Students may not be able to put their fingers on the reason schoolwork so often frustrates and bores them, but its lack of genuine intellectual challenge is surely a major factor.

Here, again, is why the study of immediate, firsthand experience—the mall, the school, the street—can be so engaging. Its inherent complexity demands the use of every known thought process, and the level of difficulty automatically adjusts to that which is most appropriate for the individual student.

The Appeal of the Simplistic

In times of uncertainty, easy answers have great appeal. This is such an era, and well-meaning politicians and policy makers are quick to supply them.

Unfortunately, more often than not, behind legislation and new initiatives lies a gross lack of understanding of education. Many share the view of Standardisto Louis Gerstner, Jr., CEO of IBM, who apparently believes that educating has to do primarily with "the distribution of information." If only it could be that simple. Teaching, real teaching, involves the altering of the images of reality in the minds of others, a challenge inherently far more complex than those presented by rocket science.

The educational establishment has itself to blame for the fact that so many who do not know what they are doing are promoting simplistic approaches to educating. The establishment has drifted along thoughtlessly, assuming that the major curricular issues have been solved and that all that is needed now is a bit of touching up of what was taught last year, a task that can be handled by the subject-matter specialists.

In eras when knowledge changed little from generation to generation, that view was probably an acceptable one. Today, it is not. The perspectives of subject-matter specialists are too narrow; their interest in the whole, of which their specializations are parts, is too restricted; the rate of societal change is too rapid for reform of the "touch-ing up" sort. Freezing the status quo in place, assuming that what the young should be taught is merely what the educated happen to know, ensures that, as the years pass, school curricula will bear less and less relationship to reality.

There are other wrongheaded views shared by many Standardistos—that somehow just "raising the bar" increases students' ability to clear it, that before the standards movement there were no standards, that the talent wasted by one-size-fits-all programs is not worth developing, that students who will be turned into "failures" by the standards will not present a serious problem, that standardized tests tell us something really important, that market forces have a magical ability to cure the ills of education, that extrinsic rewards are dependable motivators, and so on. However, behind the standards juggernaut and impelling it forward is the single, primary, simplistic, and unexamined assumption that what the next generation most needs to know is what this generation knows. Surface that assumption and carefully examine it, and every other Standardisto assumption will begin to show itself in a different light.

Teaching to lists of what is "important" that have been devised by the elders is the ultimate "back-to-basics" program. If we proceed down the road we are now on and succeed in replicating ourselves, we will have an America in which everyone understands and is comfortable with everyone else—as we slide toward oblivion.

Note

1. E. D. Hirsch, Jr., *Cultural Literacy: What Every American Needs to Know* (Boston: Houghton Mifflin, 1987).

MARION BRADY (mbrady@digital.net) is an education consultant living in Cocoa, Fla.

Unit 2

Unit Selections

Key Points to Consider

❖ How can parents and teachers provide children and adolescents with experiences that promote their cognitive, social, and emotional development?

❖ Why is an accurate perception of self important to children's self-esteem?

❖ What is the truth about high schools and adolescent cliques?

 **Links** **www.dushkin.com/online/**

These sites are annotated on pages 4 and 5.

Development

The study of human development provides us with knowledge of how children and adolescents mature and learn within the family, community, and school environments. Educational psychology focuses on description and explanation of the developmental processes that make it possible for children to become intelligent and socially competent adults. Psychologists and educators are presently studying the idea that biology as well as the environment influence cognitive, personal, social, and emotional development and involve predictable patterns of behavior.

Jean Piaget's theory regarding the cognitive development of children and adolescents is perhaps the best known and most comprehensive. According to this theory, the perceptions and thoughts that young children have about the world are often quite different when compared to adolescents and adults. That is, children may think about moral and social issues in a unique way. Children need to acquire cognitive, moral, and social skills in order to interact effectively with parents, teachers, and peers. If human intelligence encompasses all of the above skills, then Piaget may have been correct in saying that development is the child's intelligent adaptation to the environment.

Today the cognitive, moral, social, and emotional development of children takes place in a rapidly changing society. A child must develop positive conceptions of self within the family as well as at school in order to cope with the changes and become a competent and socially responsible adult. In "What Do We Know From Brain Research?" Pat Wolfe and Ron Brandt discuss the potential that such research has for teaching and learning, while the articles "Play an Endangered Species" and "Self-Esteem and Beyond" discuss the cognitive and social skills of children. Adolescence brings with it the ability to think abstractly and hypothetically and to see the world from many perspectives. Adolescents strive to achieve a sense of identity by questioning their beliefs and tentatively committing to self-chosen goals. Their ideas about the kinds of adults they want to become and the ideals they want to believe in sometimes lead to conflicts with parents and teachers. Adolescents are also sensitive about espoused adult values versus adult behavior. The articles in this unit discuss the cognitive, social, and emotional changes that confront adolescents and also suggest ways in which the family and school can help meet the needs of adolescents.

What Do We Know from Brain Research?

The recent explosion of neuroscientific research has the exciting potential to increase our understanding of teaching and learning. But it's up to educators to carefully interpret what brain science means for classroom practice.

Pat Wolfe and Ron Brandt

In July 1989, following a congressional resolution, President Bush officially proclaimed the 1990s the "Decade of the Brain." And indeed in the past nine years, we have seen an unprecedented explosion of information on how the human brain works. Thousands of research projects, books, magazine cover stories, and television specials regale us with new facts and figures, colorful PET scans, and at times, suspiciously simple ways to improve our memories, prevent Alzheimer's, and make our babies geniuses.

Our knowledge of brain functioning has been revolutionized. And many of the new findings have changed medical practice. We have a much better understanding of mental illnesses and the drugs that ameliorate them. Treatment for tumors, seizures, and other brain diseases and disorders has become much more successful.

But what about the educational applications of these new findings? Have we learned enough to incorporate neuroscientific findings into our schools? Is it possible that the Decade of the Brain will usher in the Decade of Education?

Interpreting Brain Research for Classroom Practice

Brain science is a burgeoning new field, and we have learned more

> **A child's brain at birth has all the brain cells, or neurons, that it will ever have.**

about the brain in the past 5 years than in the past 100 years. Nearly 90 percent of all the neuroscientists who have ever lived are alive today. Nearly every major university now has interdisciplinary brain research teams.

But almost all scientists are wary of offering prescriptions for using their research in schools. Joseph LeDoux from New York University and author of *The Emotional Brain* (1996) says, "There are no quick fixes. These ideas are very easy to sell to the public, but it's too easy to take them beyond their actual basis in science." Susan Fitzpatrick, a neuroscientist at the McDonnell Foundation, says scientists don't have a lot to tell educators at this point. She warns,

Anything that people would say right now has a good chance of not being true two years from now because the understanding is so rudimentary and people are looking at things at such a simplistic level. (1995, p. 24)

Researchers especially caution educators to resist the temptation to adopt policies on the basis of a single study or to use neuroscience as a promotional tool for a pet program. Much work needs to be done before the results of scientific studies can be taken into the classroom. The reluctance of scientists to sanction a quick marriage between neuroscience and education makes sense. Brain research does not—and may never—tell us specifically what we should do in a classroom. At this point it does not "prove" that a particular strategy will increase student understanding. That is not currently the purpose of neuroscience research. Its purpose is to learn how the brain functions. Neuroscience is a field of study separate from the field of education, and it is unrealistic to expect brain research to lead directly to pedagogy. So how do we use the current findings?

We need to critically read and analyze the research in order to separate the wheat from the chaff. If educators do not develop a functional understanding of the brain and its processes, we will be vulnerable to pseudoscientific fads, inappropriate generalizations, and dubious programs.

Then, with our knowledge of educational practice, we must determine if and how brain research informs that practice. Educators have a vast background of knowledge about teaching and learning. This knowledge has been gained from educational research, cognitive science, and long experience. Given this knowledge base, educators are in the best position to know how the research does—or does not—supplement, explain, or validate current practices.

Although we must be cautious about many neuroscientific findings, a few are quite well established. Some validate what good educators have always done. Others are causing us to take a closer look at educational practice.

Finding One

The brain changes physiologically as a result of experience. The environment in which a brain operates determines to a large degree the functioning ability of that brain.

Researchers agree that at birth, humans do not yet possess a fully operational brain. The brain that eventually takes shape is the result of interaction between the individual's genetic inheritance and everything he or she experiences. Ronald Kotulak, in his book *Inside the Brain* (1996), uses the metaphor of a banquet to explain the relationship between genes and the environment.

> The brain gobbles up the external environment through its sensory system and then reassembles the digested world in the form of trillions of connections which are constantly growing or dying, becoming stronger or weaker depending on the richness of the banquet. (p. 4)

The environment affects how genes work, and genes determine how the environment is interpreted. This is a relatively new understanding. It wasn't too many years ago that scientists thought the brain was immutable or fixed at birth. Scientists had known for some time that with a few specialized exceptions, a child's brain at birth has all the brain cells, or neurons, that it will ever have. Unlike tissue in most other organs, neurons do not regenerate, so researchers assumed that the brain you had at birth was the brain you were stuck with for life.

However, Marian Diamond and her colleagues at the University of California at Berkeley pioneered research in the mid-1960s showing that brain structures are modified by the environment (Diamond & Hopson, 1998). Her research established the concept of neural plasticity—the brain's amazing ability to constantly change its structure and function in response to external experiences. A further finding that should please us all is that dendrites, the connections between brain cells, can grow at any age. Researchers have found this to be true

in humans as well as in animals. Contrary to folk wisdom, a healthy older person is not necessarily the victim of progressive nerve cell loss and diminishing memory and cognitive abilities.

So our environment, including the classroom environment, is not a neutral place. We educators are either growing dendrites or letting them wither and die. The trick is to determine what constitutes an enriched environment. A few facts about the brain's natural proclivities will assist us in making these determinations.

1. The brain has not evolved to its present condition by taking in meaningless data; an enriched environment gives students the opportunity to make sense out of what they are learning, what some call the opportunity to "make meaning."

> Babies don't talk one week, tie their shoes the next, and then work on their emotional development.

2. The brain develops in an integrated fashion over time. Babies don't talk one week, tie their shoes the next, and then work on their emotional development. An enriched environment addresses multiple aspects of development simultaneously.

3. The brain is essentially curious, and it must be to survive. It constantly seeks connections between the new and the known. Learning is a process of active construction by the learner, and an enriched environment gives students the opportunity to relate what they are learning to what they already know. As noted educator

Phil Schlechty says, "Students must do the work of learning."

4. The brain is innately social and collaborative. Although the processing takes place in our students' individual brains, their learning is enhanced when the environment provides them with the opportunity to discuss their thinking out loud, to bounce their ideas off their peers, and to produce collaborative work.

Finding Two

IQ is not fixed at birth.

This second finding is closely linked to the first. Craig Ramey, a University of Alabama psychologist, took on the daunting task of showing that what Diamond did with rats, he could do with children. His striking research (Ramey & Ramey, 1996) proved that an intervention program for impoverished children could prevent children from having low IQs and mental retardation.

Ramey has directed studies of early educational intervention involving thousands of children at dozens of research centers. The best programs, which started with children as young as six weeks and mostly younger than four months, showed that they could raise the infants' scores on intelligence tests by 15 to 30 percent. It is important to note that although IQ tests may be useful artifacts, intelligence is probably much more multifaceted. Every brain differs, and the subtle range of organizational, physiological, and chemical variations ensures a remarkably wide spectrum of cognitive, behavioral, and emotional capabilities.

Finding Three

Some abilities are acquired more easily during certain sensitive periods, or "windows of opportunity."

At birth, a child's cerebral cortex has all the neurons that it will ever have. In fact, in utero, the brain produces an overabundance of neurons, nearly twice as many as it will need. Beginning at about 28 weeks of prenatal development, a massive pruning of neurons begins, resulting in the loss

Brain Fact
Enriching the Environment

Marian Diamond and her team of researchers at the University of California at Berkeley have been studying the impact of enriched and impoverished environments on the brains of rats. Diamond believes that enriched environments unmistakably influence the brain's growth and learning. An enriched environment for children, Diamond says,

■ Includes a steady source of positive emotional support;

■ Provides a nutritious diet with enough protein, vitamins, minerals, and calories;

■ Stimulates all the senses (but not necessarily all at once!);

■ Has an atmosphere free of undue pressure and stress but suffused with a degree of pleasurable intensity;

■ Presents a series of novel challenges that are neither too easy nor too difficult for the child at his or her stage of development;

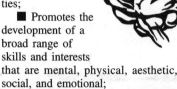

■ Allows social interaction for a significant percentage of activities;

■ Promotes the development of a broad range of skills and interests that are mental, physical, aesthetic, social, and emotional;

■ Gives the child an opportunity to choose many of his or her efforts and to modify them;

■ Provides an enjoyable atmosphere that promotes exploration and the fun of learning;

■ Allows the child to be an active participant rather than a passive observer.

Diamond, M., & Hopson, J. (1998). *Magic trees of the mind: How to nurture your child's intelligence, creativity, and healthy emotions from birth through adolescence* (pp. 107–108). New York: Dutton.

of one-third to one-half of these elements. (So we lose up to half our brain cells before we're born.) While the brain is pruning away excess neurons, a tremendous increase in dendrites adds substantially to the surface area available for synapses, the functional connections among cells. At the fastest rate, connections are built at the incredible speed of 3 billion a second. During the period from birth to age 10, the number of synaptic connections continues to rise rapidly, then begins to drop and continues to decline slowly into adult life.

Much credit for these insights into the developing brain must be given to Harry Chugani and Michael Phelps at the UCLA School of Medicine. Phelps co-invented the imaging technique called Positron Emission Tomography (PET), which visually depicts the brain's energy use. Using PET scans, Chugani has averaged the energy use of brains at various ages. His findings suggest that a child's

peak learning years occur just as all those synapses are forming (1996). Chugani states that not only does the child's brain overdevelop during the early years, but that during these years, it also has a remarkable ability to adapt and reorganize. It appears to develop some capacities with more ease at this time than in the years after puberty. These stages once called "critical periods" are more accurately described as "sensitive periods" or "windows of opportunity."

Probably the prime example of a window is vision. Lack of visual stimulation at birth, such as that which occurs with blindness or cataracts, causes the brain cells designed to interpret vision to atrophy or be diverted to other tasks. If sight is not restored by age 3, the child will be forever blind. . . . Similarly, the critical period for learning spoken language is totally lost by about age 10. If a child is born deaf, the 50,000 neural pathways that would normally activate the auditory cells remain silent, and the sound of the human voice, essential for learning language, can't get through. Finally, as the child grows older, the cells atrophy and the ability to learn spoken language is lost.

Not all windows close as tightly as those for vision and language development. Although learning a second language also depends on the stimulation

> # The brain is essentially curious, and it must be to survive.

of the neurons for the sounds of that language, an adult certainly can learn a second language and learn to speak it quite well. However, it is much more difficult to learn a foreign language after age 10 or so, and the language will probably be spoken with an accent. We might say that learning a second language is not a window that slams shut—it just becomes harder to open.

The implications of the findings regarding early visual, auditory, motor, cognitive, and emotional development are enormous. Indeed, in many places work has already begun to enrich prenatal and early childhood environments. One example is the application of the research with premature infants. Premature babies who are regularly touched in their incubators gain weight at twice the rate of those who are not touched. Preemies whose parents visit them regularly vocalize twice as much in the third week as babies who are visited infrequently or not at all.

The research findings on early development are in stark contrast with the current situation in society.

■ An estimated 12 percent of infants born in this country suffer significant reduction of their cognitive ability as a result of preterm birth; maternal smoking, alcohol use, or drug use in pregnancy; maternal and infant malnutrition; and postbirth lead poisoning or child abuse (Newman & Buka, 1997). Many of these factors could be eliminated with education programs for parents (or future parents). Twenty-five percent of all pregnant women receive no prenatal care.

■ The early years, which are most crucial for learning, receive the least emphasis in federal, state, and local programs. We spend at least seven times more on the elderly than we do on children from birth to age 5.

■ About half of all children in the United States are in full-time day care within the first year. Yet many day care centers not only are underfunded, but they are also staffed by untrained, low-paid workers and have too high an adult/child ratio. (Thirty-eight states do not require family child care providers to have *any* training prior to serving children.)

■ Our present system generally waits until children fall behind in school, then places them in special education programs. With intense early intervention, we could reverse or prevent some adverse effects. It is possible that the billions of dollars spent on special education services might be better spent on early intervention.

Finding Four

Learning is strongly influenced by emotion.

The role of emotion in learning has received a good deal of press in the past few years. Daniel Goleman's *Emotional Intelligence* (1995) and Joseph LeDoux's *The Emotional Brain* (1996) have been instrumental in increasing our understanding of emotion.

Emotion plays a dual role in human learning. First, it plays a positive role in that the stronger the emotion connected with an experience, the stronger the memory of that experience. Chemicals in the brain send a message to the rest of the brain: "This information is important. Remember it." Thus, when we are able to add emotional input into learning experiences to make them more meaningful and exciting, the brain deems the information more important and retention is increased.

In contrast, LeDoux has pointed out that if the emotion is too strong (for example, the situation is perceived by the learner to be threatening), then learning is decreased. Whether you call this "downshifting" or decreasing the efficiency of the rational thinking cortex of the brain, it is a concept with many implications for teaching and learning.

Expect More Findings

On the horizon are many more studies that may have implications for the education of the human brain from birth through old age. Current research areas include these:

■ The role of nutrition in brain functioning

■ How brain chemicals affect mood, personality, and behavior

■ The connection between the mind/brain and the body

Rather than passively wait for research findings that might be useful, educators should help direct the search to better understand how the brain learns. James McGaugh of the University of California at Irvine has suggested that we educators need to be more proactive and tell the scientists, "Here's what we need to know. How can you help us?"

Should the Decade of the Brain lead to an enlightened Decade of Education? Eventually, yes. Along with cognitive research and the knowledge base we already have, findings from the neurosciences can provide us with important insights into how children learn. They can direct us as we seek to enrich the school experience for all children—the gifted, the creative, the learning disabled, the dyslexic, the average students, and all the children whose capabilities are not captured by IQ or other conventional measures. We can help parents and other caregivers understand the effects of maternal nutrition and prenatal drug and alcohol use and the role of early interaction and enriched environments. Brain research can also offer valuable guidance to policymakers and school administrators as they strive to focus their priorities.

Does what we are learning about the brain matter? It must, because our children matter.

References

Chugani, H. T. (1996). *Functional maturation of the brain.* Paper presented at the Third Annual Brain Symposium, Berkeley, California.

Diamond, M., & Hopson, J. (1998). *Magic trees of the mind: How to nurture your child's intelligence, creativity, and healthy emotions from birth through adolescence.* New York: Penguin Putnam.

Fitzpatrick, S. (1995, November). Smart brains: Neuroscientists explain the mystery of what makes us human. *American School Board Journal.*

Goleman, D. (1995). *Emotional intelligence: Why it can matter more than IQ.* New York: Bantam.

Kotulak, R. (1996). *Inside the brain: Revolutionary discoveries of how the mind works.* Kansas City, MO: Andrews & McMeely.

LeDoux, J. (1996). *The emotional brain: The mysterious underpinnings of emotional life.* New York: Simon & Schuster.

Newman, L., & Buka, S. L. (1997). *Every child a learner: Reducing risks of learning impairment during pregnancy and infancy.* Denver, CO: Education Commission of the States.

Ramey, C. T., & Ramey, S. L. (1996). *At risk does not mean doomed.* National Health/Education Consortium Occasional Paper #4. Paper presented at the meeting of the American Association of Science, February 1996.

Pat Wolfe is an independent educational consultant. She can be reached at 555 Randolph St., Napa, CA 94559 (e-mail: wolfe@napanet.net).
Ron Brandt is Editor Emeritus of *Educational Leadership* and an independent educational consultant. He may be reached at 1104 Woodcliff Dr., Alexandria, VA 22308-1058 (e-mail:ronbrandt@erols.com).

Play

An Endangered Species

In their rush to increase teaching hours, many districts are eliminating recess and free time—and something valuable is being lost

By Sheila G. Flaxman

Children know a simple truth that many administrators seem to have forgotten: Play is a necessary part of growing up.

Unfortunately, in their frantic quest to raise standardized test scores and give children a competitive advantage at ever-earlier ages, many school districts have targeted "nonessential" activities as cutting into crucial instructional time. The result: Recess and nonacademic free time are being shortened and even eliminated. A widespread belief is that schools should be solely devoted to academics and play can occur outside of the educational system.

I believe that this is a dangerous proposition. Playtime—recess play or unorganized inside play—is a vital educational activity all its own. It allows children at all ages to use initiative and imagination, to be creative and social. Children left to their own devices will explore, experiment, test, err, and try again, all at their own pace. They will use their bodies and expend energy that might otherwise erupt when they need to be focused and alert.

The Value of Free Playtime

Free play is a critically important factor in normal development from birth through childhood. Early in the 20th century, pioneer child-development specialists such as Switzerland's Jean Piaget and Russian psychologist Lev Vygotsky recognized the value of such activity. Vygotsky believed that play leads directly to the development of a child's conceptual abilities, enabling him or her to master abstract thought, among other skills. Piaget, who developed a widely accepted theory of intellectual development, noted that through the joys of recreation "knowledge arises neither from objects nor the child, but from interactions between the child and those objects."

Play Involves Free Choice

A lot of what is passed off as "play" in schools—the use of games, toys, and puzzles that teach academic concepts—does not promote the enriching qualities of play that involves free choice, that is nonliteral and self-motivated. Nonliteral, by definition, is nonrealistic. Children direct and invent this kind of play—no one presents them with a task or a set of standards to follow. This means that the use of materials, the environment, the rules of the game, and the roles of the participants all flow from the children's imaginations and their sense of reality.

Children engage in such play because they enjoy it—it's self-directed. They do not play for rewards; they enjoy the doing, not the end result. Once they get bored, they go on to do something else—and continue to learn and grow.

But is this activity really as important as traditional academic areas of the curriculum? Teachers of young children are often obligated to explain and justify the value of play to administrators and parents anxious to know why their children aren't learning at a faster

From *Instructor,* September 2000, p. 39. © 2000 by Scholastic, Inc. Reprinted by permission.

Free Play: 10 Benefits to Children

1 Muscular development and control of large muscles, fine motor skills, and eye-hand coordination.

2 Speech development through social interactions during play.

3 Social development: parallel play leading to cooperative play.

4 Language-skill development through dramatic play to clarify ideas.

5 Problem solving and creative thinking—probably the most important skills for living in the world today.

6 Increased consciousness of the cause-and-effect involved in a sequence of events.

7 Therapeutic value in providing opportunities for "safe" acting-out behaviors.

8 Opportunities for self-talk, a useful tool for teachers as they listen to children at play.

9 Development of self-confidence while trying new things in a nonjudgmental environment.

10 Learning cooperation and values by putting themselves in the "shoes" of others.

rate. Such critics believe that play takes valuable time away from more important activities and allows children to hide in a fantasy world instead of facing the realities of the here and now.

Preparation for Adulthood

The view held by critics of play is countered by the work of experts such as Piaget. He maintained that infants and young children learn new concepts through a two-part method: discovering a process and then practicing it. Seen in this light, play is the best preparation for adulthood, especially in our highly technological, competitive society. That's because play, whether in the classroom, at recess, or outdoors, is all about discovering and practicing. It allows children to form an understanding of the social, emotional, moral, and intellectual concepts to which they are being introduced at every turn as they rapidly develop.

This is especially important today, when children are being exposed to so much, so early. Play helps them make sense of and internalize all the stimuli by which they are being bombarded; it provides emotional release from the increasing stress of modern life.

Many recess activities, especially those that require coordinated efforts, teach children how to work together, how to take turns, and how to reciprocate. They offer concrete evidence that, by following some basic rules for the good of the group, the children can keep playing and having fun. If we allow children the freedom to experiment with language, higher-order thinking skills, and new ways of sharing a toy, they will make discoveries that help them throughout life.

The social skills learned during free recreation are also closely related to the establishment of moral guidelines. We bemoan the fact that children do not have appropriate role models. Yet moral development arises from the ability of a child to put him- or herself in the other child's shoes—a lesson of play.

It's Good for the Body, Too

The most forward-thinking workplaces today recognize the need for employees to stretch, exercise, and move around—many provide a designated space in which to do so. If adult workers are happier, healthier, and more productive thanks to such respite, imagine the benefits for young students.

Daily media stories of out-of-control young people should be a warning that kids need safe, healthy outlets for physical energy. Plus, there is an ever-increasing amount of research documenting the poor physical condition of children today. Yet schools persist in curtailing the time allotted for children to run, skip, stretch, jump—play. Why don't more administrators realize that active play develops healthy bodies while teaching children to enjoy exercise?

In your classroom and school, take the opportunity to fight for free play as an integral part of a child's day. When playtime is threatened, so is a child's chance to grow.

Sheila G. Flaxman has been an early-childhood teacher and administrator for 35 years. She lives and works in Little Rock, Arkansas.

Re-evaluating Significance of Baby's Bond With Mother

By SANDRA BLAKESLEE

Challenging a popular belief about human development, a researcher claims to have found that the security of a baby's attachment to its mother does not influence how well-adjusted that child will be later in life.

Events like divorce, disease and accidents are far more important in shaping a child's well-being at age 18 than any early bonding with its mother, said the researcher, Dr. Michael Lewis, a professor of pediatrics and psychiatry at the University of Medicine and Dentistry of New Jersey and director of the Institute for the Study of Child Development at the Robert Wood Johnson Medical School in New Brunswick.

The study is one of a number of research projects on attachment, a field that is gaining attention as experts debate what happens to infants and children when both mother and father work outside the home.

Dr. Lewis based his conclusion on a study of 84 children who were examined at age 1 in terms of maternal

An attack on the gold standard for understanding how babies and children develop

attachment—a popular measure of social adjustment and mental health—and again at age 18 in terms of adult attachment to family and friends.

Secure attachment in infancy did not protect children from being maladjusted at age 18, Dr. Lewis said, nor did insecure attachment in infancy predict trouble in adolescence. He reported his findings at a recent meeting of the International Society on Infant Studies in Atlanta and in a book "Altering Fate—Why the Past Does Not Predict the Future,"

published last year by the Guilford Press.

The new finding attacks the gold standard for understanding how babies and children develop: the so-called infant maternal attachment measure, which infers well-being from the reactions of babies who are temporarily separated then reunited with their mothers.

According to many experts in child development, how the baby reacts to the mother's return each time is critically important. In general, if the baby cries, goes to the mother and is comforted, the child is securely attached. If the baby ignores the mother and is ambivalent to her return or if the baby cries but refuses to be consoled, the baby is insecurely attached.

To the adherents of attachment theory, this little mini-drama speaks volumes about the child's psychological health and profoundly influences that child's developmental course.

From *New York Times*, August 4, 1998. © 1998 by The New York Times. Reprinted by permission.

Attachment theory is an offshoot of psychoanalysis and carries many of Sigmund Freud's ideas into modern practice, said Dr. Robert Cairns, director of the Center for Developmental Science at the University of North Carolina in Chapel Hill. It argues that early mother-infant relationships create "internal representations" in the baby's brain and that these shadows lay the foundation for psychological well-being and human personality throughout life. The mother is the critical figure. Early events are more primary than later events. Given these beliefs, the challenge became how to measure these "internal representations" in babies who cannot talk, Dr. Cairns said.

Figuring that behavior might imply something important about a baby's mind, researchers in the early 1970's devised a test called the Strange Situation. The test has many permutations but basically a mother and her 12-month-old baby enter a room in which they meet a stranger and find many interesting toys. After a few minutes, the mother leaves and the stranger plays with the baby.

After two minutes, the mother returns and the baby's behavior is observed. A little later, the mother leaves the child alone again, waits two minutes and comes back in.

The original goal was to find a measure that would, in five minutes, identify the structure of the course of human personality development, he said. The infant's external behavior is said to capture his or her internal model of the attachment relationship, Dr. Lewis said, "even though neglected and abused children often show secure attachment." Moreover, the nature of this early attachment emerges later in life, especially during stressful times.

A good attachment will protect you while a poor attachment will make you more vulnerable, he said.

This view now dominates infant and child psychiatry. The cardinal rule is that the mother-child relationship is vital for early life and determines subsequent social adjustment.

Psychiatric literature on adolescence treats attachment as a stable individual characteristic, like brown eyes. Some theorists claim that adults choose mates based on infant attachment status; insecurely attached individuals will seek securely attached people to balance out their weakness.

But life is not so simple, Dr. Lewis said. What happens to infants is important but the notion that our early reactions are frozen into the brain, unmalleable by later experience, is open to question. To see if early attachment correlates with later adjustment, Dr. Lewis found 84 children who had been evaluated at age 1—49 securely attached, 35 insecurely attached—and who were now seniors in high school. Each person was interviewed for an hour at home to measure adult attachment. Among other things, the teen-agers were asked to describe early relationships with their parents, to generate adjectives for each parent and provide memories to support the adjectives.

Interviews were scored by trained observers who examined how specific memories were integrated into a general understanding of the parent-child relationship. A teen-ager was deemed securely attached if he presented a coherent story about his relationship with his parents. A teenager was considered insecurely attached if that story was fragmented, ambivalent or incoherent.

Among securely attached infants, 57 percent were considered well-adjusted at age 18 and 43 percent were found to be maladjusted, Dr. Lewis said. Among insecure infants, 74 percent were considered secure at age 18 and 26 percent were believed to have remained insecure.

Dr. Lewis asserts that the critical factor in human development is not security of attachment at age 1 but subsequent experiences in family life. There are many critical periods in every child's life. Divorce played a primary role in their adjustment and "to understand a child's emotional and social development, you have to look at his current life," he

said. He added: "We don't so much remember the past as we reconstruct it in the light of present events. Accidents and chance encounters are a major part of life. The task is always adaptation to the present."

The proponents of attachment theory, however, are not ready to give up on a method that in their view works. For example, Dr. Alan Sroufe, a leading attachment expert at the University of Minnesota in Minneapolis, conducted a long-term study several years ago and found that, in his sample, infant attachment can predict psychopathology at age 17. "I disagree with Mike Lewis," Dr. Sroufe said, "His study is weaker than ours and he used fewer children. I'm not surprised he didn't find correlations. I also disagree with him on logical grounds. Your behavior is always a product of your history and your present circumstances."

Do life's dramas at 1 play out at 18?

Similarly, Dr. Jay Belsky, a professor of human development at Pennsylvania State University in University Park and another well-known proponent of attachment theory, argues that infant day care can disrupt attachment and may harm children in the long run. "To understand the present, you have to understand what the child brings to the circumstances," Dr. Belsky said. "Of course it matters how development proceeds, but what happens early in life makes a difference."

The debate is over how much of a difference. Critics of attachment theory, including Dr. Lewis, say that most researchers place far too much importance on what happens in the first year or two of life.

Some proponents of the theory even argue that critical mother-infant bonding begins at birth. "Years ago, I visited a program in Philadelphia to foster the social and emotional development of children of teen-aged inner-city mothers," Dr. Lewis said. "The program consisted of placing the naked newborn child on the naked belly of the mother, as if early bonding would somehow inoculate the child against all future problems."

Dr. Irving Lazar, a professor emeritus of child development at Vanderbilt University in Nashville, is even more critical of attachment theorists. "Of course babies need good mothers," he said.

"It's important to feel loved and secure. But the so-called attachment measure is ludicrous. The one-time observation of a baby's reaction to its mother's return has no meaningful consequences." All it does is make mothers feel guilty, he said.

Dr. Cairns said that animal studies mostly supported Dr. Lewis.

Studies of other mammals separated from their mothers, including the monkey experiments of Dr. Harry Harlow in which babies were raised without mothers, show no permanent damage to the deprived animals, he said. Dr. Harlow's monkeys treated their first-born babies "like basketballs" and that is what got reported, Dr. Cairns said, but babies born later to those same mothers were well-cared for.

The mothers adapted.

When pressed, people on both sides of the debate will say "of course both past and present are important," Dr. Cairns said, "but they really don't mean it." Many have entrenched ideological positions which, if confined to an ivory tower, might be amusing. These arguments, though, have important policy consequences for American society, he said.

If the first year of life is all-important, then why bother investing huge sums in later intervention programs? But if the first year of life is not that important, and it is the quality of your whole childhood that matters, how could we possibly change things?

FOR PARENTS PARTICULARLY

Self-Esteem and Beyond

HELEN ALTMAN KLEIN

Parents often view high self-esteem as the most important gift they can give to their children. To achieve this goal, many parents provide a stream of positive, supportive messages. They fear that negative comments will inflict lasting damage. Parenting books, pediatricians, and the media all support the importance of self-esteem.

The intent is a good one. Children need strength in a sometimes inhospitable world. In schools, we can see children who have heard so much criticism that they no longer try to do anything. We know that children, like adults, can be defeated by accepting an image of themselves as inadequate. Therapists are convinced of the damage that negative messages can do to social, academic, and professional functioning. People are especially vulnerable if they enter adulthood with a poor sense of self-worth.

Children do need praise and positive feedback. Unconditional praise, however, can be useless and even destructive. Think of the child who receives praise that is independent of the quality of the work produced. Consider the impact of hearing only about successes and never about limits. Ponder the impact of children believing that they are better and more worthy than everyone else. One of my favorite cartoons shows two mothers talking:

Mother 1: Jamie got an "F" on his report card. It is going to damage his self-esteem. It will destroy his self-image!

Mother 2: Are you going to find a tutor for him so he can do better? Are you going to ground him?

Mother 1: Of course not! I'm going to sue the school!

The concept of self-esteem needs to be revisited. Hearing parents blame the teacher for poor grades will not help an underachieving child work harder to achieve future goals. Neither does it help a child to have a parent devalue another child's accomplishments. When parents devalue athletics to a child who is weaker in that area, the child is unlikely to respect the athletic achievements of others in the future. Parents need to think about the long-term impact of their unconditional praise or other comments.

The very young child builds self-esteem around self-appraisal. At first, children's self-appraisal is based mostly on feeling loved and valued by their parents. As children's cognitive complexity matures, their concept of self extends beyond self-appraisal. They see beyond the all-or-nothing stance of "loved" or "not loved." This more mature view of self includes self-perceptions, and is multidimensional.

Susan Harter (1993) has explored this more complex concept of self-perception. School-age children can understand, for example, that their social capabilities may be very different from their athletic skills. They can also differentiate among scholastic competence, behavioral conduct, and physical appearance. This more mature view of self comes from their developing mental ability. It also emerges from their experiences in the world. As children encounter the demands of school, they incorporate new information about themselves. Many adults can remember being selected last for a gym team or receiving the most time-outs in class. They also remember winning a spelling bee or being elected class president. These experiences explain why some children's self-esteem fluctuates during the early school years. By high school, most young people have a good understanding of their abilities. They know their strengths and limits on many fronts.

High self-esteem is a necessary first step towards successful adjustment. It is, however, not enough. Accurate self-appraisal is the next, equally critical, step for maturity. Our children need help in developing an accurate self-perception. Parents should try to raise children who are fundamentally satisfied with the person they are, but who also have an honest, accurate appraisal of their strengths and weaknesses. Children should be able to acknowledge their limitations. This will encourage them to work hard to improve in areas where they are less able. It will also help them respect the abilities of those who excel in areas where they themselves do not. Parents can do several things to help their children develop an accurate self-perception:

From *Childhood Education*, Summer 2000, p. 240. Reprinted by permission of Helen Altman Klein and the Association for Childhood Education International. © 2000 by ACEI.

- **Encourage your child to value a wide range of competencies.** The early years of school present many challenges to children. On a typical day, a 2nd-grader may be asked to read out loud, complete a work sheet of arithmetic problems, learn a new song, participate in a relay race, and stand quietly in line. Depending on the child, some of these demands may be easy and others may require considerable effort. We cannot do everything with equal success. We should, instead, have a respect for a range of ability.

- **Accept and acknowledge weaknesses and limitations.** If the child reports that he is "terrible" in a certain activity, it is important to assess the accuracy of this belief. If it is false, the child needs to rethink this self-perception. If it is true, it is an important signal for change. Successful adults use failures and difficulties to decide where to put their energies. We should not demand perfection from our children. We need to help them make a commitment to maximize their potentials. An accurate self-perception helps children know where to devote their effort.

- **Encourage children's attempts to change.** Children often need our help in their efforts to change. The fearful child may need extra encouragement to make it through a visit to the dentist for the first time without incident. We may be able to ease the social activities of a shy child by orchestrating a visit by another child. It may be useful to provide extra help for a child who is struggling with long division. A child who receives the support needed to make progress will be better able to tackle challenges throughout life.

- **Support children when they work hard.** It is important that children make a concerted effort to do their work on their own. Many parents are tempted to help their children with homework. As it gets late in the evening, we may want to lend a hand so that the work can be completed. We know that we can do better, neater work. We believe the teacher will be impressed. Many a scout badge and 4H project has been completed with the help of an eager older sibling. We need to remember, however, that the goals for which our child worked the hardest are prized the most. When children assume responsibility for their own actions, they can best value the outcomes.

- **Applaud real successes.** It is good to acknowledge an "A" earned by an academically gifted child. It is much more important to acknowledge the clumsy child who has practiced faithfully and given his all to, for example, learning to dribble a soccer ball. Children know the difference between make-work and real accomplishments. As children gain mastery in real skills, they should take pride in their accomplishments. We need to celebrate their successes. Children also grow when they recognize the strengths of siblings and friends. As children accept their own strengths, they find it easier to accept and applaud those of others.

- **Foster a respect for others who excel in different areas.** We all need people whose skills and abilities differ from our own. I cannot fix my car, but my career depends on its safe and reliable functioning. I cannot carry a tune, but I receive joy from musicians who perform with seeming ease and effortlessness. The skills of others enrich our lives in many areas. We should not devalue the areas where our children do not perform well. To do so is to devalue the skills of children who are different and who excel in those areas. Good self-esteem does not depend on others being "not good."

Our goals for our children need to go beyond self-esteem. The wonder of children lies in their special pattern of skills and potentials. Children thrive with a good and honest appreciation of their own abilities and from a drive to make the best of them. Children need to take on responsibility for developing their own excellence. This includes a commitment to action, and a willingness to appreciate and acknowledge the strengths of others.

References

Harter, S. (1993). Developmental changes in self-understanding across the 5 to 7 shift. In A. Sameroff & M. Haith (Eds.), *Reason and responsibility: The passage through childhood* (pp. 207–236). Chicago: University of Chicago Press.

BEYOND LITTLETON

How Well Do You Know Your Kid?

The new teen wave is bigger, richer, better educated and healthier than any other in history. But there's a dark side, and too many parents aren't doing their job.

By Barbara Kantrowitz and Pat Wingert

JOCKS, PREPS, PUNKS, GOTHS, GEEKS. They may sit at separate tables in the cafeteria, but they all belong to the same generation. There are now 31 million kids in the 12-to-19 age group, and demographers predict that there will be 35 million teens by 2010, a population bulge bigger than even the baby boom at its peak. In many ways, these teens are uniquely privileged. They've grown up in a period of sustained prosperity and haven't had to worry about the draft (as their fathers did) or cataclysmic global conflicts (as their grandparents did). Cable and the Internet have given them access to an almost infinite amount of information. Most expect to go to college, and girls, in particular, have unprecedented opportunities; they can dream of careers in everything from professional sports to politics, with plenty of female role models to follow.

But this positive image of American adolescence in 1999 is a little like yearbook photos that depict every kid as happy and blemish-free. After the Littleton, Colo., tragedy, it's clear there's another dimension to this picture, and it's far more troubled. In survey after survey, many kids—even those on the honor roll—say they feel increasingly alone and alienated, unable to connect with their parents, teachers and sometimes even classmates. They're desperate for guidance, and when they don't get what they need at home or in school, they cling to cliques or immerse themselves in a universe out of their parents' reach, a world defined by computer games, TV and movies, where brutality is so common it has become mundane. The parents of Eric Harris and Dylan Klebold have told friends they never dreamed their sons could kill. It's an extreme case, but it has made a lot of parents wonder: do we really know our kids?

Many teens say they feel overwhelmed by pressure and responsibilities. They are juggling part-time jobs and hours of homework every night; sometimes they're so exhausted that they're nearly asleep in early-morning classes. Half have lived through their parents' divorce. Sixty-three percent are in households where both parents work outside the home, and many look after younger siblings in the afternoon. Still others are home by themselves after school. That unwelcome solitude can extend well into the evening; mealtime for this generation too often begins with a forlorn touch of the microwave.

In fact, of all the issues that trouble adolescents, loneliness ranks at the top of the list. University of Chicago sociologist Barbara Schneider has been studying 7,000 teenagers for five years and has found they spend an average of 3½ hours alone *every day*. Teenagers may claim they want privacy, but they also crave and need attention—and they're not getting it. Author Patricia Hersch profiled eight teens who live in an affluent area of northern Virginia for her 1998 book, "A Tribe Apart." "Every kid I talked to at length eventually came around to saying without my asking that they wished they had more adults in their lives, especially their parents," she says.

Loneliness creates an emotional vacuum that is filled by an intense peer culture, a critical buffer against kids' fear of isolation. Some of this bonding is normal and appropriate; in fact, studies have shown that the human need for acceptance is almost a biological drive, like hunger. It's especially intense in early adolescence, from about 12 to 14, a time of "hyper self-consciousness," says David Elkind, a professor of child development at Tufts University and author of "All Grown Up and No Place to Go." "They become very self-centered and spend a lot of time thinking about what others think of them," Elkind says. "And when they think about what others are thinking, they make the error of thinking that everyone is thinking about *them*." Dressing alike is a refuge, a way of hiding in the group. When they're 3 and scared, they cling to a security blanket; at 16, they want body piercings or Abercrombie shirts.

If parents and other adults abdicate power, teenagers come up with their own rules. It's "Lord of the Flies" on a vast scale. Bullying has become so extreme and so common that many teens just accept it as part of high-school life in the '90s. Emory University psychologist Marshall Duke, an expert on children's friendships, recently asked 110 students in one of his classes if any of them had ever been threatened in high school. To his surprise, "they all raised their hand." In the past, parents and teachers served as mediating forces in the classroom jungle. William Damon, director of the Stanford University Center for Adolescence, re-

Peril and Promise: Teens by the Numbers

They watch too much television, and their parents may not be around enough, but today's teenagers are committing fewer crimes, having fewer babies and generally staying out of serious trouble. Here's a look at who they are—and what they're up to:

Demographics

THE BREAKDOWN
Teenagers account for roughly 10 percent of the U.S. population.

Teens (13–19)

White
18,199,000   66%

Black
3,992,000   15

Hispanic
3,723,000   14

Asian, Pac. Islander
1,030,000   4

American Indian, Eskimo and Aleut
275,000   1

PARENTS AT WORK
Parents work more, so their teenagers are often left unsupervised.

Families with employed parents

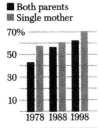

■ Both parents
▨ Single mother

70%
50
30
10
      1978 1988 1998

KIDS HAVING KIDS: A TREND ON THE DECLINE
The birthrate among teens has fallen dramatically, down 16 percent overall.

Birthrates for females 15–19

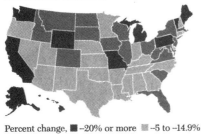

Percent change, ■ –20% or more ▨ –5 to –14.9%
1991–97   ■ –15 to –19.9%

DROP IN CRIME
In 1997, kids were responsible for 17 percent of violent-crime arrests.

Arrests per 100,000 juveniles 10–17

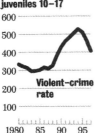

600
500
400
300
200   **Violent-crime rate**
100
      1980 85   90   95

Lifestyle

SEXUAL ACTIVITY
Almost one out of five teenagers is still a virgin by the age of 20.

Percentage of teens who have had sexual intercourse, 1995

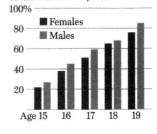

100%
80   ■ Females
60   ▨ Males
40
20
   Age 15 16   17   18   19

COOLEST BRANDS

Boys	Girls
Nike	Nike
Sony	adidas
Tommy Hilfiger	Tommy Hilfiger
Nintendo	The Gap
adidas	Old Navy

FAVORITE TV SHOWS

Boys	Girls
'The Simpsons'	'Dawson's Creek'
'South Park'	'Friends'
'MTV'	'7th Heaven'
'Home Improve.'	'The Simpsons'
'Friends'	'Buffy the V.S.'

LESS OF THE BAD STUFF: SMOKING, DRINKING AND DOING DRUGS
Today, teens say, they misbehave less than kids in the recent past. The percentage who, in the last 30 days, admit to having used ...

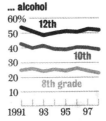

... alcohol
60% **12th**
50
40
30   **10th**
20
10   8th grade
   1991   93   95   97

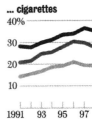

... cigarettes
40%
30
20
10
   1991   93   95   97

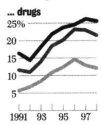

... drugs
25%
20
15
10
5
   1991   93   95   97

Home life

PASSING THE HOURS
Kids spend more time partying than studying each week. They also like tube time.

Activity	percentage of teens	/hours
Watching TV	98%	11.0
Listening to CDs, tapes, etc.	96	9.9
Doing chores	84	4.1
Studying	59	3.7
Going to parties	58	4.0
Going to religious functions	51	2.5
Working at a regular paid job	32	4.7

WHAT WERE WE TALKING ABOUT?
Parents and kids both say they're discussing important life issues.

Issue discussed	parents	/kids
Alcohol/drugs	98%	90%
How to handle violent situations	83	80
Basic facts of reproduction	76	80
AIDS	78	75

● **85%** of teens said that **Mom** cares 'very much' about them. **58%** said the same about **Dad.**

● **25%** of teens said that their **mom** is 'always' home when they return from school. **10%** said their **dad** was.

● Do parents let teenagers make their own decisions about weekend **curfew**? **66%** said no.

● How much are teens '**understood**' by their family members? **35%** said 'quite a bit.'

SPENDING HABITS
Teens average just under $100 in total weekly spending.

Weekly spending

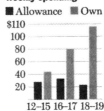

■ Allowance ▨ Own

$110
100
80
60
40
20
   12–15 16–17 18–19

RESEARCH BY BRET BEGUN. SOURCES: CENSUS BUREAU; BLS; NAT'L CENTER FOR JUVENILE JUSTICE; NCHS; TEENAGE RESEARCH UNLIMITED; MONITORING THE FUTURE STUDY, UNIV. OF MICHIGAN; KAISER FAMILY FOUNDATION; NAT'L LONGITUDINAL STUDY OF ADOLESCENT HEALTH; JUPITER COMMUNICATIONS; GREENFIELD ONLINE; THE ALAN GUTTMACHER INST.

Online

HOOKED UP
47% of teens are using the computer to go online this year.

Percentage of teens who go online

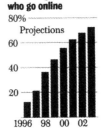

80%
   Projections
60
40
20
   1996 98   00   02

WHAT DO THEY DO?
They keep up with each other—and what's out there.

Top 10 activities

E-mail	83%
Search engine	78
Music sites	59
General research	58
Games	51
TV/movie sites	43
Chat room	42
Own Web page	38
Sports sites	35

EVERY MOVE THEY MAKE
With age comes online freedom. Here's how parents say they monitor their kids while they're on the Net.

	Age 11–15	16–18
Sit with them while online	38%	9%
Kids can log on only with an adult	34	5
Mainly use for online games	28	15
Limit hours for kids' use	47	21
Know which Web sites kids can visit	68	43
Kids are online whenever they want	54	75
Use the Net more than watching TV	19	22

calls writing a satirical essay when he was in high school about how he and his friends tormented a kid they knew. Damon got an "A" for style and grammar, but the teacher took him aside and told him he should be ashamed of his behavior. "That's what is supposed to happen," Damon says. "People are supposed to say, 'Hey, kid, you've gone too far here'." Contrast that with reports from Littleton, where Columbine students described a film class nonchalantly viewing a murderous video created by Eric Harris and Dylan Klebold. In 1999 this apparently was not remarkable behavior.

When they're isolated from parents, teens are also more vulnerable to serious emotional problems. Surveys of high-school students have indicated that one in four considers suicide each year, says Dr. David Fassler, a child and adolescent psychiatrist in Burlington, Vt., and author of "Help Me, I'm Sad: Recognizing, Treating and Preventing Childhood and Adolescent Depression." By the end of high school, many have actually tried to kill themselves. "Often the parents or teachers don't realize it was a suicide attempt," he says. "It can be something ambiguous like an overdose of nonprescription pills from the medicine cabinet or getting drunk and crashing the car with suicidal thoughts."

Even the best, most caring parents can't protect their teenagers from all these problems, but involved parents can make an enormous difference. Kids do listen. Teenage drug use (although still high) is slowly declining, and even teen pregnancy and birthrates are

down slightly—largely because of improved education efforts, experts say. More teens are delaying sex, and those who are sexually active are more likely to use contraceptives than their counterparts a few years ago.

In the teenage years, the relationship between parents and children is constantly evolving as the kids edge toward independence. Early adolescence is a period of transition, when middle-school kids move from one teacher and one classroom to a different teacher for each subject. In puberty, they're moody and irritable. "This is a time when parents and kids bicker a lot," says Laurence Steinberg, a psychology professor at Temple University and author of "You and Your Adolescent: A Parents' Guide to Ages 10 to 20." "Parents are caught by surprise," he says. "They discover that the tricks they've used in raising their kids effectively during childhood stop working." He advises parents to try to understand what their kids are going through; things do get better. "I have a 14-year-old son," Steinberg says, "and when he moved out of the transition phase into middle adolescence, we saw a dramatic change. All of a sudden, he's our best friend again."

IN MIDDLE ADOLESCENCE, ROUGHLY THE first three years of high school, teens are increasingly on their own. To a large degree, their lives revolve around school and their friends. "They have a healthy sense of self," says Steinberg. They begin to develop a unique sense of identity, as well as their own values and beliefs. "The danger in this

time would be to try to force them to be something you want them to be, rather than help them be who they are." Their relationships may change dramatically as their interests change; in Schneider's study, almost three quarters of the closest friends named by seniors weren't even mentioned during sophomore year.

Late adolescence is another transition, this time to leaving home altogether. "Parents have to be able to let go," says Steinberg, and "have faith and trust that they've done a good enough job as parents that their child can handle this stuff." Contrary to stereotypes, it isn't mothers who are most likely to mourn in the empty nest. They're often relieved to be free of some chores. But Steinberg says that fathers "suffer from thoughts of missed chances."

That should be the ultimate lesson of tragedies like Littleton. "Parents need to share what they really believe in, what they really think is important," says Stanford's Damon. "These basic moral values are more important than math skills or SATs." Seize any opportunity to talk—in the car, over the breakfast table, watching TV. Parents have to work harder to get their points across. Ellen Galinsky, president of the Families and Work Institute, has studied teenagers' views of parents. "One 16-year-old told us, 'I am proud of the fact that [my mother] deals with me even though I try to push her away. She's still there'." So pay attention now. The kids can't wait.

With ANNE UNDERWOOD

BEYOND LITTLETON

The Truth About High School

From who's in which clique to where you sit in the cafeteria, every day can be struggle to fit in.

BY JERRY ADLER

IT WAS ONE CARELESS MOMENT IN THE cafeteria that she now believes will haunt her forever, or at least until graduation, whichever comes first. Blond, smart, athletic and well off, she must have thought she could get away with sitting down with a couple of gawky skaters from the fringe of high-school society, if only to interview them about hip-hop music for the school newspaper. She should have known that in high school, appearance outweighs motive by 100 to 1. There were giggles and stares, then loss of gossip privileges and exile from her seat at the center table next to the jocks. Now, a year later, recovered from a bout of anorexia as she tried to starve her way back into favor, she has found new friends. But the formerly cool sophomore, too humiliated to bear being identified, views her years in a West Coast high school as "hell."

It should come as no surprise, given the events of two weeks ago, that teenagers can turn their social lives into a matter of life and death. Since the invention of high school, adolescents have been forming cliques and mentally ranking them— it is, says David Zinn, adolescent psychiatrist at Chicago's Beacon Therapeutic Center, excellent practice for an adult society "dominated by hierarchies." The relative positions of some groups have shifted over time, reflecting changes in adult society: jocks are, like their adult models, bigger than ever; cheerleaders are less exalted, perhaps because girls are now playing more sports themselves; while kids are still doing drugs, they've lost some of their demimonde glamor. In general, Zinn believes, high-school kids are more tolerant of differences than they were a gen-

eration ago. Minority kids, penetrating deep into the heartland, are less likely to be regarded as exotic freaks. But one of the biggest changes, says University of North Carolina pediatrician William Coleman, is driven by simple loneliness. As adolescents spend less and less time with their parents, cliques increasingly fill the emotional vacuum, and the high-school game of acceptance or rejection is being played for even higher emotional stakes.

Athletes enforce the social code at most high schools, which helps explain why they're usually at the top. "It's pretty common," says senior Lowell Crabb, a varsity football and baseball player at South Pasadena High, near Los Angeles, "to see jocks picking on the fat kid or the wimpy kid, or anybody who's different." Jocks were like that even in the old days, before their games were

From *Newsweek*, May 10, 1999, pp. 56-58. © 1999 by Newsweek, Inc. All rights reserved. Reprinted by permission.

90% of Americans say parents aren't spending enough time with their teens;

56% say teens don't have enough places to go to help them stay out of trouble

broadcast on the school's in-house cable channel, their teams were ranked nationally by USA Today and big-city newspapers sent reporters around to interview them. Now Chicago psychiatrist Marc Slutsky believes their aggression is a response to the increased pressure they labor under. While schools have grown more and more concerned with nurturing students' academic self-esteem, athletics are becoming increasingly performance-driven and professional. "These kids get the least sensitive treatment," he says. "All that pressure on them saying 'don't screw up' gets displaced onto others."

Once high schools were divided simply into the in-crowd and everyone else. But as they have grown larger they have spawned a fabulous diversity of gangs, cliques, crews and posses. These include athletes and preppies and wanna-be gangsters; pot-smoking skaters and sullen punks; gays and nerds and, yes, morbid, chalk-faced Goths. Cliques proclaim their identities with uniforms that are surprisingly similar from coast to coast. Chinos and button-down shirts mark kids as preppies a thousand miles from Andover; baggy jeans signify hip-hop on a Laotian kid in Iowa no less than on a homeboy straight out of BedStuy.

Long before most people had heard of Columbine High School, the black trench coat was a potent symbol for kids in places like central Texas who would rather suffocate than conform to how the cool kids thought they should dress.

In contrast to a generation ago, cliques are much more likely to have both boys and girls in them, Zinn says, a development he traces to early exposure to sexual imagery on television. "Familiarity with the opposite sex comes much earlier now," he says. "You don't find as much mystery or excitement attached to it."

The lush diversity of cliques has made student life more democratic. "This isn't like a pyramid with one group on top," says Eva Greenwald, a senior at Oak Park and River Forest High School near Chicago, population 2,700. "Think of us as living in a lot of different bubbles." Conversely, in schools this size students can live not just apart from their peers, but almost unaware of them. Andrew, a senior athlete and honor student at Cal High School in Whittier, Calif. eats his lunch with his friends every day in the quad. After four years at Cal, "I have no idea what goes on in the cafeteria," he says. "I've actually never been in there."

Some students jealously guard their turf. At Glenbrook South High School, in the Chicago suburb of Glenview, the groups even take their names from their perches: the fashionable "wall people" who favor a bench along the wall outside the cafeteria, and the punkish "trophy-case" kids who sit on the floor under a display of memorabilia. When freshman Stephanie Hernandez sat at the wall one day last fall, she was ordered off the bench by a football player, and hasn't sat there since. "It's just a piece of plastic with holes in it, but they love it," she says. "OK, you can have your bench."

Must life be like this? Experiments in creating egalitarian high-school cultures have met with mixed results. The Paideia School, founded

A Teen Who's Who

Jocks rule and nerds still struggle for acceptance just about everywhere. But many schools have unique cliques. A look at Illinois' Glenbrook South High:

Trophy-Case Kids Named for their hangout under the school awards case. They're punkish in black hooded sweatshirts.

Wall Kids Mostly seniors, mostly popular. Lots of preppies and "Abercrombies." Their turf: a wall outside the cafeteria.

Bandies Musicians, they stick to themselves outside rehearsal room. Not especially cool or uncool, just good friends.

Backstage People Theater and arts types (both genders) lounge on couches backstage to talk, do homework and take naps.

Student-Council Kids Clean-cut, popular. Lunch-time hangout: the council office.

in 1971 as a liberal alternative to the white-flight academies springing up in Atlanta, sought to pre-empt jock culture by decreeing that every student had to be on a sports team. "I'm not a jock, I'm an athlete," says junior Will Arnold, a distinction that might seem superfluous for the captain of the Ultimate Frisbee team. This system has worked well, but it was tested last year when both the boys' and girls' basketball teams made it to the state finals, and hero-worship reared its unfamiliar head. "It can be seductive," headmaster Paul Bianchi says. "People like to see their names in the paper." Glenbrook South, home of the wall kids and trophy-case kids, makes an extraordinary effort at inclusiveness, offering something like 70 clubs and 23 sports and both regular and alternative student newspapers and theater groups. But still, says principal David Smith, there's no avoiding the fact that "adolescence is a tribal society. It's just the nature of the thing."

Fitting in is partly a matter of choice. Wearing black trench coats to school is not just a neutral fashion choice, but a way of flaunting one's indifference to the ruling cliques, which is precisely why the cool kids find it so infuriating. But fitting in is also a gift. To be popular, "either you have money, you look good or you play football," says Steve Walker, the gregarious captain of the football team at Merritt Island High School, 50 miles east of Orlando, Fla. Lacking those, you could try throwing a really great party, he says, but "other than that, I couldn't tell you, because I've been popular all my life. As long as I show up, the party's going to be OK."

In some ways, the system works, assigning kids the roles they're comfortable with. As an experiment one day last month, Lauren Barry, a pink-haired trophy-case kid at Glenbrook, switched identities with a well-dressed girl from "the wall." Barry walked around all day in the girl's expensive jeans and Doc Martens, carrying a shopping bag from Abercrombie & Fitch. "People kept saying, 'Oh, you look so pretty',"

she recalls. "I felt really uncomfortable." It was interesting, but the next day, and ever since, she's been back in her regular clothes. The lines drawn by teenagers are frequently unfair, often hurtful and generally enforced by physical and psychological intimidation. Which is why it's worth bearing in mind that high school only seems as if it lasts forever.

With John McCormick and Karen Springen in Chicago, Daniel Pedersen in Atlanta, Nadine Joseph in San Francisco, Ana Figueroa in Los Angeles and Beth Dickey in Melbourne, Fla.

Unit Selections

Key Points to Consider

❖ What information should parents and teachers of disabled students seek in order to best serve their needs?

❖ Who are the gifted and talented? How can knowledge of their characteristics and learning needs help to provide them with an appropriate education?

❖ What cultural differences exist in our society? How can teacher expectations affect the culturally or academically diverse child? How would multicultural education help teachers deal more effectively with these differences?

❖ What are some of the criticisms concerning multicultural programs?

 **Links**   **www.dushkin.com/online/**

These sites are annotated on pages 4 and 5.

The Equal Educational Opportunity Act for All Handicapped Children (Public Law 94-142) gives disabled children the right to an education in the least-restrictive environment, due process, and an individualized educational program that is specifically designed to meet their needs. Professionals and parents of exceptional children are responsible for developing and implementing an appropriate educational program for each child. The application of these ideas to classrooms across the nation at first caused great concern among educators and parents. Classroom teachers whose training did not prepare them for working with the exceptional child expressed

negative attitudes about mainstreaming. Special resource teachers also expressed concern that mainstreaming would mitigate the effectiveness of special programs for the disabled and would force cuts in services. Parents feared that their children would not receive the special services they required because of governmental red tape and delays in proper diagnosis and placement.

It has been more than two decades since the implementation of P.L. 94-142, which was amended by the Individuals with Disabilities Education Act (IDEA) in 1991 and introduced the term "inclusion." Inclusion tries to assure that disabled children will be fully integrated within the classroom. Many of the above concerns have been studied by psychologists and educators, and their findings have often influenced policy. For example, research has indicated that inclusion is more effective when regular classroom teachers and special resource teachers work cooperatively with disabled children.

The articles concerning the educationally disabled confront some of these issues. Susan Lei Lani Stewart presents "Good Questions to Ask: When a Child With a Developmental Delay Joins Your Class," and the author of "Does My Child Need Ritalin?" offers a description of attention deficit hyperactivity disorder and effective ways to treat it. Other exceptional children are the gifted and talented. These children are rapid learners who can absorb, organize, and apply concepts more effectively than the average child. They often have IQs of 140 or more and are convergent thinkers (i.e., they give the correct answer to teacher or test questions). Convergent thinkers are usually models of good behavior and academic performance, and they respond to instruction easily; teachers generally value such children and often nominate them for gifted programs. There are other children, however, who do not score well on standardized tests of intelligence because their thinking is more divergent

(i.e., they can imagine more than one answer to teacher or test questions). These gifted divergent thinkers may not respond to traditional instruction. They may become bored, respond to questions in unique and disturbing ways, and appear uncooperative and disruptive. Many teachers do not understand these unconventional thinkers and fail to identify them as gifted. In fact, such children are sometimes labeled as emotionally disturbed or mentally retarded because of the negative impressions they make on their teachers. Because of the differences between these types of students, a great deal of controversy surrounds programs for the gifted. Such programs should enhance the self-esteem of all gifted and talented children, motivate and challenge them, and help them realize their creative potential. The two articles in the subsection on gifted children consider the characteristics of giftedness, and they explain how to identify gifted students and provide them with an appropriate education.

The third subsection of this unit concerns student diversity. Just as labeling may adversely affect the disabled child, it may also affect the child who comes from a minority ethnic background where the language and values are quite different from those of the mainstream culture. The term "disadvantaged" is often used to describe these children, but it is negative, stereotypical, and apt to result in a self-fulfilling prophecy whereby teachers perceive such children as incapable of learning. Teachers should provide academically and culturally diverse children with experiences that they might have missed in the restricted environment of their homes and neighborhoods. Rita Dunn, in "The Goals and Track Record of Multicultural Education," takes issue with some aspects of multicultural programs while other articles in this section address these individual differences and suggest strategies for teaching these diverse children.

PATIENT POWER

DOES MY CHILD NEED RITALIN?

Stimulants are still the most effective treatment for ADHD. The challenge is to use them wisely.

BY ANDREW ADESMAN, M.D.

AS A PEDIATRICIAN SPECIALIZING IN ATTENTION deficit hyperactivity disorder (ADHD), I sometimes envy my colleagues. When they recognize a child's asthma or an ear infection, they're seldom asked to justify the diagnosis or defend the use of established treatments. But parents are understandably squeamish about ADHD. Followers of the news know that more and more kids are being treated with Ritalin and other stimulants, and that treatment rates vary widely from one community to the next. Many conclude that we're simply drugging healthy children into submission. When I present parents with a diagnosis of ADHD they often ask, "Why can't boys just be boys?" And when I discuss stimulant therapy they ask, "Won't that speed him up?" or "Won't that make him a zombie?"

The truth is, ADHD is not an imaginary disorder. It places kids at risk of everything from school failure to drug abuse—and studies have repeatedly found that stimulants are the single most effective way to treat it. Yes, the erratic rise in treatment rates is disconcerting. But studies suggest that overdiagnosis is not common. In fact, only a small percentage of children with ADHD are receiving medication at any given time. The issue is not whether children can benefit from these drugs. The real issue, especially for a worried parent, is how to use them effectively.

The first challenge is to get a good diagnosis. It's normal for kids to become restless and inattentive at one time or another; ADHD should be considered only if these symptoms significantly interfere with

functioning. DSM-IV, the accepted guide to psychiatric disorders, defines ADHD broadly as inattention, impulsivity or hyperactivity that causes significant trouble at home and school. The DSM doesn't offer precise, numerical measures of these problems, but it does provide criteria for making a diagnosis. Besides assessing the child's behavior, academic standing and social functioning, a physician who suspects a child has ADHD should seek out independent assessments from teachers and parents. Their reponses to questionnaires can help gauge how much difficulty the child is having compared with his or her peers.

ADHD is not the only thing that keeps kids from concentrating. Hyperactivity or distractibility can also reflect social, emotional or developmental problems that exist apart from—or in addition to— ADHD. I once had a 9-year-old patient whose teachers considered him inattentive because he misunderstood directions and often asked them to repeat questions. It turned out that his hearing was mildly impaired, and more specialized tests showed he was unable to process auditory information normally.

If a child does have ADHD, medication is not the whole secret to managing it. Parents and teachers can help kids cope with the condition by establishing consistent routines, reinforcing appropriate behavior and making educational accommodations. Treatment of preschoolers should start with these behavioral interventions, and move on to medication only as a last resort.

School-age children are a different story. Stimulants such as Ritalin (methylphenidate), Dexedrine and Adderall are highly effective for kids in this group, and parents shouldn't feel guilty about employing them along with behavioral and educational interventions. None of these drugs will cure ADHD. But when they're effective, they can improve attention, reduce restlessness and foster better relations with peers, parents and teachers. Each of the three stimulant medications has roughly a 75 percent response rate—and kids who don't respond well to one of them will often respond to another. Overall, an estimated 90 percent of school-age children with ADHD respond well to treatment with these drugs.

They all have mild, dose-related side effects, such as decreased appetite at lunch and a modest delay in bedtime. Some children become moody or irritable as the medication wears off at the end of the day, and a few report headaches or stomachaches. Studies indicate that some children may grow more slowly during treatment, but no one has documented any effect on kids' ultimate height. A careful physician can minimize all these side effects by "starting low and going slow," I usually start a child at half the dose I expect will be needed, then raise it gradually to find the low-est effective dose. And I generally try all reasonable doses of one medication before switching to another.

Some critics worry that kids who respond well to stimulants in the short term may suffer adverse effects later on. But Ritalin and other amphetamines have been available for more than 40 years and been given to millions of children. Few other medications can make this claim, and certainly no other medications have been scrutinized and researched as extensively. Long-term follow-up studies to date are limited but quite reassuring. For example, some parents worry that treatment with stimulants will encourage their kids to use illicit drugs later on. The reverse is true. Although youngsters with ADHD are indeed at increased risk for drug abuse, those treated with stimulants appear less likely to develop that problem. So think twice before you rule out stimulants. You maybe depriving your child of truly effective treatment.

ADESMAN *is director of developmental and behavioral pediatrics at the Schneider Children's Hospital in New York.*

Good Questions to Ask: When a Child with a Developmental Delay Joins Your Class

Susan Lei Lani Stewart

It is always a challenge for a teacher when a child with a developmental delay joins the class. The challenge may be positive and yet overwhelming.

In my own early experience of teaching young children, although I was excited to draw children with developmental delays into the class, I often felt overwhelmed by what I did not know. Traditional questions asked of parents upon their child's enrollment did not always provide the information I needed to truly include the child with a developmental delay.

For example, whether a child has a medical diagnosis of Down syndrome or an educational assessment of a developmental delay, it is critical that the teacher consider the *uniqueness* of the child. While children with Down syndrome may have some similar characteristics, each child has individual strengths and needs. A simple diagnosis can never capture the whole individual child.

Today teachers and caregivers have a wealth of resources they can access when a child with a developmental delay joins their class. It is important to tap these resources, but unless the teacher has used or heard about the resources before, obtaining information and support can be daunting.

The questions to ask parents and specialists (that follow) are a good place to begin. These questions have emerged from my experiences in teaching young children with disabilities and delays in community preschools.

From questions to answers

Building relationships with specialists in the community will have a great impact on a teacher's program. Specialists can serve as resources for particular concerns and can refer the teacher or caregiver to literature or to others with specialized knowledge. Tapping into these resources the educator expands her ability to work with all children competently and confidently.

In areas of the United States that are remote or have few specialists, it is possible for the early childhood educator and caregiver to access helpful information by other means. Each state has an Interagency Coordinating Council (ICC) for the care and education of infants and young children with disabilities. Teachers can contact their state departments of education, health, or welfare to locate area representatives. They can use the Internet to communicate with specialists from other areas.

All of us must Read! Read! but beware, for each author has a particular bent, and information may not be based in research or theory.

Asking questions and seeking answers can seem overwhelming. However, a teacher builds a strong foundation of knowledge that she can employ in her classroom, which in turn makes teaching more pleasurable and effective.

Questions to Ask Parents

It is important to remember that parents respond to disabilities in numerous ways. Sensitivity to the family and respect are critical in fostering a positive parent-preschool relationship. Some parents may not wish to share this information with you.

1. Does your child have any medical or physical issues we should know about so that we can protect him or her from harm while at school?

Many disabling conditions have secondary issues that impact the care and education of young children with developmental delays. For example, some children with Down syndrome have *atlanto-axial subluxation,* a condition causing instability of a neck joint and having implications for physical activity.

2. Is your child eligible for special services through the school district?

This information allows the teacher to determine if there is someone with whom she may consult regarding the child's strengths, needs, and behaviors. If a child is eligible for special services through the public school system, the child will have a service coordinator and will receive services from a multidisciplinary team (MDT) of professionals.

Generally, children who have developmental delays and are between the ages of three and five receive special services through the local school district (or the lead educational agency). Infants and toddlers who have developmental delays may receive services through the local school district or through another agency such as mental health.

3. Does your child have an Individualized Family Service Plan (IFSP) or an Individualized Education Plan (IEP)?

The child who is eligible for special services must have an IFSP or IEP, authorized in the 1997 Amendments to the Individuals with Disabilities Education Act (IDEA). These plans, which guide the intervention services for individual children, are created and carried out by the MDT (i.e., service coordinator, teacher,

therapists, family, and other specialists as needed).

The information contained in an IFSP or IEP outlines the strengths of the child, areas in which the child needs additional support, specific goals for the child, how and when the goals are to be met, who will work with the child to meet those goals, how often the child will receive specific services and who will pay for those services, the location in which services will be provided (with a preference for the most natural environment), and plans for the child's transition from one program to the next program. These plans can help the teacher make adjustments in the classroom environment or curriculum to support and facilitate the development of individual children.

4. Are there any services (medical, educational, or therapeutic) that your child is receiving outside of the school district that you think we should know about?

If the parent is comfortable sharing this information, it can be beneficial for the teacher to know what different services therapists or interventionists are providing the child and family so as not to work at cross purposes. Information from therapists and interventionists can help teachers more fully include a child in the class and enable them to support the intervention efforts through classroom activities and experiences.

5. What are your expectations for your child in this class?

Although we often assume that parental desires and expectations are a driving force of the IFSP/IEP, parents may have unwritten expectations about their child's performance in the classroom. Unexpressed expectations may lead to parental dissatisfaction with the preschool experience. In offering parents an opportunity to express their expectations, the teacher implies an honest discussion of the

feasibility of meeting parental desires within the preschool environment, creating a parent-teacher relationship built on trust rather than unrealistic expectations and unmet desires.

Ideally the teacher and care provider should be part of the team of professionals acting in the interests of a child who has been identified as eligible to receive special services. For various reasons, at times a team member is overlooked in the process of planning for a child's specialized services or connecting in the information loop. Prepared with questions such as these, the teacher can become an informed and productive team member.

Questions to Ask Specialists

Confidentiality is essential for the protection of the family! Teachers should ask only specific questions of a specialist about a particular child when they have been given written permission by parents. Even if it means that a teacher could serve the child better with more knowledge about what occurs beyond the classroom, respect for the family's right to privacy is imperative.

1. What should I know about this child so that I can effectively involve her in my class and keep her from harm?

Specialists who have previously worked with a child are likely aware of strategies that are particularly effective for that child. Specialists are often trained to see environments with different eyes, which makes them a valuable resource to the teacher for information about adjusting the classroom environment to the unique needs of the individual.

2. May I get a copy of the IFSP or IEP?

When teachers are part of a child's support team, they should have a copy of the child's IFSP/IEP in their files. If the teacher is not currently a part of the child's team, she may want to request of the family that she be included so as to support the child's growth and development while in her care.

3. What are the expectations for this child in my class?

The IFSP/IEP should state explicitly what goals and objectives the child is to work on in particular settings. Professionals, like parents, may also have unwritten expectations about the child's performance in the classroom. It is helpful for teachers to know those expectations and address them appropriately.

4. As the teacher, what are the expectations of me in this child's IFSP/IEP?

If intervention is to occur in the classroom, the IFSP/IEP should state explicitly the expected role of the child's teacher. Teachers may be expected to assist the child in achieving goals and objectives, track the child's progress, assess his skills, and evaluate how well the program is supporting the child's progress toward the goals established in the IFSP/IEP.

A teacher may not be expected to work specifically with the child on his goals, but to welcome specialists into the classroom to work with the child or schedule her day to accommodate pullout services in a separate room. The variations on these themes are many. A teacher being clear at the outset as to her roles and responsibilities can prevent a lot of confusion and uncomfortable situations.

5. What can I do in the classroom to support outside intervention efforts?

If a child receives intervention services only in environments other than the classroom, the teacher can also support the child's use of new and developing skills under the guidance of the intervention specialists. Even if the classroom is not considered the primary site of intervention, all of the child's environments should work in tandem to support her growth and development so that she has multiple opportunities to practice and refine her skills.

6. How can I deal with [mention a specific concern]?

Since children typically spend a large portion of their day in preschool or child care, teachers have the opportunity to observe a child from a broad perspective and inform team members of their observations. A teacher is likely to have many questions about a child's behavior that have not been addressed previously by other team members. It may be that others have not observed the child exhibiting specific behaviors that concern the teacher.

Specialists who have worked with many different children, however, may support the teacher greatly in investigating the behaviors further and provide helpful suggestions on addressing the behaviors. Sometimes a behavior warrants specialized intervention. In any case, teachers should not hesitate to ask. Their action may alert the team to a significant concern, ease the teachers' own minds, build up their professional repertoires of teaching skills, and/or support the growth

and development of the child—all valid reasons to ask questions.

Resources

Council for Exceptional Children
1920 Association Drive
Reston, VA 22091-1589
800-328-0272, TDD: 703-264-9449
http://www.cec.sped.org
Division for Early Childhood:
http://www.dec-sped.org
Young Exceptional Children
The Division for Early Childhood of the Council for Exceptional Children—
303-620-4576
1444 Wazee Street, Suite 230
Denver, CO 80202

For further reading

Allred, K.W., R. Briem, & S.J. Black. 1998. Collaboratively addressing needs of young children with disabilities. *Young Children* 53 (5): 32–36.

Chandler, P. 1994. *A place for me: Including children with special needs in early care and education settings.* Washington, DC: NAEYC.

Murphy, D.M. 1997. Parent and teacher plan for the child. *Young Children* 52 (4): 32–36.

Olson, J., C.L. Murphy, & P.D. Olson. 1999. Readying parents and teachers for the inclusion of children with disabilities: A step-by-step process. *Young Children* 54 (3): 18–22.

Tertell, E.A., S.M. Klein, & J.L. Jewett, eds. 1998. *When teachers reflect: Journeys toward effective, inclusive practice.* Washington, DC: NAEYC.

Wolery, M., P.S. Strain, & D.B. Bailey. 1992. Reaching potentials of children with special needs. In *Reaching potentials: Appropriate curriculum and assessment for young children,* S. Bredekamp & T. Rosegrant eds. Vol. 1, 92–111. Washington, DC: NAEYC.

Wolery, M., & J.S. Wilbers, eds. 1994. *Including children with special needs in early childhood programs.* Washington, DC: NAEYC.

Susan Lei Lani Stewart, Ph.D., *is an assistant professor of education and director of the birth to kindergarten program at Salem College in Winston-Salem, North Carolina. As a preschool teacher, Susan included children with delays and disabilities in her classroom.*

Meeting the Needs of Gifted Learners in the Early Childhood Classroom

**Brooke Walker,
Norma Lu Hafenstein,
and Linda Crow-Enslow**

In one corner of an early childhood classroom, there is a cave constructed of brown butcher paper. Stalactites and stalagmites fabricated from iridescent cellophane hang from the roof of the cave. A model of a volcano, painted in bright colors, graces the window. The parts of the volcano are labeled: magma, lava, crater, crust, and ash. Inside the volcano are "gems" fashioned from glitter that sparkles when the sun shines through the window. Hanging from the classroom ceiling is a large model of the earth with the interior parts labeled: crust, mantle, outer core, and inner core. Stories written or dictated by the children, titled "When I Went to the Center of the Earth," decorate the walls.

Fifteen children, ages three and four, are engrossed in many different learning-center activities designed around the theme The Earth, their present integrated-thematic unit. In the block center three children build ramps to roll their rocks down. Brian exclaims as he knocks down a ramp, "An earthquake struck and broke my ramp."

In the math center Sarah separates rocks into sets of eight. Steven is adding up his rocks: "One plus four is five," he counts as he writes the answer in his equation book. In the science center Patty sorts rocks into "soft" and "hard" piles. George and Sally are weighing rocks on a scale, then graphing results with a teacher's help. In the art center two children create sand paintings while two others paint "pet rocks." In the language center Peter writes different rock words to put in his "Can Can," a small can

containing slips of paper with unit words on them: earth, cave, rock, mantle, plate, volcano, fault, crust, lava, fossil, core.

True learning in early childhood occurs when children involve themselves in a variety of developmentally appropriate learning experiences presented in an interdisciplinary manner. Effective early childhood teachers continually adapt and expand these experiences to respond to the individual needs of the children in their classrooms.

The vignettes above describe activities in a classroom in which an integrated-thematic curriculum has been designed to meet the needs of young gifted children. To develop an appropriate curriculum for these children, early childhood teachers need an understanding of the characteristics that distinguish such children from their peers and ways to differentiate the curriculum to address their educational needs.

Today the concept of giftedness is expanding beyond the traditional emphasis on general academic prowess (Nutall, Romero, & Kalesnick 1992). Research with preschoolers is pinpointing capabilities that may be the building blocks of giftedness in differentiated areas such as science, art, and music (Goldsmith & Feldman 1985; Wexler-Sherman, Gardner, & Feldman 1988). Recognizing this, Nutall, Romero, and

There are many types of giftedness. A person can be musically gifted, artistically gifted, athletically gifted, and so on. This article is about intellectually gifted children.

Kalesnick (1992) propose the following definition for gifted children:

> Gifted children are those showing sustained evidence of advanced capability relative to their peers in general academic skills and/or in more specific domains (music, art, science, etc.) to the extent that they need differentiated educational programming. (p. 302)

Characteristics of young intellectually gifted children

Labeling children is not a preferred method of dealing with differences; however, it is sometimes necessary in order to provide children with appropriate educational programming. Although there are always differences among children (Barbour 1992), research has demonstrated that as a group, young gifted children possess characteristics that distinguish them from their peers in the areas of cognitive, affective, and physical development.

In their cognitive development, young gifted children may demonstrate a high level of language development, an accelerated pace of thought, the ability to generate original ideas and solutions, a sensitivity to learning, and the ability to synthesize and think abstractly (Roedell, Jackson, & Robinson 1980; Hollinger & Kosak 1985; Lewis & Michaelson 1985; Parke & Ness 1988; VanTassel-Baska 1988; Lewis & Louis 1991).

These children's attention spans and interests often differ from the norm. They are able to concentrate for comparatively long periods of time on subjects that interest them. In many cases they develop "passion" areas in which they are intensely interested (Parke & Ness 1988).

There may be discrepancies between physical and intellectual development (Roedell 1990). Motor skills, often fine-motor, lag behind cognitive and conceptual abilities (Webb & Kleine 1993). Young gifted children may see in their mind's eye what they

want to draw or construct, but their motor skills do not allow them to achieve their goal (Webb 1994).

In their affective development, young gifted children often have an evaluative approach to themselves and others. They attempt to organize people and things in a search for consistency and justice. They may invent complex games and try to organize their playmates (Webb 1994).

Young gifted children are often very sensitive to their emotions and those of others (Schetky 1981). They are more aware of the world around them, of their place in it, and of the relationships between people and places, time and spaces. Their mature vocabularies and ideas and frequently uneven development make them vulnerable to social isolation if they lack interaction with children of similar abilities.

These children are still preschoolers developmentally, however, and their curriculum needs to emphasize exploration, manipulation, and play (Parke & Ness 1988). As Riley notes,

> Much of the knowledge children absorb is best acquired by exploration in the real world where they may freely, actively, construct their vision of reality, rather than being passively instructed about it. (1974, 139)

Young children learn by observing what happens when they interact with materials and people. Development of their skills is achieved through hands-on learning (Piaget & Inhelder 1969).

Developing curriculum to meet the needs of high-ability young children

While young gifted children need developmentally appropriate activities similar to those of their same-age peers, their unique characteristics dictate the need for curriculum differentiation. Children with advanced abilities require opportunities to be exposed to and use the vocabulary and concepts typically used by much older children. They need to study subjects in depth because they have

Photo courtesy of the authors

©Subjects & Predicates

unusually keen powers to make connections and perceive relationships. Curriculum should be individualized to meet their high levels of ability in particular domains.

An integrated-thematic curriculum can be adapted to meet the needs of young gifted children while also meeting the needs of the other children in the classroom. It is an enrichment tool in the highest sense. It provides children with an intellectual framework not available when studying only one content area and exposes them to many ideas not covered in traditional curricula (Van-Tassel-Baska 1988). The children described at the beginning of the article enjoy learning complex vocabulary such as magma, lava, and crust. However, their learning activities such as building a ramp with blocks or comparing soft and hard rocks are experiential and hands-on.

Providing depth

The first step in developing an integrated-thematic curriculum appropriate for young gifted children is to select an overarching theme around which to organize the year of study. The theme provides children with the opportunity to see and understand relationships while they explore concepts in depth.

For instance, teachers in our early childhood classroom example selected the theme "The Magic School Bus Explores My World and Be-

yond." It is based on the Magic School Bus series of books in which the children "ride" in a magic school bus through their different units of study. Month by month children explore a variety of social studies and science units that relate to the overall theme. Teachers select units that are rich in content and appeal to young children. Within each unit, all disciplines are represented in developmentally appropriate and meaningful ways.

In our example four units were chosen to express the exploration theme: The Human Body, The Earth, The World of the Imagination, and Rainforests. The units become meaningful as the children participate in creating unit-related environments in the classroom—during the rainforest unit the children made life-size replicas of plants, trees, and animals that live and grow in the rainforest.

Providing connections between the disciplines

In *Interdisciplinary Curriculum: Design and Implementation,* Jacobs (1989) writes that one disadvantage of integrated curriculum is that it can suffer from the "potpourri" approach: units may become samplings of knowledge without incorporating the different disciplines and skills to be covered. Teachers can avoid this problem by employing a web such as the one on the next page titled "Design for an In-Depth Integrated Unit."

When teachers design activities and lessons using this structure, they

attend to each of the disciplines and to the connections between them. The web contains opportunities for higher-level thinking and creativity. Maker (1982) includes higher-level thinking skills as essential elements in a curriculum for high-ability children. Gifted learners also have a very high potential for creative activity and should begin developing that potential as early as possible (Clark 1997).

Guiding *inquiry questions* provide a framework for the experiences in which the children engage. These types of questions provide a focus for children's exposure to key ideas and themes within and across domains of knowledge (VanTassel-Baska 1988). For example, the guiding inquiry questions for the human body unit in The Magic School Bus Explores My World and Beyond theme include the following:

1. What are the systems in the body?
2. How do they work together?
3. How does what I do affect my body?
4. How do I care for my body?

Additionally, inquiry questions lend personal meaning to the study. In answering unit questions, children are encouraged to explore how their learning relates to them personally. The last two questions address this issue specifically: "How does what I do affect my body?" and "How do I care for my body?"

"How to Develop an In-Depth Integrated Unit" is a complete web that builds on the basic skills and disciplines, using a variety of specialized

Curriculum should always be created so that high-ability and low-ability children, children with special needs, and children with special gifts can individually find it challenging and achievable.

activities relating to the human body, the chosen unit of study.

Providing opportunities to address content at different levels

Besides providing young gifted children with occasions to explore topics in depth and make connections between disciplines, a meaningful curriculum needs to furnish children with opportunities to address content at many different levels.

Individualizing means recognizing and allowing for differences in development, understanding, approach to learning, and interests when teachers plan activities so that there is sufficient variety to meet the needs and interests of each child (Dodge & Colker 1992). In the case of young gifted children, individualizing means making sure that children are allowed to develop their abilities even though they are working at a level above what is considered age or grade appropriate.

Design for an In-Depth Integrated Unit

Technology · Analyze Compare · Language Arts · Art Music · Research Inquire · Map Chart Graph · Experiment · **KEY CONCEPT** · Affective · Solve Problem · Careers · Imagine · Create · Propose Plan · Social Studies · Math Science · Produce Write Speak

1. Why is this important to learn?
2. Does this topic have sufficient depth and breadth?
3. What do I need to know and understand before beginning this unit?
4. Have I been inclusive of gender and ethnicity awareness?
5. Can this learning be applied to other areas?
6. What connections are there in the other units within the strand?
7. Are the experiences "real" in terms of problem, process, product, and audience?
8. What evaluation processes will I use?

Consider the example of Adam. When Adam entered an early childhood program at age three, he could read at a third-grade level. Participating with the class in learning to recognize the letters of the alphabet

would have been frustrating to Adam and inhibiting to his development. Teachers designed an individualized reading program for Adam in which he read books appropriate for him during times when other children were learning their letters. He was allowed to write his own stories in the writing center and read them to the class.

Individualization can be accomplished in both learning-center and group activities.

Learning-center activities

Learning centers encourage both autonomy and self-control. They allow children to take responsibility for their own learning and engage in activities that interest them (Isbell 1995). Teachers can design learning centers to meet the needs of young gifted children by generating activities that challenge the children's highest level of skill and concept development. Some of the learning-center activities presented during the human body unit include

- comparing animal bones with replicas of human bones,
- dictating or writing stories that include facts about bodies,
- weighing fruits and vegetables and graphing their differences,
- using spaghetti and meatballs to do math problems,
- creating self-portraits,
- creating skeletons from Popsicle sticks, and
- counting the number of tiles needed to equal the length of the small intestine.

Learning-center activities address different levels of ability. While one child chooses to use spaghetti and meatballs to practice counting, another child may use them to add and

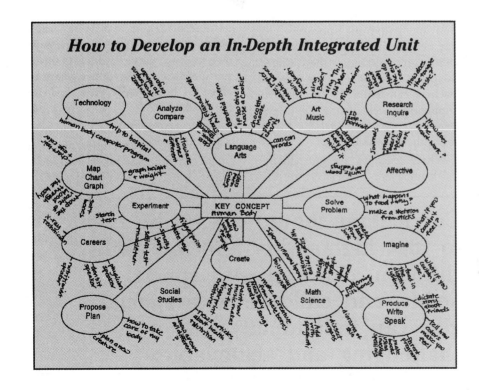

How to Develop an In-Depth Integrated Unit

Curriculum for high-ability children should never be shallowly show-offy. Curriculum for any child should be meaningful.

subtract. Some children read their stories to a teacher or a parent volunteer, while others dictate stories. A child gifted in music might write a song to fit the unit.

While all good preschool programs include choice in activities, offering activities that address the highest level of skills of the children in the class ensures that the learning needs of all children are met.

Group activities

Group activities provide the opportunity for children to develop a classroom community and learn content that is unfamiliar to all of them. During the human body unit, the children role-played blood cells passing through the heart and lungs, sang songs about the body parts, dissected animal organs (with adult help), and acted out organ functions.

The children's interests help to guide the unit of study. If a class is particularly interested in the senses, for example, more time may be spent on this topic than on others. Guest speakers and field trips are interesting to all children and provide enrichment to the curriculum for young gifted learners.

In summary

All children have unique patterns of development, individual interests, and needs. Many gifted young children, however, share some common characteristics and needs in the cognitive, physical, and social and emotional domains. An integrated-thematic curriculum, which is appropriate for all early childhood learners, can be adapted to meet gifted children's needs by providing opportunities for in-depth study and concept development. Individualizing activities to meet children's highest level of ability will ensure that high-ability young children's educational needs are met.

References

Barbour, N. B. 1992. Early childhood gifted education: A collaborative perspective. *Journal for the Education of the Gifted* 15 (2): 145–62.

Clark, B. 1997. *Growing up gifted.* 5th ed. Upper Saddle River, NJ: Prentice Hall.

Dodge, D. T., & L. J. Colker. 1992. *The creative curriculum for early childhood.* 3d ed. Mt. Rainier, MD: Gryphon House. (ERIC Document No. ED 342 487).

Goldsmith, L. T., & D. H. Feldman. 1985. Identifying gifted children: The state of the art. *Pediatric Annals* 14 (10): 709–16.

Hollinger, C., & S. Kosak. 1985. Early identification of the gifted and talented. *Gifted Child Quarterly* 29 (4): 168–71.

Isbell, R. 1995. *The complete learning center book: An illustrated guide for 32 different learning centers.* Brooklyn, NY: Gryphon.

Jacobs, H. H. 1989. The growing need for interdisciplinary curriculum content. In *Interdisciplinary curriculum: Design and implementation,* ed. H. H. Jacobs, 13–24. Alexandria, VA: Association for Supervision and Curriculum Development.

Lewis, M., & B. Louis. 1991. Young gifted children. In *Handbook of gifted education,* eds. N. Colangelo & G. Davis, 365–81. Needham Heights, MA: Allyn & Bacon.

Lewis, M., & L. Michaelson. 1985. The gifted infant. In *The psychology of gifted children: Perspectives on development and education,* ed. J. Freeman, 35–57. New York: Wiley.

Maker, C. J. 1982. *Teaching models in the education of the gifted.* Rockville, MD: Aspen.

Nutall, E. V., I. Romero, & J. Kalesnick. 1992. *Assessing and screening preschoolers: Psychological and educational dimensions.* Needham Heights, MA: Allyn & Bacon.

Parke, B., & T. Ness. 1988. Curricular decision making for the education of young children. *Gifted Child Quarterly* 32 (1): 196–99.

Piaget, J., & B. Inhelder. 1969. *The psychology of the child.* New York: Basic.

Riley, S. S. 1974. Some reflections on the value of children's play. In *Providing the best for young children,* eds. J. McCarthy & C. R. May, 138–45. Washington, DC: NAEYC.

Roedell, W. C. 1990. *Nurturing giftedness in young children.* Report No. EDO-EC-90. Reston, VA: Council for Exceptional Children. (ERIC Document No. ED 321 492).

Roedell, W., N. Jackson, & H. Robinson. 1980. *Gifted young children.* New York: Teachers College Press.

Schetky, D. H. 1981. The emotional and social development of the gifted child. *Gifted Child Today* 4 (3): 2–4.

Webb, J. T. 1994. *Nurturing social-emotional development of gifted children.* Report No. EDO-EC-93-10. Reston, VA: Council for Exceptional Children. (ERIC Document Reproduction Service No. ED 372 554).

Webb, J. T., & P. A. Kleine. 1993. Assessing gifted and talented children. In *Testing young children,* eds. J. Culbertson & D. Willis, 383–407. Austin, TX: Pro-Ed.

Wexler-Sherman, C., H. Gardner, & D. H. Feldman. 1988. A pluralistic view of early assessment: The Project Spectrum approach. *Theory into Practice* 27 (1): 77–83.

VanTassel-Baska, J. 1988. Curriculum for the gifted: Theory, research, and practice. In *Comprehensive curriculum for gifted learners,* eds. J. VanTassel-Baska, J. Feldhusen, K. Seeley, G. Wheatly, L. Silverman, & W. Foster, 1–17. Needham Heights, MA: Allyn & Bacon.

For Further Reading

Bredekamp, S., & C. Copple, eds. 1997. *Developmentally appropriate practice in early childhood programs.* Rev. ed. Washington, DC: NAEYC.

©Elisabeth Nichols

Foster, S. M. 1993. Meeting the needs of gifted and talented preschoolers. *Children Today* 22 (3): 23–30.

James, R., & L. Johnson. 1991. The preschool/primary gifted child. *Journal for the Education of the Gifted* 14 (3): 56–63.

Kitano, M. 1989. The K–3 teacher's role in recognizing and supporting young gifted children. *Young Children* 44 (3): 57–63.

Smutny, J. F., K. Veenker, & S. Veenker. 1989. *Your gifted child: How to recognize and develop the special talents in your child from birth to age seven.* New York: Ballantine.

Whitmore, J. R. 1986. *Intellectual giftedness in young children: Recognition and development.* New York: Haworth.

Wolfle, J. 1989. The gifted preschooler: Developmentally different, but still three or four years old. *Young Children* 44 (3): 41–48.

Brooke Walker, M.A., has taught at the Ricks Center for Gifted Children in Denver, Colorado, for seven years. She has made presentations on the education and development of young gifted children at state and national conferences. Her research has been published in *Gifted Child Quarterly, Roeper Review,* and *Research in Middle Level Education Quarterly.*

Norma Lu Hafenstein, Ph.D., is founder and director of the Ricks Center for Gifted Children. She consults throughout the country on giftedness and has works published in *Gifted Child Quarterly, Roeper Review,* and *Research in Middle Level Education Quarterly.*

Linda Crow-Enslow, M.A., has taught early childhood education for eight years and has presented the gifted education curriculum model used in the early childhood classrooms at state and national conferences.

Gifted Students Need an Education, Too

Gifted children have the right to an education that takes into account their special needs. Here are suggestions for how to provide it.

Susan Winebrenner

Math time is beginning in Kate Ahlgren's primary grade classroom. Her objective is to teach several concepts relating to the base 10 method of counting and computing. Her first task is to assess her students' previous mastery of these concepts. She plans to allow those students who already have a clear understanding of this week's work to spend their math time applying what they have mastered about base 10 to learning about base 5.

Kate conducts a hands-on assessment by giving all students several tasks to complete with Cuisenaire rods. As she directs students to demonstrate what happens when they count past 10, she watches specifically for students who complete each directed task quickly and correctly. Fifteen minutes later, she has identified four children who clearly need more challenging content for the rest of this week's math work. She assigns a base 10 application task for most of the students to complete with partners and takes those four youngsters aside to briefly teach them the essential elements of base 5.

The four students practice excitedly for a few minutes under Kate's supervision. She explains that they will be working together for the rest of this week on learning about base 5 because that will challenge them. She assures them that all students should be working on challenging learning tasks.

Kate gives the four advanced students several tasks similar to those she has demonstrated. They practice together while she works with the rest of the students for the duration of the math period. Just before her instruction ends, she explains to the whole class that they will notice that not all students are working on the same tasks in math. She reassures them that this is perfectly all right and that her job is to make sure

that all students are working on tasks that will help them move forward in their own learning. In this way, Kate makes differentiation the normal and acceptable condition of her classroom. She knows that when her students know something is all right with her, it will generally be all right with them, too.

Differentiated learning for high-ability students in heterogeneous classrooms is as important as it is for other children, yet the needs of the gifted are often misunderstood. Here are reasons why and suggestions for how teachers and administrators can differentiate the prescribed grade-level curriculum to meet the needs of high-ability students.

Why Provide Differentiated Learning for Gifted Students?

For the past 10 years, students who were not learning successfully were targeted for special attention. Sadly, during that same time, the needs of our most capable students have been overlooked. One reason for this neglect is the ability of gifted students to score high on assessments, which has led to the erroneous assumption that they must be learning. Another reason for ignoring their needs is that many educational leaders have misunderstood research on role modeling to mean that some gifted students should be present in all classrooms to facilitate forward progress for other students. Although students who struggle to learn can benefit from mixed-ability classes, they have plenty of positive role models in students who function well at the appropriate grade level, who are capable but not gifted learners. The discrepancy in learning ability between students who struggle to learn and gifted students is simply too wide to facilitate positive role modeling (Schunk, 1987).

Consider the range of abilities present in most classrooms. Visualize that both extremes of a learning curve are equally far removed from the norm. Students who fail to achieve the designated standards have received unprecedented attention during the past several years. They are identified for special services before they start kindergarten, experience lower student-teacher ratios, and may even have a full-time aide assigned to them for the entire school day. School districts spend much more money educating this population than they designate for the usual per-pupil expenditure.

Teachers are expected to create numerous differentiation adjustments for low-achieving students by modifying the amount of work, depth, complexity, and content of the curriculum and by linking students' learning styles and interests to the prescribed learning tasks. Politicians, community members, and teachers avidly follow the progress of these students' learning for evidence that these students are indeed moving forward.

Contrast this with the situation for gifted students, whose natural learning abilities place them as far from average as their classmates who struggle to learn. In September, many of these youngsters could take the assessments that all students in their grade will take at the end of the year and still score at or above the 95th percentile. Simply in the interests of equity, these students are as entitled to receive the same types of differentiation so readily provided to the students who struggle to learn.

To assume that gifted students are learning because they achieve acceptable standards on state assessments is unrealistic. In Colorado, Oregon, and several other states, educators have realized that the learning progress of gifted students cannot be adequately measured simply because the students meet or exceed minimum standards, so these states have specified learning expectations at exemplary levels. By setting exemplary standards, they can document the learning progress of gifted students.

© Susie Fitzhugh

perceived to be difficult (Rimm, 1990), gifted students who rarely undergo demanding learning experiences may lose confidence in their ability to perform well on challenging learning tasks. Many of these students learn to find the easiest way out, postponing their exposure to challenge in many patterns of underachievement (Rimm, 1990; Schmitz & Galbraith, 1985).

Either we must explain to parents that the promise of the school's mission statement does not apply to high-ability students, or we must commit ourselves to providing these students with appropriate and differentiated learning experiences. Whatever has been designated as suitable for students who are learning at a level commensurate with their age is not equally appropriate for students who learn at levels more typical of students several years older.

Does the Promise of Education for All Apply to Gifted Students?

Every school district's mission statement promises its parents that "[a]ll students, including those who are exceptional, are entitled to a public-supported education in which instruction is geared to their needs, interests, and developmental levels" (Reis, Burns, & Renzulli, 1992, p. 3). Unfortunately, those at greatest risk of learning the least in classrooms are those at the top range of ability. Because a sense of confidence comes primarily from being successful at something

What Are the Characteristics and Needs of Gifted Students?

Gifted students learn differently from their classmates in at least five important ways. They learn new material in much less time. They tend to remember what they have learned, making spiral curriculums and reviewing previously mastered concepts a painful experience. They perceive ideas and concepts at more abstract and complex levels than do their peers. They become passionately interested in specific topics and have difficulty moving on to other learning tasks until they feel satisfied that they have learned as much as they possibly can about their passionate interest. Finally, gifted students are able to operate on many levels of concentration simultaneously, so they can monitor classroom activities without paying direct or visual attention to them.

Gifted students have already mastered much of the grade-level work, so they should have opportunities to function at more advanced levels of complexity and depth and to tie their own passionate interests into their schoolwork.

Why Are Many Educators Reluctant to Help Gifted Students?

Many teachers are reluctant to facilitate the needs of gifted students because of the lack of teacher training in this type of differentiation, a concern that other students or parents will accuse them of unfairness, or their belief that providing differentiation for this population is elitist.

Most preservice teachers take at least one course about meeting the needs of special–education students, but few states require teachers to take any courses in how to recognize and teach gifted students. Many teachers assume that gifted kids are highly productive, always complete their work on time, get consistently high grades, and will make it on their own without much assistance. Many educators believe that a student who is unproductive in school could not possibly be gifted.

Such misconceptions about how gifted students do their work are sources of great frustration for the students, their parents, and their teachers. Most teachers in my workshops are surprised when I tell them that gifted students often resist doing their assigned work because it is designed for age-appropriate learners and usually cannot provide the challenge and sense of accomplishment that would keep gifted learners motivated to work.

Another part of the problem is confusion about whether the mandated goals must actually be *taught* to students. Realistically, teachers are only required to demonstrate that all their students have *learned* the designated standards. Students who have already mastered the required content should be allowed to demonstrate their mastery before test-preparation sessions begin and to work on alternative activities because they already know the required content. When teachers learn how to plan and provide these alternative activities routinely to students who demonstrate prior mastery, these students can make progress in their own learning during more of their time in school.

How Can Teachers Provide Differentiation for Gifted Students?

The typical approach to differentiation for gifted students in heterogeneous classes has been to offer extra credit, an expectation that doesn't work because the only students eligible for extra credit are those who often have more than enough earned credit. The practice of offering extra credit should be replaced with approaches that can motivate gifted students to become enthusiastic learners.

Compact the curriculum. The most important needs of gifted students are to have regular opportunities to demonstrate what they already know, to receive full credit for content they have already mastered, and to spend their own learning time on challenging activities that accelerate and enrich the regular curriculum (Reis, Burns, & Renzulli, 1992). Compacting the curriculum can answer these needs.

To ascertain who would benefit from a compacted curriculum for a specific topic, teachers will want to provide interested students with pre-assessment opportunities for all learning activities. Teachers should use the same methods of assessment that they plan to use at the end of a learning unit, including written tests or observed performance on designated tasks. Because the preassessment is open to all students, the learning task itself can identify those who could benefit from the specific differentiated tasks regardless of whether particular students have been designated as gifted.

Students who can demonstrate previous mastery of upcoming content are expected to pay attention to direct instruction only when instruction includes concepts they have not yet mastered. On days when the lesson content is based on what these students have already mastered, they work instead on extension activities provided by the teacher or suggested by the students themselves. They receive full credit for what they have already mastered and earn daily credit for following the teacher's expectations about on-task behavior and productivity and by developing alternative projects and activities.

Design alternative learning experiences. As part of their regular lesson planning, teachers design alternative learning experiences. These provide differentiation opportunities in terms of *content, learning processes, products, learning environment*, and *assessment*.

The *content* is different because it moves students beyond grade-level standards or is connected to students' passionate interests. The *learning processes* called upon are different because they provide depth and complexity appropriate to these students' learning abilities. *Products* differ in that they demonstrate the students' learning at advanced levels, moving beyond typical research activities to the development of individual students' talents and curiosities and the presentation of their findings to appropriate audiences.

Sometimes the *learning environment* is also different; students may pursue interests outside the regular classroom, work more independently on self-directed projects, or collaborate with other students. Even the *assessment process* is different because students receive full credit for what they have already mastered and do not have to complete all the work assigned to the rest of the class.

One particularly striking opportunity to provide alternative learning experiences presented itself when I discovered that James, one of my exceptionally gifted 6th graders, was writing a book at home on the anatomy and physiology of the human body. I pretested him and other interested students at the beginning of all language arts, reading, and writing units. James experienced differentiation in *content* because he wrote his book in class, in *learning processes* because he used sophisticated writing techniques, and in *assessment* because his grades for each unit were earned at the time of the pretest rather than at the end of the unit, with an overall grade that included an evaluation of his on-task behavior and project.

Allow differentiated pacing. For a curriculum that cannot be assessed beforehand because it is unfamiliar to all, gifted students work at their own pace to learn the required concepts and spend more time developing an expertise on a related topic of their choice.

Agree on expectations. Teachers and students work together to set up standards for evaluating productivity, behavior, and differentiated products and then agree to these standards in writing. Teachers should arrange to spend time with these students. It is important that gifted students not feel abandoned by the teacher and that they learn that everyone needs help on challenging tasks.

What Can Administrators Do To Facilitate Differentiation for Gifted Students?

Acknowledge the needs of gifted students. Acknowledge that the precedent for differentiation has been firmly set by the differentiation opportunities always available for students who struggle to learn. Because gifted learners are just as far removed from average as are children with learning problems, the differentiation that gifted students need is highly defensible and equitable.

Facilitate gifted education training for staff. Any strategies teachers learn for the benefit of their gifted students are applicable to many other students and tend to raise the learning bar for all students. One strategy, for example, is to allow students to get credit for an entire assignment by answering correctly at least four of the five most difficult problems first. This challenge motivates many students to listen more carefully to instructions so they can also qualify.

Investigate cluster grouping. Look into the practice of cluster grouping for gifted students. Cluster grouping is the practice of purposefully placing four to six gifted students together in an otherwise heterogeneous class. Their teacher must have some training in how to differentiate the curriculum for students who demonstrate previous mastery or who can learn new content faster than their classmates. Studies have demonstrated that cluster grouping can lead to improved achievement for many students at all levels of learning ability (Gentry, 1999; Winebrenner & Devlin, 1996).

Communicate your expectations. Make clear your pledge that all students, including the most capable, will be able to learn something new and challenging every day. Clarify your commitment to the goal that all students will be expected to make continuous progress in their own learning. To that end, expect gifted students to demonstrate competencies that exceed those designated as basic.

Keep the Promise

Parents of gifted learners have a right to expect that schools will fulfill the promise made to all students that children will have consistent and daily opportunities for challenging learning experiences and will demonstrate continuous forward progress in their learning. This expectation requires providing gifted students with differentiation of the regular curriculum. To complacently accept their performance at regular competency levels is to deny their equal right to an appropriate education.

References

Gentry, M. L. (1999). *Promoting student achievement and exemplary classroom practices through cluster grouping: A research-based alternative to heterogeneous elementary classrooms.* Storrs, CT: National Research Center on the Gifted and Talented.

Reis, S. M., Burns, D. E., & Renzulli, J. S. (1992). *Curriculum compacting: The complete guide to modifying the regular curriculum for high ability students.* Mansfield Center, CT: Creative Learning Press.

Rimm, S. (1990). *How to parent so children will learn.* Watertown, WI: Apple Publishing.

Schunk, D. H. (1987). Peer models and children's behavioral change. *Review of Educational Research, 57,* 149–174.

Schmitz, C., & Galbraith, J. (1985). *Managing the social and emotional needs of the gifted.* Minneapolis, MN: Free Spirit Publishing.

Winebrenner, S., & Devlin, B. (1996). *Cluster grouping of gifted students: How to provide full-time services on a part-time budget.* Reston, VA: ERIC Clearinghouse on Disabilities and Gifted Education (ERIC Digest Document Reproduction Service No. 397618).

Susan Winebrenner is an educational consultant and author of *Teaching Gifted Kids in the Regular Classroom* (Free Spirit Publishing, 2000). She may be reached at P.O. Box 398, Brooklyn, MI 49230–0398 (e-mail: ecsfirst @aol.com).

The Goals and Track Record of Multicultural Education

Paying attention to the varied learning styles of all students will do more to accomplish the goals of multicultural education than misguided programs that often divide children.

Rita Dunn

Because multicultural education is a volatile political issue—one with articulate proponents and antagonists on both sides—the research on this topic needs to be examined objectively. Many practices that schools promote make little sense in terms of how multiculturally diverse students learn. Thus, we need to examine the data concerning how poor achievement has been reversed among culturally diverse students in many schools.

What Is Multicultural Education?

Multicultural education originated in the 1960s as a response to the long-standing policy of assimilating immigrants into the melting pot of our dominant American culture (Sobol 1990). Over the past three decades, it has expanded from an attempt to reflect the growing diversity in American classrooms to include curricular revisions that specifically address the academic needs of students. In recent years, it has been distorted by some into a movement that threatens to divide citizens along racial and cultural lines (Schlessinger 1991). Generally, multicultural education has focused on two broad goals: increasing academic achievement and promoting greater sensitivity to cultural differences in an attempt to reduce bias.

Increasing Academic Achievement

Efforts intended to increase the academic achievement of multicultural groups include programs that (1) focus on the research on culturally based learning styles as a step toward determining which teaching styles or methods to use with a particular group of students; (2) emphasize bilingual or bicultural approaches; (3) build on the language and culture of African- or Hispanic-American students; and (4) emphasize math and science specifically for minority or female students (Blanks 1994). Programs in each of these categories are problematic.

■ *Culturally based learning styles.* So long as such programs include rea-

Photo courtesy of St. John's University's Center for the Study of Learning and Teaching Styles

Twenty percent of students in every culture are tactual learners—children who begin concentrating on new and difficult information by manipulating resources with their hands.

From *Educational Leadership,* April 1997, pp. 74–77. © 1997 by the Association for Supervision and Curriculum Development. All rights reserved. Reprinted by permission.

Photo courtesy of St. John's University's Center for the Study of Learning and Teaching Styles

At least 20 percent of all students in every culture are kinesthetic learners who cannot sit in their seats for very long; they learn by *doing* rather than by listening or reading.

sonable provisions for language and cultural differences, they can help students make the transition into mainstream classes. In that sense, they may be considered similar to other compensatory programs that are not multicultural in their emphasis. As a researcher and advocate of learning styles, however, I would caution against attempting to identify or respond to so-called cultural learning styles. Researchers have clearly established that there is no single or dual learning styles for the members of any cultural, national, racial, or religious group. A single learning style does not appear even within a family of four or five (Dunn and Griggs 1995).

■ *Bilingual or bicultural approaches.* Attention to cultural and language differences can be done appropriately or inappropriately. Bi- and trilingualism in our increasingly interdependent world are valuable for, and should be required of, all students. An emphasis on bilingualism for only non-English-speaking children denies English-speaking students skills required for successful interactions internationally. Today, many adults need to speak several languages fluently and to appreciate cultural similarities and differences to succeed in their work.

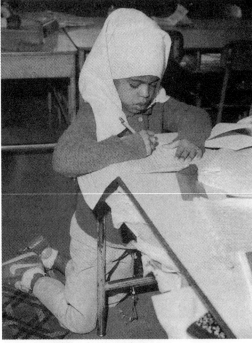

Photo courtesy of the Lafayettee Academy

Another problem arises in those classrooms in which bilingual teachers speak English ungrammatically and haltingly. Such teachers provide a poor model for non-English-speaking children, who may remain in bilingual programs for years, unable to make the transition into English-speaking classes. Ultimately, this impairs the ability of these children to move into well-paying professions and careers—the ultimate goal of most of their parents.

■ *Selective cultural programs.* Building on the language and culture of selected groups and not of others sug-

gests bias and bigotry. Parents should teach their children to appreciate and respect their native cultures; schools should teach children to appreciate and respect all cultures. If the need exists to expand attention to more cultures, let us do that. But let us stop promoting one culture over another with the inevitable result of dividing our children and diminishing their sense of belonging to the dominant culture that is uniquely American—intentionally a combination of the best of all its citizens.

■ *Minority- and gender-based grouping for math and science.* Emphasizing math and science specifically for minority or female students may be based on good intentions, but it ignores the fact that minority students and female students all learn differently from one another and differently from their counterparts—whether those be high- or low-achieving classmates. Providing resources and methods that help all students learn rapidly and well should be the focus for teaching math and science—and every other subject. Are there not males and majority students who fail those subjects? The answer is to change how those subjects are taught, not to isolate certain groups and teach them as though they all have the same style of learning.

Sensitizing Ourselves to Social Agendas

Some multicultural education programs are specifically designed to increase cultural and racial tolerance and reduce bias. These are intended to restructure and desegregate schools, increase contact among the races, and encourage minorities to become teachers; and they lean heavily on cooperative learning (Banks 1994). Sleeter and Grant (1993) describe these programs as emphasizing human relations, incorporating some compensatory goals and curricular revisions to emphasize positive contributions of ethnic and cultural groups, and using learning styles to enhance students' achievement and reduce racial tensions.

Some of these programs emphasize pluralism and cultural equity in American society as a whole, seeking to apply critical thinking skills to a critique of racism and sexism. Others emphasize multilingualism or examine issues from viewpoints other than those of the dominant culture.

In my judgment, these focuses are more political than educational or social. Critical thinking is a requirement for all—not a select few. In addition, whose thinking prevails in these programs, and what are their credentials? Being a minority member or having taken a course does not automatically make a person proficient in teaching minority or female students, or in critiquing social issues. Political debate is helpful to developing young minds; one-sided, preconceived viewpoints are not.

Curriculum and Multicultural Achievement

In the debate over New York's "Children of the Rainbow" curriculum, the ideas of multicultural education captured almost daily headlines. Opponents argued that curriculum change would not increase student achievement, whereas proponents insisted that culturally diverse students performed poorly in school because they could not relate to an American curriculum.

Drew, Dunn, and colleagues (1994) tested how well 38 Cajun students and 29 Louisiana Indian students, all poor achievers, could recall story content and vocabulary immediately and after a delay. Their recall differed significantly when they were instructed with (1) traditional versus multisensory instructional resources and (2) stories in which cultural relevance matched and mismatched students' identified cultural backgrounds. Each subject was presented with four story treatments (two culturally sensitive and two dominant American) and tested for recall immediately afterward and again one week later. The findings for Cajun subjects indicated significant differences between instructional treatments, with greater recall in each multisensory instructional condition—Cultural-Immediate, Cultural-Delayed, American-Immediate, and American-Delayed. The main effect of instructional treatment for Louisiana Indian subjects was significant as well. Recall scores were even higher when they used multisensory materials for American stories. No significant main effect emerged for test interval with either group.

> ## What determined whether students mastered the content was how the content was taught, not the content itself.

This study demonstrated that what determined whether students mastered the content was *how* the content was taught, not the content itself. The culturally sensitive curriculum did not produce significantly higher achievement for these two poorly achieving cultural groups; the methods that were used did.

Teaching Methods and Multicultural Achievement

Other studies of teaching methods revealed even more dramatic results. Before being taught with methods that responded to their learning styles, only 25 percent of special education high school students in a suburban New York school district had passed the required local examinations and state competency tests to receive diplomas. In the first year of the district's learning styles program (1987–88), that number increased to 66 percent. During the second year, 91 percent of the district's special education students were successful, and in the third year, the results remained constant at 90 percent—with a greater ratio of "handicapped" students passing state competency exams than regular education students (Brunner and Majewski 1990).

Two North Carolina elementary principals reported similarly impressive gains as a result of their learning styles programs. In an impoverished, largely minority school, Andrews (1990) brought student scores that had consistently been in the 30th percentile on the California Achievement Tests to the 83rd percentile over a three-year period by responding to students' learning styles. Shortly thereafter, Stone (1992) showed highly tactual, learning disabled (LD) elementary school students how to learn with Flipp Chutes, Electroboards,

Task Cards, and Pic-A-Holes while seated informally in rooms where levels of light matched their style preferences. The children were encouraged to study either alone, with a classmate or two, or with their teacher—based on their learning style strength. Within four months, those youngsters had achieved four months' reading gains on a standardized achievement test—better than they ever had done previously and as well as would have been expected of children achieving at normal levels.

Many professional journals have reported statistically higher scores on standardized achievement and attitude tests as a result of learning style teaching with underachieving and special education students (Dunn, Bruno, Sklar, Zenhausem, and Beaudry 1990; Dunn, Griggs, Olson, Gorman, and Beasley 1995; Klavas 1993; Lemmon 1985; Perrin 1990; Quinn 1993). Indeed, a four-year investigation by the U.S. Office of Education that included on-site visits, interviews, observations, and examinations of national test data concluded that the Dunn and Dunn Learning Styles Model was one of only a few strategies that had had a positive effect on the achievement of special education students throughout the nation (Alberg, Cook, Fiore, Friend, and Sano 1992).

What Have We Learned?

Research documents that underachieving students—whether they are from other cultures or from the dominant U.S. culture—tend to learn differently from students who perform well in our schools (Dunn and Griggs 1995; Milgram, Dunn, and Price 1993). As indicated in the examples cited earlier, schools with diverse populations reversed academic failure when instruction was changed to complement the children's learning style strengths.

In our book, *Multiculturalism and Learning Style* (Dunn and Griggs 1995), my coauthor and I summarize research findings on each of the major cultural groups in the United States—African Americans, Asian Americans, European Americans, Hispanic Americans, and Native Americans. The research clearly shows that there is no such thing as a cultural group style. There are cross-cultural and intracultural similarities and differences among all peoples. Those differences are enriching when understood and channeled positively.

Given this information, I believe it is unwise for schools with limited budgets to support multicultural education in addition to—and apart from—regular education. Instead, schools need to make their instructional delivery systems responsive to how diverse students learn (Dunn 1995).

Educational programs should not separate young children from one another. Any separation becomes increasingly divisive over time and is likely to produce the opposite of what multicultural education is intended to accomplish. Segregated children begin to feel different from and less able than the larger groups of children they see—but are apart from. These feelings can lead to emotional insecurity and a dislike of others.

The United States was founded as a nation intended to absorb people from many nations. Monocultural education in the guise of multicultural education offends the cornerstone of those intentions. The melting pot concept does not diminish one's heritage. It unites the strengths of many cultures into a single, stronger blend of culture to reflect the best of all.

References

Alberg, J., L. Cook, T. Fiore, M. Friend, and S. Sano. (1992). *Educational Approaches and Options for Integrating Students with Disabilities: A Decision Tool*. Triangle Park, N.C.: Research Triangle Institute.

Andrews, R. H. (July-September 1990). "The Development of a Learning Styles Program in a Low Socioeconomic, Underachieving North Carolina Elementary School." *Journal of Reading, Writing, and Learning Disabilities International* 6, 3: 307–314.

Banks, J. A. (1994). *An Introduction to Multicultural Education*. Boston: Allyn and Bacon.

Brunner, C. E., and W. S. Majewski (October 1990). "Mildly Handicapped Students Can Succeed with Learning Styles." *Educational Leadership* 48, 2: 21–23.

Drew, M., R. Dunn, P. Quinn, R. Sinatra, and J. Spiridakis. (1994). "Effects of Matching and Mismatching Minority Underachivers with Culturally Similar and Dissimilar Story Content and Learning Style and Traditional Instructional Practices." *Applied Educational Research Journal* 8, 2: 3–10.

Dunn, R., J. Bruno, R. I. Sklar, R. Zenhausern, and J. Beaudry. (May-June 1990). "Effects of Matching and Mismatching Minority Developmental College Students' Hemispheric Preferences on Mathematics Scores." *Journal of Educational Research* 83, 5: 283–288.

Dunn, R., S. A. Griggs, J. Olson, B. Gorman, and M. Beasley. (1995). "A Meta-Analytic Validation of the Dunn and Dunn Research Learning Styles Model." *Journal of Educational Research* 88, 6: 353–361.

Dunn, R. (1995). *Educating Diverse Learners: Strategies for Improving Current Classroom Practices*. Bloomington, Ind.: Phi Delta Kappa.

Dunn, R., and S. A. Griggs. (1995). *Multiculturalism and Learning Styles: Teaching and Counseling Adolescents*. Westport, Conn: Praeger Publishers, Inc.

Klavas, A. (1993). "In Greensboro, North Carolina: Learning Style Program Boosts Achievement and Test Scores." *The Clearing House* 67, 3: 149–151.

Lemmon, P. (1985). "A School Where Learning Styles Make a Difference." *Principal* 64, 4: 26–29.

Milgram, R. M., R. Dunn, and G. E. Price, eds. (1993). *Teaching and Counseling Gifted and Talented Adolescents: An International Learning Style Perspective*. Westport, Conn.: Praeger Publishers, Inc.

Perrin, J. (October 1990). "The Learning Styles Project for Potential Dropouts." *Educational Leadership* 48, 2: 23–24.

Quinn, R. (1993). "The New York State Compact for Learning and Learning Styles." *Learning Styles Network Newsletter* 15, 1: 1–2.

Schlessinger, A., Jr. (1991). "Report of the Social Studies Syllabus Review Committee: A Dissenting Opinion." In *One Nation, Many Peoples: A Declaration of Cultural Independence*, edited by New York State Social Studies Review and Development Committee. New York: Author.

Sleeter, C. E., and C. A. Grant. (1993). *Making Choices for Multicultural Education: Five Approaches to Race, Class, and Gender*. 2nd ed. New York: Merrill.

Sobol, T. (1990). "Understanding Diversity." *Educational Leadership* 48, 3: 27–30.

Stone, P. (November 1992). "How We Turned Around a Problem School." *Principal* 71, 2: 34–36.

Rita Dunn is Professor, Division of Administrative and Instructional Leadership, and Director, Center for the Study of Learning and Teaching Styles, St. John's University, Grand Central and Utopia Parkways, Jamaica, NY 11439. She is the author of 17 books, including ASCD's *How to Implement and Supervise Learning Style Programs* (1996).

Celebrate Diversity!

How to create a caring classroom that honors your students' cultural backgrounds

By Mary Antón-Oldenburg, Ed.D.

"I don't want to phool around, I just want to read," writes Olivia, a young Russian immigrant, during a reading-reflection time. Zena, a child of African-American and North African descent, often misses school to help her recently widowed mother care for Zena's younger siblings. Pasha's parents, who came to the United States from India with high expectations, want their first grader to be assigned harder work, while Susie, a middle-class white child, has parents who want "a typical experience" for her—she should learn to read and write, primarily through play. Though names and some details have been changed, these are all real children—and students of mine.

As a teacher, juggling the expectations and experiences of such widely diverse youngsters and their parents can be both overwhelming and enriching. It's a challenge more and more of us need to face. The young people who fill our classrooms are increasingly diverse, which is a reflection of the United States as a whole. Nearly 8 million new immigrants settled in this country between 1981 and 1990, according to the most recent figures available from the United States Census Bureau. It is estimated that 80 percent of them came here from Latin America, the Caribbean, and Asia. Experts predict that by 2020 children of color will make up close to 46 percent of America's school-age population.

While one of our most basic goals as teachers is to support the growth of the individual child, it can become complicated when that child is from a very different background than our own, whatever our ethnic origin. We need to challenge ourselves to take steps to help our students appreciate their own cultural ways, even as we help them succeed as students.

All Learning is Culturally Constructed

The culture children bring to school can have a profound effect on how they respond. One good example of this is recounted in *Teaching Other People's Children: Literacy and Learning in a Bilingual Classroom*, by Cindy Ballenger (Teachers College Press, 1999). Puzzled by her lack of success in guiding the actions of the students in her bilingual Haitian preschool class, Cindy noticed that her Haitian colleagues seemed to be having an easier time with the youngsters. These teachers used verbal patterns, she discovered, that conveyed not only a reprimand, but linked a child's behavior to concepts of universal good and bad. These messages were delivered with affection, but without the same attention to honoring the child's individual feelings as is considered "best practice" for mainstream American children. Cindy successfully learned to adapt to this pattern of talk.

Experiences such as Cindy's suggest that we may need to reconsider our current understanding of what is good practice and move toward more culturally relevant teaching. Of course, that might not seem so easy when we are faced with 25 or more students, many with different backgrounds and sets of cultural experiences. What is a teacher to do?

Multicultural Education as a Way of Life

In caring classrooms, all children must be represented. This means that multicultural content must be seen as a way of life, not an add-on. Celebrate Black History Month, but take steps to make sure that representation of African-Americans—and all groups—occurs throughout the year. Regardless of your present school population, your students will benefit from a broad education that includes many diverse points of view and incorporates diverse cultural understanding. This goal can best be accomplished by seeing the teaching of multicultural content as a thread that runs through all your curricular areas.

Here are some other ways to celebrate student diverity:

• **Learn about the backgrounds of your students.** Educate yourself about unfamiliar cultures. When you have choices in curriculum, think carefully about underrepresented groups. Go beyond the obvious holidays, heroes, and foods. And remember: You have a greater potential to increase student understanding by in-depth coverage of a few cultures than you do by devoting a number of hurried days to many cultures

With hardworking Pasha in my first-grade class, we embarked on a six-week study of the diversity of India. We were surprised to find that India has, for example, more than 100 official languages. Through exploration in film and language, culture and stories, museum visits and, yes, food, the students and I came to understand that just being from the same country does not mean that you are identical to others. We came to appreciate the multiple aspects of Indian culture, and this, in turn, helped us see that even groups that might look the same to us from their appearance have differences.

• **Encourage the teaching of multiple perspectives.** Resources abound to allow even young children to see the world from different points of view. For example, *The True Story of the Three Little Pigs,* by John Scieszka (Penguin, 1996), gives this well-worn tale a new spin by telling it from the wolf's perspective. Cut out some magazine pictures of a variety of people doing different things, and ask your students to imagine what these people are thinking. Older children will appreciate texts such as "The Bee," a poem found in *Joyful Noise: Poems for Two Voices,* by Paul Fleischman (HarperCollins, 1992), in which

the points of view of a drone and a queen bee are presented.

• **Celebrate all kinds of stories.** Storytelling style can vary widely between cultures. Researchers have found that Japanese children tell shorter narratives than their white middle-class peers. In contrast, some African-American children may tell longer stories which include events and episodes that do nor appear, on the surface, to be related. They use elaborate wordplay and elicit greater participation of the audience. Latino children may tell stories in which personal relationships are emphasized rather than ones in which events are primary.

If you encounter a child whose narratives don't quite make sense to you, consider that you may be unfamiliar with that child's storytelling style. Investigate such styles and genres, in print and on audio- and videotape, and share them with your class. Audiotape the stories students tell, and look for patterns in them. Create a class library of stories told in the styles of different cultures. Ask parents for advice and suggestions.

To learn more, read *The Need for Story: Cultural Diversity in Classroom and Community,* by Anne Haas Dyson and Celia Genishi (National Council of Teachers of English, 1994), and *Chameleon Readers: Teaching Children to Appreciate All Kinds of Good Stories,* by Allyssa McCabe (McGraw-Hill, 1995).

• **Encourage the use of a child's primary language.** Research shows that children who develop strong vocabulary and concepts in their primary language will transfer these strengths to their secondary language. If two or more of your students speak in a non-English tongue, invite them to discuss among themselves a curricular topic in that language before completing an assignment or after they finish reading. Allow for journal writing in either language. Whenever possible, provide texts in a child's primary language, for reading during quiet times of the day. Encourage parents and other community members to help you provide resources in home languages to students. And most important, encourage parents to continue to discuss high-level concepts with their children in their home language.

Learn more about teaching students whose home language is not English in *Between Worlds: Access to Second Language Acquisition,* by David E. and Yvonne S. Freeman (Heinemann, 1994).

• **Be mindful of the books you read in class and the characters you choose for class study.** Pick books that portray boys and girls from diverse cultures—but first screen these books for stereotypic presentations. Ask yourself: Does this book present this group/person in a sensitive manner? Are the illustrations appropriate, or do they include exaggeration of cultural features or images? If I were a member of this culture, would I feel positive about my image in this book? Are the setting and illustrations appropriate to the time and place in which this story occurs?

• **Teach your students to actively critique the materials that they use, the media they view.** Ask students to be aware—in the books they read and the TV and videos they watch—of who is represented and how. I encourage my students to "talk back" to portrayals that they consider inaccurate. Sometimes, we create scripts based on these verbal critiques. Helping children to talk about and even rewrite texts that contain uncomfortable stereotypes or images teaches them that books can be challenged. It empowers them to view the world with a critical eye.

• **Help students create a classroom language for challenging stereotypic statements.** Model the caring but firm statements of "We don't talk about people in that manner here" and "The way that you are talking about that person [or group] is offensive to me and to many others. I don't think you mean to be so disrespectful." Help them take ownership in expressing personal views and beliefs. Include in your modeling modulators such as: "For me," "I believe," "I am wondering," and "I think."

• **Maintain high expectations for all children!** A teacher's attitude towards a student's potential is a powerful predictor for student achievement. Treat all your students as if they are the most capable. Work from the assumption that they bring great cultural resources with them—and you may just discover a treasure trove of experience and wisdom that will enrich everyone's learning.

Mary Antón-Oldenburg, Ed.D., is a teacher-researcher in Brookline, Massachusetts with 18 years' experience in grades K–8.

Cultural and Language Diversity in the Middle Grades

JOHN MYERS and DIANE BOOTHE

Teachers today must address the challenges presented by a diverse, multicultural population of students in U.S. middle schools. In some schools in the rapidly growing Atlanta metropolitan area, for example, more than 100 different cultures are represented—and almost as many languages spoken. In 1994, there were approximately 8,000 limited-English-proficient students (commonly referred to as ESOL students) enrolled in the public schools of Georgia (Georgia Department of Education 1994). By 1998, that figure had doubled (Georgia Department of Education 1998). The number of identified middle grades ESOL students in Texas, Florida, and California far surpasses that of Georgia. Across the nation, many middle level ESOL students remain unidentified, often because they are part of a migrant population.

At the middle level, the special physical, social, and emotional needs of learners must be taken into consideration when developing ESOL curricula and instructional strategies. Just as there is no typical middle grader, there is no typical ESOL student. One thirteen-year-old ESOL student may have spent eight years in a private school in his or her country of origin and received instruction in three languages. He or she may have a greater knowledge of mathematics than the typical American student at the same grade level. Conversely, another thirteen-year-old ESOL student may have had little formal education, perhaps having spent less than five years in a rural school. Ideal instructional strategies at the middle level for helping both students—and all those in-between—take the student where he or she is, then combine materials using language that students can understand, vocabulary development activities, cooperative learning, and positive and immediate feedback. Such activities and supportive settings reduce feelings of insecurity and isolation and motivate students to excel individually and as members of the group.

Students and a Macrocultural Perspective

How else do we address diversity in our schools? We must first acknowledge that the challenges of diversity are significant. The world is changing, and today's middle graders must be prepared for life in a multicultural society. Educators at all levels must recognize their responsibility to teach with a multicultural and multiethnic perspective, regardless of the content area. Teachers at the middle level must serve as role models by treating students from different cultures equitably and by conveying to students that a diverse population in the classroom is as much an opportunity for learning as it is a challenge.

Middle grades students often have fragile self-images; their psyches bruise easily. Yet, they are inherently curious and, when motivated, enthusiastic learners. Teachers can help them to develop personal rationales for embracing diversity and see the importance of multicultural thinking. Too often, students (and teachers) are influenced by ethnocentric misconceptions that portray members of other cultures according to stereotypes, rather than as the people they really are. Young people need to develop a macrocultural view of the world, and educators must stand ready to dispel misrepresentation and unrealistic generalizations wherever they may be found.

We must also work to preserve the cultural identity and enhance the self-concepts of our diverse (often ESOL) students. Baruth and Manning (1992), in a review of studies on the effects of minority group status on personality development during identity formation, concluded that self-concept is central to a learner's development. Minority group members' perceptions of self have a direct and significant effect on their social, psychological, and intellectual development.

Steps to Take

To foster a macrocultural perspective in all of our students at the middle level, we recommend that the following steps be taken by teachers, administrators, parents, students, and community members:

1. Develop a collaborative plan focused on celebrating diversity. The plan should draw on the resources that can be contributed by students from diverse backgrounds.

2. Set an example by welcoming new Americans, especially those who are particularly isolated because of limited English proficiency.

From *The Clearing House,* March 2000, p. 239. Reprinted with permission of the Helen Dwight Reid Foundation. Published by Heldref Publications, 1319 Eighteenth St., NW, Washington, DC 20036-1802. © 2000.

3. Integrate "global learning" into the curriculum when studying geography, travel, and current events. Technological resources, such as overseas Internet sites and e-mail communication among students across national borders, can bring people from many cultures into every classroom.

4. Be proactive in challenging the validity of stereotypes. Discuss common misconceptions about all ethnic groups; remember to include erroneous concepts about Caucasians as well.

5. Use tactful, low-key humor when talking about verbal communication and nonverbal gestures that are identified with different cultural and ethnic groups.

6. Incorporate multicultural literature and art into the curriculum.

7. Use integrated thematic instruction that takes advantage of the multicultural expertise of teachers who offer exploratory courses and of people in the community.

8. Include athletic experiences and other activities from a range of cultures in p.e. classes and extracurricular programs.

9. Identify and use community resources to support instruction.

10. Use instructional strategies based on cooperative learning, group involvement, and having students take responsibility for learning activities and outcomes. Such strategies help ESOL students link up with other students. Group activities also promote cooperation and compassion, a sense of team effort, and opportunities to practice verbal skills. Such activities may focus on multicultural topics. (Or may not—culture-neutral or ethnic-neutral group activity can be ideal for helping an isolated ESOL student feel part of a learning community.)

A Cooperative Activity That Promotes Second-Language Acquisition

One group activity that works well to build a sense of community is part of a unit on ice cream. In the culminating activity, students in pairs actually make their own ice cream. The activity involves practice in predicting, measuring, following directions, and drawing conclusions and provides learning in the following areas of second-language acquisition: vocabulary development; cooperation and communication as part of a team, reducing feelings of insecurity and isolation; reinforcement for social and verbal interaction; mathematics skills; reading comprehension skills; critical-thinking skills; scientific method and laboratory skills; language arts skills (through integration of poetry); exploratory opportunities related to home arts, music, art, and technology; writing skills (through a closing narrative activity); assessment of progress in language learning; and parent involvement (through a letter-writing activity). In gathering materials for the activity, be sure to plan for the proper number of students, who will be working in pairs.

Materials required for each pair:

- 1 pint-sized freezer bag
- 1 quart-sized freezer bag
- 1/4 cup sugar
- 1/2 teaspoon vanilla
- 1 cup milk
- 3 cups crushed ice
- 1/8 cup Creamora
- 1/2 cup salt
- plastic spoons and cups
- measuring utensils

Procedures:

1. Inside the pint-sized bag, stir together the milk, Creamora, sugar, and vanilla. On a piece of paper, record observations about the physical characteristics of the mixture.

2. Seal the pint-sized bag, pressing out as much air as possible.

3. Add one-half of the ice and one-half of the salt to the quart-sized bag. Place the pint-sized bag inside the quart-sized bag. Add the rest of the ice and salt to the quart-sized bag. Seal the bag carefully.

4. Working together, hold the four corners of the quart-sized bag. Predict how long it will take for the mixture to solidify once it is shaken. Shake the bag gently until the mixture becomes solid.

5. Record both the estimated time and the actual time for the freezing (solidifying) process, along with any other observations.

6. Carefully open the quart-sized bag and remove the pint-sized bag. Record observations of the mixture.

7. Remove the mixture with a spoon and place into cups. Enjoy!

REFERENCES

Baruth, L. G., and M. L. Manning. 1992. *Multicultural education of children and adolescents.* Boston: Allyn and Bacon.

Bennett, C. I. 1995. *Comprehensive multicultural education theory and practice.* Boston: Allyn and Bacon.

Davidman, L., and P. Davidman. *Teaching with a multicultural perspective: A practical guide.* New York: Longman.

Nieto, S. 1992. *Affirming diversity.* New York: Longman.

Georgia Department of Education. 1994. *Report of language minority students in Georgia public schools.* Atlanta: Georgia Department of Education (May).

—— 1998. *Report of language minority students in Georgia public schools.* Atlanta: Georgia Department of Education (May).

John Myers is a professor and Diane Boothe is an associate professor, both in the College of Education, State University of West Georgia, Carollton, Georgia.

Voices and *Voces:*

Cultural and Linguistic Dimensions of Giftedness

by Ellen Riojas Clark and Virginia Gonzalez

It can be hard to recognize abilities in young language-minority students. Parent and teacher evaluations in conjunction with alternative assessments can capture these students' capabilities.

They are language-minority, low socioeconomic status (SES) kids. Can they be gifted? In what ways? What methods should be used to assess them? In an effort to establish the importance of identifying both linguistic and cultural giftedness in this group, two case studies look at the interaction of cognition, language, and culture—through a holistic lens of appropriate alternative assessments. Teachers' and parents' views are incorporated with dual-language testing to capture capabilities that might otherwise remain hidden. Results will show why all of these measures are necessary to get an accurate picture of the children's abilities.

We use the terms *voices* and *voces* (Spanish for *voices)* to offer a critical reflective view of the assessment of language-minority children who are gifted, and also to propose an alternative assessment model for measuring cultural nonverbal dimensions of giftedness. As part of our study of cultural and linguistic giftedness, we consider the need to establish a dialogue between cultures, in which mainstream *voices* and minority *voces* communicate their particular world views, philosophies, and ethnic identities envisioned within their social and ethnic groups. We will also argue that evaluators need to become advocates for language-minority children.

The term *voices* will be used to represent the mainstream school culture's interpretation of linguistic giftedness, illustrated by the classroom teachers' descriptions of the children's abilities. We define *voices* as: 1) the documentation of quantitative products such as scores on

VOICES
VOCES
TABLE
TABLA
EDUCATED
EDUCADO
COOPERATIVE
COOPERATIVO

standardized intelligence tests, which are highly influenced by language and learning, and 2) the interpretation of children's behaviors and the selection of performance standards that guide the curriculum-based or traditional views of giftedness, focusing only on logico-mathematical academic abilities. In contrast, the term *voces* will be used to represent the minority community interpretation of cultural giftedness, illustrated by the parents' descriptions of their children's socioemotional abilities. We define *voces* as cultural manifestations of giftedness expressed in various verbal and nonverbal forms.

The following two case studies examine the role of dominant-language assessment on the identification of linguistic giftedness and cultural factors on nonverbal giftedness.

Cultural Factors and Giftedness

As noted by Dundes, a familial environment, regardless of SES and cultural-linguistic background, is vitally important because it educates its members in the culture

Ellen Riojas Clark, Ph.D., is an associate professor, Division of Bilingual/Bicultural Studies, University of Texas at San Antonio.
Virginia Gonzalez, Ph.D., is an associate professor, Educational Curriculum & Instruction Department, Texas A&M University, College Station, Texas.

From *Educational Horizons,* Fall 1998, pp. 41-47. © 1998 by Ellen Riojas Clark and Virginia Gonzalez. Reprinted by permission.

of the home and the group and " . . . insures conformity to the accepted cultural norms and continuity from generation to generation."[1] Frasier indicated that giftedness could be expressed through different cultural and linguistic representations in low-SES children.[2] Later on, he noted that minority children do receive stimulation representative of their sociocultural environment.[3] That is, the cultural experience of minority gifted children began to be considered by researchers who tried to portray the diversity of the *voces* expressed by these children and their families. These minority *voces* are illustrated in the parents' descriptions of the two children's verbal and nonverbal giftedness presented in this article.

We have finally come to understand that minority families can nurture their children's giftedness in a culturally rich manner.

In addition, several authors have discussed the methodological problems related to the sociocultural nature of defining and measuring intelligence. For example, Darder stated, " . . . IQ testing is unable to function as a fair measurement of innate intelligence, because its primary concern is directly linked to a relative ranking of people based on criteria derived solely from the values of a selective cultural system."[4] In a previous paper, the authors noted that Hispanic mothers described their sons' giftedness using the Spanish phrases *es un niño bien educado* (literal translation: is a well-educated boy) to describe their sons' outstanding behaviors in culturally appropriate situations. Hispanic parents might also use the term *malcriado* (literal translation: ill bred) in opposition to *bien educado,* to tell their children that their behavior is inappropriate and will reflect badly on the family.[5] Thus, Hispanic gifted children (as described by their parents) can analyze a situation, determine the appropriate behavior, and perform in an exemplary manner that will reflect well on self and family.

Contemporary ethnic researchers emphasize the need to value and celebrate the diverse expressions of giftedness. We have finally come to understand that minority families can nurture their children's giftedness in a culturally rich manner. The following two case studies present a portrait of the cultural and linguistic dimensions of giftedness by using an alternative developmental assessment model.

Case studies—Oscar and Alberto

Two case studies are analyzed in this article: 1) Oscar, a 6-year-old Spanish monolingual child and 2) Alberto, a 5-year-old bilingual Spanish-English child. Pseudonyms are used for both children in order to protect their identities. The boys were attending a bilingual kindergarten classroom when they were referred for assessment for possible giftedness by their teachers. Background information was collected using the Home Language Survey[6] and the Parents' and Teachers' Ratings of Cognitive, Linguistic, and Social Skills.[7]

The families and home environments of the two children are similar. Oscar and Alberto both came from low-SES, traditional, intact, Hispanic families that provided secure, well-structured, and stable environments for the children. That is, in spite of limited economic resources, these families provided a nurturing home environment. In both families, mothers and fathers were present in the household; both mothers were housewives and both fathers held blue collar jobs. None of the parents had much formal schooling; they had attended the *escuela secundaria* (the equivalent of a junior high school in the United States). The parents of both children were immigrants from Mexico, and both children were born in the U.S. Oscar's parents have resided here for fifteen years; Alberto's parents for four. Both families lived in a low-SES Hispanic *barrio* in a middle-sized city near the Mexican border.

Both Oscar and Alberto were the youngest of three children. Spanish was used as the primary language in each home and both sets of parents noted a recent increase of English use, indicating the influence of schooling on both children's language abilities.

We believe that including parents and teachers enriches assessment, because they are "experts" in daily life behaviors in natural settings, and they are also social agents for the development of language-minority children.

Alternative development assessment model

An "ethnic-researcher" developmental approach including nonverbal and verbal tasks and stimuli representing both minority and majority cultures and languages as the major component for accurately identifying cultural and linguistic giftedness in bilingual children was used to evaluate Oscar and Alberto.[8] During early childhood, individuals acquire language as a tool for thinking. Research has shown that minority children perform at higher cognitive developmental levels in nonverbal than in verbal tasks.[9] Current research indicates the need to use alternative assessments across contexts by multiple informants for language-minority children.[10] We believe that including parents and teachers enriches assessment, because they are "experts" in daily life behaviors in natural settings, and they are also social agents for the development of language-minority children. Thus, following these recommendations, the two case studies presented here use alternative measures that have a strong data-driven base:

1. Home Language Survey
2. Parents' and Teachers' Ratings of Children's Cognitive, Linguistic, and Social Abilities
3. Qualitative Use of English and Spanish Tasks
4. Cartoon Conservation Scales

Standardized tests used as comparison measures:

1. Language Assessment Scales (LAS)
2. Test of Nonverbal Intelligence-2 (TONI-2)

A **home language survey,** as well as parent and teacher ratings were used to get a clearer picture of the children's abilities. Parents were asked to: 1) rate their and their children's Spanish and English proficiency; 2) rate the frequency of use of Spanish and English at home; 3) provide the ages of the children in the home; and 4) provide background information for both parents.[11] **Parents' and teachers' ratings** involve describing the child's linguistic and cognitive abilities both at home and school, including selecting descriptors of the child's abilities and writing additional comments.[12]

QUEST in Spanish and English was chosen because it reliably explains verbal and nonverbal concept formation in bilingual children as a two-way universal and culturally-linguistically bound process influenced by cognition, culture, and language. Based on this model, five verbal and nonverbal classification tasks (labeling, defining, sorting, verbal justification of sorting, and category clue) were designed to assess bilingual children's general and linguistic-gender conceptual processes.[13]

The **Cartoon Conservation Scale** (CCS) includes Piagetian tasks with drawings done in a "comic-book" format providing concrete images. Each item involves a story that the child finishes in a way that she or he thinks "makes it true." The structure of the CCS presents eight conservation subscales: number, substance, length, distance, egocentricity, horizontality of water, volume or displacement of water, and probability.[14]

Results: A Comparison of Oscar and Alberto
Parents' Assessments

Parents' descriptions of their children's cognitive, linguistic, and social abilities are based on the parents' rating scales. The parents' *voces* describe the cultural dimensions of their gifted children's cognitive, linguistic,

and social skills using terms conveying a different meaning in Spanish than the literal translation in English—expressing differences between the Hispanic and mainstream American cultures. Despite these differences, these minority parents also valued education and the attainment of academic goals in their children.

When Oscar's parents described his cognitive and linguistic abilities, they used Spanish. A translated version of their descriptions is: "My son is very intelligent. He is always asking about something that is new to him, he wants it explained very well and then he never forgets it, . . . once a story is read to him he can retell the story and doesn't forget any details, . . . he learns everything very rapidly, and has great abilities." Oscar's parents used the expression in Spanish *"es un niño ejemplar"* to describe his cognitive abilities. A literal translation of this Spanish expression is "he is an example of a child," but in Spanish the cultural connotation is that "the child has an outstanding social behavior that shows maturity and wiseness." In describing Oscar's linguistic abilities, his parents stated that speaking to him was like speaking with an adult. The child's problem-solving abilities were described in terms of his adult-like speech and reasoning. Oscar's parents reported that he gave them advice in how to face problematic household situations; a translation of their description is: "Mami, when you have a problem you must always be patient." In addition, Oscar's parents described him as an imaginative and independent child who liked to do puzzles and drawings, had good writing skills, and enjoyed reading.

The interpersonal skills of being cooperative, independent, and able to understand social rules were used by Alberto's parents also as examples of his gifted problem-solving abilities.

Alberto's parents described their son's cognitive abilities using Spanish: *"Mi hijo es* (My son is) *atrevido* (risk-taker), *intenso* (intense), *curioso* (witty), *persistente* (persistent), *listo* (quick), *inteligente* (studious, applied), *laborioso* (hard-worker) *y* (and) *sabio* (wise)." The translation of some Spanish terms into English indicates a variation in connotative meanings, such as in the word *inteligente.* Alberto's parents described his cognitive abilities as very advanced for his chronological age: "He is observant, and has a long attention span; he is good in math; he likes to do puzzles, and takes apart things and puts them back together again; and he has good navigating skills." They perceived Alberto's willingness to help solve problems as adult-like behavior because he analyzed situations, determined what needed to be done, and did it without being asked. Alberto's parents described his social and interpersonal skills in Spanish: "*Mi hijo es* (My son is) *simpático* (charming), *empático* (sentimental), *cooperativo* (cooperative), *abierto* (open-minded), *servicial* (helpful), *sano* (moral), *amistoso* (friendly), *considerado* (considerate), *seguro* (confident), *impulsivo* (sure), *y respetuoso* (respectful). *Es un niño ejemplar* (he is an example of a child)." The interpersonal skills of being cooperative, independent, and able to understand social rules were used by Alberto's parents also as examples of his gifted problem-solving abilities.

Teachers' Assessments

Teachers' descriptions of the children's cognitive, linguistic, and social abilities were collected using the teachers' rating scales. They implement the curriculum endorsed by the mainstream school culture, and because of this they represent the *voices* in their descriptions of the children's abilities. But teachers cannot divorce themselves from their cultural identities, reflected in the strategies, methodologies, and educational philosophies that they choose to endorse. Due to this individual choice, teachers also represent the *voces* in their descriptions of the children's abilities.

Oscar's teacher reported that he had good reasoning skills in math and he problem-solved using math manipulatives. She talked about Oscar's motivation for learning, mentioning that he was "very knowledgeable in many areas" and that "he showed excitement in putting puzzles together without the outline." She explained Oscar's "very expanded vocabulary" as the result of his family travel experiences and his ability to relate knowledge from his real-world experience to classroom activities. When playing, she described him as creative and independent; and when working with others, she described him as a leader who "organizes groups," and as a responsible child who volunteered for cleaning up in the classroom without being told.

Alberto's teacher described him as eager to learn, intrinsically motivated, persistent, and committed to finishing tasks. His teacher also mentioned that Alberto liked to assemble things and draw, and had good problem-solving skills. Like his parents, his teacher mentioned Alberto's advanced language skills as exemplified by his large vocabulary and very good story-telling skills. His teacher considered Alberto to be independent, very helpful, cooperative, caring, friendly, observant, thoughtful, talkative, and adventurous.

Alternative Assessments
Oscar's QUEST performance (in Spanish)

Oscar performed at a concrete level in nonverbal tasks, and at a functional level in verbal tasks. Even though Oscar could: 1) not label all the items, he could still define them verbally at a concrete level; and 2) sort

items nonverbally at the concrete level, he could not articulate the reasons why he had grouped the objects into categories and subcategories. Thus, we conclude that Oscar showed nonverbal cultural giftedness, but did not show linguistic giftedness.

Alberto's QUEST performance (in Spanish and English)

Alberto's performance in English was much lower than in Spanish, demonstrating the effect of assessing a minority child in his first language and culture on his verbal and nonverbal cognitive development. His performance was also higher for animal than for food items, which represented different cultural and linguistic possible categorizations. Based on Alberto's metalinguistic and concrete performance in QUEST in Spanish, he was diagnosed as culturally and linguistically gifted.

CCS performance

The subscales passed by Oscar and Alberto in Spanish were conservation of number and length, horizontality, and probability. In addition, Oscar passed the scale of volume, and Alberto passed the scale of egocentricity, both in Spanish. Both children's performance at the concrete level indicated advanced cognitive development.

Therefore, not only the language used in testing is important, but also the cultural stimuli and perspectives used to interpret their performance.

Standardized Test Performance

On the **Test of Nonverbal Intelligence** (TONI-2),[15] Oscar's score indicated average intelligence; Alberto's score indicated superior intelligence. Both Oscar's scores (4 in Spanish and 1 in English) on the **Language Assessment Scales**[16] and his teacher's language ratings, indicated that he was Spanish monolingual. Alberto was found to be bilingual, but also Spanish-dominant, based upon his scores on the LAS (4 in Spanish and 2 in English) and his similar parents' and teachers' ratings.

Discussion and Conclusions
Gifted or Not?

Can a monolingual, minority, low-SES child be gifted? Oscar's case indicates "yes," the child can be culturally or nonverbally gifted as evidenced by alternative developmental measures (QUEST and CCS) administered in Spanish. Oscar's case shows that nonverbal cultural giftedness is *not* associated with the degree of bilingualism, but with the degree of sensitivity of alternative assessments to measure minority cultural representations influencing cognition. Therefore, not only the language used in testing is important, but also the cultural stimuli and perspectives used to interpret their performance. As for Alberto, we discovered that he shows not only nonverbal but also verbal giftedness in Spanish as evidenced by QUEST and CCS. Our analysis of Alberto's case leads us to be positive about the stimulating role of not only two cultures but also two languages on cognitive development.

Both case studies also show that nonverbal cultural giftedness in language-minority children cannot be measured by nonverbal standardized intelligence tests. Moreover, there were also differences between both children's performance in nonverbal and verbal tasks in QUEST Spanish and the TONI-2. Within a developmental perspective, these differences may indicate that cognition results from the dynamic interaction between internal and external factors. Thus, it is possible that Alberto was positively influenced by being bilingual because he was more intelligent nonverbally than Oscar, who was only monolingual Spanish. Then, these two children presented differences in their range of cognitive developmental potential, and also in how cultural and linguistic factors contributed to the actualization of their potentials.[17]

The Home Environment

Several researchers have noted the important role of the family in offering mentoring and support to minority children in order to be successful in the mainstream educational environment. For instance, Van Tassel-Baska pointed out that it is not only what economic resources are present in the family that have been traditionally associated with parental occupation and educational level, but what coping strategies low-SES at-risk children are able to learn from supportive positive role models in their families. He found that African-American and Asian-American adolescents who had been identified as gifted and succeed academically in school, had "families which served as a major source of encouragement and influence . . . [and] . . . had at least one parent who was dominant and monitored the child's progress through school very closely."[18] For these adolescents, the support of extended family members was important (usually the maternal grandmother) because they transmitted positive values, provided guidance, and nurtured their self-concept and self-esteem.[19]

By analyzing the home environments of both children, we see that both fathers self-reported that they were proficient in English, and both mothers self-reported that they were limited English-proficient. Even though primarily Spanish was used to communicate in both households, only Alberto started to learn English; Oscar remained monolingual Spanish. Thus, we believe that individual differences precede cultural and linguistic differences, and that any language-minority child is first an individual and then a member of a particular linguistic and cultural community.

Based on these cases, it seems that: 1) a monolingual child can be culturally or nonverbally gifted; 2) the level of nonverbal cognitive development influences the rate and amount of first- and second-language acquisition; and 3) cultural and linguistic factors do not affect every child in the same manner given individual differences.

However, the Hispanic voces *of the parents described giftedness also as a socially and emotionally mature behavior expressed by their children in appropriate contexts of their minority culture.*

Voces and *voices:* **Integrating parents' and teachers' perspectives**

We found both similarities and differences between the teachers' and the parents' descriptions of the cognitive, linguistic, and social abilities of the two cases. The teachers' *voices* representing the school mainstream culture coincided with the parents' *voces* when they were describing giftedness as an advanced verbal and logico-mathematical intelligence. However, the Hispanic *voces* of the language-minority children's parents described giftedness also as a socially and emotionally mature behavior expressed by their children in appropriate contexts of their minority culture.

Lay people from the majority culture also have the tendency to emphasize successful behaviors in a real-life sociocultural context when describing "intelligent" individuals.[20] In contrast, Sternberg also found that "experts," professionals trained in psychology, defined intelligence using the traditional scholastic aptitude skills measured by standardized IQ tests referring only to the verbal and logico-mathematical domains of intelligence.[21] There is an interesting relationship between CCS, QUEST, and the parents' and teachers' views of the children. CCS and QUEST results show that the children were operating at higher cognitive developmental levels for their ages. The parents' view of their children is that they were gifted because their "adult-like" behaviors were at a higher developmental level. The teachers' view of the children emphasized their academic skills and logico-mathematical developmental abilities.

Integrating the teachers' *voices* and the minority parents' *voces* in this study builds on the concept of exploring the potential of cross-cultural benefits and resources advocated by Serpell.[22] We have also learned that children from low-SES households whose family members provide adequate emotional nurturing, transmit positive educational values, and celebrate their academic success, do function as empathic role models and mentors.

In conclusion, we believe that cultural and linguistic giftedness does exist among minority monolingual or unbalanced bilingual children, but we can only observe its psychological expressions in behaviors measured through sensitive alternative assessments like QUEST and CCS. We want to advocate the need to give language-minority children and their parents the opportunity to express their *voces*. Our view of giftedness is enhanced and elaborated by the perspectives of the *voces* of minority homes, communities, and people in interaction with the traditional *voices* of our mainstream American school culture.

1. A. Dundes, *The Study of Folklore* (New Jersey: Prentice Hall, 1965), 2, 294, 297.

2. M.M. Frasier, "The Identification of Gifted Black Students: Developing New Perspectives," *Journal for the Education of the Gifted* 10, no. 3. (1987): 155–180.

3. M.M. Frasier, Disadvantaged and Culturally Diverse Gifted Students," *Journal for the Education of the Gifted* 14, no. 3 (1991): 234–245.

4. A. Darder, *Culture and Power in the Classroom: A Critical Foundation for Bicultural Education* (New York: Bergin & Garvey, 1991).

5. V. Gonzalez and E.R. Riojas-Clark, "Folkloric and Historical Dimensions of Giftedness," in V. Gonzalez, ed., *Language and Cognitive Development in Second Language Learning: Educational Implications for Children and Adults* (Needham Heights, Mass.: Allyn & Bacon, 1999), 1–18.

6. V. Gonzalez, "A Model of Cognitive, Cultural, and Linguistic Variables Affecting Bilingual Spanish/English Children's Development of Concepts and Language," doctoral dissertation (Austin, Tex.: The University of Texas at Austin, ERIC Document Reproduction Service No. ED 345 562, 1991).

7. V. Gonzalez, "A Model of Cognitive, Cultural, and Linguistic Variables Affecting Bilingual Spanish/English Children's Development of Concepts and Language," *Hispanic Journal of Behavioral Sciences* 16, no. 4 (1994): 396–421.

8. V. Gonzalez and T.D. Yawkey, "The Assessment of Culturally and Linguistically Diverse Students: Celebrating Change," *Educational HORIZONS* 73, no. 1, (1993): 41–49.

9. Gonzalez, "A Model of Cognitive, Cultural, and Linguistic Variables," 1991; Gonzalez, "A Model of Cognitive, Cultural, and Linguistic Variables," 1994; and V. Gonzalez, P. Bauerle, and M. Felix-Holt, "Theoretical and Practical Implications of Assessing Cognitive and Language Development in Bilingual Children with Qualitative Methods," *The Bilingual Research Journal* 20, no. 1 (1996): 93–131.

10. J. Cummins, "Interdependence of First-and-Second-Language Proficiency in Bilingual Children," in E. Bialystock, ed., *Language Processing in Bilingual Children* (Cambridge, England: Cambridge University Press, 1991), 70–89; J.W. Oller, Jr., "Challenged Bilinguals," *NABE NEWS* 17, no. 4 (1994): 15–16, 18; R.J. Samuda, "Towards Nondiscriminatory Assessment: Principles and Applications," in R.J. Samuda, et al., eds., *Assessment and Placement of Minority Students* (Toronto, Canada: C. J. Hogrefe, 1991), 173–189; and J.S. Renzulli, "The National Research Center on the Gifted and Talented: The Dream, the Design, and the Destination," *Gifted Child Quarterly* 35, no. 2 (1991): 73–80.

11. Gonzalez, "A Model of Cognitive, Cultural, and Linguistic Variables," 1991.

12. M. Fleming, et al., *Parents' and Teachers' Ratings of Minority Children's Cognitive, Linguistic, and Social Abilities* (Tucson, Ariz.: The University of Arizona and Tucson Independent School District, 1992).

13. Gonzalez, "A Model of Cognitive, Cultural, and Linguistic Variables," 1991; Gonzalez, "A Model of Cognitive, Cultural, and Linguistic Variables," 1994; and V. Gonzalez, *Cognition, Culture, and Language in Bilingual Children: Conceptual and Semantic Development* (Bethesda, Md.: Austin & Winfield, 1995).

14. E.A. De Avila, *Cartoon Conservation Scales (CCS)* (San Antonio, Tex.: Stephen Jackson & Associates, 1976).

15. L. Brown, R.J. Sherbenou, and S.K. Johnsen, *Test of Nonverbal Intelligence-2 (TONI-2)* (Austin, Tex.: Pro-Ed, 1990).

16. E. A. De Avila and S. E. Duncan, *The Language Assessment Scales (LAS)* (Monterey, Calif.: CTB/McGraw-Hill, 1986).

17. Gonzalez and Yawkey, "Assessment of Culturally and Linguistically Diverse Students."

18. J. Van Tassel-Baska, "The Role of the Family in the Success of Disadvantaged Gifted Learners," *Journal for the Education of the Gifted* 13, no. 1 (1989): 22–36.

19. Ibid.

20. R.J. Sternberg, *Beyond IQ: A Triarchic Theory of Human Intelligence* (New York: Cambridge University Press, 1984).

21. Ibid.

22. R. Serpell, "Assessment Criteria for Severe Intellectual Disability in Various Cultural Settings," *International Journal of Behavioral Development* 11, no. 1 (1988): 117–144.

Unit Selections

Key Points to Consider

❖ Compare and contrast the different approaches to learning. What approach do you think is best, and why? What factors are important to your answer (e.g., objectives, types of students, setting, personality of the teacher)?

❖ What are some principles for effective teaching that derive directly from brain research and different conceptualizations of intelligence?

❖ What teaching strategies could you use to promote greater student retention of material? What are good ways to attract and keep students' attention? Must a teacher be an "entertainer"? Why or why not?

❖ How can a teacher promote positive self-esteem, values, character, caring, and attitudes? How are they related to cognitive learning? How much emphasis should be put on cultivating character or positive student interactions? How would you create a "caring" classroom? Discuss whether or not this would interfere with achievement of cognitive learning targets.

❖ If you wanted to create a constructivistic classroom in the subject area and/or grade in which you want to teach, what would the classroom look like? What would you emphasize, and how would your actions reflect constructivist principles and research on intelligence?

❖ How can teaching for standards be integrated with differentiation? How is it possible to use different instructional strategies to help all students obtain high standards?

 **Links**   **www.dushkin.com/online/**

These sites are annotated on pages 4 and 5.

Learning can be broadly defined as a relatively permanent change in behavior or thinking due to experience. Learning is not a result of change due to maturation or temporary influences. Changes in behavior and thinking of students result from complex interactions between their individual characteristics and environmental factors. A continuing challenge in education is understanding these interactions so that learning can be enhanced. This unit focuses on approaches within educational psychology that represent different ways of viewing the learning process and related instructional strategies. Each approach to learning emphasizes a different set of personal and environmental factors that influence certain behaviors. While no one approach can fully explain learning, each is a valuable contribution to our knowledge about the process and the improvement of student performance.

The discussion of each learning approach includes suggestions for specific techniques and methods of teaching to guide teachers in understanding student behavior and in making decisions about how to teach. The articles in this section reflect a recent emphasis on applied research conducted in schools, research on the brain, and on constructivist theories.

Researchers have recently made significant advances in understanding the way our brain works. Information processing refers to the way that the mind receives sensory information, stores it as memory, and recalls it for later use. This procedure is basic to all learning, no matter what teaching approach is taken, and we know that the method used in processing information determines to some extent how much and what we remember. The essays in the first subsection present some of the fundamental principles of brain functioning, information processing and cognition, and human intelligences.

In the past, behaviorism was the best-known approach to learning. Most practicing and prospective teachers are familiar with concepts such as classical conditioning, reinforcement, and punishment, and there is no question that behaviorism has made significant contributions to understanding learning. But behaviorism has also been subject to much misinterpretation, in part because it seems so simple. In fact, the effective use of behavioristic principles is complex and demanding, as the article on praise points out.

Constructivist learning theory is currently the predominant approach to learning that is recognized by educational psychologists. According to constructivists, it is important for students to actively create and reorganize knowledge. There is a need for students to interpret within meaningful contexts so that what is learned is well connected with existing knowledge. Two articles are devoted to constructivist learning. The first shows how to incorporate constructivism principles with inquiry learning, another important approach to teaching/learning, to encourage critical thinking. The second article reviews the essence of a constructivist culture.

Social psychological learning emphasizes the affective, social, moral, and personal development of students. Social psychology is the study of the nature of interpersonal relationships in social situations. In education, this approach looks at teacher-pupil relationships and group processes to derive principles of interaction that affect learning. One article in this section examines the application of social psychological principles. It examines character education, morals, and values, traits that are becoming more important in light of recent incidents of school violence and children's access to all types of information on the Internet.

Instructional strategies are the teacher behaviors and methods of conveying information that affect learning. Teaching methods or techniques can vary greatly, depending on objectives, group size, types of students, and personality of the teacher. For example, discussion classes are generally more effective for enhancing thinking skills than are individualized sessions or lectures. For the final subsection, four articles have been selected that show how teachers can use principles of cognitive psychology and intelligence in their teaching. The first article emphasizes the importance of an appropriate classroom environment that will encourage and support students' thinking.

Differentiated instruction is quickly becoming a major teaching technique, as discussed in two articles by national expert Carol Tomlinson. In her first article she presents her research on differentiated instruction to illustrate essential principles and practice. In her second article she considers differentiation in light of another recent trend in instruction—standards-based teaching. Finally, technology is also becoming a pervasive opportunity for teaching and learning. The fourth article examines one aspect of this field, the Internet, with applications to the classroom.

Learning and Instruction

Brain Basics:
Cognitive Psychology and Its Implications for Education

Richard L. Bucko

The human brain is a unique creation composed of a hundred billion neurons connected by trillions of synapses. For millennia, people have asked how this three-pound mass of soft tissue inside the human skull performs such tasks as writing letters, solving problems, and contemplating the universe. These questions are now finding answers through recent findings about the way the human brain works. The general field of study is known as cognitive science. When applied to the study of human cognition, it is known as cognitive psychology. When applied to the field of education, it is known as brain-based learning. Brain-based learning may be the most important influence on the way we teach since the first school was founded.

Knowledge of brain-based learning will be essential to educators of the future because good teaching requires an understanding of how the brain receives, processes, and produces information. As our understanding of cognitive psychology grows, learning problems will be addressed analytically, with an understanding of the damage to connections that causes these problems. Brain-based learning can be the foundation of pragmatic future education reform based on clear evidence of how children learn.

This article will address key research findings about brain research, the thinking skills movement, popular literature on the brain, and implications for schools.

Key Findings about Brain Functions

Three technological innovations are now allowing neuroscientists to analyze and observe the connection between the various areas of the brain. First, neural imaging allows researchers to observe the inner workings of the brain. As subjects see colors or words, various areas of the brain light up on imaging screens. Different brain regions can be observed handling letters of the alphabet, numbers, tastes, and smells. In a bilingual person, one area will handle one language while another deals with the second language.

Second, molecular biology is revealing the operations of genes and molecules inside brain cells. One example is from the work of Eric Kandel at Columbia University. He discovered a short string of chemical molecules, called CREB, which serves as a switch to turn certain genes in the brain on and off. CREB is needed to change short-term memory into long-term memory. As we age,

From *ERS Spectrum*, Summer 1997, pp. 20–25. © 1997 by Educational Research Service. Reprinted by permission.

CREB is less plentiful, a fact that may partially explain memory loss as we enter later years. Even the sense of smell is managed by over 1,000 genes controlling neurons that respond to various smells, connecting these odors to associated behaviors, memories, and thoughts (Flam 1996).

Third, computers have given us an exact way to think about information processing by helping us to learn how processing is localized.

The convergence of brain scans, molecular biology, and computers has opened the way for researchers to localize the regions where different concepts are stored and to observe how these regions are joined together in thought and consciousness (Hilts 1995).

The Way the Brain Works—

The wiring of the brain is far more complex than the most powerful supercomputer. We have billions of neurons and many more supporting cells within the confines of our heads. One amazing finding is that the physical structure of these cells changes as they respond to the environment and experience. When confronted with changes to our surroundings or new experiences, brain cells grow or shrink and new thread-like connections between neurons are established, or old ones are strengthened. If a person is blinded, for example, the other sensory portions of the brain will become stronger.

Today, brain researchers consider the brain to be organized in both a focal and diffuse manner, depending on what functions are being addressed. Basic sensory and motor functions are controlled by specific areas, while higher mental functions involve a constellation of areas across the brain.

Complex thinking requires memory applications from several locations. It may involve visual or auditory memories, concept identification, and language usage. All of this occurs while other portions of the brain are aware of sensations of feeling, temperature, visual stimuli, sounds, and possibly tangential thoughts—and all the while that thinker's brain is responsible for maintaining balance while walking and chewing gum. This is what is meant by the term *parallel processing*, the ability of the brain to perform many tasks at once.

Human speech has provided a rich area for the study of the way information travels through the brain. An incredible array of "category deficits" in human thinking arise from damage to the brain. Examples include people whose overall functioning is normal but who cannot recall the names of animals; people who can write words but not numbers; and people who can recognize faces of loved ones but cannot say their names. The range extends from unnoticeable gaps to an almost complete inability to understand language.

When studied in detail, in many patients and with the assistance of imaging equipment, the various disabilities give us a good picture of how the brain organizes and manipulates information. For example, damage to a particular part of the back of the brain can cause a person to fail to recognize categorical relationships such as a violin as a musical instrument, or robin as a bird, or any other individuals as belonging to particular categories.

After more than a century of study, cases like this have allowed researchers to tentatively identify about 20 categories that the brain uses to organize knowledge. These include plants, animals, body parts, colors, numbers, verbs, facial expressions, and sounds. There are certainly many more (Hilts 1995).

In mapping emotions, opposites such as happiness and sadness are not registered in the same place in the brain. They entail different and independent patterns of activity in different locations. Because happiness and sadness involve separate brain areas, we can have bittersweet emotions, such as when we fondly think of a deceased loved one.

In a memory, connections are made to areas of the brain that may control memory of visual images, odors, sounds, and certain words. This is a vital point for educators. Connections between the various brain areas are the foundation of thinking and knowing. Connections allow us to put two or more memory images together. These images may be of sounds, sights, ideas, or emotions. The ability to *associate* or *connect* these images stored in different areas of the brain allows us to be "smart." By connecting these images at the speed of electricity, we are able to create a simple thought, such as "I am going to take the dog out," or a more complex one, such as "It is my wife's birthday—it will make her happy if I send her flowers." We will address the implications for the classroom shortly.

Levels of Brain Function—

There is value in identifying the three levels of brain function that are addressed in a school or workplace. The nature of the organization of brain functions and their connections to one another form the *first* level of brain performance, known as neurological development. The *second* level is subskill performance. This requires the connections of several parts of the brain that are required to perform the *third*, or skill level. For example, eye-hand coordination, visual integration, and cognitive recall are subskills required to perform the skill of writing; all of these subskills contribute to writing performance.

When we think of skill performance in analytical terms, we can become more effective teachers who systematically analyze the performance of individual students. The learning difficulties or strengths of the individual are affected by developmental levels and relative strengths within a skill or subskill.

Male/Female Differences—

Yes, there are differences in the structure of male and female brains. One example is the larger size of the corpus callosum (a structure that joins the left and right hemispheres) in females. Another is the tendency of female brains to develop in a rather uniform manner, while male brains do not.

Differences in brain organization appear to result in variations in cognitive abilities. Most significantly, it is generally true that females tend to be more fluent than males in the use of language, and males tend to be better at spatial analysis. Less definite research indicates that boys excel in mathematical ability and tend to be more aggressive than females. Efforts to explain sex differences tend to focus on one or more of the following: different brain organization, hormonal effects on cerebral function, genetic sex-linkage, maturation rate, and environment (Kolb and Whishaw 1996).

The sex-based concept of left-brain dominance (highly verbal, logical thinker and basically rational) verses right brain dominance (less verbal, spatial memory strength, and intuitive processor), is receiving little support in the recent research. It is, at best, inconclusive. Each hemisphere relies heavily on the other, thereby producing a synergy that cannot be separated. According to Renate and Geoffrey Caine (1991), "schools should provide the opportunity to develop all abilities even as we continue to prefer some over others" (p. 34).

The Thinking Skills Movement

As John Dewey pointed out in the 1930s, thinking can be done well or badly, and good thinking, like good manners, can be taught. Thinking occurs in the formation of beliefs, and in making decisions and solving problems. If good thinking can be taught, it can have far-reaching applications well beyond the classroom.

Since 1956, Bloom's *Taxonomy of Educational Objectives* has provided one of the fundamental frameworks for teachers to teach thinking skills in the classroom. Writers and workshop presenters use this well-organized structure for the teaching of thinking. Bloom's Taxonomy was a notable effort—but it has not been borne out by the last few decades of research on cognitive processes (Hart 1986).

Some Bloom advocates try to adapt the taxonomy to current brain research. Adapting Bloom's model of higher and lower forms of cognition to classroom instruction may have some merit, but other approaches to developing thinking, language, and metacognitive processing seem to have more potential.

Through the 1980s, "thinking skills" was a key buzzword in teacher training. Prominent theorists included Perkins, Costa and Adler. D. N. Perkins wrote of intelligence as the combination of *Power* (natural ability/IQ), *Tactics* (thinking strategy) and *Content* combining to form *Intelligence*. Thus,

Intelligence = Power + Tactics + Content

The "unnaturalness of good thinking" required that thinking be taught in a variety of ways. Perkins described

"thinking frames" or tactics/strategies that enhance intelligence.

In 1980, the Association for Supervision and Curriculum Development published a compilation of the works of various authors entitled *Developing Minds*. Edited by Arthur Costa, the book presented useful ways to enhance thinking in such content areas as writing, reading, science, and math. It included 18 articles by 18 different authors on programs for teaching thinking.

Hundreds of additional books and articles added to the vast array of materials about teaching thinking. But all of this activity took place with no clear idea of how the mind received, processed, or produced information.

It is interesting how little we have heard in recent years about "thinking skills." Is it no longer important, or was it void of valid content? Is the vacuum of knowledge about the brain being filled by meaningful and applicable cognitive research?

As early as 1986, Mortimer Adler was one of the few voices presenting an alternative view about teaching thinking. He supported content-based instruction that involved reading, writing, measuring, testing, and trying to draw conclusions. When practical thinking applications were applied to content instruction, meaningful thinking instruction took place. This approach is supported today through research that tells us that making connections with the brain is the key to long-term memory and the ability to apply classroom learning in other contexts.

For centuries, humans have recognized the importance of quality thinking. What has changed in recent years is the advance of technology that has enabled researchers to study, even to observe, what takes place when we think. It is interesting, but not surprising, that some of the foremost thinkers about thinking during the 1980s (Hart 1986) have become leaders in the application of the science of cognition and brain-based learning.

The Recent Brain Literature

Since the early 1980s, there have been a number of books on best-seller lists that have used findings about the brain as subject matter that has fascinated millions of readers. Two books by Oliver Sacks, *The Man Who Mistook His Wife for a Hat* (1987) and *An Anthropologist on Mars* (1995) depict unusual case studies of behavioral abnormalities caused by neurological damage. This seems to have a fascination for many readers.

Howard Gardner documented the concept that the brain possesses many forms of intelligence in his 1983 book *Frames of Mind*. By the 1990s, the concept of multiple intelligence had caught on in many schools. His book and its variants continued selling in the popular market. Educators are familiar with his important theory that there are at least seven intelligences: mathematical, musical, kinesthetic, linguistic, spatial, intrapersonal, and interpersonal. A strength in one does not predict a strength in another. Gardner's Harvard-based research was state-of-the-art and played a strong role in raising the consciousness of educators toward the importance of learning more about the brain. Like the popular books previously mentioned, it also raised the interest level of the general public.

The *Triarchic Mind* followed in 1988 with a description of three forms of intelligence. Robert Sternberg presented his "triarchic theory" of intelligence using three manifestations: 1) the internal world of the individual, which is the traditional view of intelligence, 2) the relationship of that intelligence to the environment around us, and 3) the relationship of intelligence to experiences we have had since the time we were born.

Emotional Intelligence (1995), by Daniel Goleman, is a serious look at the importance of those factors not measured on an IQ test. Goleman argues that our view of intelligence is far too narrow. He uses brain and behavioral research to demonstrate the factors involved when people of high IQ fail at life and those of modest IQ do extremely well. Emotional intelligence includes persistence, impulse control, enthusiasm, empathy, and social awareness.

In line with the current interest in character education, the recent book *Moral Intelligence* (1997), by Robert Coles, again uses the term intelligence in a title. Coles makes the point that during the elementary school years the child becomes a moral creature—it is the time when the conscience is, or is not, created.

These important years are the time when the malleable mind is being formed. Children are eager to absorb the world that is placed around them—the good or the bad, the moral or the immoral. The brain is a sponge during these young years when it is capable of gaining vast amounts of information. Too often our society forgets that the early years are the most important time to direct our efforts in school and at home. It is the fortunate child who is nurtured in both.

Although his work has focused on educational disabilities, Melvin Levine has been a guiding light to educators on the role of brain function. As a researcher, pediatrician, and professor at the University of North Carolina, he has been able to develop his ideas about how the developing brain functions. As a lecturer and as the author of several books, most notably, *Educational Care* (1994), he has been able to extend his influence to many schools.

Educational Care provides a guide for parents and teachers to collaborate in the management of children with school-related problems. Through the development of diagnostic instruments that integrate neurological, behavioral, and developmental findings, he has been able to better understand the workings of a child's mind and plan better ways to teach those with educational difficulties.

Applications in Education

Learning and Memory—

Cognitive psychologists have identified two separate types of memory systems. The "what" memory system holds facts such as faces, names, and dates. The "how-to" memory preserves skills such as reading or sewing. Memories of both types are stored in the short-term holding area behind the forehead where they remain for a few moments. Some of these memories are converted to long-term storage that may last for years. "What" memory tends to fade quickly, but "how-to" memory can last a lifetime (Hilts 1995).

Conversion of short-term into long-term memory involves the growth of new connections between neurons. Certain memory-enhancing strategies, such as repetition and association, are effective ways of growing connections between neurons. Actual changes to the brain occur—the size of a brain area grows or shrinks, depending on experience and practice. Memory is generally considered to be a five-step process: 1) acquisition, 2) registration, 3) storage, 4) access, 5) transfer.

Thematic instruction provides connections among storage areas of the brain, therefore reinforcing memory through dispersal. The more areas that are "touched" by the stimulus, the greater the probability of long-term retention.

Cooperative learning also provides connections to other parts of the brain through integration with other content topics or through social interaction.

Opportunities to think and speak about a topic, as well as to listen and do hands-on activities, will also enhance the probability of long term retention.

Creation of many strong connections between areas of the brain provides the key to memory enhancement. As Gardner would say, this is influenced by an individual's strength in the specific area of intelligence being addressed. The important point for educators is that the brain's *thinking* function involves retaining information and connecting the information storage locations when necessary.

John Bruer makes a strong case for the relevance of prior knowledge in his 1993 book *Schools for Learning*. A good teacher will consciously use an "anticipatory set" (capture students' attention and relate the topic to prior knowledge), because the way we understand and remember new material depends on how it relates to what we already know. Learning is an active process as well as a constructive one. Our brains make sense of what we experience by actively connecting it with prior knowledge.

The Learning Environment—

The emotional condition of one's mind can have a great influence on the brain's ability to retain information. If the learner's mind is stressed by fear and anxiety, maximum learning cannot occur. Too much of the mind's energy and attention is expended on the emotion and not on the intended learning. When divorce, peer pressure, the birth of a sibling, or other stress-causing circumstances occur, learning suffers.

Climate is a term often used to describe the character and culture of a school. A pleasant, academic orientation enhances the mind's readiness to accept and retain information. Friendly classmates, pleasant surroundings, gentle colors, cleanliness, and abundant classical music are possible ingredients of a healthy learning climate.

Far too little effort is spent in creating school environments that increase the ability to learn. The classroom is often a very unnatural environment. School typically requires long hours of attention in a sitting position—a task far more difficult for some than others.

Success for an adult in a home or work setting generally does not require being in one chair or room for an extended time. In those settings, social interaction, motivation, and energy, as well as a variety of other task-specific skills, are essential. Teaching, for example, requires energy, motivation, verbal and interpersonal skills, as well as the ability to use effective instructional strategies. Yet, the degree to which such skills are recognized and used to the greatest advantage during a typical school day is generally minimal.

The Mind/Body Connection—

Sometimes we forget that the brain benefits from care of the entire body. Good nutrition and exercise are fundamental to optimum school performance. Aerobic activity feeds the brain with oxygen and glucose—essential to increasing nerve connections. Children who exercise regularly do better in school according to many studies.

Getting more physical activity into the school day is a challenge, but it can be achieved through large-group music aerobics, class recess that involves significant activity, and gym classes that involve real movement. Classroom learning benefits from added activity. Physical movement involving lesson content enhances brain function and learning. Studies have found that young children learn subtraction faster and retain it longer when it is presented in a variety of forms, including physical activity such as moving classmates as numbers in an equation or calculating comparable distances or times for outdoor runs.

Music and the Arts—

Like physical education classes, music and the arts can be powerful forces in the effort to create learning connections. Plato said that music "is a more potent instrument than any other for education." He was prescient in his understanding that music trains the brain for advanced forms of thinking.

In a recent University of California study, two groups of three year olds were the subject of a unique experiment. One group took piano lessons and sang daily in chorus. The other did not have music as part of their curriculum. After eight months, the musical group performed far better on a puzzle completion task (Blakeslee 1995). This skill could translate into better math and engineering skills.

Studies such as this support the belief that early music training may improve a child's ability to reason. While it may not be practical to provide students with daily classes with a music teacher, playing classical music during quiet work times in class and in the hallways can significantly increase student exposure.

The possibilities for the integration of history, math, and language into music, art, and drama are endless. Classroom dramatizations, the use of geometry in art, and other cross-curricular possibilities are only limited by the teacher's imagination.

Summary

The neurological system of each student contains a variety of skill strengths and weaknesses that influence school performance. The task is to think of the brain as an organ for learning and to match instruction and the learning environment to the way that the brain most effectively gathers and retains information.

The following practices, some of which are already used in many classrooms, can help us attune schooling to what brain-based learning research tells us:

- Use a wide variety of instruction geared toward different types of intelligence.
- Incorporate movement into instructional activities.
- Make greater use of instructional strategies that build connections among the different brain functions, such as thematic instruction and cooperative learning.
- Do more to promote students' physical fitness.
- Stress the importance of early music training to enhance children's cognitive skills, and integrate music into other subject areas.
- Create pleasant, relaxed classroom environments through pleasing colors, classical music, and cleanliness.
- Relate new topics to students' prior knowledge in order to strengthen their long-term memory of content.
- Teach critical thinking skills by applying them to content instruction through reading, writing, measuring, testing, and trying to draw conclusions.

Schools have been slow to implement instruction that reflects what we know about the brain and learning. There are many reasons—inertia, the fear of taking a chance, lack of time to reflect on and plan for change, and difficulties in communicating to educators what *does* make a difference.

Change in education is notoriously slow. Wisely, we don't want to be reckless with our children. But as more and more evidence supports the power of understanding cognitive psychology, we are on the eve of a learning revolution that could change our schools for the better.

References

Adler, Mortimer. (1986). "Why Critical Thinking Programs Won't Work." *Education Week* (September 17, 1986).

Blakeslee, Sandra. (1995). *New York Times (Science Times)*, May 16, 1995: C1.

Bloom, Benjamin et al. (1956). *Taxonomy of Educational Objectives: The Classification of Educational Goals.* New York: Longmans Green.

Bruer, John T. (1993). *Schools for Learning.* Cambridge, MA: MIT Press.

Caine, Renate and Geoffrey Caine. (1991). *Making Connections: Teaching and the Human Brain.* Alexandria, VA: Association for Supervision and Curriculum Development.

Coles, Robert. (1997). *The Moral Intelligence of Children.* New York: Random House.

Costa, Arthur L., editor. (1985). *Developing Minds* Alexandria, VA: Association for Supervision and Curriculum Development.

Flam, Faye. (1996). "Tracking Down Thoughts." *The Philadelphia Inquirer* (May 20, 1996): E-3.

Gardner, Howard (1983). *Frames of Mind.* New York: Basic Books.

Gardner, Howard. (1995). "Reflections on Multiple Intelligences." *Phi Delta Kappan* (November 1995).

Goleman, Daniel. (1995). *Emotional Intelligence.* New York: Bantam Books.

Hart, Leslie A. (1986). "A Response: All Thinking Paths Lead to the Brain." *Educational Leadership* (May 1986).

Hilts, Phillip. (1995). "Brain's Memory System Comes Into Focus." *The New York Times* (May 30, 1995): C1.

Kolb, Bryan and Ian Q. Whishaw. (1996). *Fundamentals of Human Neuropsychology.* W. H. Freeman and Co.

Levine, Melvin. (1987). *Developmental Variation and Learning Disorders.* Boston, MA: Educators Publishing Service.

Levine, Melvin. (1994). *Educational Care.* Boston, MA: Educators Publishing Service.

Perkins, D. N. (1986). "Thinking Frames." *Educational Leadership* (May, 1986).

Sacks, Oliver. (1987). *The Man Who Mistook His Wife For a Hat.* New York: Harper Perennial.

Sacks, Oliver. (1995). *An Anthropologist on Mars.* New York: Vintage Books.

Sternberg, Robert J. (1988). *The Triarchic Mind.* New York: Viking.

Richard L. Bucko is Principal of George C. Baker School in Moorestown Township Public Schools, New Jersey (enrollment 2,800). Dr. Bucko has published and presented in the area of effective instruction, and his study of the subject of brain-based learning is a continuation of his interest in this area.

In Search of . . .
Brain-Based Education

BY JOHN T. BRUER

The "In Search of . . ." television series is no way to present history, Mr. Bruer points out, and the brain-based education literature is not the way to present the science of learning.

WE HAVE almost survived the Decade of the Brain. During the 1990s, government agencies, foundations, and advocacy groups engaged in a highly successful effort to raise public awareness about advances in brain research. Brain science became material for cover stories in our national newsmagazines. Increased public awareness raised educators' always simmering interest in the brain to the boiling point. Over the past five years, there have been numerous books, conferences, and entire issues of education journals devoted to what has come to be called "brain-based education."

Brain-based educators tend to support progressive education reforms. They decry the "factory model of education," in which experts create knowledge, teachers disseminate it, and students are graded on how much of it they can absorb and retain. Like many other educators, brain-based educators favor a constructivist, active learning model. Students should be actively engaged in learning and in guiding their own instruction. Brain enthusiasts see neuroscience as perhaps the best weapon with which to destroy our outdated factory model.[1] They argue that teachers should teach for meaning and understanding. To do so, they claim, teachers should create learning environments that are low in threat and high in challenge, and students should be actively engaged and immersed in complex experiences. No reasonable parent or informed educator would take issue with these ideas. Indeed, if more schools

From *Phi Delta Kappan*, May 1999, pp. 649-657. © 1999 by John T. Bruer. Reprinted by permission.

THE DANGER WITH MUCH OF THE BRAIN-BASED EDUCATION LITERATURE IS THAT IT BECOMES EXCEEDINGLY DIFFICULT TO SEPARATE THE SCIENCE FROM THE SPECULATION.

taught for understanding and if more teachers had the resources to do so, our schools would be better learning environments.

However, there is nothing new in this critique of traditional education. It is based on a cognitive and constructivist model of learning that is firmly rooted in more than 30 years of psychological research. Whatever scientific evidence we have for or against the efficacy of such educational approaches can be found in any current textbook on educational psychology.[2] None of the evidence comes from brain research. It comes from cognitive and developmental psychology; from the behavioral, not the biological, sciences; from our scientific understanding of the mind, not from our scientific understanding of the brain.

To the extent that brain-based educators' recipe for school and classroom change is well grounded in this behavioral research, their message is valuable. Teachers should know about short- and long-term memory; about primacy/recency effects; about how procedural, declarative, and episodic memory differ; and about how prior knowledge affects our current ability to learn. But to claim that these are "brain-based" findings is misleading.

While we know a considerable amount from psychological research that is pertinent to teaching and learning, we know much less about how the brain functions and learns.[3] For nearly a century, the science of the mind (psychology) developed independently from the science of the brain (neuroscience). Psychologists were interested in our mental functions and capacities—how we learn, remember, and think. Neuroscientists were interested in how the brain develops and functions. It was as if psychologists were interested only in our mental software and neuroscientists only in our neural hardware.

Deeply held theoretical assumptions in both fields supported a view that mind and brain could, and indeed should, be studied independently.

It is only in the past 15 years or so that these theoretical barriers have fallen. Now scientists called cognitive neuroscientists are beginning to study how our neural hardware might run our mental software, how brain structures support mental functions, how our neural circuits enable us to think and learn. This is an exciting and new scientific endeavor, but it is also a very young one. As a result we know relatively little about learning, thinking, and remembering at the level of brain areas, neural circuits, or synapses; we know very little about how the brain thinks, remembers, and learns.

Yet brain science has always had a seductive appeal for educators.[4] Brain science appears to give hard biological data and explanations that, for some reason, we find more compelling than the "soft" data that come from psychological science. But seductive appeal and a very limited brain science database are a dangerous combination. They make it relatively easy to formulate bold statements about brain science and education that are speculative at best and often far removed from neuroscientific fact. Nonetheless, the allure of brain science ensures that these ideas will often find a substantial and accepting audience. As Joseph LeDoux, a leading authority on the neuroscience of emotion, cautioned educators at a 1996 brain and education conference, "These ideas are easy to sell to the public, but it is easy to take them beyond their actual basis in science."[5]

And the ideas are far-ranging indeed. Within the literature on the brain and education one finds, for example, that brain science supports Bloom's Taxonomy, Madeline Hunter's effective teaching, whole-language instruction, Vygotsky's theory of social learning, thematic instruction, portfolio assessment, and cooperative learning.

The difficulty is that the brain-based education literature is very much like a docudrama or an episode of "In Search of . . ." in which an interesting segment on Egyptology suddenly takes a bizarre turn that links Tutankhamen with the alien landing in Roswell, New Mexico. Just where did the episode turn from archaeological fact to speculation or fantasy? That is the same question one must constantly ask when reading about brain-based education.

Educators, like all professionals, should be interested in knowing how basic research, including brain science, might contribute to improved professional practice. The danger with much of the brain-based education literature, as with an "In Search of . . ." episode, is that it becomes exceedingly difficult to separate the science from the speculation, to sort what we know from what we would like to be the case. If our interest is enhancing teaching and learning by applying sci-

ence to education, this is not the way to do it. Would we want our children to learn about the Exodus by watching "In Search of Ramses' Martian Wife"?

We might think of each of the numerous claims that brain-based educators make as similar to an "In Search of . . ." episode. For each one, we should ask, Where does the science end and the speculation begin? I cannot do that here. So instead I'll concentrate on two ideas that appear prominently in brain-based education articles: the educational significance of brain laterality (right brain versus left brain) and the claim that neuroscience has established that there is a sensitive period for learning.

Left Brain, Right Brain: One More Time

"Right Brain versus left brain" is one of those popular ideas that will not die. Speculations about the educational significance of brain laterality have been circulating in the education literature for 30 years. Although repeatedly criticized and dismissed by psychologists and brain scientists, the speculation continues.[6] David Sousa devotes a chapter of *How the Brain Learns* to explaining brain laterality and presents classroom strategies that teachers might use to ensure that both hemispheres are involved in learning.[7] Following the standard line, the *left hemisphere* is the logical hemisphere, involved in speech, reading, and writing. It is the analytical hemisphere that evaluates factual material in a rational way and that understands the literal interpretation of words. It is a serial processor that tracks time and sequences and that recognizes words, letters, and numbers. The right hemisphere is the intuitive, creative hemisphere. It gathers information more from images than from words. It is a parallel processor well suited for pattern recognition and spatial reasoning. It is the hemisphere that recognizes faces, places, and objects.

According to this traditional view of laterality, left-hemisphere-dominant individuals tend to be more verbal, more analytical, and better problem solvers. Females, we are told, are more likely than males to be left-hemisphere dominant. Right-hemisphere-dominant individuals, more typically males, paint and draw well, are good at math, and deal with the visual world more easily than with the verbal. Schools, Sousa points out, are overwhelmingly left-hemisphere places in which left-hemisphere-dominant individuals, mostly girls, feel more comfortable than right-hemisphere-dominant individuals, mostly boys. Hemispheric dominance also explains why girls are superior to boys in arithmetic —it is linear and logical, and there is only one correct answer to each problem—while girls suffer math anxiety when it comes to the right-hemisphere activities of algebra and geometry. These latter disciplines, unlike arithmetic, are holistic, relational, and spatial and also allow multiple solutions to problems.

Before we consider how, or whether, brain science supports this traditional view, educators should be wary of claims about the educational significance of gender differences in brain laterality. There are tasks that psychologists have used in their studies that reveal gender-based differences in performance. Often, however, these differences are specific to a task. Although males are superior to females at mentally rotating objects, this seems to be the only spatial task for which psychologists have found such a difference.[8] Moreover, when they do find gender differences, these differences tend to be very small. If they were measured on an I.Q.-like scale with a mean of 100 and a standard deviation of 15, these gender differences amount to around five points. Furthermore, the range of difference within genders is broad. Many males have better language skills than most females; many females have better spatial and mathematical skills than most males. The scientific consensus among psychologists and neuroscientists who conduct these studies is that whatever gender differences exist may have interesting consequences for the scientific study of the brain, but they have no practical or instructional consequences.[9]

Now let's consider the brain sciences and how or whether they offer support for some of the particular teaching strategies Sousa recommends. To involve the right hemisphere in learning, Sousa writes, teachers should encourage students to generate and use mental imagery: "For most people, the left hemisphere specializes in coding information verbally while the right hemisphere codes information visually. Although teachers spend much time talking (and sometimes have their students talk) about the learning objective, little time is given to developing visual cues." To ensure that the left hemisphere gets equal time, teachers should let students "read, write, and compute often."[10]

What brain scientists currently know about spatial reasoning and mental imagery provides counterexamples to such simplistic claims as these. Such claims arise out of a folk theory about brain laterality, not a neuroscientific one.

Here are two simple spatial tasks: 1) determine whether one object is above or below another, and 2) determine whether two objects are more or less than one foot apart. Based on our folk theory of the brain, as spatial tasks both of these should be right-hemisphere tasks. However, if we delve a little deeper, as psychologists and neuroscientists tend to do, we see that the information-processing or computational demands of the two tasks are different.[11] The first task requires that we place objects or parts of objects into broad categories—up/down or left/right—but we do not have to determine how far up

or down (or left or right) one object is from the other. Psychologists call this *categorical* spatial reasoning. In contrast, the second task is a spatial *coordinate* task, in which we must compute and retain precise distance relations between the objects.

Research over the last decade has shown that categorical and coordinate spatial reasoning are performed by distinct subsystems in the brain.[12] A subsystem in the brain's *left* hemisphere performs categorical spatial reasoning. A subsystem in the brain's *right* hemisphere processes coordinate spatial relationships. Although the research does point to differences in the information-processing abilities and biases of the brain hemispheres, those differences are found at a finer level of analysis than "spatial reasoning." It makes no sense to claim that spatial reasoning is a right-hemisphere task.

Based on research like this, Christopher Chabris and Stephen Kosslyn, leading researchers in the field of spatial reasoning and visual imagery, claim that any model of brain lateralization that assigns conglomerations of complex mental abilities, such as spatial reasoning, to one hemisphere or the other, as our folk theory does, is simply too crude to be scientifically or practically useful. Our folk theory can neither explain what the brain is doing nor generate useful predictions about where novel tasks might be computed in the brain.[13] Unfortunately, it is just such a crude folk theory that brain-based educators rely on when framing their recommendations.

Visual imagery is another example. From the traditional, folk-theoretic perspective, generating and using visual imagery is a right-hemisphere function. Generating and using visual imagery is a complex operation that involves, even at a crude level of analysis, at least five distinct mental subcomponents: 1) to create a visual image of a dog, you must transfer long-term visual memories into a temporary visual memory store; 2) to determine if your imagined dog has a tail, you must zoom in and identify details of the image; 3) to put a blue collar on the dog requires that you add a new element to your previously generated image; 4) to make the dog look the other way demands that you rotate your image of the dog; and 5) to draw or describe the imagined dog, you must scan the visual image with your mind's eye.

There is an abundance of neuroscientific evidence that this complex task is not confined to the right hemisphere. There are patients with brain damage who can recognize visual objects and draw or describe visible objects normally, yet these patients cannot answer questions that require them to generate a mental image. ("Think of a dog. Does it have a long tail?") These patients have long-term visual memories, but they cannot use those memories to generate mental images. All these patients have damage to the rear portion of the left hemisphere.[14]

Studies on split-brain patients, people who have had their two hemispheres surgically disconnected to treat severe epilepsy, allow scientists to present visual stimuli to one hemisphere but not the other. Michael Gazzaniga and Kosslyn showed split-brain patients a lower-case letter and then asked the patients whether the corresponding capital letter had any curved lines.[15] The task required that the patients generate a mental image of the capital letter based on the lower-case letter they had seen. When the stimuli were presented to the patients' left hemispheres, they performed perfectly on the task. However, the patients made many mistakes when the letter stimuli were presented to the right hemisphere. Likewise, brain-imaging studies of normal adult subjects performing imagery tasks show that both hemispheres are active in these tasks.[16] Based on all these data, brain scientists have concluded that the ability to generate visual imagery depends on the left hemisphere.

One of the most accessible presentations of this research appears in *Images of Mind*, by Michael Posner and Mark Raichle, in which they conclude, "The common belief that creating mental imagery is a function of the right hemisphere is clearly false."[17] Again, different brain areas are specialized for different tasks, but that specialization occurs at a finer level of analysis than "using visual imagery." Using visual imagery may be a useful learning strategy, but if it is useful it is not because it involves an otherwise underutilized right hemisphere in learning.

The same problem also subverts claims that one hemisphere or the other is the site of number recognition or reading skills. Here is a simple number task, expressed in two apparently equivalent ways: What is bigger, two or five? What is bigger, 2 or 5? It involves recognizing number symbols and understanding what those symbols mean. According to our folk theory, this should be a left-hemisphere task. But once again our folk theory is too crude.

Numerical comparison involves at least two mental subskills: identifying the number names and then comparing the numerical magnitudes that they designate. Although we seldom think of it, we are "bilingual" when it comes to numbers. We have number words—e.g., *one, two*—to name numbers, and we also have special written symbols, Arabic numerals—e.g., 1, 2. Our numerical bilingualism means that the two comparison questions above place different computational demands on the mind/brain. Using brain-recording techniques, Stanislaus Dehaene found that we identify number words using a system in the brain's left hemisphere, but we identify Arabic numerals using brain areas in both the right and left hemispheres. Once we identify either the number words or the Arabic digits as symbols for numerical quantities, a distinct neural subsystem in the

THE FUNDAMENTAL PROBLEM WITH THE RIGHT-BRAIN VERSUS LEFT-BRAIN CLAIMS IN THE EDUCATION LITERATURE IS THAT THEY RELY ON INTUITIONS AND FOLK THEORIES ABOUT THE BRAIN.

brain's right hemisphere compares magnitudes named by the two number symbols.[18]

Even for such a simple number task as comparison, both hemispheres are involved. Thus it makes no neuroscientific sense to claim that the left hemisphere recognizes numbers. Brain areas are specialized, but at a much finer level than "recognizing numbers." This simple task is already too complex for our folk theory to handle. Forget about algebra and geometry.

Similar research that analyzes speech and reading skills into their component processes also shows that reading is not simply a left-hemisphere task, as our folk theory suggests. Recognizing speech sounds, decoding written words, finding the meanings of words, constructing the gist of a written text, and making inferences as we read all rely on subsystems in both brain hemispheres.[19]

There is another different, but equally misleading, interpretation of brain laterality that occurs in the literature of brain-based education. In *Making Connections,* Renate Caine and Geoffrey Caine are critical of traditional "brain dichotomizers" and warn that the brain does not lend itself to such simple explanations. In their view, the results of research on split brains and hemispheric specialization are inconclusive—"both hemispheres are involved in all activities"—a conclusion that would seem to be consistent with what we have seen in our brief review of spatial reasoning, visual imagery, number skills, and reading.

However, following the folk theory, they do maintain that the left hemisphere proc-

esses parts and the right hemisphere processes wholes. In their interpretation, the educational significance of laterality research is that it shows that, within the brain, parts and wholes always interact. Laterality research thus provides scientific support for one of their principles of brain-based education: the brain processes parts and wholes simultaneously. Rather than number comparison or categorical spatial reasoning, the Caines provide a more global example: "Consider a poem, a play, a great novel, or a great work of philosophy. They all involve a sense of the 'wholeness' of things and a capacity to work with patterns, often in timeless ways. In other words, the 'left brain' processes are enriched and supported by 'right brain' processes."[20]

For educators, the Caines see the two-brain doctrine as a "valuable metaphor that helps educators acknowledge two separate but simultaneous tendencies in the brain for organizing information. One is to reduce information to parts; the other is to perceive and work with it as a whole or a series of wholes."[21] Effective brain-based educational strategies overlook neither parts nor wholes, but constantly attempt to provide opportunities in which students can make connections and integrate parts and wholes. Thus the Caines number among their examples of brain-based approaches whole-language instruction,[22] integrated curricula, thematic teaching, and cooperative learning.[23] Similarly, because we make connections best when new information is embedded in meaningful life events and in socially interactive situations, Lev Vygotsky's theory of social learning should also be highly brain compatible.[24]

To the extent that one would want to view this as a metaphor, all I can say is that some of us find some metaphors more appealing than others. To the extent that this is supposed to be an attempt to ground educational principles in brain science, the aliens have just landed in Egypt.

Where did things go awry? Although they claim that laterality research in the sense of hemispheric localization is inconclusive, the Caines do maintain the piece of our folk theory that attributes "whole" processing to the right hemisphere and "part" processing to the left hemisphere. Because the two hemispheres are connected in normal healthy brains, they conclude that the brain processes parts and wholes simultaneously. It certainly does—although it probably is not the case that wholes and parts can be so neatly dichotomized. For example, in visual word decoding, the right hemisphere seems to read words letter by letter—by looking at the parts—while the left hemisphere recognizes entire words—the visual word forms.[25]

But again, the parts and wholes to which the brain is sensitive appear to occur at quite a fine-grained level of analysis—categories versus coordinates, generating versus scanning visual images, identifying number words versus Arabic digits. The Caines' ex-

ample of part/whole interactions—the left-hemisphere comprehension of a text and the right-hemisphere appreciation of wholeness—relates to such a highly complex task that involves so many parts and wholes at different levels of analysis that it is trivially true that the whole brain is involved. Thus their appeal to brain science suffers from the same problem Kosslyn identified in the attempts to use crude theories to understand the brain. The only brain categories that the Caines appeal to are parts and wholes. Then they attempt to understand learning and exceedingly complex tasks in terms of parts and wholes. This approach bothers neither to analyze the brain nor to analyze behaviors.

The danger here is that one might think that there are brain-based reasons to adopt whole-language instruction, integrated curricula, or Vygotskian social learning. There are none. Whether or not these educational practices should be adopted must be determined on the basis of the impact they have on student learning. The evidence we now have on whole-language instruction is at best inconclusive, and the efficacy of social learning theory remains an open question. Brain science contributes no evidence, pro or con, for the brain-based strategies that the Caines espouse.

The fundamental problem with the right-brain versus left-brain claims that one finds in the education literature is that they rely on our intuitions and folk theories about the brain, rather than on what brain science is actually able to tell us. Our folk theories are too crude and imprecise to have any scientific, predictive, or instructional value. What modern brain science is telling us—and what brain-based educators fail to appreciate—is that it makes no scientific sense to map gross, unanalyzed behaviors and skills—reading, arithmetic, spatial reasoning—onto one brain hemisphere or another.

Brains Like Sponges: The Sensitive Period

A new and popular, but problematic, idea found in the brain-based literature is that there is a critical or sensitive period in brain development, lasting until a child is around 10 years old, during which children learn faster, easier, and with more meaning than at any other time in their lives. David Sousa presented the claim this way in a recent commentary in *Education Week*, titled "Is the Fuss About Brain Research Justified?"

As the child grows, the brain selectively strengthens and prunes connections based on experience. Although this process continues throughout our lives, it seems to be most pronounced between the ages of 2 and 11, as different development areas emerge and taper off. . . . These so-called "windows of opportunity" represent critical periods when the brain demands certain types of input to create or consolidate neural networks, especially for acquiring language, emotional control, and learning to play music. Certainly, one can learn new information and skills at any age. But what the child learns during that window period will strongly influence what is learned after the window closes.[26]

In a recent *Educational Leadership* article, Pat Wolfe and Ron Brandt prudently caution educators against any quick marriage between brain science and education. However, among the well-established neuroscientific findings about which educators can be confident, they include, "Some abilities are acquired more easily during certain sensitive periods, or 'windows of opportunity.' " Later they continue, "During these years, [the brain] also has a remarkable ability to adapt and reorganize. It appears to develop some capacities with more ease at this time than in the years after puberty. These stages once called 'critical periods' are more accurately described as 'sensitive periods' or 'windows of opportunity.' "[27] Eric Jensen, in *Teaching with the Brain in Mind,* also writes that "the brain learns fastest and easiest during the school years."[28]

If there were neuroscientific evidence for the existence of such a sensitive period, such evidence might appear to provide a biological argument for the importance of elementary teaching and a scientific rationale for redirecting resources, restructuring curricula, and reforming pedagogy to take advantage of the once-in-a-lifetime learning opportunity nature has given us. If teachers could understand when sensitive periods begin and end, the thinking goes, they could structure curricula to take advantage of these unique windows of opportunity. Sousa tells of an experienced fifth-grade teacher who was upset when a mother asked the teacher what she was doing to take advantage of her daughter's windows of opportunity before they closed. Unfortunately, according to Sousa, the teacher was unaware of the windows-of-opportunity research. He warns, "As the public learns more about brain research through the popular press, scenes like this are destined to be repeated, further eroding confidence in teachers and in schools."[29]

This well-established neuroscientific "finding" about a sensitive period for learning originated in the popular press and in advocacy documents. It is an instance where neuroscientists have speculated about the implications of their work for education and where educators have uncritically embraced that speculation. Presenting speculation as fact poses a greater threat to the public's confidence in teachers and schools than does Sousa's fifth-grade teacher.

During 1993, the *Chicago Tribune* ran Ron Kotulak's series of Pulitzer-Prize-win-ning articles on the new brain science. Kotulak's articles later appeared as a book titled *Inside the Brain: Revolutionary Discoveries of How the Mind Works.* Kotulak, an esteemed science writer, presented the first explicit statement that I have been able to find on the existence of a sensitive period between ages 4 and 10, during which children's brains learn fastest and easiest.[30] Variations on the claim appear in the Carnegie Corporation of New York's 1996 publication, *Years of Promise: A Comprehensive Learning Strategy for America's Children,* and in *Building Knowledge for a Nation of Learners,* published by the Office of Educational Research and Improvement of the U.S. Department of Education.[31]

A report released in conjunction with the April 1997 White House Conference on Early Brain Development stated, "[B]y the age of three, the brains of children are two and a half times more active than the brains of adults—and they stay that way throughout the first decade of life. . . . This suggests that young children—particularly infants and toddlers—are biologically primed for learning and that these early years provide a unique window of opportunity or prime time for learning.[32]

If the sensitive period from age 4 to age 10 is a finding about which educators can be confident and one that justifies the current fuss about brain science, we would expect to find an extensive body of neuroscientific research that supports the claim. Surprisingly, brain-based enthusiasts appeal to a very limited body of evidence.

In Kotulak's initial statement of the sensitive-period claim, he refers to the brain-imaging work of Dr. Harry Chugani, M.D., at Wayne State University: "Chugani, whose imaging studies revealed that children's brains learned fastest and easiest between the ages of 4 and 10, said these years are often wasted because of lack of input."[33]

Years of Promise, the Carnegie Corporation report, cites a speech Kotulak presented at a conference on Brain Development in Young Children, held at the University of Chicago on 13 June 1996. Again referring to Chugani's work, Kotulak said that the years from 4 to about 10 "are the wonder years of learning, when a child can easily pick up a foreign language without an accent and learn a musical instrument with ease."[34] *Years of Promise* also cites a review article published by Dr. Chugani that is based on remarks he made at that Chicago conference.[35] *Rethinking the Brain,* a report based on the Chicago conference, also cites the same sources, as does the U.S. Department of Education document. What's more, Wolfe, Brandt, and Jensen also cite Chugani's work in their discussions of the sensitive period for learning.

A 1996 article on education and the brain that appeared in *Education Week* reported, "By age 4, Chugani found, a child's brain uses more than twice the glucose that an adult brain uses. Between the ages 4 and 10, the amount of glucose a child's brain uses remains relatively stable. But by age 10, glucose utilization begins to drop off until it reaches adult levels at age 16 or 17. Chugani's findings suggest that a child's peak learning years occur just as all those synapses are forming."[36]

To be fair, these educators are not misrepresenting Chugani's views. He has often been quoted on the existence and educational importance of the sensitive period from age 4 until age 10.[37] In a review of his own work, published in *Preventive Medicine,* Chugani wrote:

> The notion of an extended period during childhood when activity-dependent [synapse] stabilization occurs has recently received considerable attention by those individuals and organizations dealing with early intervention to provide "environmental enrichment" and with the optimal design of educational curricula. Thus, it is now believed by many (including this author) that the biological "window of opportunity" when learning is efficient and easily retained is perhaps not fully exploited by our educational system.[38]

Oddly, none of these articles and reports cite the single research article that provides the experimental evidence that originally motivated the claim: a 1987 *Annals of Neurology* article.[39] In that 1987 article, Chugani and his colleagues, M. E. Phelps and J. C. Mazziota, report results of PET (positron emission tomography) scans on 29 epileptic children, ranging in age from five days to 15 years. Because PET scans require the injection of radioactive substances, physicians can scan children only for diagnostic and therapeutic purposes; they cannot scan "normal, healthy" children just out of scientific curiosity. Thus the 1987 study is an extremely important one because it was the first, if not the only, imaging study that attempted to trace brain development from infancy through adolescence.

The scientists administered radioactively labeled glucose to the children and used PET scans to measure the rate at which specific brain areas took up the glucose. The assumption is that areas of the brain that are more active require more energy and so will take up more of the glucose. While the scans were being acquired, the scientists made every effort to eliminate, or at least minimize, all sensory stimulation for the subjects. Thus they measured the rate of glucose uptake when the brain was (presumably) not engaged in any sensory or cognitive processing. That is, they measured resting brain-glucose metabolism.

One of their major findings was that, in all the brain areas they examined, metabolic levels reached adult values when children were approximately 2 years old and contin-

NEITHER
CHUGANI, HIS
CO-AUTHORS,
NOR OTHER
NEUROSCIENTISTS
HAVE STUDIED
HOW QUICKLY
OR EASILY
5-YEAR-OLDS
LEARN AS OPPOSED
TO 15-YEAR-OLDS.

ued to increase, reaching rates twice the adult level by age 3 or 4. Resting glucose uptake remained at this elevated level until the children were around 9 years old. At age 9, the rates of brain glucose metabolism started to decline and stabilized at adult values by the end of the teenage years. What the researchers found, then, was a "high plateau" period for metabolic activity in the brain that lasted from roughly age 3 to age 9.

What is the significance of this high plateau period? To interpret their findings, Chugani and his colleagues relied on earlier research in which brain scientists had counted synapses in samples of human brain tissue to determine how the number and density of synaptic connections change in the human brain over our life spans. In the late 1970s, Peter Huttenlocher of the University of Chicago found that, starting a few months after birth and continuing until age 3, various parts of the brain formed synapses very rapidly.[40] This early, exuberant synapse growth resulted in synaptic densities in young children's brains that were 50% higher than the densities in mature adult brains. In humans, synaptic densities appear to remain at these elevated levels until around puberty, when some mechanism that is apparently under genetic control causes synapses to be eliminated or pruned back to the lower adult levels.

With this background, Chugani and his colleagues reasoned as follows. There is other evidence suggesting that maintaining synapses and their associated neural structures accounts for most of the glucose that the brain consumes. Their PET study measured changes in the brain's glucose consumption over the life span. Therefore, they reasoned, as the density and number of synapses wax and wane, so too does the rate of brain-glucose metabolism. This 1987 PET study provides important indirect evidence

about brain development, based on the study of living brains, that corroborates the direct evidence based on counting synapses in samples of brain tissue taken from patients at autopsy. In the original paper, the scientists stated an important conclusion: "Our findings support the commonly accepted view that brain maturation in humans proceeds at least into the second decade of life."[41]

However, if you read the 1987 paper by Chugani, Phelps, and Mazziota, you will not find a section titled "The Relationship of Elevated Brain Metabolism and Synaptic Densities to Learning." Neither Chugani nor any of his co-authors have studied how quickly or easily 5-year-olds learn as opposed to 15-year-olds. Nor have other neuroscientists studied what high synaptic densities or high brain energy consumption means for the ease, rapidity, and depth of learning.

To connect high brain metabolism or excessive synaptic density with a critical period for learning requires some fancy footwork— or maybe more accurately, sleight of hand. We know that from early childhood until around age 10, children have extra or redundant synaptic connections in their brains. So, the reasoning goes, during this high plateau period of excess brain connectivity, "the individual is given the opportunity to retain and increase the efficiency of connections that, through repeated use during a critical period, are deemed to be important, whereas connections that are used to a lesser extent are more susceptible to being eliminated."[42] This, of course, is simply to assume that the high plateau period is a critical period.

Linking the critical period with learning requires an implicit appeal to another folk belief that appears throughout the history of the brain in education literature. This common assumption is that periods of rapid brain growth or high activity are optimal times, sensitive periods, or windows of opportunity for learning.[43] We get from Chugani's important brain-imaging results to a critical period for learning via two assumptions, neither of which is supported by neuroscientific data, and neither of which has even been the object of neuroscientific research. The claim that the period of high brain connectivity is a critical period for learning, far from being a neuroscientific finding about which educators can be confident, is at best neuroscientific speculation.

Chugani accurately described the scientific state of affairs in his *Preventive Medicine* review. He *believes,* along with some educators and early childhood advocates, that there is a biological window of opportunity when learning is easy, efficient, and easily retained. But there is no neuroscientific evidence to support this belief. And where there is no scientific evidence, there is no scientific fact.

Furthermore, it would appear that we have a considerable amount of research ahead of us if we are to amass the evidence

for or against this belief. Neuroscientists have little idea of how experience before puberty affects either the timing or the extent of synaptic elimination. While they have documented that the pruning of synapses does occur, no reliable studies have compared differences in final adult synaptic connectivity with differences in the experiences of individuals before puberty. Nor do they know whether the animals or individuals with greater synaptic densities in adulthood are necessarily more intelligent and developed. Neuroscientists do not know if prior training and education affect either loss or retention of synapses at puberty.[44]

Nor do neuroscientists know how learning is related to changes in brain metabolism and synaptic connectivity over our lifetimes. As the developmental neurobiologist Patricia Goldman-Rakic told educators, "While children's brains acquire a tremendous amount of information during the early years, most learning takes place after synaptic formation stabilizes."[45] That is, a great deal, if not most, learning takes place after age 10 and after pruning has occurred. If so, we may turn into efficient general learning machines only after puberty, only after synaptic formation stabilizes and our brains are less active.

Finally, the entire discussion of this purported critical period takes place under an implicit assumption that children actually do learn faster, more easily, and more deeply between the ages of 4 and 10. There are certainly critical periods for the development of species-wide skills, such as seeing, hearing, and acquiring a first language, but critical periods are interesting to psychologists because they seem to be the exception rather than the rule in human development. As Jacqueline Johnson and Elissa Newport remind us in their article on critical periods in language learning, "In most domains of learning, skill increases over development."[46]

When we ask whether children actually do learn more easily and meaningfully than adults, the answers we get are usually anecdotes about athletes, musicians, and students of second languages. We have not begun to look at the rate, efficiency, and depth of learning across various age groups in a representative sample of learning domains. We are making an assumption about learning behavior and then relying on highly speculative brain science to explain our assumption. We have a lot more research to do.

So, despite what you read in the papers and in the brain-based education literature, neuroscience has *not* established that there is a sensitive period between the ages of 4 and 10 during which children learn more quickly, easily, and meaningfully. Brain-based educators have uncritically embraced neuroscientific speculation.

The pyramids were built by aliens—to house Elvis.

A February 1996 article in *Newsweek* on the brain and education quoted Linda

Darling-Hammond: "Our school system was invented in the late 1800s, and little has changed. Can you imagine if the medical profession ran this way?"[47] Darling-Hammond is right. Our school system must change to reflect what we now know about teaching, learning, mind, and brain. To the extent that we want education to be a research-based enterprise, the medical profession provides a reasonable model. We can only be thankful that members of the medical profession are more careful in applying biological research to their professional practice than some educators are in applying brain research to theirs.

We should not shrug off this problem. It is symptomatic of some deeper problems about how research is presented to educators, about what educators find compelling, about how educators evaluate research, and about how professional development time and dollars are spent. The "In Search of . . ." series is a television program that provides an entertaining mix of fact, fiction, and fantasy. That can be an amusing exercise, but it is not always instructive. The brain-based education literature represents a genre of writing, most often appearing in professional education publications, that provides a popular mix of fact, misinterpretation, and speculation. That can be intriguing, but it is not always informative. "In Search of . . ." is no way to present history, and the brain-based education literature is not the way to present the science of learning.

1. Renate Nummela Caine and Geoffrey Caine, Making *Connections: Teaching and the Human Brain* (New York: Addison-Wesley, 1994); idem, "Building a Bridge Between the Neurosciences and Education: Cautions and Possibilities," *NASSP Bulletin*, vol. 82, 1998, pp. 1–8; Eric Jensen, *Teaching with the Brain in Mind* (Alexandria, Va.: Association for Supervision and Curriculum Development, 1998); and Robert Sylvester, *A Celebration of Neurons* (Alexandria, Va.: Association for Supervision and Curriculum Development, 1995).

2. See, for example, Michael Pressley and C. B. McCormick, *Advanced Educational Psychology for Educators, Researchers, and Policymakers* (New York: HarperCollins, 1995).

3. John T. Bruer, *Schools for Thought: A Science of Learning in the Classroom* (Cambridge, Mass.: MIT Press, 1993); and idem, "Education and the Brain: A Bridge Too Far," *Educational Researcher*, November 1997, pp. 4–16.

4. Susan F. Chipman, "Integrating Three Perspectives on Learning," in Sarah L. Friedman, Kenneth A. Klivington, and R. W. Peterson, eds., *The Brain, Cognition, and Education* (Orlando, Fla.: Academic Press, 1986), pp. 203–32.

5. *Bridging the Gap Between Neuroscience and Education: Summary of a Workshop Cosponsored by the Education Commission of the States and the Charles A. Dana Foundation* (Denver: Education Commission of the States, 1996), p. 5.

6. Chipman, op. cit.; Howard Gardner, *Art, Mind, and Brain: A Cognitive Approach to Creativity* (New York: Basic Books, 1982);

Mike Rose, "Narrowing the Mind and Page: Remedial Writers and Cognitive Reductionism," *College Composition and Communication*, vol. 39, 1988, pp. 267–302; and Jerre Levy, "Right Brain, Left Brain: Fact and Fiction," *Psychology Today*, May 1985, p. 38.

7. David A. Sousa, *How the Brain Learns: A Classroom Teacher's Guide* (Reston, Va.: National Association of Secondary School Principals, 1995).

8. M. C. Linn and A. C. Petersen, "Emergence and Characterization of Sex Differences in Spatial Ability: A Meta-Analysis," *Child Development*, vol. 56, 1985, pp. 1470–98.

9. Sally Springer and Georg Deutsch, *Left Brain, Right Brain* (New York: W. H. Freeman, 1993).

10. Sousa, pp. 95, 99.

11. Christopher F. Chabris and Stephen M. Kosslyn, "How Do the Cerebral Hemispheres Contribute to Encoding Spatial Relations?," *Current Directions in Psychology*, vol. 7, 1998, pp. 8–14.

12. Ibid.

13. Ibid.

14. Martha Farah, *Visual Agnosias* (Cambridge, Mass.: MIT Press, 1991).

15. Stephen M. Kosslyn et al., "A Computational Analysis of Mental Image Generation: Evidence from Functional Dissociations in Split-Brain Patients," *Journal of Experimental Psychology: General*, vol. 114, 1985, pp. 311–41.

16. Stephen M. Kosslyn et al., "Two Types of Image Generation: Evidence for Left and Right Hemisphere Processes," *Neuropsychologia*, vol. 33, 1995, pp. 1485–1510.

17. Michael I. Posner and Mark E. Raichle, *Images of Mind* (New York: Scientific American Library, 1994), p. 95.

18. Stanislaus Dehaene, "The Organization of Brain Activations in Number Comparison," *Journal of Cognitive Neuroscience*, vol. 8, 1996, pp. 47–68.

19. Mark Jung Beeman and Christine Chiarello, "Complementary Right- and Left-Hemisphere Language Comprehension," *Current Directions in Psychology*, vol. 7, 1998, pp. 2–7.

20. Caine and Caine, p. 37.

21. Ibid., p. 91.

22. Ibid., pp. 9, 48, 91.

23. Ibid., pp. 127–30.

24. Ibid., pp. 47–48.

25. Beeman and Chiarello, op. cit.

26. David A. Sousa, "Is the Fuss About Brain Research Justified?," *Education Week*, 16 December 1998, p. 35.

27. Pat Wolfe and Ron Brandt, "What Do We Know from Brain Research?," *Educational Leadership*, November 1998, p. 12.

28. Jensen, p. 32.

29. Sousa, "Is the Fuss About Brain Research Justified?," p. 35.

30. Ronald Kotulak, *Inside the Brain: Revolutionary Discoveries of How the Mind Works* (Kansas City: Andrews McMeel, 1996), p. 46.

31. *Years of Promise: A Comprehensive Learning Strategy for America's Children* (New York: Carnegie Corporation of New York, 1996), pp. 9–10; and Office of Educational Research and Improvement, *Building Knowledge for a Nation of Learners* (Washington, D.C.: U.S. Department of Education, 1996).

32. Rima Shore, *Rethinking the Brain: New Insights into Early Development* (New York: Families and Work Institute, 1997), pp. 21, 36.

33. Kotulak, p. 46.

34. Ronald Kotulak, "Learning How to Use the Brain," 1996, available on the Web at http://www.newhorizons.org/ofc_21cliusebrain.html.

35. Harry T. Chugani, "Neuroimaging of Developmental Nonlinearity and Developmental Pathologies," in R. W. Thatcher et al., eds., *Developmental Neuroimaging* (San Diego: Academic Press, 1996), pp. 187– 95.

36. Debra Viadero, "Brain Trust," *Education Week*, 18 September 1996, pp. 31–33.

37. *Better Beginnings* (Pittsburgh: Office of Child Development, University of Pittsburgh, 1997); A. DiCresce, "Brain Surges," 1997, available on the Web at www.med.wayne.edu/wmp97/brain.htm; and Lynell Hancock, "Why Do Schools Flunk Biology?," *Newsweek*, 19 February 1996, pp. 58–59.

38. Harry Chugani, "A Critical Period of Brain Development: Studies of Cerebral Glucose Utilization with PET," *Preventive Medicine*, vol. 27, 1998, pp. 184–88.

39. Harry T. Chugani, M. E. Phelps, and J. C. Mazziota, "Positron Emission Tomography Study of Human Brain Function Development," *Annals of Neurology*, vol. 22, 1987, pp. 487–97.

40. Peter R. Huttenlocher, "Synaptic Density in Human Frontal Cortex—Developmental Changes of Aging," *Brain Research*, vol. 163, 1979, pp. 195–205; Peter R. Huttenlocher et al., "Synaptogenesis in Human Visual Cortex—Evidence for Synapse Elimination During Normal Development," *Neuroscience Letters*, vol. 33, 1982, pp. 247–52; Peter R. Huttenlocher and Ch. de Courten, "The Development of Synapses in Striate Cortex of Man," *Human Neurobiology*, vol. 6, 1987, pp. 1-9; and Peter R. Huttenlocher and A. S. Dabholkar, "Regional Differences in Synaptogenesis in Human Cerebral Cortex," *Journal of Comparative Neurology*, vol. 387, 1997, pp. 167-78.

41. Chugani, Phelps, and Mazziota, p. 496.

42. Chugani, "Neuroimaging of Developmental Nonlinearity," p. 187.

43. Herman T. Epstein, "Growth Spurts During Brain Development: Implications for Educational Policy and Practice," in S. Chall and A. F. Mirsky, eds., *Education and the Brain* (Chicago: University of Chicago Press, 1978), pp. 343-70; and Chipman, op. cit.

44. Patricia S. Goldman-Rakic, Jean-Pierre Bourgeois, and Pasko Rakic, "Synaptic Substrate of Cognitive Development: Synaptogenesis in the Prefrontal Cortex of the Nonhuman Primate," in N. A. Krasnegor, G. R. Lyon, and P. S. Goldman-Rakic, *Development of the Prefrontal Cortex: Evolution, Neurobiology, and Behavior* (Baltimore: Paul H. Brooks, 1997), pp. 27-47.

45. *Bridging the Gap*, p. 11.

46. Jacqueline S. Johnson and Elissa L. Newport, "Critical Period Effects on Universal Properties," *Cognition*, vol. 39, 1991, p. 215.

47. Hancock, p. 59.

JOHN T. BRUER is president of the James S. McDonnell Foundation, St. Louis.

Educators Need to Know About the Human Brain

Illustration by Jim Hummel

In this response to John Bruer's article in the May 1999 **Kappan,** *Mr. Brandt argues that, used in conjunction with knowledge from other sources, findings from neuroscience are yielding additional insights into the learning process—and that educators would be foolish to ignore this growing body of knowledge. Mr. Bruer was offered an opportunity to provide a rejoinder, but he chose instead to refer readers back to his May article.*

BY RON BRANDT

IN THE MAY 1999 *Kappan,* John Bruer condemns irresponsible claims regarding the use of brain research in education.[1] A well-informed scientist, Bruer is right to critique what he considers misinterpretations, but I think he is mis-taken when he discourages educators from trying to understand and apply what is known. Used in conjunction with knowledge from other sources, including cognitive science, educational research, and professional experience, findings from neuroscience are yielding additional insights into the learning process.

In earlier articles Bruer stated flatly, "Right now, brain science has little to offer educational practice or policy" and urged attention instead to cognitive science.[2] But there is no need to erect a Berlin Wall between cognitive science and neuroscience; they are two sides of the same coin. In his *Kappan* article, Bruer recognizes this, noting that, in the past 15 years or so, "theoretical barriers have fallen."

Neuroscientists complain that, historically, cognitivists have shown little interest in the neurological substrate of the cognition they study. If true, such an attitude would be understandable, because until the last decade, few means were available for scientists to investigate the brain directly. Under the circumstances, according to Francis Crick, co-discoverer of the structure of DNA, cognitive psychologists adopted a "functionalist" perspective:

> Just as it is not necessary to know about the actual wiring of a computer when writing programs for it, so a functionalist investigates the information processed by the brain, and the computational processes the brain performs on this information, without considering the neurological implementation of these processes. He usually regards such considerations as totally irrelevant or, at best, premature.[3]

This may be unfair. As evidenced by the lucid explanations of brain research in his new book, *The Myth of the First Three Years*,[4] Bruer is very knowledgeable about neuroscience. But as Crick and some other neuroscientists say, the field of cognitive science must now be broadened to incorporate the flood of new knowledge emerging from brain research. Neuroscientist Joseph LeDoux—contending that cognitive science has ignored emotions, the subject of his research—argues the need for a new, more inclusive field he calls "mind science."[5]

Scholarly Quarrels Serve a Purpose

Educators are used to scholarly quarrels; positions advanced by some researchers are almost invariably contradicted by others. One re-

sult is that practitioners seldom look to research for guidance. With so many inconsistencies, how are they to know whose claims are right? But such disagreements are part of how science works. Leslie Brothers, a psychiatrist who writes about the relationships between neuroscience and other fields, notes that among brain researchers, "Unexpected findings strain existing paradigms. Back and forth struggles regarding the proper context and significance of the findings ensue. Ultimately sometimes after many years of discussion old frameworks for understanding are replaced by new ones."[6] In the meantime, those unwilling to wait must decide for themselves—after weighing contrasting views—what seems to make the most sense.

In my reading of the books scientists have been writing about the brain, I have come across several debates that are important to educators. I will briefly highlight two such disagreements and explain possible reasons for them. Then I will cite a few examples of why I think findings from neuroscience—when combined with other knowledge—can be enlightening.

Enrichment in Early Childhood

One of the brain-related issues especially interesting to educators is the place of "enrichment" in early education. Science writer Janet Hopson and anatomist Marian Diamond have written about research conducted since the 1960s establishing that rats allowed to play with toys and other rats have thicker, heavier brains than rats kept in isolation. The extra weight and thickness is mostly because their brains have formed more connections among neurons. Researchers have also found that the growth of rats' brains in response to experience (and apparent shrinkage from lack of it) occurs not just in the weeks following birth, but at all ages. Even more interesting, the same is true for hu-

mans. Bruer, who downplays the concept of "enrichment," nevertheless calls "the ability of the mature brain to change and reorganize . . . a new, exciting finding of brain science."[7]

So what is in dispute? Whether the findings justify calls for improving the care and education of children. Diamond and Hopson recommend a set of experiences at each age level from birth to adolescence that they believe constitute "enrichment" for humans.[8] Bruer cautions that enriched conditions for rats, which he prefers to call "complex," are really just approximations of rats' natural environment in the wild. Most human children are not kept in cages, so we have no way of knowing what would be the equivalent of an enriched environment for humans. Bruer wants educators to understand the possibility of cultural bias in a loaded word like "enrichment." Experiences like those suggested by Diamond and Hopson may be valuable, he implies, but they do not necessarily affect children's brains in the same way complex environments affect the brains of rats.

Michael Gazzaniga, a prolific author who worked with Roger Sperry on the well-publicized research on split-brain patients, also objects to the idea that certain experiences automatically improve children's brains. "[Following a] White House conference on babies and brains," Gazzaniga writes, "the *New York Times* published an editorial saying neuroscience had informed us that the brain needs crafting during development, and reading is the way to do it. . . . This kind of casual reasoning drives serious scientists to distraction."[9] Offering what he considers a more accurate position, Gazzaniga declares that "the brain is not primarily an experience-storing device that constantly changes its structure to accommodate new experience. From the evolutionary perspective it is a dynamic computing device that is largely rule driven; it stores information by manipulating the value of simple arithmetic variables."[10]

Educators concerned about the quality of child care in our society must decide which interpretation of the enrichment research seems most reasonable. The issue, they should remember, is not whether children's lives will be better if they have access to books, music, and interesting games—they will, of course—but whether these things are necessary for brain development.

Constructivism Wrong?

Closely related to the enrichment issue (because it also involves the brain's plasticity) and having many implications for education is a controversy between researchers whose work builds on discoveries that many capabilities are "built in" and other scientists who are equally impressed with the brain's ability to change with experience. Diamond and Hopson say, "When you look at the way a child's brain develops, one thing becomes absolutely obvious . . . *input from the environment helps shape the human brain.*"[11] Gazzaniga, however, rejects the idea of "so-called plasticity." He claims that when "clever neuroscientists . . . intervene and stimulate neurons in abnormal and bizarre ways, . . . the brain simply responds differently, and hence the resulting networks are different. This response hardly suggests that the brain is plastic in the sense that it has rewired itself."[12]

Gazzaniga and other neuroscientists who emphasize the evolutionary perspective are so convinced that "brains accrue specialized systems (adaptations) through natural selection" that they ridicule the idea, much cherished by educators, of constructivism.[13] Gazzaniga attacks neuroscientist Terry Sejnowski, who he says

marries the questionable neurobiology he reviews to the work of Jean Piaget, then suggests children learn domains of knowledge by interacting with the environment. . . . The constructivist view of the brain is that it has a common mechanism that solves the struc-

ture of all problems. . . . This sort of assertion leaves us breathless because if we know anything, it is that any old part of the brain can't learn any old thing.[14]

Another evolutionary scientist, Steven Pinker, blames educators for trying to teach mathematics and reading with a constructivist philosophy, which he describes as "a mixture of Piaget's psychology with counterculture and postmodern ideology." American students, he charges, perform poorly because they are taught in accord with this "wrong" idea. "The problem," Pinker writes, "is that the educational establishment is ignorant of evolution."[15]

Educators who understand what cognitive scientists mean when they describe learning as construction[16] have cause to resent Pinker's charges and to wonder who is ignorant of what. Beyond being offended, however, we need to understand the reason he takes such a position.

The Evolved Modular Brain

Richard Restak, a Washington neurologist who has written numerous books about the brain, provides a piece of the puzzle by describing the brain as "modular." Researchers now understand, he writes, that brains are "arranged according to a distributed system composed of large numbers of modular elements linked together . . . . [N]o . . . area holds sway over all the others, nor do all areas of the brain 'report' to an overall supervisory center."[17] This decentralized organization, which is presumably the result of millions of years of evolution, incorporates numerous systems for performing particular tasks, such as recognizing faces, throwing objects, and counting. Each ability probably developed in response to a particular environmental challenge.

It may be helpful for educators to understand that human brains are apparently "pre-wired" for capabilities such as oral language and rudi-

mentary mathematics (in the sense that particular neurons seem dedicated to these purposes from birth). In other words, these capabilities are not created entirely through experience; children's brains are not blank slates.

Knowing that this is really their message, perhaps we can be tolerant of scientists who, as they seek to establish the concept of the evolved modular brain, think it necessary to wage verbal warfare on the equally valid idea that brains also learn from experience. Francis Crick summarizes the interrelationship succinctly: "The brain at birth, we now know, is not a tabula rasa but an elaborate structure with many of its parts already in place. Experience then tunes this rough-and-ready apparatus until it can do a precision job."[18]

You Can't Derive Pedagogy From Biology, But . . .

With the conflicts over enrichment, plasticity, and evolved capabilities as background, I now return to the original question about the usefulness of brain research to education. My position is simply this: if we had no other knowledge about human behavior and learning, we could certainly not derive much pedagogy from findings about the physical brain. But that is not the case. We do have a great deal of knowledge about learning, which we have acquired in several different ways. As Bruer argues, psychology, especially cognitive psychology, is a key source of that knowledge. We can also draw on other social sciences, such as anthropology, along with educational research and professional experience. When brain research is combined with knowledge from these other sources, it can further illuminate our understanding.

A practical example is Fast ForWord, a research-based program for students with a particular kind of learning disability. Neuroscientists Paula Tallal and Michael Merzenich developed the program based on research documenting brain plasticity in monkeys and on findings that some children have difficulty hearing phonemes, especially consonants, because their brains do not process spoken language quickly enough.[19] If they do not hear the difference between "*b*" and "*p*," for example, they cannot develop phonemic awareness, which reading experts now agree is an essential prerequisite for learning to read.

Fast ForWord consists of computer games that first teach students to distinguish between similar sounds, using artificially slowed speech, and then challenge them gradually to increase their recognition speed. Using the program several hours a day, many children are said to make as much progress in four to six weeks as they would in two years of intensive work with a therapist.

Fast ForWord is a good illustration because it builds on what was already known about reading instruction and the problems of learning-disabled students. For example, in a comprehensive review of the voluminous research on reading, Marilyn Adams had already identified the critical necessity of phonemic awareness.[20] Without that kind of information, and without other knowledge, including that accrued in recent decades about the design of computer games, Fast ForWord might not have been as effective.

Understanding Ourselves And Our Students

Most of us, though, are not in a position to devise new programs or approaches. An important benefit for us of knowledge about the brain may be increased understanding of what we commonly observe about human behavior. I have begun keeping a list of questions that I think neuroscience is helping to answer. Here are three: Why do people often not use in one situation what they have learned someplace else? Why do people sometimes do things such

as buying a particular kind of car or picking a fight in school for reasons they are not completely aware of? Why do students often not remember what they have been taught?

Information from brain research cannot provide definitive answers to questions such as these, but, combined with what we already know, it can add to our understanding. For example, the problem of "transfer of training" has plagued educators for at least a century. School curricula were changed when researchers could find no evidence that Latin and other classical studies improved students' general academic abilities. Advocates of character education and thinking skills have found, to their chagrin, that students who have been taught a strategy often fail to use it when circumstances are different. Researchers even have labels to describe knowledge that is not transferred: it is called "inert" or "situational."

The transfer problem becomes clearer when we know about the brain's modular structure explained above. As mentioned, many scientists now believe this structure is the result of evolution. "Evolutionary theory has generated the notion that we are a collection of adaptations — brain devices that allow us to do specific things. . . . Many systems throughout the brain contribute to a single cognitive function."[21] While these systems are certainly in communication with one another, they are also somewhat independent. Knowing this, educators must take steps to strengthen connections among cognitive functions that might otherwise remain relatively separate. Stanislaus Dehaene, a French mathematician turned neuroscientist, says a priority for mathematics teachers must be integration of the brain's various mathematics systems:

If my hypothesis is correct, innumeracy is with us for a long time, because it reflects one of the fundamental properties of our brain: its modularity, the compartmentalization of mathematical knowledge within multiple partially

autonomous circuits. In order to become proficient in mathematics, one must go beyond these compartmentalized modules and establish a series of flexible links among them. . . . A good teacher is an alchemist who gives a fundamentally modular human brain the semblance of an interactive network.[22]

Another commonly observed characteristic of people, including children in schools, is our tendency to do things without always knowing why. A contributing factor is probably our emotions, which, though still poorly understood, are now being studied by neuroscientists. They have identified connections among the amygdala, the hippocampus, and the frontal lobes, revealing that fear and probably other emotions are processed in the same approximate location (the frontal lobes) where personal and social decisions are made.[23] When we understand that emotions, which probably are the effects of various chemical neurotransmitters,[24] help determine what we remember but that they are usually unconscious (when they become conscious we call them feelings), we can begin to see how emotions may influence our decisions without our knowing it.

A third question that brain research helps answer is why we remember some things but forget others. Every teacher has been exasperated by students who insist they were never taught something when they obviously were. Knowing how memory works not only helps us understand this familiar problem but gives us some clues for what to do about it. The most fundamental thing scientists have learned about memory is that we do not store memories whole and therefore do not retrieve them that way either. When we remember something, we actually reconstruct it by combining elements of the original experience. Neuroscientist Antonio Damasio explains that a memory "is recalled in the form of images at many brain sites rather than at a single site. Although we have the illusion that everything comes together in a single anatomical theater, recent evidence suggests that it does not. Probably the relative simultaneity of activity at different sites binds the separate parts of the mind together."[25]

Our ability to re-create the memory to recombine all or most of the elements (which are stored in millions of neurons) depends on the strength of the original experience, including the emotional load. Daniel Schacter, an expert on memory and the brain, says it concisely: "For better or worse, our recollections are largely at the mercy of our elaborations; only those aspects of experience that are targets of elaborative encoding processes have a high likelihood of being remembered subsequently."[26] Why, then, do students forget what they have been taught? Because the information served no useful purpose in their lives, was thus devoid of emotional impact, and was not "elaborately encoded."

Thinking, Learning, and Feeling All Have a 'Neural Substrate'

My purpose here is not to insist on the correctness of these interpretations or to argue that brain research alone tells us how to run schools. I wish only to show that knowledge about brain functioning is relevant, especially when used to supplement what we know from other sources. Today's educators are fortunate to be living at a time when we are finally beginning to really understand the learning process, including its neural substrate. We are coming to recognize, as Francis Crick says in *The Astonishing Hypothesis,* that all our thoughts, behaviors, and feelings are the result of chemical and electrical activity in the brain and related neural structures. Never again should we talk about psychological phenomena without recognizing that all of them are "brain-based."

Much remains unclear, and we surely will misinterpret some findings as we try to make sense of the partial information currently available. If so, we must be open to clarification, some of which will come with newer findings. But with today's challenges, educators would be foolish to ignore the growing body of knowledge about our brains.

Notes

1. John T. Bruer, "In Search of . . . . Brain-Based Education," *Phi Delta Kappan,* May 1999, pp. 649–57.
2. John T. Bruer, "Brain Science, Brain Fiction," *Educational Leadership,* November 1998, p. 14. See also John T. Bruer, "Education and the Brain: A Bridge Too Far," *Educational Researcher,* November 1997, pp. 4–16.
3. Francis Crick, *The Astonishing Hypothesis: The Scientific Search for the Soul* (New York: Scribner, 1994), p. 18.
4. John T. Bruer, *The Myth of the First Three Years* (New York: Free Press, 1999).
5. Joseph LeDoux, *The Emotional Brain* (New York: Simon & Schuster, 1996), p. 68.
6. Leslie Brothers, *Friday's Footprint: How Society Shapes the Human Mind* (New York: Oxford University Press, 1997), p. 48.
7. Bruer, "Brain Science, Brain Fiction," p. 18.
8. Marian Diamond and Janet Hopson, *Magic Trees of the Mind: How to Nurture Your Child's Intelligence, Creativity, and Healthy Emotions from Birth Through Adolescence* (New York: Dutton, 1998).
9. Michael S. Gazzaniga, *The Mind's Past* (Berkeley: University of California Press, 1998), p. 29.
10. Ibid., p. 35.
11. Diamond and Hopson, p. 63 (emphasis in the original).
12. Gazzaniga, p. 48.
13. Ibid., p. 9.
14. Ibid., pp. 13–15.
15. Steven Pinker, *How the Mind Works* (New York: Norton, 1997), pp. 341–42. When I complained to Pinker about these comments, he replied in a personal message sent in May 1999 that "ultimately we do not disagree on much" and that in his future writings he would take my observations into account.
16. *Learner-Centered Psychological Principles: A Framework for School Reform and Redesign* (Washington, D.C.: American Psychological Association, 1997).
17. Richard Restak, *The Modular Brain* (New York: Scribner, 1994), pp. 35, xvi–xvii.
18. Crick, p. 10.
19. Beverly A. Wright et al., "Deficits in Auditory Temporal and Spectral Resolution in Language-Impaired Children," *Nature,* 8 May 1997, pp. 176–78.
20. Marilyn J. Adams, *Beginning to Read: Thinking and Learning About Print* (Urbana: Center for the Study of Reading, University of Illinois, 1990).
21. Gazzaniga, p. 10.
22. Stanislaus Dehaene, *The Number Sense: How the Mind Creates Mathematics* (New York: Oxford University Press, 1997), p. 139.
23. LeDoux, op. cit.
24. Candace Pert, *Molecules of Emotion* (New York: Scribner, 1997).
25. Antonio R. Damasio, *Descartes' Error* (New York: Grosset/Putnam, 1994), p. 84.
26. Daniel L. Schacter, *Searching for Memory* (New York: Basic Books, 1996), p. 56.

RON BRANDT is an independent writer and consultant living in Arlington, Va. He was executive editor of Educational Leadership *from 1978 to 1995.*

ABILITY AND EXPERTISE

It's Time to Replace the Current Model of Intelligence

BY ROBERT J. STERNBERG

BILLY HAS an IQ of 121 on a standardized individual intelligence test, and Jimmy has an IQ of 94 on the same test. What do these scores, and the difference between them, mean? The conventional answer to this question is that they represent a kind of intellectual predestination: The two children possess inborn gifts that are relatively fixed and will, to a large extent, predict their future achievement. So no one will be surprised if Billy goes on to do well in high school and gets into a good college—or if Jimmy barely gets through school and ends up with a minimum-wage job—because that's what this familiar and widely accepted model of human intelligence would lead us to expect.

But a scientific model is just a way of fitting together pieces of information and things we have observed into a pattern that makes sense. It does not represent the certain or only way of arranging the pieces, and models can be and often are modified or even discarded when we make new discoveries or look at what we know in new

ways. This happened, for example, in the early seventeenth century, when the Ptolemaic model of the solar system, in which all the heavenly bodies were said to revolve around the earth, was replaced by the Copernican, sun-centered, model of the solar system.

Many psychologists now question the simple identification of IQ with ability, which the old model of human intelligence posits. They believe that abilities are too broad and too complex to be measured by the kind of IQ test that Billy and Jimmy took. They also believe that environment and genetics play a part and, furthermore, that abilities are not a fixed quantity: They can be modified by education and experience. I'd like to propose a further, and important, building block for this new model of human intelligence—namely that the difference in Billy's and Jimmy's IQ scores simply means that the two children are at a different stage in developing the expertise measured by the IQ test. Furthermore, I suggest that people who study abilities and those who study ex-

From the Spring 1999 issue of the *American Educator*, pp. 10-13, 50-51. Reprinted by permission of the *American Educator*, the quarterly journal of the American Federation of Teachers, and Robert J. Sternberg.

pertise are really talking about the same thing. What we are measuring when we administer a Wechsler Intelligence Scale for Children (WISC) or an Iowa Test of Basic Skills (ITBS) or an SAT are the same. They are not different in kind but only in the point at which we are measuring them.

In the Eye of the Beholder

When we give an achievement test, we accept the idea that we are testing a form of expertise, but this is equally true when we administer an IQ test. What differs is the level of expertise we measure and, probably more important, the way we perceive what we are measuring. The familiar IQ/ability model creates a certain expectation: that one kind of accomplishment (IQ test scores) will predict—and, in fact, lead to—another kind of accomplishment (grades or scores on achievement tests). And of course we also use different words to describe the two kinds of accomplishment.

But this way of looking at the two kinds of test scores is a familiar convenience rather than a psychological reality. Solving problems on a verbal-analogies test or a test of mathematical problem solving, which are supposed to test a child's abilities, calls for expertise just the way so-called achievement tests do: You can't do well on these so-called tests of ability without knowing the vocabulary or having some familiarity with problem-solving techniques. The chief difference between ability and achievement tests is not what they measure but the point at which they measure it. IQ and other tests of ability are, typically, administered early in a child's school career, whereas various indications about school performance, such as grades or achievement test scores, are collected later. However, all of the various kinds of assessments are of the same kind, psychologically. They all test—to some extent—what you know and how well you can use it. What distinguishes ability tests from the other kinds of assessments is how the ability tests are used (usually, predictively), rather than what they measure. There is no qualitative distinction.

But if the distinction between what these tests measure does not exist, how do we come to make it? The answer is a complicated story, but the principal reason is historical accident. Briefly, the two kinds of testing were developed separately and used on different groups of people. IQ/ability testing, which originated in Alfred Binet's testing of young children, focused on exceptionally low levels of performance and came to be viewed primarily as predictive. Early studies of expertise were done with adults. They focused on exceptionally high levels of performance and came to be viewed as measures of achievement.

The Traditional Model

According to the traditional model of fixed individual differences, the capabilities that a child inherits interact with the child's environment to produce, at an early age, a relatively fixed potential for achievement. Children fulfill this potential to a greater or lesser degree. Thus, if a child who scores well on ability tests does well in school, we say he is living up to his potential. If, as sometimes happens, his achievement does not match his test scores, we call him an *underachiever*—or if the kid confounds expectations by working hard and doing well, he gets the label of *overachiever*. Ironically, ability test scores are considered a better indicator of what a child can achieve (or should achieve) than what the child actually does. A test of verbal analogies, in this view, might actually tell us more about a person's verbal abilities than the person's comprehension of the reading he or she does in everyday life; or a test of mathematical problem-solving skills might be viewed as more informative than the mathematical problem solving the person does on the job.

According to this model, the more intelligent students (that is, the ones with higher IQs) do better in school. As a result, they are likely to attend selective colleges, go on to professional schools, and eventually get well-paying jobs and enjoy other forms of success. The less intelligent do worse in school and may drop out. At best, they probably have to be satisfied with low-status credentials that reflect hard work rather than ability, and their role in the labor market is to fill the jobs that the more intelligent people don't want to do.

This is the view Richard Herrnstein and Charles Murray present in *The Bell Curve* (1994), and as people who have read the book will remember, it assigns African Americans as a group to the status of an underclass, based on the average "potential" of group members displayed in IQ and other ability tests. Herrnstein and Murray's use of the traditional model has occasioned a great deal of controversy. However, the view of IQ as fixed and determinant is, unfortunately, consistent with many current educational practices and common views about intellectual competence.

Developing Expertise

The idea that abilities are a form of developing expertise offers a more flexible and optimistic view of human capabilities, and one that is more in line with what we are discovering about human intelligence. Children become experts in the skills needed for success on ability tests in much the same ways that they become experts in doing anything else—through a combination of genetic endowment and experience (Ericsson, 1996). To do well on a test, a child needs to acquire, store, and learn how to use at least two kinds of knowledge: explicit knowledge of a domain and implicit or tacit knowledge of a field. Knowledge of a domain is subject-matter knowledge: In American history, for example, it would be the facts, trends, and major ideas about the political, economic, and social development of our country. Implicit knowledge is the kind of knowledge one needs to be successful in a field but which is not part of the subject matter and often is not even talked about. For example, in American history, the role of the Federalist Papers in the shaping of the U.S. Constitution would be explicit knowledge; how to use the library or Internet to research an essay about the Federalist Papers and how to take and organize notes and carry the paper through successive drafts to completion would be implicit knowledge.

Tests measure both explicit and implicit knowledge: knowledge of the subject matter and knowledge about how to take a test. This is as true of ability tests as it is of achievement tests. A verbal-analogies test, for example, measures explicit knowledge of vocabulary and a student's ability to reason with this knowledge, but the test also measures implicit knowledge of how to take a test. Thus, the student has to work within certain time limits and choose the best answer from a list of answers no one of which is exactly right.

To translate the gaining of expertise on test-taking into procedural terms, students need

- direct instruction in how to solve test-like problems—usually this takes place in school;
- practice in solving such problems, again usually in academic contexts;
- an opportunity to watch others, such as teachers or other students, solve test-like problems;
- practice thinking about such problems, sometimes mentally simulating what to do when confronting them;
- rewards for successful solutions (good grades, praise from teachers, other kinds of recognition), thereby reinforcing such behavior.

The difference between Billy's score of 121 and Jimmy's 94 also reflects a number of personal and cultural factors, and they do not all pertain to what we usually consider expertise. For example, the two boys may possess different degrees of "test-wiseness," that is, understanding the tricks of taking tests (Millman, Bishop, and Ebel, 1965; Bond and Harman, 1994). They may feel differing levels of anxiety and/or alertness on the day they are tested, and this would probably show itself in their scores. Cultural differences between them may lead to different attitudes about the importance of doing well on a test, particularly one that clearly does not "count." Most important of all, the boys

may be at different levels of developing expertise in the skills that the test measures.

Individual Differences

But saying that IQ tests and other assessments of ability are testing the same thing as achievement tests and that the expertise revealed is not fixed should not be taken to mean that everybody has the same intellectual capacity. The difference in expertise that Billy and Jimmy reveal on their IQ tests may indicate an underlying difference in their capacities. However, IQ tests do not directly measure these differences and neither do any of the other ways in which we currently seek to measure ability (see, for example, Vygotsky, 1978). Individual differences in developing expertise result in much the same way as in most kinds of learning: from (a) the rate of learning (which can be caused by the amount of direct instruction received, the amount of problem solving done, the amount of time and effort spent in thinking about problems, and so on); and from (b) the asymptote of learning—that is, the limit set by ability to what a student can ultimately achieve, given unlimited training. This limit, or asymptote, can be caused by differences in numbers of schemas—the networks of information on various subjects stored in our memories—the organization of schemas, efficiency in using schemas, and so on (see Atkinson, Bower, and Crothers, 1965). For example, children can learn how to solve the various kinds of mathematical problems found in tests of mathematical abilities, whether through regular schooling, a special course, or through assimilation of everyday experience. When they learn, they will learn at different rates, and reach different asymptotes. Ultimately the differences represent genetic and environmental factors that are interacting in ways that we cannot now measure.

Various Kinds of Expertise

As I've already noted, the so-called ability tests typically come earlier in a student's school career than the various types of achievement tests, but what IQ tests measure is not psychologically prior. Achievement tests might just as well be used to predict scores on ability tests—and sometimes they are, as for instance, when school officials try to predict a student's college admissions test scores on the basis of the student's grades. When we look at the test of abilities as though they are psychologically prior, we are confusing the order in which students usually take these tests with some kind of psychological ordering. But in fact, our temporal ordering implies no psychological ordering at all. The recent change in the meaning of the acronym *SAT* (from Scholastic Aptitude Test to Scholastic Assessment Test) reflects the recognition that what was called an aptitude test measures more than just "aptitude"—indeed, it hints at the interchangeability of the two kinds of tests. Nevertheless, the SAT is still widely used as an ability test, and the SAT-II, which more directly measures subject-matter knowledge, as a set of achievement tests.

Tests that claim to measure ability through questions employing vocabulary, reading comprehension, verbal analogies, arithmetic problem solving, and the like are all, in part, tests of achievement. Even abstract-reasoning tests measure achievement in dealing with geometric symbols, which is a skill taught in Western schools (Laboratory of Comparative Human Cognition, 1982). Indeed, if we examine the content of ability tests, it is clear that they measure achievement that the students taking the test should have accomplished several years back. We could just as well use academic performance to predict ability-test scores. The problem with the traditional model is not that it proposes a correlation between ability tests and other forms of achievement. That undoubtedly exists. It is rather the traditional model's proposing that the capacities measured by the tests *cause* later success—or failure—instead of merely preceding it.

An Illusion of Causality

The notion that success on ability tests predicts success in many other areas gains credibility from the fact that some of the skills or qualities that make people more expert at taking tests are also likely to make them successful in other aspects of life in our culture. Taking a test, say, of verbal or figural analogies, or of mathematical problem solving, typically requires skills such as (a) puzzling out what someone else wants (here, the person who wrote the test), (b) command of English vocabulary, (c) reading comprehension, (d) allocation of limited time, (e) sustained concentration, (f) abstract reasoning, (g) quick thinking, (h) symbol manipulation, and (i) suppression of anxiety and other emotions that can interfere with test performance. These skills are also part of what is required for successful performance in school and in many kinds of job performance. Thus, an expert test-taker is likely also to have skills that will be involved in other kinds of expertise as well, such as expertise in getting high grades in school.

To the extent that the expertise required for one kind of performance overlaps with the expertise required for another kind of performance, there will be a correlation

between performances. However, the expertise that ability tests measure is not the cause of school or job expertise; it is itself an expertise that overlaps with school or job expertise. Differences in test scores, academic performance, and job performance are all effects of different levels of expertise.

The New Model

The notion of *developing* expertise means that people are constantly in the process of developing expertise when they work within a given domain. Individuals can differ in rate and asymptote of development. However, the main constraint in achieving expertise is not some fixed prior level of capacity, of the kind measured by IQ tests. It is the degree to which students are purposefully engaged in working and teachers in helping them. This involves direct instruction, active participation, role modeling, and reward.

The model of developing expertise has five key elements: metacognitive skills, learning skills, thinking skills, knowledge, and motivation. The elements all influence one another, both directly and indirectly. For example, learning leads to knowledge, but knowledge facilitates further learning.

1. Metacognitive skills. Metacognitive skills refer to students' understanding and control of their own learning. These skills would include what a student knows about writing papers or solving arithmetic word problems, both in regard to the steps that are involved and how these steps can be executed effectively (Sternberg 1985, 1986, 1988; Sternberg and Swerling, 1996).

2. Learning skills. Learning skills are sometimes divided into explicit learning, which occurs when we make an effort to learn, and implicit learning, which occurs when we simply pick up information without any particular effort. Examples of learning skills are distinguishing relevant from irrelevant information; putting together the relevant information; and relating new information to information already stored in memory (Sternberg, 1985, 1986).

3. Thinking skills. There are three main sets of thinking skills. Critical (analytical) thinking skills include analyzing, critiquing, judging, evaluating, comparing and contrasting, and assessing. Creative thinking skills include creating, discovering, inventing, imagining, supposing, and hypothesizing. Practical thinking skills include applying, using, and practicing (Sternberg, 1985, 1986, 1994, 1997). They are the first step in translating thought into real-world action.

4. Knowledge. There are two main kinds of knowledge that are relevant in academic learning. Declarative knowledge is of facts, concepts, principles, laws, and the like. It is "knowing that." Procedure knowledge is of procedures and strategies. It is "knowing how." Of particular importance is procedural tacit knowledge, which involves knowing how the system in which one is operating functions (Sternberg, Wagner, Williams & Horvath, 1995).

5. Motivation. There are a number of different kinds of motivation, and in one or another of its forms, motivation is probably indispensable for school success. Without it, the student never even tries to learn (McClelland, 1985; McClelland, Atkinson, Clark, and Lowell, 1976; Bandura, 1977, 1996; Amabile, 1996; Sternberg and Lubart, 1996).

6. Context. All of the elements discussed above are characteristics of the learner. However, it is a mistake to assume, as conventional tests usually do, that factors external to the student's mastery of the material play no part in how well the student does on a test. Such contextual factors include whether the student is taking the test in his or her native language, whether the test emphasizes speedy performance, the importance to the student of success on the test, and the student's familiarity with the kinds of material on the test.

Novices—beginning learners—work toward expertise through deliberate practice. But this practice requires an interaction of all five of the key elements in the model. At the center, driving the elements, is motivation. Without it, nothing happens. Motivation drives metacognitive skills, which in turn activate learning and thinking skills, which then provide feedback to the metacognitive skills, enabling the student's level of expertise to increase (see also Sternberg, 1985). The declarative and procedural knowledge acquired through the extension of the thinking and learning skills also results in these skills being used more effectively in the future.

All of these processes are affected by, and can in turn affect, the context in which they operate. For example, if a learning experience is in English but the learner has only limited English proficiency, his or her learning will be inferior to that of someone with more advanced English language skills. Or if material is presented orally to someone who is a better visual learner, that individual's performance will be reduced.

Eventually, as the five elements influence one another, the student reaches a kind of expertise at which he or she becomes a reflective practitioner who is able to consciously use a certain set of skills. But expertise occurs at many levels. The expert first-year graduate or law student, for example, is still a far cry from the expert professional. People thus cycle through many times, on the way to successively higher levels of expertise.

Implications for the Classroom

The model of abilities as a form of developing expertise has a number of immediate implications for education, in general, and classroom practice, in particular.

First, teachers and all who use ability and achievement tests should stop distinguishing between what the two kinds of tests assess. The measurements are not different in kind but only in the point at which they are being made.

Second, tests measure *achieved* levels of developing expertise. No test—of abilities or anything else—can specify the highest level a student can achieve.

Third, different kinds of assessments—multiple-choice, short answer, performance-based, portfolio—complement one another in assessing multiple aspects of developing expertise. There is no one "right" kind of assessment.

Fourth, instruction should be geared not just toward imparting a knowledge base, but toward developing reflective analytical, creative, and practical thinking with a knowledge base. Students learn better when they think to learn, even when their learning is assessed with straightforward multiple-choice memory assessments (Sternberg, Torff, and Grigorenko, 1998).

The model I've proposed here views students as novices who are capable of becoming experts in a variety of areas. The traditional model, which posits fixed individual differences—and typically bases the kind of instruction a student gets on these differences—holds many students back from attaining the expertise they are capable of. It is true that for various reasons (including, perhaps, genetic as well as environmentally based differences), not all individuals will reach the same ultimate level of expertise. But they should all be given the opportunity to reach new levels of competence well beyond what they, and in some cases, others may think possible. The fact that Billy and Jimmy have different IQs tells us something about differences in what they now do. It does not tell us anything about what ultimately they will be able to achieve.

References

Amabile, T. M. (1996). *Creativity in context.* Boulder, CO: Westview.

Atkinson, R. C., Bower, G. H., & Crothers, E. J. (1965). *An introduction to mathematical learning theory.* New York: John Wiley & Sons.

Bandura, A. (1977). Self-efficacy: Toward a unifying theory of behavioral change. *Psychological Review, 84,* 181–215.

Bandura, A. (1996). *Self-efficacy: The exercise of control.* New York: Freeman.

Bond, L., & Harman, A. E. (1994). Test-taking strategies. In R. J. Sternberg (Ed.), *Encyclopedia of human intelligence* (Vol. 2, pp. 1073–1077). New York: Macmillan.

Ericsson, A. (Ed.) (1996). *The road to excellence.* Mahwah, NJ: Erlbaum.

Herrnstein, R. J., & Murray, C. (1994). *The bell curve*. New York: Free Press.

Laboratory of Comparative Human Cognition (1982). Culture and intelligence. In R. J. Sternberg (Ed.), *Handbook of human intelligence* (pp. 642–719). New York: Cambridge University Press.

McClelland, D. C. (1985). *Human motivation*. New York: Scott Foresman.

McClelland, D. C., Atkinson, J. W., Clark, R. A., & Lowell, E. L. (1976). *The achievement motive*. New York: Irvington.

Millman, J., Bishop, H., & Ebel, R. (1965). An analysis of test-wiseness. *Educational and Psychological Measurement*, 25, 707–726.

Sternberg, R. J. (1985). *Beyond IQ: A triarchic theory of human intelligence*. New York: Cambridge University Press.

Sternberg, R. J. (1986). *Intelligence applied*. Orlando, FL: Harcourt Brace College Publishers.

Sternberg, R. J. (1988). *The triarchic mind: A new theory of human intelligence*. New York: Viking-Penguin.

Sternberg, R. J. (1994). Diversifying instruction and assessment. *The Educational Forum*, 59(1), 47–53.

Sternberg, R. J. (1997). *Successful intelligence*. New York: Plume.

Sternberg, R. J., & Lubart, T. I. (1995). *Defying the crowd: Cultivating creativity in a culture of conformity*. New York: Free Press.

Sternberg, R. J., & Lubart, T. I. (1996). Investing in creativity. *American Psychologist*, 51, 677–688.

Sternberg, R. J., & Spear-Swerling, L. (1996). *Teaching for thinking*. Washington, DC: APA Books.

Sternberg, R. J., Torff, B., & Grigorenko, E. L. (1998). Teaching triarchically improves school achievement. *Journal of Educational Psychology*, 90, 374–384.

Sternberg, R. J., Wagner, R. K., Williams, W. M., & Horvath, J. (1995). Testing common sense. *American Psychologist*, 50, 912–927.

Vygotsky, L. S. (1978). *Mind in society: The development of higher psychological processes*. Cambridge, MA: Harvard University Press.

This work was supported by the U.S. Office of Educational Research and Improvement (Grant R206R50001), but this support does not imply endorsement of positions taken or conclusions reached.

Robert J. Sternberg is IBM Professor of Psychology in the Department of Psychology at Yale University. His areas of specialization are human abilities and cognition. A long version of this article appeared in **Educational Researcher,** *April 1998.*

CAUTION— PRAISE CAN BE DANGEROUS

By Carol S. Dweck

THE SELF-ESTEEM movement, which was flourishing just a few years ago, is in a state of decline. Although many educators believed that boosting students' self-esteem would boost their academic achievement, this did not happen. But the failure of the self-esteem movement does not mean that we should stop being concerned with what students think of themselves and just concentrate on improving their achievement. Every time teachers give feedback to students, they convey messages that affect students' opinion of themselves, their motivation, and their achievement. And I believe that teachers can and should help students become high achievers who also feel good about themselves. But how, exactly, should teachers go about doing this?

In fact, the self-esteem people were on to something extremely important. Praise, the chief weapon in their armory, is a powerful tool. Used correctly it can help students become adults who delight in intellectual challenge, understand the value of effort, and are able to deal with setbacks. Praise can help students make the most of the gifts they have. But if praise is not handled properly, it can become a negative force, a kind of drug that, rather than strengthening students, makes them passive and dependent on the opinion of others. What teachers—and parents—need is a framework that enables them to use praise wisely and well.

Where Did Things Go Wrong?

I believe the self-esteem movement faltered because of the way in which educators tried to instill self-esteem. Many people held an intuitively appealing theory of self-esteem, which went something like this: Giving students many opportunities to experience success and then praising them for their successes will indicate to them that they are intelligent. If they feel good about their intelligence, they will achieve. They will love learning and be confident and successful learners.

Much research now shows that this idea is wrong. Giving students easy tasks and praising their success tells students that you think they're dumb.[1] It's not hard to see why. Imagine being lavishly praised for something you think is pretty Mickey Mouse. Wouldn't you feel that the person thought you weren't capable of more and was trying to make you feel good about your limited ability?

But what about praising students' ability when they perform well on challenging tasks? In such cases, there would be no question of students' thinking you were just trying to make them feel good. Melissa Kamins, Claudia Mueller, and I decided to put this idea to the test.

Mueller and I had already found, in a study of the relationship between parents' beliefs and their children's expectations, that 85 percent of parents thought they needed to praise their children's intelligence in order to assure them that they were smart.[2] We also knew that many educators and psychologists thought that praising children for being intelligent was of great benefit. Yet in almost 30 years of research, I had seen over and over that children who had maladaptive achievement patterns were already obsessed with their intelligence—and with proving it to others. The children worried about how smart they looked and feared that failing at some task—even a relatively unimportant one—meant they were dumb. They also worried that having to work hard in order to succeed at a task showed they were dumb. Intelligence seemed to be a label to these kids, a feather in their caps, rather than a tool that, with effort, they could become more skillful in using.

In contrast, the more adaptive students focused on the process of learning and achieving. They weren't worried about their intelligence and didn't consider every task a measure of it. Instead, these students were more likely to concern themselves with the effort and strategies they needed in order to master the task. We wondered if praising children for being intelligent, though it seemed like a positive thing to do, could hook them into becoming dependent on praise.

Praise for Intelligence

Claudia Mueller and I conducted six studies, with more than 400 fifth-grade students, to examine the effects of praising children for being intelligent.[3] The students were from different parts of the country (a Midwestern town and a large Eastern city) and came from varied ethnic, racial, and socioeconomic backgrounds. Each of the studies involved several tasks, and all began with the students working, one at a time, on a puzzle task that was challenging but easy enough for all of them to do quite well. After this first set, we praised one-third of the children for their *intelligence*. They were told: "Wow, you got *x* number correct. That's a really good score. You must be smart at this." One-third of the children were also told that they got a very good score, but they were praised for their *effort*: "You must have worked really hard." The final third were simply praised for their *performance*, with no comment on why they were successful. Then, we looked to see the effects of these different types of praise across all six studies.

We found that after the first trial (in which all of the students were successful) the three groups responded similarly to questions we asked them. They enjoyed the task equally, were equally eager to take the problems home to practice, and were equally confident about their future performance.

In several of the studies, as a followup to the first trial, we gave students a choice of different tasks to work on next. We asked whether they wanted to try a challenging task from which they could learn a lot (but at which they might not succeed) or an easier task (on which they were sure to do well and look smart).

The majority of the students who had received praise for being intelligent the first time around went for the task that would allow them to keep on looking smart. Most of the students who had received praise for their effort (in some studies, as many as 90 percent) wanted the challenging learning task. (The third group, the students who had not been praised for intelligence or effort, were right in the middle and I will not focus on them.)

These findings suggest that when we praise children for their intelligence, we are telling them that this is the name of the game: Look smart; don't risk making mistakes. On the other hand, when we praise children for the effort and hard work that leads to achievement, they want to keep engaging in that process. They are not diverted from the task of learning by a concern with how smart they might—or might not—look.

The Impact of Difficulty

Next, we gave students a set of problems that were harder and on which they didn't do as well. Afterwards, we repeated the questions we had asked after the first task: How much had they enjoyed the task? Did they want to take the problems home to practice? And how smart did they feel? We found that the students who had been praised for being intelligent did not like this second task and were no longer interested in taking the problems home to practice. What's more, their difficulties led them to question their intelligence. In other words, the same students who had been told they were smart when they succeeded now felt dumb because they had encountered a setback. They had learned to measure themselves from what people said about their performance, and they were dependent on continuing praise in order to maintain their confidence.

In contrast, the students who had received praise for their effort on the easier task liked the more difficult task just as much even though they missed some of the problems. In fact, many of them said they liked the harder problems even more than the easier ones, and they were even more eager to take them home to practice. It was wonderful to see.

Moreover, these youngsters did not think that the difficulty of the task (and their relative lack of success) reflected on their intelligence. They thought, simply, that they had to make a greater effort in order to succeed. Their interest in taking problems home with them to practice on presumably reflected one way they planned to do this.

Thus, the students praised for effort were able to keep their intellectual self-esteem in the face of setbacks. They still thought they were smart; they still enjoyed the challenge; and they planned to work toward future success. The students who had been praised for their intelligence received an initial boost to their egos, but their view of themselves was quickly shaken when the going got rough. As a final test, we gave students a third set of problems that were equal in difficulty to the first set—the one on which all the students had been successful. The results were striking. Although all three groups had performed equally well on the first trial, the students who had received praise for their intelligence (and who had been discouraged by their poor showing on the second trial) now registered the worst performance of the three groups. Indeed, they did significantly worse than they had on the first trial. In contrast, students who were praised for working hard performed the best of the three groups and significantly better than they had originally. So the different kinds of praise apparently affected not just what students thought and felt, but also how well they were able to perform.

Given what we had already seen, we reasoned that when students see their performance as a measure of their intelligence, they are likely to feel stigmatized when they perform poorly and may even try to hide the fact. If, however, students consider a poor performance a temporary setback, which merely reflects how much effort they have put in or their current level of skill, then it will not be a stigma. To test this idea, we gave students the opportunity to tell a student at another school about the task they had just completed by writing a brief description on a prepared form. The form also asked them to report their score on the second, more difficult trial.

More than 40 percent of the students who had been praised for their intelligence lied about their score (to improve it, of course). They did this even though they were reporting their performance to an anonymous peer whom they would never meet. Very few of the students in the other groups exaggerated their performance. This suggests that when we praise students for their intelligence, failure becomes more personal and therefore more of a disgrace. As a result, students become less able to face and therefore deal with their setbacks.

The Messages We Send

Finally, we found that following their experiences with the different kinds of praise, the students believed different things about their intelligence. Students who had received praise for being intelligent told us they thought of intelligence as something innate—a capacity that you just had or didn't have. Students who had been praised for effort told us they thought of intelligence more in terms of their skills, knowledge, and motivation—things over which they had some control and might be able to enhance.

And these negative effects of praising for intelligence were just as strong (and sometimes stronger) for the high-achieving students as for their less successful peers. Perhaps it is even easier to get these youngsters invested in looking smart to others. Maybe they are even more attuned to messages from us that tell them we value them for their intellects.

How can one sentence of praise have such powerful and pervasive effects? In my research, I have been amazed over and over again at how quickly students of all ages pick up on messages about themselves—at how sensitive they are to suggestions about their personal qualities or about the meaning of their actions and experiences. The kinds of praise (and criticism) students receive from their teachers and parents tell them how to think about what they do—and what they are.

This is why we cannot simply forget about students' feelings, their ideas about themselves and their motivation, and just teach them the "facts." No matter how objective we try to be, our feedback conveys messages about what we think is important, what we think of them, and how they should think of themselves. These messages, as we have seen, can have powerful effects on

many things including performance. And it should surprise no one that this susceptibility starts very early.

Melissa Kamins and I found it in kindergarten children.[4] Praise or criticism that focused on children's personal traits (like being smart or good) created a real vulnerability when children hit setbacks. They saw setbacks as showing that they were bad or incompetent—and they were unable to respond constructively. In contrast, praise or criticism that focused on children's strategies or the efforts they made to succeed left them hardy, confident, and in control when they confronted setbacks. A setback did not mean anything bad about them or their personal qualities. It simply meant that something needed to be done, and they set about doing it. Again, a focus on process allowed these young children to maintain their self-esteem and to respond constructively when things went wrong.

Ways of Praising

There are many groups whose achievement is of particular interest to us: minorities, females, the gifted, the underachieving, to name a few. The findings of these studies will tell you why I am so concerned that we not try to encourage the achievement of our students by praising their intelligence. When we worry about low-achieving or vulnerable students, we may want to reassure them they're smart. When we want to motivate high-achieving students, we may want to spur them on by telling them they're gifted. Our research says: Don't do that. Don't get students so invested in these labels that they care more about keeping the label than about learning. Instead of empowering students, praise is likely to render students passive and dependent on something they believe they can't control. And it can hook them into a system in which setbacks signify incompetence and effort is recognized as a sign of weakness rather than a key to success.

This is not to say that we shouldn't praise students. We can praise as much as we please when they learn or do well, but should wax enthusiastic about their strategies, not about how their performance reveals an attribute they are likely to view as innate and beyond their control. We can rave about their effort, their concentration, the effectiveness of their study strategies, the interesting ideas they came up with, the way they followed through. We can ask them questions that show an intelligent appreciation of their work and what they put into it. We can enthusiastically discuss with them what they learned. This, of course, requires more from us than simply telling them that they are smart, but it is much more appreciative of their work, much more constructive, and it does not carry with it the dangers I've been describing.

What about the times a student really impresses us by doing something quickly, easily—and perfectly? Isn't it appropriate to show our admiration for the child's ability? My honest opinion is that we should not. We should not be giving students the impression that we place a high value on their doing perfect work on tasks that are easy for them. A better approach would be to apologize for wasting their time with something that was too easy, and move them to something that is more challenging. When students make progress in or master that more challenging work, that's when our admiration—for their efforts—should come through.

A Challenging Academic Transition

The studies I have been talking about were carried out in a research setting. Two other studies[5] tracked students with these different viewpoints in a real-life situation, as they were making the transition to junior high school and during their first two years of junior high. This is a point at which academic work generally becomes more demanding than it was in elementary school, and many students stumble. The studies compared the attitudes and achievement of students who believed that intelligence is a fixed quantity with students who believed that they could develop their intellectual potential. We were especially interested in any changes in the degree of success students experienced in junior high school and how they dealt with these changes. For the sake of simplicity, I will combine the results from the two studies, for they showed basically the same thing.

First, the students who believed that intelligence is fixed did indeed feel that poor performance meant they were dumb. Furthermore, they reported, in significantly greater numbers than their peers, that if they did badly on a test, they would seriously consider cheating the next time. This was true even for students who were highly skilled and who had a past record of high achievement.

Perhaps even worse, these students believed that having to make an effort meant they were dumb—hardly an attitude to foster good work habits. In fact, these students reported that even though school achievement was very important to them, one of their prime goals in school was to exert as little effort as possible.

In contrast to the hopelessly counterproductive attitude of the first group, the second group of students, those who believed that intellectual potential can be developed, felt that poor performance was often due to a lack of effort, and it called for more studying. They saw effort as worthwhile and important—something necessary even for geniuses if they are to realize their potential.

So once again, for those who are focused on their fixed intelligence and its adequacy, setbacks and even effort bring a loss of face and self-esteem. But challenges, setbacks, and effort are not threatening to the self-esteem of those who are concerned with developing their potential; they represent opportunities to learn. In fact, many of these students told us that they felt smartest when things were difficult; they gained self-esteem when they applied themselves to meeting challenges.

What about the academic achievement of the two groups making the transition to junior high school? In both studies, we saw that students who believed that intelligence was fixed and was manifest in their performance did more poorly than they had in elementary school. Even many who had been high achievers did much less well. Included among them were many students who entered junior high with high intellectual self-esteem. On the other hand, the students who believed that intellectual potential could be developed showed, as a group, clear gains in their class standing, and many blossomed intellectually. The demands of their new environment, instead of causing them to wilt because they doubted themselves, encouraged them to roll up their sleeves and get to work.

These patterns seem to continue with students entering college. Research with students at highly selective universities found that, although they may enter a situation with equal self-esteem, optimism, and past achievement, students respond to the challenge of college differently: Students in one group by measuring themselves and losing confidence; the others by figuring out what it takes and doing it.[6]

Believing and Achieving

Some of the research my colleagues and I have carried out suggests that it is relatively easy to modify the views of young children in regard to intelligence and effort in a research setting. But is it possible to influence student attitudes in a real-life setting? And do students become set in their beliefs as they grow older? Some exciting new research shows that even college students' views about intelligence and effort can be modified—and that these changes will affect their level of academic achievement.[7] In their study, Aronson and Fried taught minority students at a prestigious university to view their intelligence as a potentiality that could be developed through hard work. For example, they created and showed a film that explained the neural changes that took place in the brain every time students confronted difficulty by exerting effort. The students who were instructed about the relationship between intelligence and effort went on to earn significantly higher grades than their peers who were not. This study, like our intelligence praise studies, shows that (1) students' ideas about their intelligence can be influenced by the messages they receive, and (2) when these ideas change, changes in performance can follow.

But simply getting back to basics and enforcing rigorous standards—which some students will meet and some will not—won't eliminate the pitfalls I have been describing. This approach may convey, even more forcefully, the idea that intelligence is a gift only certain students possess. And it will not, in itself, teach students to value learning and focus on the *process* of achievement or how to deal with obstacles. These students may, more than ever, fear failure because it takes the measure of their intelligence.

A Different Framework

Our research suggests another approach. Instead of trying to convince our students that they are smart or simply enforcing rigorous standards in the hopes that doing so will create high motivation and achievement, teachers should take the following steps: first, get students to focus on their potential to learn; second, teach them to value challenge and learning over looking smart; and third, teach them to concentrate on effort and learning processes in the face of obstacles.

This can be done while holding students to rigorous standards. Within the framework I have outlined, tasks are challenging and effort is highly valued, required, and rewarded. Moreover, we can (and must) give students frank evaluations of their work and their level of skill, but we must make clear that these are evaluations of their current level of performance and skill, not an assessment of their intelligence or their innate ability. In this framework, we do not arrange easy work or constant successes, thinking that we are doing students a favor. We do not lie to students who are doing poorly so they will feel smart: That would rob them of the information they need to work harder and improve. Nor do we just give students hard work that many can't do, thus making them into casualties of the system.

I am not encouraging high-effort situations in which students stay up studying until all hours every night, fearing they will displease their parents or disgrace themselves if they don't get the top test scores. Pushing students to do that is not about valuing learning or about orienting students toward developing their potential. It is about pressuring students to prove their worth through their test scores.

It is also not sufficient to give students piles of homework and say we are teaching them about the importance of effort. We are not talking about quantity here but about teaching students to seek challenging tasks and to engage in an active learning process.

However, we as educators must then be prepared to do our share. We must help students acquire the skills they need for learning, and we must be available as constant resources for learning. It is not enough to keep harping on and praising effort, for this may soon wear thin. And it will not be effective if students don't know *how* to apply their effort appropriately. It is necessary that we as educators understand and teach students how to engage in processes that foster learning, things like task analysis and study skills.[8]

When we focus students on their potential to learn and give them the message that effort is the key to learning, we give them responsibility for and control over their achievement—and over their self-esteem. We acknowledge that learning is not something that someone gives students; nor can they expect to feel good about themselves because teachers tell them they are smart. Both learning and self-esteem are things that students achieve as they tackle challenges and work to master new material.

Students who value learning and effort know how to make and sustain a commitment to valued goals. Unlike some of their peers, they are not afraid to work hard; they know that meaningful tasks involve setbacks; and they know how to bounce back from failure. These are lessons that cannot help but serve them well in life as well as in school.

These are lessons I have learned from my research on students' motivation and achievement, and they are things I wish I had known as a student. There is no reason that every student can't know them now.

Endnotes

1. Meyer, W. U. (1982). Indirect communications about perceived ability estimates. *Journal of Educational Psychology, 74,* 888–897.
2. Mueller, C. M., & Dweck, C. S. (1996). Implicit theories of intelligence: Relation of parental beliefs to children's expectations. Paper presented at the Third National Research Convention of Head Start, Washington, D.C.
3. Mueller, C. M., & Dweck, C. S. (1998). Intelligence praise can undermine motivation and performance. *Journal of Personality and Social Psychology; 75,* 33–52.
4. Kamins, M., & Dweck, C. S. (1999). Person vs. process praise and criticism: Implications for contingent self-worth and coping. *Developmental Psychology.*
5. Henderson, V., & Dweck, C. S. (1990). Achievement and motivation in adolescence: A new model and data. In S. Feldman and G. Elliott (Eds.), *At the threshold: The developing adolescent.* Cambridge, MA: Harvard University Press; *and* Dweck, C. S., & Sorich, L. (1999). Mastery-oriented thinking. In C. R. Snyder (Ed.). *Coping.* New York: Oxford University Press.
6. Robins, R. W. & Pals, J. (1998). Implicit self-theories of ability in the academic domain: A test of Dweck's model. Unpublished manuscript, University of California at Davis; *and* Zhao, W., Dweck, C. S., & Mueller, C. (1998). Implicit theories and depression-like responses to failure. Unpublished manuscript, Columbia University.
7. Aronson, J., & Fried, C. (1998). Reducing stereotype threat and boosting academic achievement of African Americans: The role of conceptions of intelligence. Unpublished manuscript, University of Texas.
8. Brown, A. L. (1997). Transforming schools into communities of thinking and learning about serious matters. *American Psychologist, 52,* 399–413.

Carol S. Dweck is a professor of psychology at Columbia University, who has carried out research on self-esteem, motivation, and academic achievement for thirty years. Her new book, Self-Theories: Their Role in Motivation, Personality, and Development, *was just published by The Psychology Press.*

Constructivist Theory in the Classroom

Internalizing Concepts through Inquiry Learning

MARY M. BEVEVINO, JOAN DENGEL, and KENNETH ADAMS

Why should I care about Rwanda?
How does the Malaysian conflict concern me? How will it apply to my life?
World War I? Nobody's even alive from that conflict!
Why do we have to learn this stuff?

Every social studies teacher has heard these or similar student questions and complaints. What lies behind the fact that some students see so little value in learning about social studies? Teachers point out that students have trouble applying and transferring knowledge, that they do not have enough problem-solving skills, or that they do not understand the importance of what they are asked to learn. Students frustrate us when they cannot integrate previously learned and new concepts, even more so when they take absolutely no interest in our attempts to guide them into problem-solving practice.

Teachers can make learning meaningful when they employ activities that call on students to use their prior knowledge and experiences to construct their own frames of thought (Johnson et al. 1996). Through such inquiry learning approaches, we put students into situations that demand critical thinking and encourage the internalizing of major concepts. Inquiry activities also give students the opportunity to express, confront, and analyze preconceptions and misconceptions in an active, nonthreatening way. In this article, we explore the learning-cycle inquiry model, as outlined in figure 1.

Constructing Knowledge through Inquiry Learning

Planning the Learning Cycle

The learning cycle is an inquiry approach originating with the Science Curriculum Improvement Study (Trowbridge and Bybee 1990). Robert Karplus and his colleagues based the learning cycle format on Piaget's cognitive development principles. Students "learn through their own involvement and action. . . . The goal is to allow students to apply previous knowledge, develop interests, and initiate and maintain a curiosity toward the materials at hand" (Trowbridge and Bybee 1990, 306).

Using the learning cycle format, the teacher can create a series of activities that are personally meaningful for students and give students opportunities to practice critical thinking skills. A simplified version of the plan outlined here can be completed in one class period; this plan is particularly useful in a ninety-minute class, but it can also be constructed to extend over several class periods.

In this inquiry format, the students first tackle a teacher-created problematic situation by conceptualizing questions, constructing hypotheses, and reaching consensus on solutions.

Next, they discuss and debate their proposed solutions with the class. Finally, they apply their contextualized insights to an important historical issue, researching and analyzing events and societal conditions of the time, proposing solutions to the controversial issue, and deciding on the best solutions. In the activities described here, students come to a consensus about mutually beneficial and workable alternatives to armed conflict.

The Teacher's Duties

During this inquiry-based set of activities, the teacher sets the stage and selects the student groups that will participate in the activities. The teacher decides the issue to be studied, selects the activities, gives the directions, and sets up the problematic situations. He or she acts as a catalyst, encouraging students to propose hypotheses and to analyze the validity of previously gained personal and academic knowledge. By offering suggestions for problem solving and for shaping the learning cycle itself, he or she also encourages the students to reflect on the process. The teacher's job is to nurture divergent solutions and to help students to recognize and expand their ability to think critically. In *Piaget for Educators* (1990), Bybee observed that

[m]any educators are confronted with the task of facilitating development from concrete to formal levels of thought. To do so requires educators to understand the major differences between the two stages. Since both concrete and formal periods are concerned with logical thought, what are some basic differences between the periods? There are two differences. In the formal operational period, mental action no longer requires actual objects, events, or situations. For . . . students [at the concrete level], the realm of the real is possible. For formal students, the realm of the possible is real. (135)

Because any inquiry-based strategy is a complicated style of learning, the learning cycle format is not one to be used every day. For the teacher, planning a series of flexible activities requires a complex set of decisions. This learning format should be used when a complicated, controversial historical issue is to be studied, when the issue is crucial to course content, and when the teacher wants

---

FIGURE 2
Logic and Mutual Benefit Tests

The Logic Test:	All proposed solutions to the problem must rest on factual evidence, previous knowledge and experience, and logical reasoning; emotional responses unsubstantiated by logical decision making will not be allowed.
The Mutual Benefit Test:	Any solution must be agreed upon by all members of the group and must show evidence of some degree of benefit for all members of the group.

---

the students to construct their own knowledge. The maturity level and prior knowledge of the students are also considerations when choosing a specific historical issue (Clark and Starr 1991).

The plan described here targets the issue of conflict, specifically in the context of World War I; the problems and conditions leading to war; and alternatives to armed conflict. To have the students consider the issue, the teacher first employs the concept of the family structure as a microcosmic example of the large-scale balance of power clashes leading up to the outbreak of World War I. The roles in Phase 1 are appropriate for juniors and seniors because students at that level generally have experience as wage earners and as consumers, have siblings or have friends who do, and are usually involved in both concrete and abstract thinking processes.

Phase 1: Exploration

The first phase demands that the students use prior knowledge and experience to solve a problem or series of problems. Students are clustered into groups of four to carry out a simulation game in which the students in each group act as siblings. The game encourages the students to experience conflict and come to consensus regarding balance of power, territorial allocations, work, and economic resources. In other words, it allows a complicated issue to be explored in a simplified way. Martorella (1991) noted that simulations "enable many students to relate easily to and become highly interested in a problem that they might not otherwise take very seriously. Furthermore, they allow students to assume control over their own learning and to be less dependent on the teacher" (225). The teacher structures the exploration by preparing a simulation that examines the concepts to be developed throughout the learning cycle.

To set up a simulation that will illustrate conflicts over territory, employment, economic resources, and balance

---

FIGURE 1
The Learning Cycle

Phase 1: Exploration	Students address a problem, make hypotheses, and predict solutions.
Phase 2: Discussion and Presentation of New Content	Students and the teacher discuss the result of Phase 1; the teacher introduces new concepts through a mini lecture.
Phase 3: Application and Expansion	Students use knowledge gained from Phases 1 and 2 to address a new problem.

of power, the teacher assigns roles to each of the four members of the group; the roles are defined as any combination of brothers and sisters, aged 17, 13, 9, and 5, who live with their parents in a two-bedroom apartment. Using the logic and mutual benefit guidelines (figure 2), the brothers and sisters must come to consensus on three problems: allocation of space, assignment of work, and allocation of economic resources.

This simulation should generate varying levels of controversy as the students recognize that their own ideas, needs, opinions, and conclusions are not necessarily compatible with those of others in the group. Students gain practice in engaging in and resolving controversy—essential skills for citizens in a democratic society. Each person in the group works for positive compromise that will permit the members to move forward with the most benefit to each (Martorella 1991).

Phase 2: Discussion and Presentation of New Content

Phase 2 of this learning cycle has three main components:

- The students share their proposed solutions.
- The students describe the conflicts they experienced in their groups and the strategies they used to come to consensus.
- The teacher introduces new content relative to the historical issue that then will be analyzed in Phase 3.

The second phase uses guided discussion and the lecture format to examine student solutions to the simulation game. The class also discusses the group dynamics that they have just experienced. These discussions require "the greatest attention and guidance on the teacher's part to ensure productive and meaningful results" (Martorella 1991, 224). This phase thus begins with each group reporting its solutions to the three problems while the teacher outlines the elements of each group's solutions on the board (thereby creating a visual display of the acceptability of divergent solutions). Each solution is scrutinized by the class according to the logic and mutual benefit tests. The teacher then poses questions that explore the conflicts that can arise when people decide on territorial problems, employment and work, and economic concerns. He or she asks the students about the dynamics of the group decision-making progress, pointing out that power can be used to benefit or disrupt group decision making. The teacher addresses the shifting of the balance of power within each group and the personalities in the groups and their impact on the struggle to reach consensus.

The use of the learning cycle can clarify students' thought processes and correct their misconceptions. The students have the opportunity to explain, to argue, and to debate their ideas. "This process can result in disequilibrium and the possibility of developing more adequate concepts and patterns of reasoning" (Trowbridge and By-

bee 1990, 306). The discussion period in Phase 2 requires the highest levels of critical thinking as students respond to open-ended teacher questions "that call for the application of individual values, that encourage personal input, and that require the student to make decisions related to attitudes, outlooks, and personal beliefs" (Mumford 1991, 194). The teacher encourages the development of student frames of thinking with questions such as the following:

- Why did you divide your room in that manner?
- What factors led you to decide on that arrangement?
- What must you be illustrating about your beliefs concerning the roles of smaller children in a family?
- What power struggles did you face during the attempt to reach consensus?
- What did those struggles reveal about the use of power in family decision making?
- How did the arrangement made by your group conform to the mutual benefit test?
- What is the value of applying the logic and mutual benefit tests to family decision making?
- How do those tests help to balance out the effect of power on your family's decision-making process?

Such questions help the students make connections, pursue logical thought processes, and recognize how their individual values, attitudes, and personal beliefs shape their decisions.

Using the lecture format, the teacher then introduces concepts such as territorialism, expansionism, employment, wages, economic and natural resource factors, tilting the balance of power, the struggle for economic dominance of power, and mediation strategies. He or she then draws parallels between the family controversy microcosm and the macrocosmic controversies that lead to worldwide conflict, at the same time introducing concepts related to conflict between nations, such as imperialism, nationalism, industrial growth, colonialism, and milita-

---

FIGURE 3
Historical Antecedents of World War I

1389	The Ottoman Empire conquers Serbia.
1850–1914	Europe experiences the pinnacle of nationalism.
1862–1890	Bismarck dominates European affairs.
1890	Kaiser Wilhelm ascends to power, demanding that Bismarck resign.
1912	Serbia gains independence from Turkish rule, yet many Serbs live in territories (e.g., Bosnia) ruled by Austria-Hungary.
1914	Archduke Ferdinand is assassinated on June 28.

FIGURE 4
Treaties Showing Interactions and Shifting Relationships of Nations Prior to World War I

1881	Bismarck signs an alliance with Austria-Hungary and Russia.
1882	The Triple Alliance of Germany, Austria-Hungary, and Italy is formed.
1894	Wilhelm reaffirms the alliance with Austria-Hungary and Italy but excludes Russia.
1894	France and Russia sign an alliance creating a rival block.
1904	France signs the *Entente Cordiale* with Great Britain, leading to close military and diplomatic ties.
1907	Great Britain signs an alliance with Russia.
1905–1911	Competition for colonies brings Germany and France to the brink of war.
1912	Balkan states attack the Ottoman Empire.

rism. The teacher explains how historical antecedents influence personalities and events (figure 3). He or she also reviews treaties made prior to the war, demonstrating the interactions and shifting relationships that occurred among the affected nations (figure 4).

Phase 3: Application and Expansion

Phase 3 of the learning cycle requires the students to apply the knowledge, skills, and insights acquired in Phases 1 and 2 to a new situation or to creatively extend their knowledge into new areas of exploration. It also challenges misconceptions and assists students in the expansion of their preconceptual understanding of selected concepts.

This particular plan calls for students with newfound insights to analyze conditions and events occurring in Germany, France, and England from 1900 to 1913 related to territorialism, employment, availability of economic and natural resources, personalities, and attempts at mediation. The students' goal is to determine the causes for World War I.

Pondering these issues, small groups of students engage in research to create a composite picture of the major powers, describing their national agendas, nationalistic divisiveness, colonial expansion into Africa and the Pacific Islands; the dynamics among the nations; and each country's perception of its own power, reputation, and competitiveness. After the groups present their composite descriptions to the class, the analysis of divergent solutions

begins. In their small groups, students must come up with viable alternative solutions that meet the logic and mutual benefit tests, solutions that might have been employed to resolve the conflicts related to territory, employment, economics, and balance of power that precipitated the outbreak of international armed conflict in 1914. As a final activity, each group proposes its alternative solutions. The students and teacher discuss each proposal, analyzing its strengths and possible weaknesses. The learning cycle ends with the whole class coming to a consensus as to the best solutions offered.

Conclusion

Inquiry lessons that encourage students to develop their own frames of thought are complicated and time consuming to plan but extremely effective in the classroom. They give teachers a way to personalize and contextualize the great forces of history in such a manner that students can relate the importance of a historical issue to their own lives. Thus, learning about history becomes a personally interesting and deeply internalized experience.

REFERENCES

Bybee, R. W. 1990. *Piaget for educators.* 2nd ed. Prospect Heights, Ill.: Waveland Press.

Clark, L. H., and I. S. Starr. 1991. *Secondary and middle school teaching methods.* 6th ed. New York: Macmillan.

Johnson, J. A., V. L. Dupuis, D. Murial, G. E. Hall, and D. M. Gollnick. 1996. *Introduction to the foundations of American education.* 3rd ed. Boston: Allyn and Bacon.

Martorella, P. H. 1991. *Teaching social studies in middle and secondary schools.* New York: Macmillan.

Trowbridge, L. W., and R. W. Bybee. 1990. *Becoming a secondary school science teacher.* Columbus: Merrill.

SUGGESTED READINGS

Boorstin, D., and B. M. Kelley. 1990. *A history of the United States since 1861.* Englewood Cliffs, N.J.: Prentice-Hall.

Ellis, E. G., and A. Esler. 1997. *World history: Connections to today.* Englewood Cliffs, N.J.: Prentice-Hall.

Henson, K. T. 1993. *Methods and strategies for teaching in secondary and middle schools.* 2nd ed. White Plains, N.Y.: Longman.

Johnson, D. W., and R. T. Johnson. 1988. Critical thinking through structured controversy. *Educational Leadership* 45:58–64.

Kim, E. C., and R. D. Kellough. 1991. *A resource guide for secondary school teaching: Planning for competencies.* 5th ed. New York: Macmillan.

Levine, J. M. 1989. *Secondary instruction: A manual for classroom teaching.* Boston: Allyn and Bacon.

Mary M. Bevevino is a professor of education, Joan Dengel is an associate professor of education, and Kenneth Adams is an associate professor of education, all at Edinboro University of Pennsylvania.

The Challenges of Sustaining a Constructivist Classroom Culture

Illustration by John Berry

Mr. Windschitl sees articulating these challenges as a significant step in helping educators create and sustain a classroom culture that values diversity in learning and offers a new vision of the roles of teachers and learners—the culture of constructivism.

BY MARK WINDSCHITL

MS. HUGHES' sixth-grade classroom is a noisy place, and if you come to visit you may have a hard time finding her. Today, students are clustered in small groups, bent over note cards and diagrams they have assembled in order to determine whether they can design a habitat that can support Australian dingoes and marmosets.

The students have just participated in three days of discussion and reading about interrelationships among mammals. They are divided into four groups, each of which has negotiated with Ms. Hughes to devise a complex problem to work on that reflects their interests and abilities. One group chose a design problem: creating a habitat for a local zoo that will support at least three kinds of mammals naturally found in the same geographic area.

> # Constructivism is a culture— not a fragmented collection of practices.

The students are now engaged for the next two weeks on this project. They find and share dozens of resources, many of which are spread out on tables and on the floor around the room. Allen brings to class a video he shot at the zoo last week so that everyone can see what different habitats look like. Michelle loads a CD-ROM on mammals that she brought from home, and James donates one of his mother's landscape architecture books for ideas on how to diagram spaces and buildings.

During the next two weeks, these students will develop an understanding of how mammal species interact with one another, cope with the environment, and follow the natural cycles of reproduction. Concepts such as "competition for resources" and "reproductive capacity"—whose definitions in other classes might have been memorized—arise instead from a meaningful and multifaceted context. These concepts are built on the experiences of the students and are essential, interconnected considerations in the success of the habitat design. This is one of the many faces of the constructivist classroom.

A growing number of teachers are embracing the fundamental ideas of constructivist learning—that their students' background knowledge profoundly affects how they interpret subject matter and that students learn best when they apply their knowledge to solve authentic problems, engage in "sense-making" dialogue with peers, and strive for deep understanding of core ideas rather than recall of a laundry list of facts. Unfortunately, much of the public conversation about constructivism has been stalled on its philosophical contrasts with more traditional approaches to instruction. Constructivists have offered varying descriptions of how classrooms can be transformed, usually framed in terms of these contrasts. And although these descriptions have prompted educators to reexamine the roles of teachers, the ways in which students learn best, and even what it means to learn, the image of what is possible in constructivist classrooms remains too idealized.

To all the talk about theory, educators must add layers of dialogue about real classroom experiences and concerns about those experiences. An essential part of this dialogue is the articulation of the pedagogical, logistical, and political challenges that face educators who are willing to integrate constructivism into their classroom practice. The new discourse shifts the emphasis from comparisons between constructivism and traditional instruction to the refinement of constructivist practices in real classrooms. This frank conversation about challenges is equally valuable for sympathetic administrators—being informed and reflective about these issues is a necessary prerequisite to offering support for the classroom teacher.

In this article, I characterize and categorize these challenges and describe the kinds of administrative support necessary to create and sustain a culture of constructivist teaching in schools. First, however, it is necessary to examine constructivism as a philosophy on which a systemic classroom culture can be based rather than to view it as a set of discrete instructional practices that may be inserted into the learning environment whenever necessary. The challenges I describe here are challenges precisely because they cause us to reconsider and dare us to change the comfortable (and often unstated) norms, beliefs, and practices of the classroom culture we are so familiar with. Constructivism is more than a set of teaching techniques; it is a coherent pattern of expectations that underlie new relationships between students, teachers, and the world of ideas.

Constructivism as Culture

Constructivism is premised on the belief that learners actively create, interpret, and reorganize knowledge in individual ways. These fluid intellectual transformations occur when students reconcile formal instructional experiences with their existing knowledge, with the cultural and social contexts in which ideas occur, and with a host of other influences that serve to mediate understanding. With respect to instruction, this belief suggests that students should participate in experiences that accommodate these ways of learning. Such experiences include problem-based learning, inquiry activities, dialogues with peers and teachers that encourage making sense of the subject matter, exposure to multiple sources of information, and opportunities for students to demonstrate their understanding in diverse ways.

However, before teachers and administrators adopt such practices, they should understand that constructivism cannot make its appearance in the classroom as a set of isolated instructional methods grafted on to otherwise traditional teaching techniques. Rather, it is a culture—a set of beliefs, norms, and practices that constitute the fabric of school life. This culture, like all other cultures, affects the way learners can interact with peers, relate to the teacher, and experience the subject matter. The children's relationships with teachers, their patterns of communication, how they are assessed, and even their notion of "what learning is good for" must all be connected, or the culture risks becoming a fragmented collection of practices that fail to reinforce one another. For example, the constructivist belief that learners are capable of intellectual autonomy must coincide with the belief that students possess a large knowledge base of life experiences and have made sense out of much of what they have experienced. These beliefs are linked with the practice of problem-based learning within relevant and authentic contexts and with the norm of showing mutual respect for one another's ideas in the classroom.

Portraying the constructivist classroom as a culture is important because many challenges for the teacher emerge when new rituals take root or when familiar norms of behavior are transformed into new patterns of teacher/student interaction.[1] By contrast, if discrete practices that have been associated with constructivism (cooperative learning, performance assessments, hands-on experiences) are simply inserted as special activities into the regular school day, then it remains business as usual for the students. Teachers and students do not question their vision of learning, no one takes risks, and hardly a ripple is felt.

Throughout this article then, challenges become apparent when we question the fundamental norms of the classroom—the images and beliefs we hold of teachers and students, the kinds of discourse encouraged in the classroom, the way authority and decision making are controlled, and even what

"counts" as learning. I begin with a subtle but powerful influence on classroom instruction.

Images of Teaching: The Chains That Bind Us

Most of us are products of traditional instruction; as learners, we were exposed to teacher-centered instruction, fact-based subject matter, and a steady diet of drill and practice.[2] Our personal histories furnish us with mental models of teaching, and these models of how we were taught shape our behavior in powerful ways. Teachers use these models to imagine lessons in their classrooms, develop innovations, and plan for learning.[3] These images serve to organize sets of beliefs and guide curricular actions.[4] Teachers are more likely to be guided not by instructional theories but by the familiar images of what is "proper and possible" in classroom settings.[5]

Unfortunately, the signs and symbols of teacher-centered education and learning by transmission, which are likely to be a part of teachers' personal histories, persist in classrooms today.[6] In this environment, it is assumed that the more quiet and orderly the classrooms are, the more likely it is that learning is taking place. Individual desks face the front of the room, where the teacher occupies a privileged space of knowing authority; students work individually on identical, skill-based assignments to ensure uniformity of learning. Value statements are embedded everywhere in this environment.

Constructivist teachers envision themselves emerging boldly from the confines of this traditional classroom culture, but the vision first requires critical reflection. Teachers must ask themselves, "Is my role to dispense knowledge or to nurture independent thinkers? How do I show respect for the ideas of the students? Am I here to learn from the students?" Teachers must struggle to develop a new, well-articulated rationale for instructional decisions

and cannot depend on their previous teaching or learning experiences for much help in shaping their choice of methods; shifting the centers of authority and activity in accordance with this rationale requires persistence. For example, teachers can be uncomfortable with their apparent lack of control as students engage with their peers during learning activities and may be unwilling to allow supervisors who visit the classroom to observe this kind of environment. Teachers may reconsider their ideas of student-centered learning in favor of conforming to the more traditional images of the teacher as the hub of classroom discourse and attention.[7]

New Demands on the Teacher

Constructivist instruction, especially that which is based on design tasks or problem solving, places high demands on the teacher's subject-matter understanding. The teacher must not only be familiar with the principles underlying a topic of study but must also be prepared for the variety of ways these principles can be explored.

For example, if students are studying density in science class, the teacher must support the understanding of one group of students who want to approach the concept from a purely abstract, mathematical perspective as they construct tables, equations, and graphs to develop their knowledge. In this case, the teacher must understand these different representations of information and how they are interrelated. Another group of students may plan to recount the story of the Titanic, emphasizing the role that density played in the visibility of the iceberg, the ballast of the ship, and the sinking itself. Here, the teacher must be intellectually agile, able to apply his or her mathematical understanding of density to a real-life, inevitably more complex situation.

Teachers in different subject areas may allow students varying degrees of latitude in exploring content and will differ in how they accept student "constructions" of core curricular ideas. Mathematics is characterized by rule-based propositions and skills that may be open to discovery via many experiential pathways. Most forms of mathematics problems, however, have only one right answer. And if students are allowed to explore problems by their own methods, teachers may find it difficult to see exactly how the students are making sense of the problem-solving process—not all constructions are created equal. Science and social studies present the same challenges, although science is less axiomatic than mathematics, and the issues explored in social studies are open to wider interpretation. Dealing with the "correctness" of student constructions is an ongoing concern, and the arguments have barely been introduced here, but reflection on these issues helps teachers develop a critical awareness of disciplinary "truths" and the viability of various ways of knowing the world.

Crafting instruction based on constructivism is not as straightforward as it seems.

In addition to the necessity for flexible subject-matter knowledge, constructivism places greater demands on teachers' pedagogical skill. Crafting instruction based on constructivism is not as straight-

forward as it seems. Educators struggle with how specific instructional techniques (e.g., lecture, discussion, cooperative learning, problem-based learning, inquiry learning) fit into the constructivist model of instruction. Regardless of the particular techniques used in instruction, students will always construct and reorganize knowledge rather than simply assimilate information from teachers or textbooks. The question is not whether to use lecture or discussion, but how to use these techniques to complement rather than dominate student thinking. For example, constructivist principles suggest that students should experience the ideas, phenomena, and artifacts of a discipline before being exposed to formal explanations of them. Students might begin units of instruction in science class by manipulating a pendulum, in math class by constructing polygons, or in social studies by reading letters from Civil War battlefields. Only after these experiences do teachers and students together suggest terminology, explanations, and conceptual organization.

Even though designing instruction is important, constructivist teaching is less about the sequencing of events and more about responding to the needs of a situation.[8] Teachers must employ a sophisticated range of strategies to support individual students' understandings as they engage in the problem-based activities that characterize constructivist classrooms. These strategies include scaffolding, in which the task required of the learner is strategically reduced in complexity; modeling, in which the teacher either thinks aloud about or acts out how she would approach a problem; and coaching, guiding, and advising, which are loosely defined as providing learners with suggestions of varying degrees of explicitness.[9] The teacher is challenged to select the proper strategy and implement it with skill.

Problem-based activities exemplify another core value of the construc-

tivist culture—collaboration. Students are witness to and participate in one another's thinking. Learners are exposed to the clear, cogent thinking of some peers as well as to the inevitable meandering, unreflective thought of others. Students do require training to function effectively in these groups.[10] However, even with training, many capable students are simply not interested in helping their peers, and negative consequences of group work—such as bickering, exclusion, and academic freeloading—are common.[11] These consequences can be minimized if the teacher is familiar with the principles of cooperative learning. And so, having students work together requires that the teacher have additional competencies in cooperative learning strategies and management skills particular to decentralized learning environments.

A final pedagogical challenge involves independent student projects. Depending on the degree of structure the teacher imposes in a classroom, students will have some latitude in choosing problems or design projects that relate to the theme under study. Often, students determine with the teacher suitable criteria for problems and for evidence of learning. Negotiation about criteria prompts questions such as: Is the problem meaningful? Important to the discipline? Complex enough? Does it relate to the theme under study? Does it require original thinking and interpretation, or is it simply fact finding? Will the resolution of this problem help us acquire the concepts and principles fundamental to the theme under study? Because curricular materials are often filled with prepared questions and tasks, teachers seldom have occasion to introduce their students to this idea of "problems about problems." Clearly, teachers must develop their own ability to analyze problems by reflecting on the nature of the discipline and refining their ideas through extended dialogue with colleagues and experiences with students.

Logistical and Political Challenges

Effective forms of constructivist instruction call for major changes in the curriculum, in scheduling, and in assessment.[12] When students are engaged in problem solving and are allowed to help guide their own learning, teachers quickly find that this approach outgrows the 50-minute class period. This situation often means that the teacher will have to negotiate with administrators and other teachers about the possibilities of block scheduling and integrating curricula. If teachers can team with partners from other subject areas, they can extend the length of their class periods and develop more comprehensive themes for study that bridge the worlds of science, social studies, math, and the arts.

The purpose of integrated curricula and extended class periods is to allow students to engage in learning activities that will help them develop deep and elaborate understandings of subject matter. These understandings may be quite different in nature from student to student. Thus there is a need for forms of assessment that allow students to demonstrate what they know and that connect with rigorous criteria of excellence. These are not the paper-and-pencil, objective tests in which learners recognize rather than generate answers or create brief responses to questions in which they have little personal investment. Rather, students are required to produce journals, research reports, physical models, or performances in the forms of plays, debates, dances, or other artistic representations. Assessing these products and performances requires well-designed, flexible rubrics to maintain a link between course objectives and student learning. Designing these rubrics (through negotiation with students) builds consensus about what "purpose" means in a learning activity, about the nature of meaningful criteria, and about how assessments reflect the efficacy of the teacher as a promoter of understanding.

The final and perhaps most politically sensitive issue confronting teachers is that the diversity of understandings emerging from constructivist instruction does not always seem compatible with state and local standards. For example, student groups engaged in science projects on photosynthesis may have radically different approaches to developing their understanding of this phenomenon. One group may choose to focus on chemical reactions at the molecular level while another group may examine how oxygen and carbon dioxide are exchanged between animals and plants on a global scale. These two groups will take disconcertingly divergent paths to understanding photosynthesis.

This kind of project-based learning must be skillfully orchestrated so that, however students choose to investigate and seek resolutions to problems, they will acquire an understanding of key principles and concepts as well as the critical thinking skills that are assessed on standardized tests. Proponents of project-based learning have demonstrated that these kinds of learning outcomes are entirely possible.[13] Artful guidance by the teacher notwithstanding, it can be unsettling for teachers to reconcile the language of "objectives, standards, and benchmarks" with the diversity of understandings that emerge in a constructivist classroom.

Conclusions and Recommendations

How does a school community support the instructional expertise, academic freedom, and professional collaboration necessary to sustain a constructivist culture? First, a core group of committed teachers must systematically investigate constructivism in order to understand its principles and its limitations. The ideas behind constructivism seem intuitive and sensible, but teachers and administrators must go beyond the hyperbole and the one-shot-workshop acquaintance with constructivism. Interested faculty members should conduct a thorough reading campaign, and at least one or two teachers should extend their experience by participating in advanced workshops, attending classes, and witnessing how constructivist cultures operate in other schools. Stipends and released time can be provided for a cadre of lead teachers to attend classes, do extra reading, adapt curriculum, and offer their own workshops to fellow teachers. Workshop topics could include the constructivist implementation of cooperative learning, scaffolding techniques, problem-based learning, or multifaceted assessment strategies.

The faculty members must openly discuss their beliefs about learners and about their roles as teachers. If these beliefs are left unexamined or unchallenged, then individuals have feeble grounding for their personal philosophies. Just as problematically then, everyone operates on different, untested assumptions. And all decisions about curriculum, instruction, and assessment are built on such assumptions.

Personal philosophies of education are particularly important when constructivism is used to furnish underlying principles—important because constructivism means risk taking and a divergence from business as usual. Sooner or later, teachers will be asked, "Why do you teach that way?" Whatever form that question takes, teachers must be able to justify the choices they make. This task will not be as intimidating if the teacher has mindfully linked the aspects of his or her constructivist philosophy to the various dimensions of classroom experience and to the larger goals of education.

The process of making these beliefs explicit can also strengthen teachers' resolve to move beyond the traditional images of what is proper and possible in the classroom. It can make clear to them the characteristics and limitations of the system that encouraged images of teachers as dispensers of information and students as passive recipients of knowledge. Accordingly, teachers must try to arrive at a new vision of their role. This vision must include serving as a facilitator of learning who responds to students' needs with a flexible understanding of subject matter and a sensitivity to how the student is making sense of the world.

Teachers and their principals must be prepared to go on record with these beliefs in discussions with parent groups and the school board. Educators should always have a rationale for what and how they teach; however, because constructivism is so contrary to historical norms, it is even more important in this case that the rationale be well founded, coherent, and applicable to the current school context. Community members will undoubtedly be suspicious of teaching methods that are so different from the ones they remember as students and that sound too much like a laissez-faire approach to learning.

Administrators must also take the lead in supporting a "less is more" approach. The compulsion to cover material is antithetical to the aim of constructivist instruction—the deep and elaborate understanding of selected core ideas. Textbooks, which are often the de facto curriculum, have become encyclopedic, and administrators should make teachers feel secure about using a variety of other resources. They should also provide funds to purchase alternative classroom materials. Furthermore, ad-

ministrators must be open to suggestions for block scheduling and for integrating curricula, perhaps even arranging for interested teachers to be placed together in team-teaching situations that are premised on the constructivist approach.

To strengthen the school's position on accountability, assessment specialists who understand constructivism can be brought in to connect local standards with instruction and with evidence that learning is taking place. Teachers will undoubtedly appreciate assistance in investigating and evaluating a variety of assessment strategies.

The list of challenges I have described here is not exhaustive. There are certainly others, and the challenges outnumber the solutions at the moment. But articulating these challenges is a significant step in helping educators create and sustain a classroom culture that values diversity in learning and offers a new vision of the roles of teachers and learners—the culture of constructivism.

Notes

1. Pam Bolotin-Joseph, "Understanding Curriculum as Culture," in Pam Bolotin-Joseph, Stevie Bravman, Mark Windschitl, Edward Mikel, and Nancy Green, eds., *Cultures of Curriculum* (Mahwah, N.J.: Erlbaum, forthcoming).
2. Thomas Russell, "Learning to Teach Science: Constructivism, Reflection, and Learning from Experience," in Kenneth Tobin, ed., *The Practice of Constructivism in Science Education* (Hillsdale, N.J.: Erlbaum, 1993), pp. 247–58.
3. Corby Kennison, "Enhancing Teachers' Professional Learning: Relationships Between School Culture and Elementary School Teachers' Beliefs, Images, and Ways of Knowing" (Specialist's thesis, Florida State University, 1990).
4. Kenneth Tobin, "Constructivist Perspectives on Teacher Learning," in idem, ed., pp. 215–26; and Kenneth Tobin and Sarah Ulerick, "An Interpretation of High School Science Teaching Based on Metaphors and Beliefs for Specific Roles," paper presented at the annual meeting of the American Educational Research Association, San Francisco, 1989.
5. Kenneth Zeichner and Robert Tabachnick, "Are the Effects of University Teacher Education Washed Out by School Experience?," *Journal of Teacher Education*, vol. 32, 1981, pp. 7–11.
6. Adriana Groisman, Bonnie Shapiro, and John Willinsky, "The Potential of Semiotics to Inform Understanding of Events in Science Education," *International Journal of Science Education*, vol. 13, 1991, pp. 217–26.
7. James H. Mosenthal and Deborah Ball, "Constructing New Forms of Teaching: Subject Matter Knowledge in Inservice Teacher Education," *Journal of Teacher Education*, vol. 43, 1992, pp. 347–56.
8. David Lebow, "Constructivist Values for Instructional Systems Design: Five Principles Toward a New Mindset," *Educational Technology, Research, and Development*, vol. 41, no. 3, 1993, pp. 4–16.
9. Jeong-Im Choi and Michael Hannafin, "Situated Cognition and Learning Environments: Roles, Structures, and Implications for Design," *Educational Technology, Research, and Development*, vol. 43, no. 2, 1995, pp. 53–69.
10. David W. Johnson, Roger T. Johnson, and Karl A. Smith, *Active Learning: Cooperation in the College Classroom* (Edina, Minn.: Interaction Book Company, 1991).
11. Robert E. Slavin, *Cooperative Learning* (Boston: Allyn and Bacon, 1995).
12. Phyllis Blumenfeld et al., "Motivating Project-Based Learning: Sustaining the Doing, Supporting the Learning," *Educational Psychologist*, vol. 26, 1991, pp. 369–98.
13. Ibid.9

MARK WINDSCHITL is an assistant professor of curriculum and instruction in the College of Education, University of Washington, Seattle.

Keeping in Character

A Time-Tested Solution

The positive outcomes of for-character education, the authors contend, counter such misleading pictures as the one sketched by Alfie Kohn in his February Kappan *article.*

BY JACQUES S. BENNINGA
AND EDWARD A. WYNNE

Illustration by Mario Noche

I N THE February 1997 *Kappan*, Alfie Kohn attacked modern character education for a myriad of alleged deficiencies. This essay constitutes our response to his criticisms. The basic structure of true "for-character" education relies on an approach that

- is relevant for students of all ages;
- has been time-tested and refined over 2,500 years;
- is as responsive to today's children as it was to yesterday's;
- has broad support among American citizens, including teachers and students; and

- has a research base to justify its continuation.

Increasing Disorder

Before we turn to particulars, it is important for readers to understand exactly why we and so many other American adults are worried about the character of the nation's youth. It is not, as Kohn implies, because we dislike young people. Instead, it is because

we love them and want them to stop killing and abusing themselves and one another at record rates.

Statistics document the record-breaking rates of distress afflicting young Americans and form an essential backdrop for any discussion of for-character practices. The annual rates of death of young (15- to 19-year-old) white males by homicide and suicide are at their highest points since national record-keeping began in 1914.[1] The rates of out-of-wedlock births to young (15- to 19-year-old) white females are also at or near their highest points since national record-keeping began in 1936. What's more, these high rates have occurred dur-

ANY FOR-CHARACTER

SCHOOL OR CLASSROOM

WILL INCLUDE

A NUMBER OF

FOR-CHARACTER

ACTIVITIES.

ing an era of generally more accessible contraception, abortion, and sex education. All these indicators focus on whites—members of our most advantaged group. This suggests that the "causes" for the bulk of the disorder only incidentally involve poverty and race.

As if we needed any more bad news, the Centers for Disease Control released an important report in February 1997. That report found that "nearly three-quarters of all the murders of children in the industrialized world occur in the United States" and that the U.S. has the "highest rates of childhood homicide, suicide, and firearms-related deaths of any of the world's 26 richest nations."[2]

All these relatively precise measures of disorder indirectly measure many other uncountable forms of profound despair, injury, and wrongdoing that affect the young.

- Most murders of young persons are committed by young murderers.
- Every identified young death by homicide undoubtedly subsumes many other less violent crimes, such as battery, woundings, and beatings.
- Out-of-wedlock births are also indices of victimization of vulnerable females by males or of risky acts of promiscuity.
- The suicides are also indicators of previously attempted suicides and other symptoms of deep depression.

High school students themselves are very well situated to see what is happening among their peers. They clearly recognize that many deeply flawed contemporary education policies have enmeshed our young in a disorderly, low-demand world—a world in which too many adults confuse being caring with being permissive. Recent evidence from a national sample of high school students shows that 50% of the respondents said that "schools fail to challenge pupils to do their best," 71% said that there were "too many disruptive students," 79% said that learning would im-

prove if "schools ensured students got their work done on time and completed their assignments," 86% said that schools should teach students the value of "hard work," 71% would require after-school classes for students who get D's and F's in major subjects, 73% said requiring exit tests before graduation would cause students to learn more, and 50% said that "too many students get away with being late to class or not doing their work."[3] As we will show, these student opinions are quite congruent with the for-character approach.

Some Qualifications

We have both done considerable research and writing on issues involving student character. For instance, each of us, acting separately and with the help of local educators, has organized school recognition programs, one in the Chicago area and the other in the Fresno area. These programs identify elementary and secondary schools that maintain exemplary character formation policies and curricula. Over 13 yearly cycles, approximately 400 elementary, middle, and secondary schools have participated in these programs. Thus we have examined a variety of good, bad, and indifferent for-character activities. From that base, after some important background information, we will assess Kohn's key contentions.

One other qualification should be expressed. Many of Kohn's criticisms are essentially aimed at the ambitious claims made for packaged character education curricula. We and many leading figures in the character education movement are not sanguine about expecting notable results from any such quick-fix approach.[4] However, well-conceived packages may be useful if they are part of a holistic school- or classroom-wide for-character approach. Indeed, it is to express our distance from quick-fix activities that we use the phrase "for-character education" rather than the more common "character education." Such use stresses the need to integrate for-character elements into many typical school activities. Thus there can be for-character policies, for-character cocurricular activities, and even for-character lunchroom policies. To further stress the issue of systematically planning for-character activities, one of the authors even published a list of 100 for-character activities that can be used in and around schools.[5] Though 100 is not a sacred number, the point is that any for-character school or classroom will include a number of for-character activities, most of which will be integrated into its day-to-day operations.

Character and For-Character Education

The word *character* derives from the Greek word "to mark" or "to engrave" and is associated with the writings of philosophers such as Plato and Aristotle.

People with good character habitually display good behavior, and these people are known by their behavior. Thus a generous person may be seen giving notable gifts, or a brave person may perform heroic acts. A courteous person behaves properly and with civility toward others.

There may be no specific consensus on a list of desirable character traits or habits. But considerable agreement exists on the desirable virtues—moral qualities regarded as good or meritorious—that underlie these traits. Throughout history thoughtful philosophers and educators have been concerned about the cultivation of such virtues as honesty, kindness, courage, perseverance, and loyalty and about the cultivation of their concomitant traits. The renewed interest in such virtues is evident in the huge success of *The Book of Virtues,* by William Bennett. The book is a collection of inspiring classic literature for children and adults. It addresses 10 particular virtues. In recent years, we have also witnessed the publication of a spate of nonsectarian character-oriented books by psychologists, educators, and distinguished scholars.[6]

The consensus is that traits—and, to some degree, virtues—are not innate. They must be acquired through learning and practice in homes, schools, neighborhoods, churches, and other agencies. They must be transmitted to be internalized. However, a child's state of mind *is* relevant to this process. That is, for-character educators do not advocate having children behave solely according to a set of principles or rules without understanding them. Rather, for-character educators agree with William Frankena, who proposed that "we regard the morality of principles and the morality of traits of character, or being and doing, not as rival kinds of morality between which we must choose, but as two complimentary aspects of the same morality."[7]

The character tradition stresses the importance of whole environments operating systematically to foster good character formation. But environments mean not only the physical elements surrounding students, but also the people surrounding them, the good or bad examples they provide, and the expectations they establish. Profound character education involves managing classrooms or whole schools so that they will advance student character.

Here is where Alfie Kohn missed the mark. His criticisms extend far beyond the defects of relying solely on packages. He takes offense because for-character educators have developed a perspective, a "particular style of moral training." And it is true that there are good and bad ways to teach character. Kohn then proposes his alternative to character education. Let us, in his words, get straight to the educational point. His alternative is a set of various approaches that we have met before, collected under the umbrella of developmental education. The umbrella currently includes such panaceas as the whole-language approach, constructivism, and, most recently, democratic education. These approaches have already been tried in our own era, without generating either "good people" or notable academic learning.[8]

True, the policies have attractive labels. But such labels are deceptive. Who, for example, could be against democratic education? Yet such ambiguous labels are riddled with inconsistencies that foreclose careful analysis. For example, many educators now favor emotive terminology, such as "educating for democracy," without being able to define or evaluate the policies advocated to advance such ends. Various notions, such as self-esteem education and inclusion, are now contained in the "democratic education" package. Few of these programs have undergone rigorous evaluation to determine their effects, and, when they have been evaluated, the results often fail to support their ambitious claims.

But that doesn't seem to matter to some. In the words of educational theorist Amy Guttman, democratic education "commits us to accepting nondiscriminatory and nonrepressive policies as legitimate even when they are wrong."[9] Even when such practices lead to lower academic achievement, she states, they are necessary to advance the "virtues of citizenship," and even when student participation threatens to produce disorder within schools, it may be defended on "democratic grounds."[10]

These conceptions of democracy are probably not what America's founders had in mind two centuries ago, but they seem to be exactly what Alfie Kohn believes. That is, he wants us to engage elementary school children in "deep, critical reflection about certain ways of being"; to teach reflection over diligence, respect, patriotism, and responsibility; to teach self-determination and skepticism over self-control and obedience. He does not suggest where skepticism should begin or end. Still, he is at least skeptical about patriotism: he compares the Pledge of Allegiance to the Flag to a form of "loyalty oath to the Fatherland" (with its obvious Nazi overtones). It would seem consistent with such cynicism to approve as well of 10-year-olds' skepticism toward their parents, although wiser students may choose to reserve their skepticism for persons who recommend such questionable doctrines.

The Five Questions

Kohn poses five basic questions that might be asked of character education programs. In answer to the first question—"At what level are problems addressed?"—Kohn reiterates the liberal argument that crime and urban decay are political outcomes of unemployment and the consolidation of great wealth in the hands of the few. These "bad things" are the cause of any character problems our young people might have. In other words, "It's all someone else's fault!" Our reply is brief, since we are neither criminologists nor economists—but neither, we believe, is Kohn.

- The data we have already cited on steadily rising youth disorder dealt just with whites. Presumably, such a group, even though afflicted with disorder, is not composed of poor inner-city residents.

- The long-term economic trends affecting most young white Americans involve economic improvements over their parents. Our college students, when we ask them for a show of hands on such matters, usually agree that they will be better off than their parents regarding such things as length of education, quality of housing, length of life span, and quality of health. It appears that the long-term increase in disorder is not caused by the spread of grinding poverty.

- The causal connection, if any, between crime and personal income is actually hotly debated. As James Wilson and Richard Herrnstein have emphasized, the overall statistical relationship between crime and the unemployment rate is not very strong.[11] Though many criminals may be poorly educated and are often unemployed, the factors underlying the development of the criminal personality are more complicated.

View of Human Nature

Next, Kohn addresses for-character's view of human nature. And surprise, the for-character educators do not see everything as sweetness and roses. "Fix-the-kids," say prominent for-character educators, who take a "dim view of human nature" (William Kilpatrick), who hold a "pessimistic view of human nature" (Edward Wynne), who say that "children are self-centered" (Kevin Ryan), and who seek to "control [children's] impulses and defer [their] gratification" (Amitai Etzioni).

Kohn is absolutely right! We are horrified and distressed at the harm so many young people are doing to themselves and to one another. We also desperately want to change the destructive conduct of many young people—to protect them and their possible victims. As for being anti-youth, our opinions and prescriptions are generally similar to those approved by young people themselves, as reported in the national high school student poll quoted near the beginning of this article. Are the students also anti-youth?

If modern for-character educators are not utopian in their attitudes toward children, they certainly are not alone. In a recent national survey of American

adults, 72% of the respondents said there was an excess of "drugs and violence in their local schools." When the responses were broken down by race, the comparable figures were 58% (whites) and 80% (blacks).[12] Are the blacks who think there's too much violence in their children's schools also anti-youth?

There are important historic precedents for our current concerns. Many of history's best minds have realized that most children and adults don't naturally set about "doing good for intrinsic reasons," as Kohn would suggest. A revealing dialogue from Plato's *Republic* (Book II) is instructive. Glaucon, a character in *The Republic,* maintains in a discussion with Socrates that it is natural for people to pursue their own interests despite the needs of others or the need for an orderly society. As evidence, Glaucon tells the story of Gyges, an otherwise rather decent shepherd. Gyges found a magic ring that enabled him to become invisible. The result? Gyges "seduced the queen and with her help attacked and murdered the king and seized the throne."[13] Of course, the tale of Gyges is a story—all made up. However, does anyone doubt the psychological truth of the ring story? When people receive uncontrolled power, there is a real possibility that they will abuse it. Or, as James Madison put it, "If men were angels, no government would be necessary."

Similarly, Horace Mann, the founder of public education in the U.S., believed that "moral education is a primal necessity of social existence. The unrestrained passions of men are not only homicidal, but suicidal."[14] But contrary to what Kohn would surmise, Mann hoped to form a literate, diligent, productive, and responsible citizenry committed to the conception that the best society was one in which people governed themselves through elected officials and representative institutions. Both Aristotle and Plato advocated a curriculum of music, literature, mathematics, and gymnastics that would result in a "well-balanced and harmonious character."

It would certainly be wrong to characterize these men or the contemporary for-character educators mentioned by Kohn as promoting a totalitarian educational agenda based on their conceptions of an unschooled human nature. To the contrary, it seems more reasonable to conclude that the current for-character perspective represents the collective and rather consistent perspective of the best minds of the past 2,500 years. Such a conclusion seems more promising than the utopian, New Age perspective proposed by Kohn.

Furthermore, the Founders of our nation, from their extensive reading of history, concluded that the greatest threat to democracy was the danger of tyranny that might evolve from the failure of powerful men to meet their civic responsibilities. To prevent such destructive patterns, citizens had to possess such virtues as self-discipline, responsibility, and prudence. Lacking such virtuous citizens, any democracy would gradually decay into a morass of selfishness and jealousy.

John Adams and his wife Abigail exemplified this "republican virtue" in their role as parents. Adams, absent for long periods from his family, wrote to his wife, "Train [our children] to virtue. Habituate them to industry, activity, and spirit."[15] Similarly, George Washington compiled and learned early a set of 110 "Rules of Civility and Decent Behavior in Company and Conversation," which thereafter governed his private behavior and tempered his impulsiveness.[16] The models left us by these men are still worth emulating.

Rather than holding a dark, bleak vision of human nature, these leaders had purpose and courage in the face of danger and suffering. They were indifferent to material circumstances and believed that their legacies would consist of the good and virtuous lives they lived. It is understandable that some citizens in our hedonistic and pedestrian era (What is the going price for a night in Lincoln's bed?) have trouble interpreting their heroic stoicism. Still, we owe it to our young people to try and hold high models up before them. Kohn has missed the point here.

The Ultimate Goal

Kohn next attacks for-character educators for their "profoundly conservative, if not reactionary, agenda." Rather than teach the virtuous life, he wants educators to train children as "advocates for social justice." Rather than set standards for behavior, he wants educators to promote skepticism in children. Rather than, as Aristotle suggested, "learning that there are things which one is expected to do even when all concerned are aware that one does not feel like doing them . . . [and] that there are things worth doing and aiming for which are not immediately pleasant,"[17] Kohn wants us to emphasize "the cultivation of autonomy so that children come to experience themselves as 'origins' rather than 'pawns.'" Thus children should be allowed to participate "in making decisions about their learning and about how they want their classroom to be." We should, Kohn states, stress compassion over loyalty, cooperation over competition, autonomy over punctuality, self-determination over self-control. In truth, those of us concerned with the formation of character engage in no such dichotomous thinking. We want to develop all the virtues.

But children cannot be treated like miniature adults. Nowhere is this issue better exemplified than in recent public service television spots for the United Negro College Fund. In these brief ads, small children are pictured piloting advanced aircraft, sitting behind corporate desks, and teaching in a university classroom, while the announcer suggests: "A mind is a terrible thing to waste." The point behind these gripping presentations is clear: children are only *potentially* capable of doing the jobs suggested by the images. They are certainly not ready in the early stages of life for the responsibilities that are inherent in adult positions. They need encouragement and training to realize their potential. Their minds are not those of adults. As both Piaget and Kohlberg have shown us, they are not miniature versions of what they will become. Rather, they are, as we now know, thinkers of a qualitatively different kind from the thinkers we hope they will become. This point seems to have been overlooked by Kohn, who seems to believe that by defining the best outcomes for adults we can infer direct implications for classrooms of children. This is just not so.

Allowing students too much freedom to "cultivate autonomy" and too much freedom to "make decisions about their learning" can be detrimental. Three quick examples may suffice to make this obvious point.

- A *New York Times* article (independently verified by one of the authors) told of one "democracy first" public high school in which a discussion took place among the students and teachers—the whole school community—about whether the students should be allowed to bring knives and to have sex on a school picnic. (They eventually voted the proposal down.)[18]

- Robert Howard described an elementary school classroom in which the students, with their classroom teacher's approval, decided that a student who was guilty of spitting on a classmate was to be punished by standing in the middle of his classmates who would each, in turn, spit on the offender. (A more experienced teacher intervened and stopped the punishment.)[19]

- Timothy Lensmire invited the students in his third-grade writing project to insert the names of fellow pupils in the stories they composed. He wrote a book on the project and its outcomes. The young authors discovered that using the names of classmates gave them the power to embarrass and shame their peers. Some students so named became very upset. Eventually, Lensmire was distressed about the pain and selfishness his innovation was generating, but—like Hamlet—he could not decide what to do. Fortunately, the principal stepped in and ended the project. Lensmire's book was sympathetically reviewed in an academic journal.[20] The reviewer disapproved of the principal's intrusion, calling it "institutionalized violence," and commented that, if the project had continued, Lensmire could have transformed his classroom into a court and could have had his writers and injured students hold an in-class lawsuit over the conflict—that is, if someone did not beat up someone else first.

A CERTAIN WELL-ROUNDEDNESS
IS DESIRABLE, AND AN
EXCESS IN ANY ONE VIRTUE
CAN LEAD TO IMBALANCES.

These activities bear some vague, though distorted and uninformed, resemblance to our republican form of government. We say "distorted" because they involve so little accountability for the misuse of student power. Nothing happens to authors who recklessly hurt other students' feelings. As for the picnic, if the "no knives and no sex" resolution had failed, would the students have been collectively liable for any harmful—or deadly—results? These are just the sort of in-school activities that cultivate poor character in students. Though we feel such activities are comparatively rare in our schools, we believe many readers will be able to identify less dramatic examples of similar tendencies.

What For-Character Educators Want

So what do for-character educators want? What is our ultimate goal? Simply stated, we want children and adolescents to learn to feel a sense of belonging to and responsibility for others. This goal and its rationale come from the work of Emile Durkheim almost 100 years ago. In Durkheim's view, morality and religion, the *collective conscience* as he called them, are the cohesive bonds that hold the social order together. A breakdown of these values, he believed, would lead to social instability and individual feelings of anxiety and dissatisfaction, sometimes resulting in depression, suicide, and other forms of disorder.

Durkheim exhaustively studied the topic of suicide.[21] He concluded that it—and by extension other types of youth disorder—was largely caused by the affliction of not being immediately needed. Suicide was not particularly related to poverty or to evident social injustice. Instead, people with simple, proximate obligations to others (e.g., mothers, manual laborers, teachers) tended to choose to live through the inevitable "slings and arrows of outrageous fortune." They rejected suicide because it was a betrayal of those immediate obligations. (Who will feed the chickens? Who will change the baby's diapers?) These notions are certainly generalizable. Conversely, people with abstract

and unclear obligations to others are much more prone to suicide. Young people, especially in our country and in our era, are one class with very remote and vague obligations to others.

Recent sociological studies have reached conclusions generally congruent with Durkheim's broad propositions.[22] One of the authors once examined records of adolescents who had committed suicide. One pitiful file told of a boy whose last act before committing suicide was to kill his beloved dog. Once the ties of responsibility were destroyed, the boy no longer had any obligation to endure the typical buffets of life. In effect, we are often saved by our obligations to others.

Durkheim's theory implies that the young are ignored, unwanted, and lacking in serious responsibilities. The solution involves creating more structured and intense responsibilities. Thus he implies that being extremely permissive toward the young makes things worse. When people are really important to us, we surround their conduct with many forms of constraint and their misconduct with notable and fast consequences. We demand that the surgeon who will cut us open first wash his or her hands. When we go to an expensive restaurant for a fine meal, we want the waiter to display a little style. When we're playing a sport to win, we want our teammates to go all out. We put people who are really important to us under pressure, and so they feel important.

But too many of today's young people are rarely expected to help support their families, nor are they called on to carry out demanding household chores. Instead, their most typical characteristic is that they are often not very much needed by anyone else. They are ignored. Their roles are largely ornamental. If many of them died, the day-to-day work of the world would continue for the immediate future. People given such freedom can find themselves bored and tempted toward irresponsible and dangerous behavior. The traditional character prescription still applies: "For Satan finds some mischief still for idle hands to do."

We believe that children need age-appropriate but significant responsibilities, in order to feel socially integrated and respected. Adults with authority (i.e., parents, teachers, coaches) should feel comfortable disciplining youngsters who fail to carry out those significant duties. It is, furthermore, the responsibility of adults to critically examine children's and adolescents' social environments and to design and manage them so those environments help our young people grow into mature and moral adults.

These intuitions, based on our collective research, are corroborated by findings about what works with regard to for-character education. Activities in which students assume responsibility (including the acceptance of authority and consequences) for their own learning and behavior and the learning and behavior of others "will result in positive changes in selected prosocial character traits." Moreover, "classroom and school climates that embody such factors as clear standards, mutual respect between students and teachers, and shared governance have been found to be associated with some limited, but nonetheless important, positive changes in student character."[23]

Which Values?

In his fourth question, Kohn wonders, "Which values" should we teach? We agree with him that "whether or not we deliberately adopt a character or moral education program, we are always teaching values." We would say, more precisely, we are always teaching virtues. But which virtues? Though Kohn agrees with the teaching of noncontroversial virtues, such as fairness or honesty, he objects to such "conservative" and "potentially controversial" guidelines as "work hard and complete your tasks." Here again, Kohn rebukes for-character educators for sneaking in their propagandistic biases—e.g., the Protestant work ethic or obedience. He would prefer that we teach empathy and skepticism.

The for-character tradition recognizes that no single virtue should always dominate, although the virtues are systematically related to form a unity of perspective. Virtuous people we know or read about and admire—e.g., George Washington, Martin Luther King, Mother Teresa—all possessed a measure of the Socratic virtues: wisdom, temperance, justice, and courage. A certain well-roundedness is desirable, and an excess in any one virtue can lead to imbalances. For example, the fictional Hamlet was reflective and loyal, but indecisive. Richard Nixon was diligent and farsighted, but also vindictive.

We do not feel qualified to strongly recommend any particular mix of values to educators or parents. We are far more concerned with the openness of the decision-making process, realizing that conflicts do occur over moral priorities. Since their inception American public schools have successfully and regularly resolved conflicts over what should be taught. Such disputes are the day-to-day routines of our democratic processes. Differences are scrutinized, pros and cons are subjected to public debate, compromises are negotiated, and votes are cast.

There are, of course, many sources that offer specific answers to the question of which virtues we should teach. One such set is embodied in the principles laid out in the U.S. Constitution, the Bill of Rights, and other founding documents (e.g., justice, the rights and responsibilities of citizenship, freedom of the press, freedom of religion, and so on). Another set of answers is the common core of virtues alluded

to throughout this article: honesty, love, compassion, duty, respect, responsibility, diligence, and so on. A third set of answers can be found in the growing number of communities that have adopted common core virtues for their own children. Yet another set of answers can be found in the six pillars growing out of the Aspen Declaration of 1992: caring, civic virtue and citizenship, justice and fairness, respect, responsibility, and trustworthiness. Since America is the world's most religious industrialized country, it would be incongruous if some of that tradition did not influence the setting of priorities with regard to virtue. This might touch on such matters as chastity, the sanctity of marriage, honoring one's parents or others in authority, or displaying charity. The list goes on.

What Is Our Theory of Learning?

The pedagogical principles we advocate are simple and direct.

- Identify and list the virtues and relevant behavior traits one hopes children will learn. (There are a variety of virtues to choose from and a variety of sources for those virtues.)
- Establish those identified virtues or traits as goals for students and the faculty.
- Provide occasions for students, either individually or as part of well-designed groups, to practice the behaviors associated with such traits or virtues.
- Praise students, either individually or as a group—publicly or privately—when desirable behavior, consistent with expectations, is displayed.
- Identify undesirable traits and prohibit them. Publicize and justify such prohibitions, and establish and enforce clear, unpleasant, and appropriate consequences for such misbehavior by individuals or groups.
- Use the school's formal curriculum and ceremonies to support such activities.
- Hire, train, and retain staff members who actively support such policies.[24]

Kohn characterizes this approach as nothing more than "exhortation and directed recitation . . . teaching as a matter of telling and compelling." Teachers in for-character classrooms, he states, are encouraged to engage in a variety of measures to get students to conform: praising children who respond correctly, prohibiting wrongdoing, and inculcating habits such as perseverance, delay of gratification, and self-control. He's correct. But this approach is far more than simplistic "exhortation." We believe that straightforward tactics will improve academic and for-character learning and help save students' lives.

As to for-character vocabulary, we intend such words as *instill in, transmit to,* and *habit formation* to describe the process of character development and mature moral decision making. These are, however, not our words. They are the words of Plato and Aristotle, of Kant and Piaget. They are the collective knowledge of our best minds over time.

So how do schools best help shape the character of the young? Our answer is clear. Effective schools share the same systemic characteristics researchers have observed in highly effective parents.[25] Similarly, less-effective schools share characteristics of less-effective, laissez-faire parents. That is, well-grounded teachers and schools set high expectations and nourish children's earned sense of competence and self-reliance. They rely on extrinsic control, clarity, consistency, nurture, and honesty of communication to shape their students' character. They are primarily concerned for the well-being of the children. We believe that schools with these characteristics are more likely to graduate students who are accomplished academically and who demonstrate the habits and character traits that lead to productive citizenship. We believe that this is what good schools have always been about.

The Bog of Intrinsic Motivation

Kohn strongly opposes all measures that involve incentives, since they rely on external motivation. His position is, in effect, that, as long as such constraints are applied, students will not be free. That is, they will not practice learning for intrinsic reasons. The matter can be put in a more critical way: Kohn is less interested in stimulating students toward excellence in academics or character formation than many other educators. His case requires him to find strong evidence that recognition, praise, and other earned rewards do not habituate people to be kind, honest, or diligent. In other words, well-deserved praise does not encourage people to make a habit of their praised conduct. This is a rather fantastic position, countered by recent research and everyday experience.[26]

Allow us to provide just one instance of such everyday experience of the deep power of extrinsic motivation over learning. As part of a study of a typical suburban high school, one of the authors identified various systems to motivate learning that were used in that school. Each system was accompanied by its own unique intrinsic and extrinsic rewards. The most powerful and effective learning systems were associated with interscholastic competitive team athletics.

This "discovery" simply represents the researcher's having stumbled into a widely recognized pattern. In many schools, a great deal of attention is given to athletics. Much of this attention consists of public praise, publicity, and other forms of conspicuous display. The point so often forgotten, though, is that such extrinsic motivation systems work very well! Student athletes work long and hard to learn how to improve their skills, and often they succeed. The members of the swimming team, for example, practiced arduously for four hours a day over the 20-day Christmas vacation. And when the members of the girls' varsity volleyball team returned to school in the fall, their coach publicly tested each player to see if she had managed to improve her jumping and speed since their last practices. All the other school teams applied equivalent begin-the-season tests. It was understood by the athletes that training started well before each season began. Obviously, extrinsic motivation to learn has not turned off student athletes; it has just made them work harder at learning their skills.

Finally, Kohn offers his example of a good school program that promotes children's moral and social development. He presents the Child Development Project (CDP), whose premise is that, "by meeting children's needs, we increase the likelihood that they will care about others." However, one of the authors helped conduct a four-year direct comparison of students in CDP schools with students attending a public school with a strong for-character program.

In contrast to the CDP schools, the for-character school established specific, measurable goals, standards, and performance indicators; conducted frequent, systematic assessments of performance; measured and rated school performance relative to the goals and published the results; publicly recognized schools, classes, and individuals for achieving goals; and supported school personnel in their efforts to achieve school goals. In other words, it was not the type of school in which Kohn would enroll his children.

Although there were major differences between the CDP program and the for-character program, both seem to have had positive effects in students, and, of the hundreds of variables studied, there were numerous areas in which neither program was significantly or consistently differentiated from the other.[27] But the teachers in the for-character school, as opposed to teachers in the CDP schools, rated their school as more businesslike, creative, and innovative, with more involved and supportive parents, a more supportive and accessible principal, a more traditional academic focus, a pleasanter atmosphere, and better relations between teachers and students. And students in the for-character school scored higher on measures of self-esteem in the third and fourth grades than did students in the CDP schools. These positive results in a school with clear for-character policies should not extinguish other experiments designed to improve student character. However, the results do counter such misleading pictures as the one sketched by Alfie Kohn.

1. The U.S. Department of Health and Human Services, Public Health Service, Bureau of Vital Statistics, and predecessor agencies have compiled annual vital statistics reports on specific topics for appropriate years (homicide and suicide, 1914–94; out-of-wedlock births, 1940–93).

2. Judith Haveman, "A Nation of Violent Children: A New Survey Finds the Epidemic Is Confined Almost Exclusively to the U.S.," *Washington Post National Weekly Edition,* 17 February 1997, p. 34.

3. Jean Johnson and Steve Farkas, *Getting By: What American Teenagers Really Think About Their Schools* (New York: Public Agenda, 1997).

4. Over the past few years many books have documented exemplary programs in character education. None of these school programs relied primarily on packaged character education programs, though some did use them. See Jacques S. Benninga, ed., *Moral, Character, and Civic Education in the Elementary School* (New York: Teachers College Press, 1991); Philip F. Vincent, *Promising Practices in Character Education: Nine Success Stories from Around the Country* (Chapel Hill, N.C.: Character Development Group, 1996); and Edward A. Wynne, *A Year in the Life of an Excellent Elementary School* (Lancaster, Pa.: Technomics, 1993).

5. "List of 100 For-Character Activities and Policies," in Edward A. Wynne and Kevin Ryan, *Reclaiming Our Schools: A Handbook on Teaching Character, Academics, and Discipline* (New York: Merrill, 1997), pp. 197–202.

6. See, for example, Stephen L. Carter, *Integrity* (New York: HarperCollins, 1996); William Damon, *Greater Expectations: Overcoming the Culture of Indulgence in America's Homes and Schools* (New York: Free Press, 1996); Jack Frymier et al., *Values on Which We Agree* (Bloomington, Ind.: Phi Delta Kappa Educational Foundation, 1995); Gertrude Himmelfarb, *The Demoralization of Society: From Victorian Virtues to Modern Values* (New York: Alfred A. Knopf., 1995); William Kilpatrick, Gregory Wolfe, and Suzanne M. Wolfe, *Books That Build Character: A Guide to Teaching Your Child Moral Values Through Stories* (New York: Simon & Schuster, 1994); Alex Molnar, ed., *The Construction of Children's Character: 96th NSSE Yearbook, Part II* (Chicago: National Society for the Study of Education, University of Chicago Press, 1997); and Wynne and Ryan, op. cit.

7. William K. Frankena, *Ethics* (Englewood Cliffs, N.J.: Prentice-Hall, 1963), p. 53.

8. See, for example, Robert E. Slavin, "Reforming State and Federal Policies to Support Adoption of Proven Practices," *Educational Researcher,* December 1996, p. 4, in which Slavin comments that "year after year, the achievement of American children remains unchanged. . . . Yet, in what other area of American life would we be satisfied to say that things have simply become no worse over the past quarter century?" Slavin was writing about the academic achievement of youths; we have shown that the moral indicators have declined over this same time period.

9. Amy Gutmann, *Democratic Education* (Princeton, N.J.: Princeton University Press, 1987), p. 288.

10. Ibid.

11. James Q. Wilson and Richard J. Herrnstein, *Crime and Human Nature.* (New York: Simon & Schuster, 1985).

12. Jean Johnson and John Immerwahr, *First Things First: What Americans Expect from the Public Schools* (New York: Public Agenda, 1994).

13. Plato, *The Republic,* trans. H.D. P. Lee (Baltimore: Penguin Books, 1955), pp. 90–91.

14. Horace Mann, as quoted in Lori Sanford Wiley, *Comprehensive Character-Building Classroom* (Manchester, N.H.: Character Development Foundation, 1997), p. 28.

15. Lawrence Cremin, *American Education: The Colonial Years.* (New York: Harper Torchbook, 1970), p. 479.

16. Richard Brookhiser, "A Man on Horseback," *Atlantic,.* January 1996, p. 61.

17. Sarah Broadie, *Ethics with Aristotle* (New York: Oxford University Press, 1991), p. 109.

18. Edward A. Wynne, "Character and Academics in the Elementary School," in Benninga, ed., p. 142.

19. Robert W. Howard, "Lawrence Kohlberg's Influence on Moral Education in Elementary Schools," in Benninga, ed., pp. 61–62.

20. John Willinsky, "The Underside of Empowerment," *Educational Researcher,* March 1995, pp. 31–32.

21. Emile Durkheim, *Suicide: A Study in Sociology,* trans. John A. Spaulding and George Simpson (Glencoe, ILL.: Free Press, 1951).

22. R. W. Marris, "Sociology of Suicide," in Seymour Perlin, ed., *A Handbook for the Study of Suicide* (New York: Oxford University Press, 1975), pp. 93–112.

23. James S. Leming, *Character Education: Lessons from the Past, Models for the Future* (Camden, ME.: Institute for Global Ethics, 1993), p. 16.

24. Edward A. Wynne, "Transmitting Character in Schools—Some Common Questions and Answers," *The Clearing House,"* January/February 1995, *pp. 151–53.*

25. See Eleanor Maccoby, *Social Development: Psychological Growth and the Parent/Child Relationship* (New York: Harcourt Brace Jovanovich, 1980), pp. 382–383; and Diane Baumrind, "The Development of Instrumental Competence Through Socialization," in Anne D. Pick, ed., *Minnesota Symposium on Child Psychology,.* vol. 7 (Minneapolis: University of Minnesota Press, 1973).

26. Judy Cameron and W. David Pierce, "The Debate About Rewards and Intrinsic Motivation: Protests and Accusations Do Not Alter the Results," *Review of Educational Research,.* vol. 66, 1996, pp. 39–51.

27. Jacques S. Benninga et al., "Effects of Two Contrasting School Task and Incentive Structures on Children's Social Development," *Elementary School Journal,.* vol. 92, 1991, pp. 149–67.

JACQUES S. BENNINGA is a professor of education and director of the Bonner Center for Character Education and Citizenship at California State University, Fresno. EDWARD A. WYNNE is a professor of education at the University of Illinois, Chicago, and editor of the For-Character Education Web Page (www.uic.edu/~edaw/main.html).

Improving Student Thinking

BARRY BEYER

Believe it or not, our students—regardless of age or grade level—not only *can* think but they *do.* They make decisions, attack problems, pose hypotheses, evaluate information, and even make inferences. Unfortunately, of course, many don't carry out these operations very skillfully or consistently, or at all the appropriate times or places, at least in our classes. Consequently, they often fail to develop the kinds of subject matter understandings, insights, and knowledge that we try so hard to help them develop. Isn't there something we can do in our classrooms to help our students improve the quality of their thinking, so they can think better and learn the subjects they study as well as they really could and as well as we would like them to?

The answer, happily, is a resounding *yes!*

Research, exemplary classroom practice, and accumulated teaching experience indicate that there are at least four things you and I can do right now in our classrooms that will improve the abilities and inclinations of our students to think better than they do when left on their own. And, we can do these *at the same time* that we engage our students in achieving the various subject matter learning objectives called for by our curricula. Specifically, we can

- provide a classroom learning environment that makes thinking possible and students willing to engage in it;
- make the invisible substance of thinking visible and explicit;
- guide and support student execution of newly encountered, difficult, or complex thinking operations during their initial efforts to apply them; and
- integrate instruction in thinking with instruction in subject matter.

Before we consider some of the many ways to incorporate these approaches into our daily teaching, however, it is important to note that *improving* thinking differs considerably from *facilitating* thinking. The latter consists of making thinking easier. It is commonly a one-time intervention to help students overcome a temporary obstacle or to ease them through a difficult thinking task. Improving thinking,

on the other hand, means making thinking work better—more rapidly, accurately, "expertly"—in the long run than it does now. This requires a continuing, systematic, long-term effort to move students toward achieving and maintaining the highest levels possible of skilled, self-directed, self-correcting thinking. The four approaches described here are especially useful for achieving that goal.

Providing Thoughtful Learning Environments

Unless the learning environments of our classrooms nurture and support student thinking, especially higher-order thinking, our students are unlikely to be very receptive to serious efforts on our part to help them improve their thinking. Among the features of such learning environments two stand out as especially crucial: (1) repeated opportunities to engage in meaningful thinking beyond the level of recall and (2) encouragement to engage and remain engaged in such thinking. By ensuring that our classrooms consistently exhibit these features, we make them "thinker-friendly" as well as "thinking-friendly." Specialists call such classrooms thoughtful classrooms (Wiggins 1987).

Providing Thinking Opportunities

The secret to providing repeated classroom opportunities to engage in thinking is to engage students in productive learning tasks. These are tasks that require students to produce knowledge new to them, rather than simply to reproduce information or knowledge claims already presented to them in texts, lectures, or media. One powerful way to do this is to frame learning assignments or lessons around thoughtful questions.

A thoughtful question is a question that—to produce an acceptable response—requires students to go substantially beyond where they are and, like the crew of the Enterprise, "to boldly go where no man has gone before." To answer these questions, students must locate and use information they may not yet possess as well as restructure familiar information to produce something they do not already know. "What did Columbus discover?" is not a

From *The Clearing House*, May/June 1998, pp. 262–267. © 1998 by Barry Beyer.

very thoughtful question. "Who discovered Columbus—and why?" is much more thoughtful.

Thoughtful questions stimulate thinking and trigger additional related questions. They engage students in defining terms; posing hypotheses; identifying, finding, assessing, and manipulating data; making and testing inferences; generating and evaluating conclusions and arguments; and applying concepts, principles, and other kinds of knowledge. They are not yes/no questions. They cannot be answered simply by recall. They do not have a single preferred "right" answer (Newmann 1990; Wiggins 1987). Organizing lessons, units, or topics around such questions provides students continued opportunities to engage in all kinds of thinking to generate worthwhile and meaningful subject matter learning.

Productive learning activities also provide considerable opportunities for sustained thinking. Activities like judging the accuracy of a given claim or body of information or generating a strong argument in support of a conclusion may require as few as only one or two classroom periods (Beyer 1997). Longer tasks such as the following provide even more opportunities for continued student thinking:

Create and justify the "good citizenship merit badge" requirements for a specific kind of person in a given culture or place at a particular time in history, such as for a Nez Perce youth in the 1870s, an enslaved or free African American in the 1850s, or a king's vassal in the Middle Ages.

Organizing our lessons around thoughtful questions and productive learning tasks helps make thinking a central part of student learning in our classrooms.

Encouraging Student Thinking

Providing opportunities to think, however, is fruitless unless students take advantage of them. And, as we all know, too many students frequently do not! It is thus also essential that we encourage students to seize and sustain engagement in thinking opportunities if we are to create and maintain a thoughtful learning environment.

The kind of encouragement required here is not the redouble-your-effort kind derived from simple cheerleading or from exhortations like, "Think! Think again! Now think harder!" On the contrary, it is the kind of encouragement that *emboldens* students to engage in thinking. This means providing them some tangible aid, prompt, or other support that gives them reason to feel that they will or can succeed at the task at hand.

We can provide such encouragement by arranging students so they face each other as well as by surrounding them with bulletin board displays of quotations, cartoons, puzzles, and copies of their own work that illustrate the importance and value of good thinking. Providing wait time for them to think before we accept their responses to our questions or claims and before we respond to their assertions or answers also serves that purpose (Rowe

1974). So, too, does our modeling the behaviors and dispositions of skillful thinking and helping our students exhibit these behaviors and dispositions. Rather than cutting thinking off with remarks such as, "Good answer!," we can build on their responses to sustain continued thinking by, for instance, asking for evidence to support the accuracy of a response or for examples or more details or assumptions underlying it.

We can also encourage student thinking by minimizing or eliminating the negative risks of thinking (Lipman 1991; Nickerson 1988–89). We can consistently emphasize the positive value of rejected hypotheses and "wrong answers" in leading us to valid hypotheses and "answers." We can constantly employ the language of thinking by using precise thinking terms to denote the specific cognitive actions, skills, conditions, or products in which we wish to engage students. For instance, instead of asking, "What do you think will happen next?" we should ask, "What do you *predict* will happen next?" (Olson and Astington 1990; Perkins 1992). And we can keep classroom discourse focused on truth and proof rather than on who says what, welcome and explore divergent or unusual views, and reward the validated products of high-risk thinking (Newmann 1990).

When engaging in new or difficult thinking tasks is a normal and expected part of our classrooms and "emboldening boosts" are consistently given, students have reason to believe that they can engage successfully in such thinking. It is this kind of support—combined with the topics we ask them to think about—that encourages them to take advantage of the thinking opportunities we provide.

Making Thinking Visible

Before we can repair or strengthen something that is broken or is not working as well as it should be, we need to be aware of exactly how it presently functions. We also need to be aware of how it works or might work when functioning as it could or should function. This is as true of student thinking as it is of any other procedure or process. The first step in improving student thinking thus consists of making students conscious of how they presently think and how others more skilled than they carry out the same thinking operations. This means we need to make the seemingly invisible thinking processes visible and explicit, especially when our students are focusing on new or complex thinking operations.

The Invisible Substance of Thinking

What is there we can make visible and explicit about any act of thinking? Cognitive scientists assert that every thinking skill (operation, strategy, or act) consists of three elements: one or more *procedures* (series of steps and/or rules) by which it is or can be executed skillfully and efficiently; the *conditions* under which it is appropriately employed; and any *declarative knowledge* associated with it, such as the criteria employed in making judgments or evaluations or the heuristics (rules of thumb) that guide expert application of a procedure (Anderson 1983; Nickerson 1988–89). Students benefit immensely from becoming conscious of and articulating exactly how they presently execute a given thinking operation or skill as well as how experts do it, of where and when it is appropriate to employ the operation, and of anything they know—or should know—that would make its application more efficient, effective, and "expert" (Papert 1980; Vygotsky 1962).

Making the Invisible Visible

We help students make visible and explicit these normally unarticulated elements of any thinking skill in several ways. One is by engaging students in reflecting on what they did to carry out a thinking operation they have just completed. This is known as *metacognitive reflection*. Once students have completed a thinking task, we have them think back on exactly what they did mentally, step by step, to complete it, and why they took those steps. In doing this, students articulate what they recall doing, listen to how some of their peers believe they did the same thing, and then analyze these accounts to identify apparently useful, and even additional unarticulated, steps and rules. By continuously articulating and then comparing these procedural descriptions with each other and with explicit procedures employed by individuals more skilled than they in carrying out the same operation, students can spot weaknesses or omissions in the way they do it, identify steps or rules that appear to be especially useful in carrying out the thinking operation, and adapt or incorporate these into how they execute it in the future (Beyer 1997; Nickerson, Perkins, and Smith 1985; Sternberg 1984).

Another way to make the invisible of thinking visible and explicit is to model a thinking operation to be developed (Pressley and Harris 1990; Rosenshine and Meister 1992). *Modeling* consists of demonstrating step-by-step how a skill is executed, with accompanying explanation noting the key steps in the procedure and why these steps are important. If we are proficient at executing the thinking skill in question and can verbalize clearly how we do it, we ourselves can model it for our students. We may also use written protocols or videos or essays that model this procedure, if any are available. Occasionally, a student who has demonstrated skill in carrying out the thinking operation can model the procedure. Then, if we provide an immediate opportunity to apply the modeled procedure while it is still visible to them, students can attempt to replicate it. With continued practice and reflection they can adopt or adapt it to develop a skilled routine of their own for executing the skill.

The key here is making students conscious of exactly how they presently carry out a thinking act or skill (imperfect as their awareness or execution may be), of how their peers do it, and of how more skilled thinkers do it. Metacognitive reflection and modeling serve these ends well. Improving the quality of student thinking requires repeated use of both of these techniques with each thinking skill we teach.

Guiding and Supporting Student Thinking

Providing continuing guidance and support to students who are trying to apply newly encountered thinking skills proves indispensable to moving them toward skillful, autonomous use of these skills (Rosenshine and Meister 1992). Two kinds of such guidance and support prove especially effective to this end: scaffolding and cueing. Once students have become conscious of a procedure or routine for executing a new thinking operation, scaffolding and cueing can be used to guide their continuing follow-up practice and application of the procedure in a variety of contexts.

Scaffolding Thinking

A scaffold is a skeletal framework of a thinking procedure—such as a checklist—that makes the steps in that thinking procedure explicit. Students use the scaffold to steer themselves through these steps as they try to carry them out. Such devices allow students to concentrate on applying the rules and steps of an unfamiliar or complex thinking procedure to a given body of information without having also to try to recall what steps to employ. Use of thinking scaffolds minimizes procedural errors in trying to apply a newly encountered thinking skill and enables students to internalize a more effective skill-using routine sooner than they otherwise might if they had to carry out the skill, from memory, exclusively on their own (McTighe and Lyman 1988).

There are three kinds of devices that prove especially effective as scaffolds for thinking. *Procedural checklists,* such as that for decision making shown in figure 1, are the most explicit. They provide a list, in order, of the mental steps by which a specific thinking procedure can be effectively carried out. *Process-structured questions* are less explicit. Like the example in figure 1, these devices walk students through the steps in a thinking procedure not by telling them the steps directly but by asking a series of questions that require students to execute in sequence each of the steps that constitutes the given thinking procedure. *Graphic organizers,* like that in figure 1, are charts or diagrams that present visually—and occasionally with written prompts—the steps in a thinking procedure (McTighe and Lyman 1988). As students fill in the various sections of the thinking skill organizer, they move through these steps. Graphic organizers provide less explicit support and guidance than either checklists or process-structured questions but can still effectively scaffold or structure student thinking.

FIGURE 1
Scaffolds for Student Thinking

A Procedural Checklist
for Decision Making

- Identify a choosing opportunity.
- State the problem/goal.
- State the criteria of the "best" choice/decision.
- List the possible alternative choices.
- List the possible consequences of selecting each alternative.
- Evaluate each consequence in terms of the criteria identified above.
- Select the alternative that best meets the identified criteria.

Process-Structured Questions
for Decision Making

1. What do you want to make a decision about?
2. What do you want to accomplish by making this decision?
3. How will you know when you have made the "best" choice?
4. What are all the alternatives you have to choose from?
5. What are the possible consequences of each alternative—long range as well as short range?
6. What are the pluses and minuses of each consequence?
7. Which alternative is "best"? Why?

A Graphic Organizer
for Decision Making

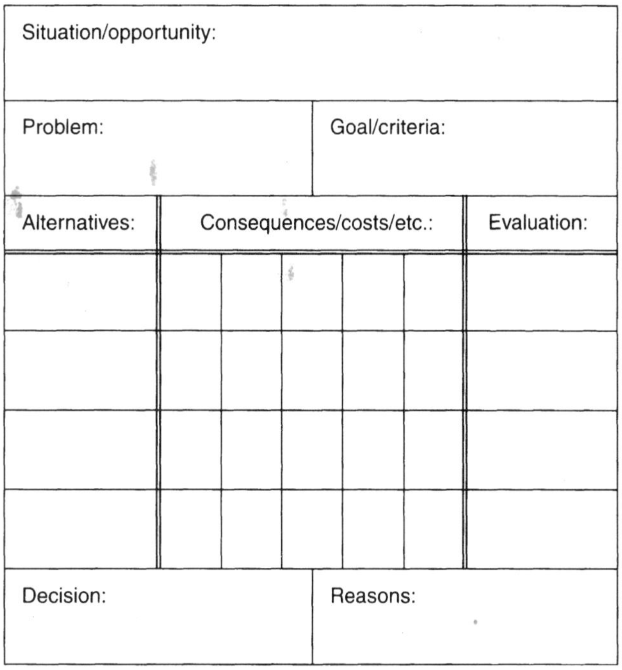

Situation/opportunity:		
Problem:	Goal/criteria:	
Alternatives:	Consequences/costs/etc.:	Evaluation:
Decision:	Reasons:	

Not all checklists, lists of questions, or graphic organizers scaffold thinking, however. Many checklists and questions trigger thinking but do not, by the way they are arranged or worded, effectively move students through the steps in a cognitive procedure. Furthermore, as commonly used, many webs, matrices, charts, and diagrams tend to represent the products of thinking—products such as concepts, generalizations, and so on—rather than a procedure by which a thinking product is generated. To be effective in scaffolding thinking, checklists, question sets, and graphic organizers must activate and present a cognitive procedure in a clear, step-by-step fashion.

Cueing Thinking

A *cue* is a prompt that reminds us of what to do or say next without telling us all that we are to do or say. Cueing thinking consists of prompting students to employ a specific thinking operation. Cues are usually much less explicit than scaffolds. They also depend much more for their effectiveness on the degree to which students have already internalized—stored in memory—under that cue label or signal the procedures and the rules that constitute the action or skill they seek to call forth. Cueing thinking proves helpful to improving student thinking only after students have become consciously aware (through metacognitive reflection and/or modeling) of an effective skill-using procedure and have had enough scaffolded practice in applying it to have stored that specific knowledge in memory.

Thinking cues take many forms (Rosenshine and Meister 1992). They range from the more explicit, such as previewing and rehearsing a skill about to be applied, to simply naming that operation, to even less explicit devices such as mnemonics and symbols. We can *preview* a thinking operation that students are about to employ by having volunteers provide its various names, report any special rules or heuristics that they know might guide its use (including the criteria it applies, if it is a critical thinking operation), tell why it is appropriate to use at this point, and define it. Asking for the definition last allows students to use the preceding volunteered information as cues for searching their memories for this definition or as information from which to construct an appropriate working definition.

We can help students *rehearse* a thinking skill they are about to practice by having volunteers report one or more routines or procedures by which it can be effectively employed and/or any rules, criteria, and heuristics that direct or inform its use. When students have been applying a skill for some time, however, merely *stating the technical label* of the skill—or words associated with it—customarily serves as a sufficient cue. *Mnemonics,* if devised or learned earlier by the students when they were first articulating or devising skilled procedures for executing a skill, also can serve as useful thinking cues. For example, consider the acronym **DECIDE** as a cue for the process of decision making:

Define goal
Enumerate alternatives
Consider consequences
Investigate effects
Determine best alternative
Execute

Acronyms like this one not only aid students in recalling the skill to employ but can actually cue the steps in a procedure for executing it (Beyer 1997).

Integrating Instruction in Thinking with Subject Matter

Thinking is affected and shaped as much by the subject matter to which it is applied as that subject matter is shaped by the kind of thinking that is employed to process it and the skill with which that thinking is applied. Efforts to improve student thinking, therefore, need to be carefully integrated into instruction in subject matter (Resnick and Klopfer 1989). *We can and should teach thinking and subject matter at the same time.*

To accomplish this, we must do at least two things. First, we must ensure that our students have repeated opportunities throughout our courses to apply the thinking skills in which they need to improve. This can be done, in part, by focusing on topics and themes within our subjects that are relevant to our students and to life today and in the future. It can also be accomplished by building student study around productive thinking activities and questions, as described above.

In addition, we must provide explicit instruction and then guided practice—as appropriate—in each thinking operation to be improved the first dozen or so times students are called upon to apply it. One way to plan for this instruction is to identify prior to beginning a course the specific thinking skills we believe our students will need to improve. Next, we can plan specific opportunities for the students, once they have first encountered the need to use these skills, to apply each at first frequently and then intermittently thereafter. Then we can design in advance the appropriate skill instruction for each point in this skill-using sequence using the subject matter our students are to be studying along the way.

Another way to provide such instruction is to be always alert while teaching to any thinking skills with which our students seem to be having difficulty. The first time we notice such difficulty we then can switch our instructional focus from subject matter to how to carry out the skill by introducing that skill. John Bransford (1993) calls this "just-in-time teaching." Appropriate guided practice can follow, over a sequence of subsequent lessons, as described above.

Both of these teaching approaches capitalize on what research tells us about student motivation to learn. And that is that students are more willing to attempt and to attend to learning a new skill when they are introduced to it and provided guidance in applying in at a time they have a perceived need to use it but realize they cannot do it effectively (Sigel 1984). Such skill lessons do not ignore the topic or subject being studied at the time. Indeed, they should use this subject matter as a vehicle for articulating the skill so students learn about this content while they also improve their proficiency in executing the skill.

Once a thinking skill has been introduced—made visible and explicit—we need to provide guided practice in it each time the students must apply it to develop further subject matter learning. Such practice not only helps students move toward skilled, autonomous use of the skill but also helps them develop the kinds of complex subject matter learning we usually wish them to develop. In guided practice of a skill, students first attend to how they executed the skill and then to the subject matter knowledge developed by its application. In time, little attention at all need be given to the skill. Upon our cue, students will soon be able to execute it effectively and eventually can do so on their own initiative. By combining instruction in thinking and subject matter in this way we capitalize on the symbiotic relationship between content and thinking: content serves as a vehicle for applying thinking and thinking serves as a tool for understanding content and producing knowledge.

Combining These Approaches to Improve Student Thinking

Many of us have long been aware of these four teaching approaches. However, we have too often elected to employ only one of them, the one that we or someone deems is "best" for us or our students. This is most unfortunate because, in order to improve the quality of student thinking and subject matter learning, we need to use all—rather than just one—of these approaches in our classrooms.

Each of the four approaches described here addresses a different element of what is required to improve thinking. Thoughtful classrooms provide the kind of nurturing thinking environment so essential for all the other approaches to "take." Making the invisible substance of thinking visible and explicit requires such an environment and establishes the baseline from which improvement can proved. Scaffolding and cueing student thinking provide the guidance and support students need to apply with increasing efficiency, ease, and what math instructors call "elegance" the thinking procedures that they are developing. And employing all of these approaches in the subject matter being studied gives purpose to and motivates continued student skill development.

Is This Worth Doing?

Is the effort to do this worth it? Of course it is. All our students think. But most of them can think better—more often—and with greater success than they now do. And many, if not most, of them certainly can learn more or better in our courses than they do now. Interestingly, research demonstrates that in classes where teachers attend continuously and explicitly to the cognitive skills needed to understand subject matter, students not only improve their proficiency in these thinking skills but they also attain higher achievement in subject matter (Estes 19723). Use of the teaching approaches described here will help us accomplish precisely these goals.

REFERENCES

Anderson, J. R. 1983. *The architecture of cognition.* Cambridge, Mass.: Harvard University Press.
Beyer, B. K. 1997. *Improving student thinking: A comprehensive approach.* Boston: Allyn and Bacon.

Bransford, J. 1993. Teaching thinking. Presentation at the ASCD National Conference on Thinking and Learning, San Antonio, Tex. (26 Feb.).
Estes, T. H., 1972. Reading in the social studies: A review of research since 1950. In *Reading in the content areas,* edited by J. Laffery. Newark, Del." International Reading Association.
Lipman, M. 1991. *Thinking in education.* Cambridge: Cambridge University Press.
McTighe, J., and F. T. Lyman, Jr. 1988. Cueing thinking in the classroom: The promise of theory embedded tools. *Educational Leadership* 45 (April): 18–24.
Newmann, F. M. 1990. Higher order thinking in teaching social studies. *Journal of Curriculum Studies* 22 (Jan.–Feb.): 41–56.
Nickerson, R. 1988–1989. On improving thinking through instruction. In *Review of research in education* (vol. 15), edited by E. Z. Rothkopf. Washington, D.C.: American Educational Research Association.
Nickerson, R. S., D. N. Perkins, and E. E. Smith. 1985. *The teaching of thinking.* Hillsdale, N.J.: Lawrence Erlbaum Associates.
Olson, D. R., and J. W. Astington. 1990. Talking about text: How literacy contributes to thought. *Journal of Pragmatics* 14: 705–21.
Papert, S. 1980. *Mindstorms: Children, computers and powerful ideas.* New York: Basic Books.
Perkins, D. 1992. *Smart schools.* New York: The Free Press.
Pressley, M., and K. R. Harris. 1990. What we really know about strategy instruction. *Educational Leadership* 48 (Sept.): 31–34.
Resnick, L., and L. E. Klopfer, eds. 1989. *Toward the thinking curriculum.* Alexandria, Va.: Association for Supervision and Curriculum Development.
Rosenshine, B. V., and C. Meister. 1992. The use of scaffolds for teaching higher level cognitive strategies. *Educational Leadership* 49 (April): 26–33.
Rowe, M. B. 1974. Wait time and rewards as instructional variables. *Journal of Research in Science Teaching* 11: 8–94.
Sigel, I. E. 1984. How can we teach intelligence? *Educational Leadership* 42 (Sept.): 38–50.
Sternberg, R. J. 1984. How can we teach intelligence? *Educational Leadership* 42 (Sept.): 38–50.
Vygotsky, L. S. 1962. *Thought and language.* Cambridge, Mass.: MIT Press.
Wiggins, C. 1987. Creating a thought-provoking curriculum. *American Educator* 11 (winter): 12–13.

Barry Beyer is professor emeritus in the Graduate School of Education at George Mason University in Fairfax, Virginia. He is the author of Improving Student Thinking: A Comprehensive Approach (*Boston: Allyn and Bacon, 1998*).

Mapping a Route Toward Differentiated Instruction

Even though students may learn in many ways, the essential skills and content they learn can remain steady. That is, students can take different roads to the same destination.

Carol Ann Tomlinson

Developing academically responsive classrooms is important for a country built on the twin values of equity and excellence. Our schools can achieve both of these competing values only to the degree that they can establish heterogeneous communities of learning (attending to issues of equity) built solidly on high-quality curriculum and instruction that strive to maximize the capacity of each learner (attending to issues of excellence).

A serious pursuit of differentiation, or personalized instruction, causes us to grapple with many of our traditional—if questionable—ways of "doing school." Is it reasonable to expect all 2nd graders to learn the same thing, in the same ways, over the same time span? Do single-textbook adoptions send inaccurate messages about the sameness of all learners? Can students learn to take more responsibility for their own learning? Do report cards drive our instruction? Should the classroom teacher be a solitary specialist on all learner needs, or could we support genuinely effective generalist-specialist teams? Can we reconcile learning standards with learner variance?

The questions resist comfortable answers—and are powerfully important. En route to answering them, we try various roads to differentiation. The concreteness of having something ready to do Monday morning is satisfying and inescapable. After all, the students will arrive and the day must be planned. So we talk about using reading buddies in varied ways to support a range of readers or perhaps developing a learning contract with several options for practicing math skills. Maybe we could try a tiered lesson or interest centers. Three students who clearly understand the chapter need an independent study project. Perhaps we should begin with a differentiated project assignment, allowing students to choose a project about the Middle Ages. That's often how our journey toward differentiation begins.

The nature of teaching requires doing. There's not much time to sit and ponder the imponderables. To a point, that's fine—and, in any case, inevitable. A reflective teacher can test many principles from everyday interactions in the classroom. In other words, philosophy can derive from action.

> We have to know where we want to end up before we start out—and plan to get there.

We can't skip one step, however. The first step in making differentiation work is the hardest. In fact, the same first step is required to make all teaching and learning effective: We have to know where we want to end up before we start out and plan to get there. That is, we must have solid curriculum and instruction in place before we differentiate them. That's harder than it seems.

Looking Inside Two Classrooms

Mr. Appleton is teaching about ancient Rome. His students are reading the textbook in class today. He suggests that they take notes of important details as they read. When they finish, they answer the questions at the end of the chapter. Students who don't finish must do so at home. Tomorrow, they will answer the questions together in class. Mr. Appleton likes to lecture and works hard to prepare his lectures. He expects students to take notes. Later, he will give a quiz on both the notes and the text. He will give students a study sheet before the test, clearly spelling out what will be on the test.

Mrs. Baker is also teaching about ancient Rome. She gives her students graphic organizers to use as they read the textbook chapter and goes over the organizers with the class so that anyone who missed details can fill them in. She brings in pictures of the art and the architecture of the period and tells how important the Romans

were in shaping our architecture, language, and laws. When she invites some students to dress in togas for a future class, someone suggests bringing in food so that they can have a Roman banquet—and they do. One day, students do a word-search puzzle of vocabulary words about Rome. On another day, they watch a movie clip that shows gladiators and the Colosseum and talk about the favored "entertainment" of the period. Later, Mrs. Baker reads aloud several myths, and students talk about the myths that they remember from 6th grade. When it's time to study for the test, the teacher lets students go over the chapter together, which they like much better than working at home alone, she says.

She also wants students to like studying about Rome, so she offers a choice of 10 projects. Among the options are creating a poster listing important Roman gods and goddesses, their roles, and their symbols; developing a travel brochure for ancient Rome that a Roman of the day might have used; writing a poem about life in Rome; dressing dolls like citizens of Rome or drawing the fashions of the time; building a model of an important ancient Roman building or a Roman villa; and making a map of the Holy Roman Empire. Students can also propose their own topic.

Thinking About the Two Classrooms

Mr. Appleton's class is not differentiated. He does not appear to notice or respond to student differences. Mrs. Baker's is differentiated—at least by some definitions. Each class has serious flaws in its foundations, however, and for that reason, Mrs. Baker's class may not be any more successful than Mr. Appletons's—and perhaps less so.

Successful teaching requires two elements: student understanding and student engagement. In other words, students must really understand, or make sense of, what they have studied. They should also feel engaged in

or "hooked by" the ways that they have learned. The latter can greatly enhance the former and can help young people realize that learning is satisfying.

Mr. Appleton's class appears to lack engagement. There's nothing much to make learning appealing. He may be satisfied by his lecture, but it's doubtful that many of the students are impressed. It is also doubtful that much real student understanding will come from the teaching-learning scenario. Rather, the goal seems to be memorizing data for a test.

Memorizing and understanding are very different. The first has a short life span and little potential to transfer into a broader world. However, at least Mr. Appleton appears clear about what the students should memorize for the test. Mrs. Baker's class lacks even that clarity.

Students in Mrs. Baker's classroom are likely engaged. It is a lively, learner–friendly place with opportunity for student movement, student choice, and peer work. Further, Mrs. Baker's list of project options draws on different student interests or talents—and she is even open to their suggestions.

Although Mrs. Baker succeeds to some degree with engagement, a clear sense of what students should understand as a result of their study is almost totally missing. Thus her careful work to provide choice and to build a comfortable environment for her learners may not net meaningful, long-term learning. Her students are studying "something about ancient Rome." Nothing focuses or ties together the ideas and information that they encounter. Activities are more about being happy than about making meaning. No set of common information, ideas, or skills will stem from completing the various projects. In essence, she has accomplished little for the long haul. Her "differentiation" provides varied avenues to "mush"— multiple versions of fog. Her students work with different tasks, not differentiated ones.

Mr. Appleton's class provides little engagement, little understanding, and scant opportunity for attending to student differences. Mrs. Baker's class provides some engagement, little understanding, and no meaningful differentiation.

An Alternative Approach

To make differentiation work—in fact, to make teaching and learning work—teachers must develop an alternative approach to instructional planning beyond "covering the text" or "creating activities that students will like."

Ms. Cassell has planned her year around a few key concepts that will help students relate to, organize, and retain what they study in history. She has also developed principles or generalizations that govern or uncover how the concepts work. Further, for each unit, she has established a defined set of facts and terms that are essential for students to know to be literate and informed about the topic. She has listed skills for which she and the students are responsible as the year progresses. Finally, she has developed essential questions to intrigue her students and to cause them to engage with her in a quest for understanding.

Ms. Cassell's master list of facts, terms, concepts, principles, and skills stems from her understanding of the discipline of history as well as from the district's learning standards. As the year evolves, Ms. Cassell continually assesses the readiness, interests, and learning profiles of her students and involves them in goal setting and decision making about their learning. As she comes to understand her students and their needs more fully, she modifies her instructional framework and her instruction.

Ms. Cassell is also teaching about ancient Rome. Among the key concepts in this unit, as in many others throughout the year, are culture, change, and interdependence. Students will be responsible for important terms, such as *republic, patrician, plebeian, veto, villa,* and *Romance language;* names of key individuals, for example, Julius Caesar, Cicero, and Virgil; and names of important places,

for instance, the Pantheon and the Colosseum.

For this unit, students explore key generalizations or principles: Varied cultures share common elements. Cultures are shaped by beliefs and val-

> Successful differentiation is squarely rooted in student engagement plus student understanding.

ues, customs, geography, and resources. People are shaped by and shape their cultures. Societies and cultures change for both internal and external reasons. Elements of a society and its cultures are interdependent.

Among important skills that students apply are using resources on history effectively, interpreting information from resources, blending data from several resources, and organizing effective paragraphs. The essential question that Ms. Cassell often poses to her students is, How would your life and culture be different if you lived in a different time and place?

Looking Inside the Third Classroom

Early in the unit, Ms. Cassell's students begin work, both at home and in class, on two sequential tasks that will extend throughout the unit as part of their larger study of ancient Rome. Both tasks are differentiated.

For the first task, students assume the role of someone from ancient Rome, such as a soldier, a teacher, a healer, a farmer, a slave, or a farmer's wife. Students base their choice solely on their own interests. They work both alone and with others who select the same topic and use a wide variety of print, video, computer, and human resources to understand what their life in ancient Rome would have been like.

Ultimately, students create a first-person data sheet that their classmates can use as a resource for their second task. The data sheet calls for the person in the role to provide accurate, interesting, and detailed information about what his or her daily schedule would be like, what he or she would eat and wear, where he or she would live, how he or she would be treated by the law, what sorts of problems or challenges he or she would face, the current events of the time, and so on.

Ms. Cassell works with both the whole class and small groups on evaluating the availability and appropriate use of data sources, writing effective paragraphs, and blending information from several sources into a coherent whole. Students use these skills as they develop the first-person data sheets. The teacher's goal is for each student to increase his or her skill level in each area.

The second task calls on students to compare and contrast their own lives with the lives of children of similar age in ancient Rome. Unlike the first task, which was based on student interest, this one is differentiated primarily on the basis of student readiness. The teacher assigns each student a scenario establishing his or her family context for the task: "You are the eldest son of a lawmaker living during the later years of the period known as Pax Romana," for example. Ms. Cassell bases the complexity of the scenario on the student's skill with researching and thinking about history. Most students work with families unlike those in their first task. Students who need continuity between the tasks, however, can continue in a role familiar from their first investigation.

All students use the previously developed first-person data sheets as well as a range of other resources to gather background information. They must address a common set of specified questions: How is what you eat shaped by the economics of your family and by your location? What is your level of education and how is that affected by your status in society? How is your life interdependent with the lives of others in ancient Rome? How will Rome change during your lifetime? How will those changes affect your life? All students must also meet certain research and writing criteria.

Despite the common elements, the task is differentiated in several ways. It is differentiated by interest because each student adds questions that are directed by personal interests: What games did children play? What was the practice of science like then? What was the purpose and style of art?

Readiness differentiation occurs because each student adds personal research and writing goals, often with the teacher's help, to his or her criteria for success. A wide range of research resources is available, including books with varied readability levels, video and audio tapes, models, and access to informed people. The teacher also addresses readiness through small-group sessions in which she provides different sorts of teacher and peer support, different kinds of modeling, and different kinds of coaching for success, depending on the readiness levels of students.

Finally, the teacher adds to each student's investigation one specific question whose degree of difficulty is based on her most recent assessments of student knowledge, facility with research, and thinking about history. An example of a more complex question is, How will your life differ from that of the previous generation in your family, and how will your grandchildren's lives compare with yours? A less complex, but still challenging question is, How will language change from the generation before you to two generations after you, and why will those changes take place?

Learning-profile differentiation is reflected in the different media that students use to express their findings: journal entries, an oral monologue, or a videotape presentation. Guidelines for each type of product ensure quality and focus on essential understandings and skills established for the unit. Students may work alone or with a "parallel partner" who is work-

ing with the same role, although each student must ultimately produce his or her own product.

At other points in the study of ancient Rome, Ms. Cassell differentiates instruction. Sometimes she varies the sorts of graphic organizers that students use when they read, do research, or take notes in class. She may use review groups of mixed readiness and then conduct review games with students of like readiness working together. She works hard to ask a range of questions that move from concrete and familiar to abstract and unfamiliar in all class discussions. She sometimes provides homework options in which students select the tasks that they believe will help them understand important ideas or use important skills best. Of course, the class also plans, works, reviews, and debates as a whole group.

Students find Ms. Cassell's class engaging—and not just because it's fun. It's engaging because it shows the connection between their own lives and life long ago. It helps them see the interconnectedness among times in history and make links with other subjects. It tickles their curiosity. And it provides a challenge that pushes each learner a bit further than is comfortable—and then supports success. Sometimes those things are fun. Often they are knotty and hard. Always they dignify the learner and the subject.

Ms. Cassell's class is highly likely to be effective for her varied learners, in part because she continually attempts to reach her students where they are and move them on—she differentiates instruction. The success of the differentiation, however, is not a stand-alone matter. It is successful because it is squarely rooted in student engagement plus student understanding.

This teacher knows where she wants her students to arrive at the end of their shared learning journey and where her students are along that journey at a given time. Because she is clear about the destination and the path of the travelers, she can effectively guide them, and she varies or

differentiates her instruction to accomplish this goal. Further, her destination is not merely the amassing of data but rather the constructing of understanding. Her class provides a good example of the close and neces-

> Differentiation is not so much the "stuff" as the "how." If the "stuff" is ill conceived, the "how" is doomed.

sary relationship between effective curriculum and instruction and effective differentiation.

The First Step Is the Compass

Mr. Appleton may have a sense of what he wants his students to know at the end of the road, but not about what his students should understand and be able to do. He teaches facts, but no key concepts, guiding principles, or essential questions. With a fact-based curriculum, differentiating instruction is difficult. Perhaps some students could learn more facts and some, fewer. Perhaps some students could have more time to drill the facts, and some, less. It's difficult to envision a defensible way to differentiate a fact-driven curriculum, probably because the curriculum itself is difficult to defend.

Mrs. Baker also appears to lack a clear vision of the meaning of her subject, of the nature of her discipline and what it adds to human understanding, and of why it should matter to a young learner to study old times. There is little clarity about facts—let alone concepts, guiding principles, or essential questions. Further, she confuses folly with engagement. She thinks that she is differentiating instruction, but without instructional clarity, her activities and projects are merely different—not differentiated. Because there is no instructional clarity, there is no basis for defensible differentiation.

Ms. Cassell plans for what students should know, understand, and be able to do at the end of a sequence of learning. She dignifies each learner by planning tasks that are interesting, relevant, and powerful. She invites each student to wonder. She determines where each student is in knowledge, skill, and understanding and where he or she needs to move. She differentiates instruction to facilitate that goal. For her, differentiation is one piece of the mosaic of professional expertise. It is not a strategy to be plugged in occasionally or often, but is a way of thinking about the classroom. In her class, there is a platform for differentiation.

Ms. Cassell helps us see that differentiated instruction must dignify each learner with learning that is "whole," important, and meaning making. The core of *what* the students learn remains relatively steady. *How* the student learns—including degree of difficulty, working arrangements, modes of expression, and sorts of scaffolding—may vary considerably. Differentiation is not so much the "stuff" as the "how." If the "stuff" is ill conceived, the "how" is doomed.

The old saw is correct: Every journey *does* begin with a single step. The journey to successfully differentiated or personalized classrooms will succeed only if we carefully take the first step—ensuring a foundation of best-practice curriculum and instruction.

Carol Ann Tomlinson is Associate Professor of Educational Leadership, Foundations and Policy at the Curry School of Education, University of Virginia, Charlottesville, VA 22903 (e-mail: cat3y@virginia.edu). She is the author of *The Differentiated Classroom: Responding to the Needs of All Learners* (ASCD, 1999).

Reconcilable Differences?

Standards-Based Teaching and Differentiation

Standards-based instruction and differentiated learning can be compatible approaches in today's classrooms.

Carol Ann Tomlinson

Recent demands for more standards-based teaching can feel like a huge impediment to encouraging differentiated instruction, especially for teachers and principals who recognize student variance and want to address it appropriately. A relatively new phenomenon (at least in its current form), standards-based instruction dominates the educational terrain in a time of great academic diversity in contemporary classrooms. In fact, standards-based instruction and the high-stakes testing that drives it can often feel like a locomotive rolling over everything in its path, including individualized learning.

When any phenomenon in education suggests that we may have to jettison common sense and good pedagogy, we must first examine it in light of what we know about high-quality instruction. In other words, if we understand how standards-based teaching does or does not align with sound teaching and learning practices, we can then approach what look like barriers to differentiation. In truth, the conflict between focusing on standards and focusing on individual learners' needs exists only if we use standards in ways that cause us to abandon what we know about effective curriculum and instruction.

Differentiation: A Way of Thinking About the Classroom

What we call *differentiation* is not a recipe for teaching. It is not an instructional strategy. It is not what a teacher does when he or she has time. It is a way of thinking about teaching and learning. It is a philosophy. As such, it is based on a set of beliefs:

- Students who are the same age differ in their readiness to learn, their interests, their styles of learning, their experiences, and their life circumstances.
- The differences in students are significant enough to make a major impact on what students need to learn, the pace at which they need to learn it, and the support they need from teachers and others to learn it well.
- Students will learn best when supportive adults push them slightly beyond where they can work without assistance.
- Students will learn best when they can make a connection between the curriculum and their interests and life experiences.
- Students will learn best when learning opportunities are natural.
- Students are more effective learners when classrooms and schools create a sense of community in which students feel significant and respected.
- The central job of schools is to maximize the capacity of each student.

By definition, differentiation is wary of approaches to teaching and learning that standardize. Standard-issue students are rare, and educational approaches that ignore academic diversity in favor of standardization are likely

Students learn best when learning opportunities are natural.

to be counterproductive in reaching the full range of learners.

Differentiation must be a refinement of, not a substitute for, high-quality curriculum and instruction. Expert or distinguished teaching focuses on the understandings and skills of a discipline, causes students to wrestle with profound ideas, calls on students to use what they learn in important ways, helps students organize and make sense of ideas and information, and aids students in connecting the classroom with a wider world (Brandt, 1998; Danielson, 1996; Schlechty, 1997; Wiggins & McTighe, 1998).

Differentiation—one facet of expert teaching—reminds us that these things are unlikely to happen for the full range of students unless curriculum and instruction fit each individual, unless students have choices about what to learn and how, unless students take part in setting learning goals, and unless the classroom connects with the experiences and interest of the individual (Tomlinson, 1995, 1999). Differentiation says, "Building on core teaching and learning practices that are solid, here's what you do to refine them for maximum individual growth."

We first need to ask, Is a given teaching or learning approach likely to have a positive impact on the core of effective teaching and learning? When we are content with the answer, we can ask further, What is the effect of the practice on individuals in an academically diverse population? The latter question always helps us refine the effectiveness of the former but cannot substitute for it.

Standards-Based Teaching

For many teachers, curriculum has become a prescribed set of academic standards, instructional pacing has become a race against a clock to cover the standards, and the sole goal of teaching has been reduced to raising student test scores on a single test, the value of which has scarcely been questioned in the public forum. Teachers feel as though they are torn in opposing directions: They are admonished to attend to student differences, but they must ensure that every student becomes competent in the same subject matter and can demonstrate the competencies on an assessment that is differentiated neither in form nor in time constraints.

To examine the dichotomy between standards-based teaching and differentiation, we must ask questions about how standards influence the quality of

teaching and learning. What is the impact of standards-based teaching on the quality of education in general? Then we can assess ways in which standards-based approaches make an impact on gifted or academically challenged students whose abilities are outside the usual norms of achievement.

- Do the standards reflect the knowledge, understandings, and skills valued most by experts in the disciplines that they represent?
- Are we using standards as a curriculum, or are they reflected in the curriculum?
- Are we slavishly covering standards at breakneck pace, or have we found ways to organize the standards within our curriculum so that students have time to make sense of ideas and skills?
- Does our current focus on standards enliven classrooms, or does it eliminate joy, creativity, and inquiry?
- Do standards make learning more or less relevant and alluring to students?
- Does our use of standards remind us that we are teaching human beings, or does it cause us to forget that fact?

If we are satisfied that our standards-based practices yield positive answers, we can look fruitfully at how to make adaptations to address the needs of academically diverse learners. If our answers are less than satisfactory, we should address the problems. Such problems inevitably point to cracks in the foundation of quality teaching and learning, and we diminish our profession by failing to attend to them. Differentiating curriculum and instruction cannot make up for ill-conceived curriculum and instruction.

Negative Cases

The following examples are recent and real. Sadly, they are not rare. They also show how good intentions can go awry.

- In one standards-driven district, primary grade teachers attended a staff-development session that they had requested and in which they had high interest. The staff developer asked them to list some concepts that they taught so that the session would be linked to what went on in their classrooms. When—even with coaching and examples—no one was able to name the concepts they taught, the staff developer asked for the topics they taught. More awkward silence followed. A few teachers said that they sometimes took a day or two to talk about holidays, such as Halloween, Christmas, or Kwanza, because young students were excited about special occasions. Other teach-

"I no longer see my curriculum as a list to be covered, and I no longer see my students as duplicates of one another."

ers explained that they no longer taught units or topics (and certainly not concepts). Their entire curriculum had become a list of skills that students learned out of context of any meaning or utility—except that the test was coming, and all 6- through 8-year-olds were expected to perform.

- A highly successful elementary school was started two decades ago to serve a student population that speaks more than 25 languages and whose homes are often marked by economic stress. The librarian in the school recently remarked,

This has always been the best place in the world to teach. The students have loved it. Their parents have trusted it. Our students have done well. The teachers have always been excited to come to work. It has been a place of energy and inspired teaching. In the last two years [since the inception of a standards-based program and high-stakes testing], I've watched us become what we were created to avoid. We are telling instead of teaching. We fight to find time to reach out to the kids. Joy in classrooms has been replaced by fear that is first felt by the teachers and then by the students. We're trying hard to keep alive what we believe in, but I'm not sure we can.

- In another standards-driven district, middle school teachers listed student names in one of there columns: *Definitely, Maybe,* and *No Hope.* The designations showed who would surely pass the standards tests, who might pass, and who had no chance of passing. The teachers separated the students into columns because, they said, there was no point in worrying about students who already knew enough to pass the test, and there was no point in wasting time on students who could not be raised to the standard. "It's the only way to go," said one teacher. "It's what we have to do to get the points on this year's test."

In all these places, teachers feel torn between an external impetus to cover the standards and a desire to address the diverse academic needs. In truth, the problem is not a contradiction between standards and appropriately responsive instruction. The problem lies in an ill-conceived interpretation and use of standards that erode the underpinnings of effective teaching and learning. The problem is not that we can't attend to the needs of individual learners, but rather that we've lost the essential frameworks of the disciplines in addi-

tion to the coherence, understanding, purpose, and joy in learning. Our first obligation is to ensure that standards-based teaching practice does not conflict with best teaching practice. Once those are aligned, differentiation—or attention to the diverse needs of learners—follows naturally.

Standards and Differentiation

There is no contradiction between effective standards-based instruction and differentiation. Curriculum tells us *what* to teach: Differentiation tells us *how.* Thus, if we elect to teach a standards-based curriculum, differentiation simply suggests ways in which we can make that curriculum work best for varied learners. In other words, differentiation can show us how to teach the same standard to a range of learners by employing a variety of teaching and learning modes.

Choose any standard. Differentiation suggests that you can challenge all learners by providing materials and tasks on the standard at varied levels of difficulty, with varying degrees of scaffolding, through multiple instructional groups, and with time variations. Further, differentiation suggests that teachers can craft lessons in ways that tap into multiple student interests to promote heightened learner interest in the standard. Teachers can encourage student success by varying ways in which students work: alone or collaboratively, in auditory or visual modes, or through practical or creative means.

Positive Cases

- Science teachers in one small district delineated the key facts, concepts, principles, and skills of their discipline for K–12. Having laid out the framework, they examined the state-prescribed standards for science and mapped them for K–12. They found that the standards in their state did a pretty good job of reflecting the facts and skills of science but did a poor job of making explicit the concepts and principles of science. With the two frameworks in front of them, the teachers could fill in gaps—and more important, could organize their curriculum in ways that were coherent and manageable. Their work helped their colleagues see the big picture of science instruction for K–12 over time, organize instruction conceptually, and teach with the essential principles of science in mind. The result was a districtwide science curriculum that made better sense to teachers and students alike, helped students think like scientists, reduced the teachers' sense of racing to cover disjointed information, and still attended to prescribed standards.

Students learn best when they can make a connection between the curriculum and their interests and life experiences.

- In a high school Algebra II class, the teacher acknowledged that some of her students lacked prerequisite skills, whereas others learned as rapidly as she could teach or even without her help. At the outset of each chapter, the teacher delineated for students the specific skills, concepts, and understandings that they needed to master for that segment of the curriculum—both to have a solid grasp of mathematics and to pass the upcoming standards exam. She helped students make connections to past concepts, understandings, and skills. She divided each week into segments of teacher-led instruction, whole-class instruction, and small-group work.

For group-work sessions, she sometimes met with students who were advanced in a particular topic to urge on their thinking, to help them solve problems in multiple ways, and to apply their understandings and skills to complex, real-life problems. Sometimes she met with students who needed additional instruction or guided assistance in applying what they were learning. Sometimes she created mixed-readiness teams of students whose goal was solving a problem in the most effective way possible. The teacher randomly called on students to present and defend their team's approach, thus maximizing the likelihood that every student had a model for solving an important problem and was able to explain the reasoning behind the solution. These problem-solving groups often evolved into teacher-created study groups that worked together to ensure that everyone had his or her questions answered. Not only did the teacher provide some class time for the study groups, but she also encouraged regular after-school meetings in her room, where she was able to monitor group progress and assist if needed. She recalls,

> The hardest thing for me was learning to teach a class where I wasn't always working with the class as a whole, but that has been rewarding, too. I know my students better. They know Algebra II better—and I think I probably understand it better, too. I haven't made a math prodigy out of everyone, of course, but I can honestly say the students like algebra better and are more confident in their capacity to learn. Their scores on the standards test improved, even though I targeted some ideas and skills more than others. I think what that fact tells me is that if I help students organize their mathematical knowledge and thinking, they can fare better in unfamiliar territory.

- In an elementary classroom, a teacher organized many of her standards around three key concepts—connections, environments, and change—and their related principles; for example, living things are changed by and change their environments. She used them to study history, science, language arts, and sometimes mathematics. Although she generally taught each of the three subjects separately, she helped students make links among them; she created activities for the students that called for reading skills in social studies, for example, and social studies skills in science. That approach, she said, allowed everyone to work with the same big ideas and skills in a lesson while she could adjust materials, activities, and projects for varied readiness levels, diverse interests, and multiple modes of learning. Bringing the students together for class discussions was no problem, she reflected, because everyone's work focused on the essentials—even though students might get to those essentials in different ways. "It took me some time to rethink the standards and how I taught them," she recalled.

> But I feel as if I'm a better teacher. I understand what I'm teaching better, and I certainly have come to understand the students I teach more fully. I no longer see my curriculum as a list to be covered, and I no longer see my students as duplicates of one another.

In these settings, teachers have retained—or, in some cases, have discovered for the first time—the essential frameworks of the disciplines and the coherence, understanding, purpose, and joy in learning. The teachers have struggled to meet their first obligation—to ensure that standards-based teaching practice is not in conflict with best teaching practice. Once the teachers aligned standards with high-quality instruction, differentiation followed naturally.

Quality and Personalization

Overwhelmed by the task, a teacher recently pleaded, "I have all these students with all these different needs; how can anyone expect me to differentiate in my classroom?" Odd as the comment sounds, she spoke for many of us. The more complex the task, the more inviting it is to retreat to the familiar—to find a standardized approach and cling to it.

Thus, we find ourselves saying, "I know I'm missing lots of my students, but if I don't hurry to cover all the standards, how will they succeed on the test?" Or, "I know it would be good to involve students in thinking and problem solving, but there's just no time." The deeper issue is about what happens when we use any approach that allows us to lose sight of

Grading Practices

The following questions help ensure that grading practices are productive for all students.

- How do learners benefit from a grading system that reminds everyone that students with disabilities or who speak English as a second language do not perform as well as students without disabilities or for whom English is their native tongue?

- What do we gain by telling our most able learners that they are "excellent" on the basis of a standard that requires modest effort, calls for no intellectual risk, necessitates no persistence, and demands that they develop few academic coping skills?

- In what ways do our current grading practices motivate struggling or advanced learners to persist in the face of difficulty?

- Is there an opportunity for struggling learners to encounter excellence in our current grading practices?

- Is there an opportunity for advanced learners to encounter struggle in our current grading practices?

—Carol Ann Tomlinson

the soul of teaching and learning. A secondary factor is that such approaches make it difficult to attend to individual differences.

Do standardizing practices fail academically diverse learners? Of course they do. Whatever practices invite us to be paint-by-number teachers will largely fail students who do not fit the template. Paint-by-number approaches will fall short for all of us—teachers and students alike—because they abandon quality. Paint-by-number approaches will fail teachers because they confuse technical expedience with artistry. They will fail students because they confuse compliance with thoughtful engagement. Any educational approach that does not invite us to teach individuals is deeply flawed.

Teaching is hard. Teaching well is fiercely so. Confronted by too many students, a schedule with breaks, a pile of papers that regenerates daily, and incessant demands from every educational stakeholder, no wonder we become habitual and standardized in our practices. Not only do we have no time to question why we do what we do, but we also experience the discomfort of change when we do ask the knotty questions. Nonetheless, our profession cannot progress and our increasingly diverse students cannot succeed if we do less.

References

Brandt, R. (1998). *Powerful teaching.* Alexandria, VA: ASCD.

Danielson, C. (1996). *Enhancing professional practice: A framework for teaching.* Alexandria, VA: ASCD.

Schlechty, P. (1997). *Inventing better schools: An action plan for educational reform.* San Francisco: Jossey-Bass.

Tomlinson, C. (1995). *How to differentiate instruction in mixed-ability classrooms.* Alexandria, VA: ASCD.

Tomlinson, C. (1999). *The differentiated classroom: Responding to the needs of all learners.* Alexandria, VA: ASCD.

Wiggins, G., & McTighe, J. (1998). *Understanding by design.* Alexandria, VA: ASCD.

Carol Ann Tomlinson is Associate Professor of Educational Leadership, Foundations, and Policy. She may be reached at the Curry School of Education, the University of Virginia, Room 287, 405 Emmet St., Charlottesville, VA 22903.

Educating the Net Generation

As technology becomes an integral part of our classrooms and schools, educators can look to the students—the Net Generation—to help make the shift to more student-centered learning.

Don Tapscott

Every time I enter a discussion about efforts to get computers into schools, someone insists that computers aren't the answer. "It won't help to just throw computers at the wall, hoping something will stick. I've seen lots of computers sitting unused in classrooms."

Digital kids are learning precisely the social skills required for effective interaction in the digital economy.

Agreed. Computers alone won't do the trick. They are a necessary but insufficient condition for moving our schools to new heights of effectiveness. We've still got to learn how best to use this technology. And I have become convinced that the most potent force for change is the students themselves.

Why look to the kids? Because they are different from any generation before them. They are the first to grow up surrounded by digital media. Computers are everywhere—in the home, school, factory, and office—as are digital technologies—cameras, video games, and CD-ROMs. Today's kids are so bathed in bits that they think technology is part of the natural landscape. To them, digital technology is no more intimidating than a VCR or a toaster. And these new media are increasingly connected by the Internet, that expanding web of networks that is attracting one million new users a month.

The Net Generation

The Net affects us all—the way we create wealth, the nature of commerce and marketing, the delivery system for entertainment, the role and dynamics of learning, and the nature of government. It should not surprise us that those first to grow up with this new medium are defined by their relationship to it. I call them the Net Generation—the N-Geners.

According to Teenage Research Unlimited (1997), teens feel that being online is as "in" as dating and partying! And this exploding popularity is occurring while the Net is still in its infancy and, as such, is painfully slow; primitive; limited in capabilities; lacking complete security, reliability, and ubiquity; and subject to both hyperbole and ridicule. Nevertheless, children love it and keep coming back after each frustrating experience. They know its potential.

What do students do on the Net? They manage their personal finances; organize protest movements; check facts; discuss zits; check the scores of their favorite team and chat online with its superstars; organize groups to save the rain forest; cast votes; learn more about the illness of their little sister; go to a virtual birthday party; or get video clips from a soon-to-be- released movie.

Chat groups and computer conferences are populated by young people hungry for expression and self-discovery. Younger kids love to meet people and talk about anything. As they mature, their communications center on topics and themes. For all ages, "E-mail me" has become the parting expression of a generation.

Digital Anxiety

For many adults, all this digital activity is a source of high anxiety. Are kids really benefitting from the digital media? Can technology truly improve the process of learning, or is it dumbing down and misguiding educational efforts? What about Net addiction? Is it useful for children to spend time in online chat rooms, and what are they doing there? Are some becoming glued to the screen? What about cyberdating and cybersex? Aren't video games leading to a violent generation? Is technology stressing kids out—as it seems to be doing to adults? Has the Net become a virtual world—drawing children away from parental authority and responsible adult influence—where untold new problems and dangers lie? What is the real risk of online predators, and can children be effectively protected? How can we shield kids from sleaze and porn? As these children come of age, will they lack the social skills for effective participation in the work force?

These questions are just a sampling of the widespread concern raised not just by cynics, moralists, and technophobes, but also by reasonable and well-meaning educators, parents, and members of the community.

Everybody, relax. The kids are all right. They are learning, developing, and thriving in the digital world. They need better tools, better access, better services—*more* freedom to explore, not less. Rather than convey hostility and mistrust, we need to change *our* way of thinking and behaving. This means all of us—parents,

educators, lawmakers, and business leaders alike.

Digital kids are learning precisely the social skills required for effective interaction in the digital economy. They are learning about peer relationships, teamwork, critical thinking, fun, friendships across geographies, self-expression, and self-confidence.

Conventional wisdom says that because children are multitasking—jumping from one computer- based activity to another—their attention span is reduced. Research does not support this view. Ironically, the same people who charge that today's kids are becoming "glued to the screen" also say that kids' attention spans are declining.

The ultimate interactive learning environment is the Internet itself.

At root is the fear that children will not be able to focus and therefore will not learn. This concern is consistent with the view that the primary challenge of learning is to absorb specific information. However, many argue—and I agree—that the content of a particular lesson is less important than learning how to learn. As John Dewey wrote,

> Perhaps the greatest of all pedagogical fallacies is the notion that a person learns only the particular thing he is studying at the time. Collateral learning . . . may be and often is more important than the spelling lesson or lesson in geography or history that is learned. (1963, p. 48)

The Challenge of Schooling

The new technologies have helped create a culture for learning (Papert, 1996) in which the learner enjoys enhanced interactivity and connections with others. Rather than listen to a professor regurgitate facts and theo-

ries, students discuss ideas and learn from one another, with the teacher acting as a participant in the learning. Students construct narratives that make sense out of their own experiences.

Initial research strongly supports the benefits of this kind of learning. For example, in 1996, 33 students in a social studies course at California State University in Northridge were randomly divided into two groups, one taught in a traditional classroom and the other taught virtually on the Web. The teaching model wasn't fundamentally changed—both groups received the same texts, lectures, and exams. Despite this, the Web-based class scored, on average, 20 percent higher than the traditional class. The Web class had more contact with one another and were more interested in the class work. The students also felt that they understood the material better and had greater flexibility to determine how they learned (Schutte, n.d.).

The ultimate interactive learning environment is the Internet itself. Increasingly, this technology includes the vast repository of human knowledge, the tools to manage this knowledge, access to people, and a growing galaxy of services ranging from sandbox environments for preschoolers to virtual laboratories for medical students studying neural psychiatry. Today's baby will tomorrow learn about Michelangelo by walking through the Sistine Chapel, watching Michelangelo paint, and perhaps stopping for a conversation. Students will stroll on the moon. Petroleum engineers will penetrate the earth with the drill bit. Doctors will navigate the cardiovascular system. Researchers will browse through a library. Auto designers will sit in the back seat of the car they are designing to see how it feels and to examine the external view.

Eight Shifts of Interactive Learning

The digital media is causing educators and students alike to shift to new ways of thinking about teaching and learning.

1. From linear to hypermedia learning. Traditional approaches to learning are linear and date back to using books as a learning tool. Stories, novels, and other narratives are generally linear. Most textbooks are written to be tackled from the beginning to the end. TV shows and instructional videos are also designed to be watched from beginning to end.

Students need better tools, better access, better services—more freedom to explore, not less.

But N-Gen access to information is more interactive and nonsequential. Notice how a child channel surfs when watching television. I've found that my kids go back and forth among various TV shows and video games when they're in the family room. No doubt that as TV becomes a Net appliance, children will increasingly depend on this nonlinear way of processing information.

2. From instruction to construction and discovery. Seymour Papert says,

> The scandal of education is that every time you teach something, you deprive a child of the pleasure and benefit of discovery. (de Pommereau, 1996, p. 68)

With new technologies, we will experience a shift away from traditional types of pedagogy to the creation of learning partnerships and learning cultures. This is not to say that teachers should not plan activities or design curriculums. They might, however, design the curriculum in partnership with learners or even help learners design the curriculum themselves.

This constructivist approach to teaching and learning means that rather than assimilate knowledge that is broadcast by an instructor, the learner constructs knowledge anew. Constructivists argue that people learn best by *doing* rather than simply by *listening*. The evidence supporting constructivism is persuasive, but that shouldn't be too surprising. When youngsters are enthusiastic about a fact or a concept that they themselves discovered, they will better retain the information and use it in creative, meaningful ways.

3. From teacher-centered to learner-centered education. The new media focus the learning experience on the individual rather than on the transmitter. Clearly, learner-centered education improves the child's motivation to learn.

The shift from teacher-centered to learner-centered education does not suggest that the teacher is suddenly playing a less important role. A teacher is equally crucial and valuable in the learner-centered context, for he or she creates and structures what happens in the classroom.

Learner-centered education begins with an evaluation of abilities, learning styles, social contexts, and other important factors that affect the student. Evaluation software programs can tailor the learning experience for each individual child. Learner-centered education is also more active, with students discussing, debating, researching, and collaborating on projects with one another and with the teacher.

4. From absorbing material to learning how to navigate and how to learn. This means learning how to synthesize, not just analyze. N-Geners can assess and analyze facts–a formidable challenge in a data galaxy of easily accessible information sources. But more important, they can synthesize. They are engaged in information sources and people on the Net, and then they construct higher-level structures and mental images.

5. From school to lifelong learning. For young baby boomers looking forward to the world of work, life often felt divided–between the period when you *learned* and the period when you *did.* You went to school and maybe to university and learned a trade or profession. For the rest of your life, your challenge was simply to keep up with developments in your field. But

---

I have become convinced that the most potent force for change is the students themselves.

things have changed. Today, many boomers reinvent their knowledge base constantly. Learning has become a continuous, lifelong process. The N-Gen is entering a world of lifelong learning from day one, and unlike the schools of the boomers, today's educational system can anticipate how to prepare students for lifelong learning.

6. From one-size-fits-all to customized learning. The digital media enables students to be treated as individuals–to have highly customized learning experiences based on their backgrounds, individual talents, age levels, cognitive styles, and interpersonal preferences.

As Papert puts it,

> What I see as the real contribution of digital media to education is a flexibility that could allow every individual to find personal paths to learning. This will make it possible for the dream of every progressive educator to come true: In the learning environment of the future, every learner will be "special." (1996, p. 16)

In fact, Papert believes in a "community of learning" shared by students and teachers:

> Socialization is not best done by segregating children into classrooms with kids of the same age. The computer is a medium in which what you make lends itself to be modified and shared. When kids get together on a project, there is abundant discussion; they show it to other kids, other kids want to see it, kids learn to share knowledge with other people— much more than in the classroom. (1997, p. 11)

7. From learning as torture to learning as fun. Maybe torture is an exaggeration, but for many kids, class is not exactly the highlight of their day. Some educators have decried the fact that a generation schooled on *Sesame Street* expects to be entertained at school—and to enjoy the learning experience. They argue that learning and entertainment should be clearly separated.

Why shouldn't learning be entertaining? In *Merriam-Webster's Collegiate Dictionary,* the third definition of the verb *to entertain* is "to keep, hold, or maintain in the mind" and "to receive and take into consideration." In other words, entertainment has always been a profound part of the learning process, and teachers throughout history have been asked to convince their students to entertain ideas. From this perspective, the best teachers were the entertainers. Using the new media, the learner also becomes the entertainer and, in doing so, enjoys, is motivated toward, and feels responsible for learning.

8. From the teacher as transmitter to the teacher as facilitator. Learning is becoming a social activity, facilitated by a new generation of educators.

The topic is saltwater fish. The 6th grade teacher divides the class into teams, asking each team to prepare a presentation on a fish of its choice. Students have access to the Web and are allowed to use any resources. They must cover the topics of history, breathing, propulsion, reproduction, diet, predators, and "cool facts." They must also address questions to others in their team or to others in the class, not to the teacher.

Two weeks later, Melissa's group is first. The students have created a shark project home page with hot links for each topic. As the students talk, they project their presentation onto a screen at the front of the class. They have video clips of different types of sharks and also a clip from Jacques Cousteau discussing the shark as an endangered species. They then use the Web to go live to Aquarius, an underwater site located off the Florida Keys. The class can ask questions of the Aquarius staff, although most inquiries are directed to the project team. One such discussion focuses on which is greater: the dangers posed by sharks to humans or the dangers posed by humans to sharks.

The class decides to hold an online forum on this topic and invites kids from classes in other countries to participate. The team asks students to browse through its project at any time, from any location, because the forum will be up for the rest of the school year. In fact, the team decides to maintain the site by adding new links and fresh information throughout the year. The assignment becomes a living project. Learners from around the world find the shark home page helpful and build links to it.

In this example, the teacher acts as consultant to the teams, facilitates the learning process, and participates as a technical consultant on the new media. The teacher doesn't have to compete with Jacques Cousteau's expertise on underwater life; her teaching is supported by his expertise.

Turning to the Net Generation

Needless to say, a whole generation of teachers needs to learn new tools, new approaches, and new skills. This will be a challenge, not just because of resistance to change by some teachers, but also because of the current atmosphere of financial cutbacks, low teacher morale, increased workloads, and reduced retraining budgets.

But as we make this inevitable transition, we may best turn to the generation raised on and immersed in new technologies. Give students the tools, and they will be the single most important source of guidance on how to make their schools relevant and effective places to learn.

References

de Pommereau, I. (1997, April 21). Computers give children the key to learning. *Christian Science Monitor,* p. 68.

Dewey, J. (1963). *Experience and education.* London: Collier Books.

Papert, S. (1996). *The connected family: Bridging the digital generation gap.* Marietta, GA: Longstreet Press.

Schutte, J. G. (n.d.). *Virtual teaching in higher education* [On-line]. Available: http://www.csun.edu/sociology/virtexp.htm.

Teenage Research Unlimited, Inc. (1996, January). Press release. Northbrook, IL: Author.

Teenage Research Unlimited, Inc. (1997, Spring). Teenage marketing and lifestyle update. Northbrook, IL: Author.

Don Tapscott is President of New Paradigm Learning Corporation and Chairman of Alliance for Converging Technologies, 133 King St. E., Ste. 300, Toronto, ON M5C 1G6, Canada (Website:http://nplc.com; e-mail: nplc@nplc.com).

Unit Selections

Key Points to Consider

❖ Discuss several ways to motivate both at-risk and typical students. What difference is there?

❖ Why should motivational style be consistent with instructional techniques?

❖ How are motivation and classroom management related?

❖ Discuss several ways to discipline both typical students and those with exceptionalities.

❖ How are classroom management and discipline different? Discuss whether discipline can be developed within students, or whether it must be imposed by teachers, supporting your argument with data derived from your reading.

 **Links**   **www.dushkin.com/online/**

These sites are annotated on pages 4 and 5.

The term *motivation* is used by educators to describe the processes of initiating, directing, and sustaining goal-oriented behavior. Motivation is a complex phenomenon, involving many factors that affect an individual's choice of action and perseverance in completing tasks. Furthermore, the reasons why people engage in particular behaviors can only be inferred; motivation cannot be directly measured.

Several theories of motivation, each highlighting different reasons for sustained goal-oriented behavior, have been proposed. We will discuss three of them: behavioral, humanistic, and cognitive. The behavioral theory of motivation suggests that an important reason for engaging in behavior is that reinforcement follows the action. If the reinforcement is controlled by someone else and is arbitrarily related to the behavior (such as money, a token, or a smile), then the motivation is extrinsic. In contrast, behavior may also be initiated and sustained for intrinsic reasons such as curiosity or mastery.

Humanistic approaches to motivation are concerned with the social and psychological needs of individuals. Humans are motivated to engage in behavior to meet these needs. Abraham Maslow, a founder of humanistic psychology, proposes that there is a hierarchy of needs that directs behavior, beginning with physiological and safety needs and progressing to self-actualization. Some other important needs that influence motivation are affiliation and belonging with others, love, self-esteem, influence with others, recognition, status, competence, achievement, and autonomy.

The dominant view of motivation in the educational psychology literature is the cognitive approach. This set of theories proposes that our beliefs about our successes and failures affect our expectations and goals concerning future per-formance. Students who believe that their success is due to their abilities and efforts are motivated toward mastery of skills. Students who blame their failures on inadequate abilities have low self-efficacy and tend to set ability and performance goals that protect their self-image.

Richard Ryan and Edward Deci, in the unit's first selection, review new research on the classic concepts of intrinsic and extrinsic motivation. They discuss the merits of each for helping students become self-regulating learners. Intrinsic forms of motivation are clearly self-regulating. Yet the authors recognize that educators cannot always rely on intrinsic motivation to promote learning. They also discuss two forms of extrinsic motivation that can also promote self regulation. One is promoting identification with the personal importance of a behavior and the second is integrated regulation where the person internalizes the instrumental value of the action. In the second article, Barry

Zimmerman discusses the role of self-efficacy in students' motivation and learning. He argues that self-efficacy predicts student effort as well as the use of self-regulating strategies such as goal setting, self-evaluation, and strategy use. The final article by Penny Hauser-Cram introduces the concept of mastery motivation. She describes how parents and caregivers can negatively affect mastery motivation by being too directive, and offers suggestions for encouraging mastery motivation. The goal is for all children to learn to persist in the face of difficulty and to seek challenge.

No matter how effectively students are motivated, teachers always need to exercise management of behavior in the classroom. Classroom management is more than controlling the behavior of students or disciplining them following misbehavior. Instead, teachers need to initiate and maintain a classroom environment that supports successful teaching and learning. The skills that effective teachers use include preplanning, deliberate introduction of rules and procedures, immediate assertiveness, continual monitoring, consistent feedback to students, and specific consequences.

The first article in this subsection describes the most current thinking about classroom management techniques that best meet the needs of learner-centered classrooms. Mary McCaslin and Thomas Good believe that teachers who value teaching for understanding need to help students internalize a commitment to certain standards of behavior, rather than settle for compliance. They suggest that this can be accomplished by teaching students to coordinate their multiple academic and social goals.

The next four articles address specific disciplinary issues facing teachers today: disciplining students in inclusive classrooms, establishing rules, dealing with confrontational students, and preventing violence in the schools. The first selection, "Teaching Students to Regulate Their Own Behavior," gives advice to teachers with inclusive classrooms about how to help students with special needs learn to regulate their own behavior, and at the same time, take some of the time demands away from the teacher. Next, David Bicard offers a framework for introducing rules in a positive matter. In the third selection, Geoff Colvin, David Ainge, and Ron Nelson observe that even effective classroom managers are sometimes faced with confrontational students. The authors discuss diffusing tactics that can minimize the likelihood of escalating conflict. Finally, Ian Elliot describes a model program for reducing violence in schools. He describes the PeaceBuilders program and the techniques adopted by schools and teachers to help students care about each other and solve problems appropriately.

Intrinsic and Extrinsic Motivations: Classic Definitions and New Directions

Intrinsic and extrinsic types of motivation have been widely studied, and the distinction between them has shed important light on both developmental and educational practices. In this review we revisit the classic definitions of intrinsic and extrinsic motivation in light of contemporary research and theory. Intrinsic motivation remains an important construct, reflecting the natural human propensity to learn and assimilate. However, extrinsic motivation is argued to vary considerably in its relative autonomy and thus can either reflect external control or true self-regulation. The relations of both classes of motives to basic human needs for autonomy, competence and relatedness are discussed. © 2000 Academic Press

Richard M. Ryan and Edward L. Deci

To be motivated means *to be moved* to do something. A person who feels no impetus or inspiration to act is thus characterized as unmotivated, whereas someone who is energized or activated toward an end is considered motivated. Most everyone who works or plays with others is, accordingly, concerned with motivation, facing the question of how much motivation those others, or oneself, has for a task, and practitioners of all types face the perennial task of fostering more versus less motivation in those around them. Most theories of motivation reflect these concerns by viewing motivation as an unitary phenomenon, one that varies from very little motivation to act to a great deal of it.

Yet, even brief reflection suggests that motivation is hardly a unitary phenomenon. People have not only different amounts, but also different kinds of motivation. That is, they vary not only in *level* of motivation (i.e., how much motivation), but also in the *orientation* of that motivation (i.e., what type of motivation). Orientation of motivation concerns the underlying attitudes and goals that give rise to action—that is, it concerns the *why* of actions. As an example, a student can be highly motivated to do homework out of curiosity and interest or, alternatively, because he or she wants to procure the approval of a teacher or parent. A student could be motivated to learn a new set of skills because he or she understands their potential utility or value or because learning the skills will yield a good grade and the privileges a good grade affords. In these examples the amount of motivation does not necessarily vary, but the nature and focus of the motivation being evidenced certainly does.

In Self-Determination Theory (SDT; Deci & Ryan, 1985) we distinguish between different types of motivation based on the different reasons or goals that give rise to an action. The most basic distinction is between *intrinsic motivation*, which refers to doing something because it is inherently interesting or enjoyable, and *extrinsic motivation*, which refers to doing something because it leads to a separable outcome. Over three decades of research has shown that the quality of experience and performance can be very different when one is behaving for intrinsic versus extrinsic reasons. One purpose of this review is to revisit this classic distinction between intrinsic and extrinsic motivation and to summarize the functional differences of these two general types of motivation.

Intrinsic motivation has emerged as an important phenomenon for educators—a natural wellspring of learning and achievement that can be systematically catalyzed or undermined by parent and teacher practices (Ryan & Stiller, 1991). Because intrinsic motivation results in high-quality learning and creativity, it is especially important to detail the factors and forces that engender versus undermine it.

From *Contemporary Educational Psychology*, Volume 25, September 20, 2000, pp. 54-67. © 2000 by Academic Press. Reprinted by permission of the publisher.

However, equally important in the current review is the explication of the very different types of motivation that fall into the category of extrinsic motivation. In the classic literature, extrinsic motivation has typically been characterized as a pale and impoverished (even if powerful) form of motivation that contrasts with intrinsic motivation (e.g., deCharms, 1968). However, SDT proposes that there are varied types of extrinsic motivation, some of which do, indeed, represent impoverished forms of motivation and some of which represent active, agentic states.

Students can perform extrinsically motivated actions with resentment, resistance, and disinterest or, alternatively, with an attitude of willingness that reflects an inner acceptance of the value or utility of a task. In the former case—the classic case of extrinsic motivation—one feels externally propelled into action; in the later case, the extrinsic goal is self-endorsed and thus adopted with a sense of volition. Understanding these different types of extrinsic motivation, and what fosters each of them, is an important issue for educators who cannot always rely on intrinsic motivation to foster learning. Frankly speaking, because many of the tasks that educators want their students to perform are not inherently interesting or enjoyable, knowing how to promote more active and volitional (versus passive and controlling) forms of extrinsic motivation becomes an essential strategy for successful teaching. We detail in this article not only the different types of motivational orientation that exist within the global extrinsic category, but moreover, their differential antecedents and consequences.

In sum, our aim in this article is to revisit the classic distinction between intrinsic and extrinsic motivation and detail the conditions that fosters each. Second, we describe a model of differing types of extrinsic motivation. Our concern here is with how teachers, parents and other socializers can lead students to internalize the responsibility and sense of value for extrinsic goals or, alternatively, how they can foster the more typically depicted "alienated" type of extrinsic motivation that is associated with low student persistence, interest, and involvement.

INTRINSIC MOTIVATION

Intrinsic motivation is defined as the doing of an activity for its inherent satisfactions rather than for some separable consequence. When intrinsically motivated a person is moved to act for the fun or challenge entailed rather than because of external prods, pressures, or rewards. The phenomenon of intrinsic motivation was first acknowledged within experimental studies of animal behavior, where it was discovered that many organisms engage in exploratory, playful, and curiosity-driven behaviors even in the absence of reinforcement or reward (White, 1959). These spontaneous behaviors, although clearly bestowing adaptive benefits on the organism, appear not to be done for any such instrumental reason, but rather for the positive experiences associated with exercising and extending one's capacities.

In humans, intrinsic motivation is not the only form of motivation, or even of volitional activity, but it is a pervasive and important one. From birth onward, humans, in their healthiest states, are active, inquisitive, curious, and playful creatures, displaying a ubiquitous readiness to learn and explore, and they do not require extraneous incentives to do so. This natural motivational tendency is a critical element in cognitive, social, and physical development because it is through acting on one's inherent interests that one grows in knowledge and skills. The inclinations to take interest in novelty, to actively assimilate, and to creatively apply our skills is not limited to childhood, but is a significant feature of human nature that affects performance, persistence, and well-being across life's epochs (Ryan & LaGuardia, in press).

Although, in one sense, intrinsic motivation exists within individuals, in another sense intrinsic motivation exists in the relation between individuals and activities. People are intrinsically motivated for some activities and not others, and not everyone is intrinsically motivated for any particular task.

Because intrinsic motivation exists in the nexus between a person and a task, some authors have defined intrinsic motivation in terms of the task being interesting while others have defined it in terms of the satisfactions a person gains from intrinsically motivated task engagement. In part, these different definitions derive from the fact that the concept of intrinsic motivation was proposed as a critical reaction to the two behavioral theories that were dominant in empirical psychology from the 1940s to the 1960s.

Specifically, because operant theory (Skinner, 1953) maintained that all behaviors are motivated by rewards (i.e., by separable consequence such as food or money), intrinsically motivated activities were said to be ones for which the reward was in the activity itself. Thus, researchers investigated what task characteristics make an activity interesting. In contrast, because learning theory (Hull, 1943) asserted that all behaviors are motivated by physiological drives (and their derivatives), intrinsically motivated activities were said to be ones that provided satisfaction of innate psychological needs. Thus, researchers explored what basic needs are satisfied by intrinsically motivated behaviors.

Our own approach focuses primarily on psychological needs—namely, the innate needs for competence, autonomy, and relatedness—but we of course recognize that basic need satisfaction accrues in part from engaging in interesting activities. Thus, we do sometimes speak of intrinsically interesting activities, but when we do so we are really only talking about tasks that, on average, many people find to be intrinsically interesting. There is considerable practical utility in focusing on task properties and their potential intrinsic interest, as it leads toward improved task design or selection to enhance motivation.

Operational Definitions

Intrinsic motivation has been operationally defined in various ways, although there have been two measures that have been most often used. Basic experimental research (e.g., Deci, 1971) has rested primarily on a behavioral measure of intrinsic motivation called the "free choice" measure. In experiments using this measure participants are exposed to a task under varying conditions (e.g., getting a reward or not). Following this period, the experimenter tells participants they will not be asked to work with the target task any further, and they are then left alone in the experimental room with the target task as well as various distractor activities. They thus have a period of "free choice" about whether to return to the activity, and it is assumed that, if there is no extrinsic reason to do the task (e.g., no reward and no approval), then the more time they spend with the target task, the more intrinsically motivated they are for that task. This measure has been the mainstay through which the dynamics of intrinsic motivation have been experimentally studied.

The other common approach to the measurement of intrinsic motivation is the use of self-reports of interest and enjoyment of the activity per se. Experimental studies typically rely on task-specific measures (e.g., Ryan, 1982; Harackiewicz, 1979). Most field studies have instead used more general, "domain" focused measures, such as one's intrinsic motivation for school (e.g., Harter, 1981).

Facilitating versus Undermining Intrinsic Motivation

Despite the observable evidence that humans are liberally endowed with intrinsic motivational tendencies, this propensity appears to be expressed only under specifiable conditions. Research into intrinsic motivation has thus placed much emphasis on those conditions that elicit, sustain, and enhance this special type of motivation versus those that subdue or diminish it. Self-Determination Theory is specifically framed in terms of social and environmental factors that *facilitate* versus *undermine* intrinsic motivation. This language reflects the assumption that intrinsic motivation, being an inherent organismic propensity, is catalyzed (rather than *caused)* when individuals are in conditions that conduce toward its expression.

Cognitive Evaluation Theory (CET) was presented by Deci and Ryan (1985) to specify the factors in social contexts that produce variability in intrinsic motivation. CET, which is considered a subtheory of self-determination theory, argues that interpersonal events and structures (e.g., rewards, communications, feedback) that conduce toward *feelings of competence* during action can enhance intrinsic motivation for that action because they allow satisfaction of the basic psychological need for competence. Accordingly, for example, optimal challenges, effectance promoting feedback, and freedom from demeaning evaluations are all predicted to facilitate intrinsic motivation.

CET further specifies that feelings of competence will *not* enhance intrinsic motivation unless they are accompanied by *a sense of autonomy* or, in attributional terms, by an *internal perceived locus of causality* (IPLOC; deCharms, 1968). Thus, people must not only experience perceived competence (or self-efficacy), they must also experience their behavior to be self-determined if intrinsic motivation is to be maintained or enhanced. Stated differently, for a high level of intrinsic motivation people must experience satisfaction of the needs both for competence and autonomy. Much of the research has focused on the effects of immediate contextual conditions that either support or thwart the needs for competence and autonomy, but some has recognized that the supports can, to some extent, come from individuals' abiding inner resources that support their ongoing feelings of competence and autonomy.

The tenets of CET, with their primary focus on the needs for competence and autonomy, were formulated to integrate a set of results from initial studies of the effects of rewards, feedback, and other external events on intrinsic motivation. Subsequently, they have been confirmed in both laboratory experiments and applied field studies, many of which have been done in classrooms.

Several early studies showed that positive performance feedback enhanced intrinsic motivation (e.g., Deci, 1971; Harackiewicz, 1979), whereas negative performance feedback diminished it (e.g., Deci & Cascio, 1972). Others (e.g., Vallerand & Reid, 1984) showed that perceived competence mediated these effects, and still others supported the hypothesis that increases in perceived competence must be accompanied by a sense of autonomy in order for the enhanced feelings of competence to result in increased intrinsic motivation (Ryan, 1982).

In fact, the majority of the research on the effects of environmental events on intrinsic motivation has focused on the issue of autonomy versus control rather than that of competence. And this issue has been considerably more controversial. The research began with the demonstration that extrinsic rewards can undermine intrinsic motivation (Deci, 1971; Lepper, Greene, & Nisbett, 1973), which we interpret in terms of the reward shifting people from a more internal to external perceived locus of causality. Although the issue of rewards has been hotly debated, a recent meta-analysis (Deci, Koestner, & Ryan, in press) confirms that virtually every type of expected tangible reward made contingent on task performance does, in fact, undermine intrinsic motivation. Furthermore, not only tangible rewards, but also threats (Deci & Cascio, 1972), deadlines (Amabile,

DeJong, & Lepper, 1976), directives (Koestner, Ryan, Bernieri, & Holt, 1984), and competition pressure (Reeve & Deci, 1996) diminish intrinsic motivation because, according to CET, people experience them as controllers of their behavior. On the other hand, choice and the opportunity for self-direction (e.g., Zuckerman, Porac, Lathin, Smith, & Deci, 1978) appear to enhance intrinsic motivation, as they afford a greater sense of autonomy.

The significance of autonomy versus control for the maintenance of intrinsic motivation has been clearly observed in studies of classroom learning. For example, several studies have shown that autonomy-supportive (in contrast to controlling) teachers catalyze in their students greater intrinsic motivation, curiosity, and the desire for challenge (e.g., Deci, Nezlek, & Sheinman, 1981; Ryan & Grolnick, 1986). Students who are overly controlled not only lose initiative but also learn less well, especially when learning is complex or requires conceptual, creative processing (Benware & Deci, 1984; Grolnick & Ryan, 1987). Similarly, studies show children of parents who are more autonomy supportive to be more mastery oriented—more likely to spontaneously explore and extend themselves—than children of parents who are more controlling (Grolnick, Deci, & Ryan, 1997).

To summarize, the CET aspect of SDT suggests that classroom and home environments can facilitate or forestall intrinsic motivation by supporting versus thwarting the needs for autonomy and competence. However, it is critical to remember that intrinsic motivation will occur only for activities that hold intrinsic interest for an individual—those that have the appeal of novelty, challenge, or aesthetic value for that individual. For activities that do not hold such appeal, the principles of CET do not apply. To understand the motivation for activities that are not experienced as inherently interesting, we need to look more deeply into the nature and dynamics of extrinsic motivation.

EXTRINSIC MOTIVATION

Although intrinsic motivation is clearly an important type of motivation, most of the activities people do are not, strictly speaking, intrinsically motivated. This is especially the case after early childhood, as the freedom to be intrinsically motivated becomes increasingly curtailed by social demands and roles that require individuals to assume responsibility for nonintrinsically interesting tasks. In schools, for example, it appears that intrinsic motivation becomes weaker with each advancing grade.

Extrinsic motivation is a construct that pertains whenever an activity is done in order to attain some separable outcome. Extrinsic motivation thus contrasts with intrinsic motivation, which refers to doing an activity simply for the enjoyment of the activity itself, rather than its instrumental value. However, unlike some perspectives that view extrinsically motivated behavior as invariantly

nonautonomous, SDT proposes that extrinsic motivation can vary greatly in the degree to which it is autonomous. For example, a student who does his homework only because he fears parental sanctions for not doing it is extrinsically motivated because he is doing the work in order to attain the separable outcome of avoiding sanctions. Similarly, a student who does the work because she personally believes it is valuable for her chosen career is also extrinsically motivated because she too is doing it for its instrumental value rather than because she finds it interesting. Both examples involve instrumentalities, yet the latter case entails personal endorsement and a feeling of choice, whereas the former involves mere compliance with an external control. Both represent intentional behavior, but the two types of extrinsic motivation vary in their relative autonomy.

Given that many of the educational activities prescribed in schools are not designed to be intrinsically interesting, a central question concerns how to motivate students to value and self-regulate such activities, and without external pressure, to carry them out on their own. This problem is described within SDT in terms of fostering the *internalization and integration* of values and behavioral regulations (Deci & Ryan, 1985). Internalization is the process of taking in a value or regulation, and integration is the process by which individuals more fully transform the regulation into their own so that it will emanate from their sense of self. Thought of as a continuum, the concept of internalization describes how one's motivation for behavior can range from amotivation or unwillingness, to passive compliance, to active personal commitment. With increasing internalization (and its associated sense of personal commitment) come greater persistence, more positive self-perceptions, and better quality of engagement.

Within SDT a second subtheory, referred to as *Organismic Integration Theory* (OIT), was introduced to detail the different forms of extrinsic motivation and the contextual factors that either promote or hinder internalization and integration of the regulation for these behaviors (Deci & Ryan, 1985). Figure 1 illustrates the OIT taxonomy of types of motivation, arranged from left to right in terms of the extent to which the motivation for one's behavior emanates from one's self.

At the far left is *amotivation*, which is the state of lacking an intention to act. When amotivated, a person's behavior lacks intentionality and a sense of personal causation. Amotivation results from not valuing an activity (Ryan, 1995), not feeling competent to do it (Deci, 1975), or not believing it will yield a desired outcome (Seligman, 1975). Theorists who have treated motivation as a unitary concept (e.g., Bandura, 1986) have been concerned only with the distinction between what we call amotivation and motivation. However, one can see from Fig. 1 that to the right of amotivation are various types of motivation that we have organized to reflect their differing degrees of autonomy or self-determination.

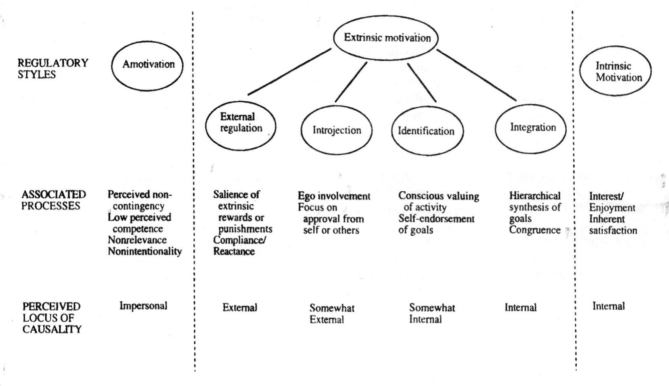

FIG. 1. A taxonomy of human motivation.

Just to the right of amotivation, is a category that represents the least autonomous forms of extrinsic motivation, a category we label *external regulation*. Such behaviors are performed to satisfy an external demand or obtain an externally imposed reward contingency. Individuals typically experience externally regulated behavior as controlled or alienated, and their actions have an *external perceived locus of causality* (EPLOC; deCharms, 1968). External regulation is the only kind of motivation recognized by operant theorists (e.g., Skinner, 1953), and it is this type of extrinsic motivation that was typically contrasted with intrinsic motivation in early lab studies and discussions.

A second type of extrinsic motivation is *introjected regulation*. Introjection describes a type of internal regulation that is still quite controlling because people perform such actions with the feeling of pressure in order to avoid guilt or anxiety or to attain ego-enhancements or pride. Put differently, introjection represents regulation by contingent self-esteem. A classic form of introjection is *ego involvement* (Nicholls, 1984; Ryan, 1982), in which a person performs an act in order to enhance or maintain self-esteem and the feeling of worth. Although the regulation is internal to the person, introjected behaviors are not experienced as fully part of the self and thus still have an EPLOC.

A more autonomous, or self-determined, form of extrinsic motivation is regulation through *identification*. Here, the person has identified with the personal impor-

tance of a behavior and has thus accepted its regulation as his or her own. A boy who memorizes spelling lists because he sees it as relevant to writing, which he values as a life goal, has identified with the value of this learning activity.

Finally, the most autonomous form of extrinsic motivation is *integrated regulation*. Integration occurs when identified regulations have been fully assimilated to the self. This occurs through self-examination and bringing new regulations into congruence with one's other values and needs. The more one internalizes the reasons for an action and assimilates them to the self, the more one's extrinsically motivated actions become self-determined. Integrated forms of motivation share many qualities with intrinsic motivation, being both autonomous and unconflicted. However, they are still extrinsic because behavior motivated by integrated regulation is done for its presumed instrumental value with respect to some outcome that is separate from the behavior, even though it is volitional and valued by the self.

At the far right hand end of the figure is intrinsic motivation. This placement emphasizes that intrinsic motivation is a prototype of self-determined activity. Yet, as implied above, this does not mean that as extrinsic regulations become more internalized they are transformed into intrinsic motivation.

The process of internalization is developmentally important, as social values and regulations are continually being internalized over the life span. Still, we do not suggest that the continuum underlying types of extrinsic motivation is a *developmental* continuum, per se. One does not have to progress through each stage of internalization with respect to a particular regulation; indeed, one can initially adopt a new behavioral regulation at any point along this continuum depending upon prior experiences and situational factors (Ryan, 1995). Some behaviors could begin as introjects, others as identifications. A person might originally get exposed to an activity because of an external regulation (e.g., a reward), and (if the reward is not perceived as too controlling) such exposure might allow the person to experience the activity's intrinsically interesting properties, resulting in an orientation shift. Or a person who has identified with the value of an activity might lose that sense of value under a controlling mentor and move "backward" into an external regulatory mode. Thus, while there are predictable reasons for movement between orientations, there is no necessary "sequence." Developmental issues are, however, evident in two ways: (1) the types of behaviors and values that can be assimilated to the self increase with growing cognitive and ego capacities and (2) it appears that people's general regulatory style does, on average, tend to become more "internal" over time (e.g., Chandler & Connell, 1987), in accord with the general organismic tendencies toward autonomy and self-regulation (Ryan, 1995).

Ryan and Connell (1989) tested the formulation that these different types of motivation do indeed lie along a continuum of relative autonomy. They investigated achievement behaviors (e.g., doing homework) among elementary school children, assessing external, introjected, identified, and intrinsic reasons for engaging in these behaviors. They found that the four types of regulation were intercorrelated according to a quasi-simplex (ordered correlation) pattern, thus providing evidence for an underlying continuum of autonomy. Differences in attitudes and adjustment were also associated with the different types of extrinsic motivation. For example, the more students were externally regulated the less they showed interest, value, or effort, and the more they indicated a tendency to blame others, such as the teacher, for negative outcomes. Introjected regulation was positively related to expending effort, but was also related to more anxiety and to poorer coping with failures. Identified regulation was associated with greater enjoyment of school and more positive coping styles. And intrinsic motivation was correlated with interest, enjoyment, felt competence, and positive coping.

Subsequent studies have extended these findings concerning types of extrinsic motivation, showing for example that more autonomous extrinsic motivation is associated with greater engagement (Connell & Wellborn, 1990), better performance (Miserandino, 1996), less dropping out (Vallerand & Bissonnette, 1992), higher quality learning (Grolnick & Ryan, 1987), and greater psychological well-being (Sheldon & Kasser, 1995),

among other outcomes. Additionally, there appears to be cross-cultural generalizability to the model as presented in Fig. 1 (e.g., Hayamizu, 1997).

Greater internalization appears, then, to yield manifold adaptive advantages (Ryan, Kuhl, & Deci, 1997), including more behavioral effectiveness (due to lessened conflict and greater access to personal resources) and greater experienced well-being. Given the clear significance of internalization for both personal experience and behavioral and performance outcomes, the critical applied issue concerns how to promote the autonomous regulation of extrinsically motivated behaviors.

Because extrinsically motivated behaviors are not inherently interesting and thus must initially be externally prompted, the primary reason people are likely to be willing to do the behaviors is that they are valued by significant others to whom they feel (or would like to feel) connected, whether that be a family, a peer group, or a society. This suggests that the groundwork for facilitating internalization is providing a sense of belongingness and connectedness to the persons, group, or culture disseminating a goal, or what in SDT we call a sense of *relatedness*. In classrooms this means that students' feeling respected and cared for by the teacher is essential for their willingness to accept the proffered classroom values. In support of this, Ryan, Stiller, and Lynch (1994) found that relatedness to teachers (and parents) was associated with greater internalization of school-related behavioral regulations.

A second issue concerns perceived *competence*. Adopting as one's own an extrinsic goal requires that one feel efficacious with respect to it. Students will more likely adopt and internalize a goal if they understand it and have the relevant skills to succeed at it. Thus, we theorize that supports for competence (e.g., offering optimal challenges and effectance-relevant feedback) facilitate internalization.

According to the SDT approach, a regulation that has been internalized may be only introjected, and that type of regulation could well leave people feeling satisfaction of their needs for competence and relatedness. However, to only introject a regulation and thus to be controlled by it will not leave the people feeling self-determined. We therefore suggest that autonomy support also facilitates internalization; in fact, it is the critical element for a regulation being integrated rather than just introjected. Controlling contexts may yield introjected regulation if they support competence and relatedness, but only autonomy supportive contexts will yield integrated self-regulation. To fully internalize a regulation, and thus to become autonomous with respect to it, people must inwardly grasp its meaning and worth. It is these meanings that become internalized and integrated in environments that provide supports for the needs for competence, relatedness, and autonomy.

Again, research has supported this reasoning. Deci, Eghrari, Patrick, and Leone (1994) experimentally demonstrated that providing a meaningful rationale for an uninteresting behavior, along with supports for autonomy and relatedness, promoted internalization and integration. Controlling contexts yielded less overall internalization, but even more interesting, the internalization that did occur in controlling contexts tended to be only introjected. In a study involving parent interviews, Grolnick and Ryan (1989) found higher levels of internalization and integration of school-related values among children whose parents were more supportive of autonomy and relatedness. Williams and Deci (1996) used a longitudinal design to show greater internalization among medical students whose instructors were more autonomy and competence supportive. These are a few of the findings in this area that suggest how supports for relatedness and competence facilitate internalization and how support for autonomy additionally facilitates the integration of behavioral regulations. When that occurs, people not only feel competent and related, but also self-determined, as they carry out extrinsically valued activities.

CONCLUSIONS

We have briefly presented self-determination theory in order to make the critical distinction between behaviors that are volitional and accompanied by the experience of freedom and autonomy—those that emanate from one's sense of self—and those that are accompanied by the experience of pressure and control and are not representative of one's self. Intrinsically motivated behaviors, which are performed out of interest and satisfy the innate psychological needs for competence and autonomy are the prototype of self-determined behavior. Extrinsically motivated behaviors—those that are executed because they are instrumental to some separable consequence—can vary in the extent to which they represent self-determination. Internalization and integration are the processes through which extrinsically motivated behaviors become more self-determined.

We reviewed studies that have specified the social contextual conditions that support intrinsic motivation and facilitate internalization and integration of extrinsically motivated tasks. The studies have been interpreted in terms of the basic psychological needs. That is, we saw that social contextual conditions that support one's feelings of competence, autonomy, and relatedness are the basis for one maintaining intrinsic motivation and becoming more self-determined with respect to extrinsic motivation. We pointed out that in schools, the facilitation of more self-determined learning requires classroom conditions that allow satisfaction of these three basic human needs—that is that support the innate needs to feel connected, effective, and agentic as one is exposed to new ideas and exercises new skills.

REFERENCES

Amabile, T. M., DeJong, W., & Lepper, M. R. (1976). Effects of externally imposed deadlines on subsequent intrinsic motivation. *Journal of Personality and Social Psychology, 34,* 92–98.

Bandura, A. (1986). *Social foundations of thought and action: A social cognitive theory.* Englewood Cliffs, NJ: Prentice–Hall.

Benware, C., & Deci, E. L. (1984). Quality of learning with an active versus passive motivational set. *American Educational Research Journal, 21,* 755–765.

Chandler, C. L., & Connell, J. P. (1987). Children's intrinsic, extrinsic and internalized motivation: A developmental study of children's reasons for liked and disliked behaviours. *British Journal of Developmental Psychology, 5,* 357–365.

Connell, J. P., & Wellborn, J. G. (1990). Competence, autonomy and relatedness: A motivational analysis of self-system processes. In M. R. Gunnar & L. A. Sroufe (Eds.), *The Minnesota symposium on child psychology* (Vol. 22, (pp. 43–77). Hillsdale, NJ: Erlbaum.

deCharms, R. (1968). *Personal causation.* New York: Academic Press.

Deci, E. L. (1971). Effects of externally mediated rewards on intrinsic motivation. *Journal of Personality and Social Psychology, 18,* 105–115.

Deci, E. L. (1975). *Intrinsic motivation.* New York: Plenum.

Deci, E. L., & Cascio, W. F. (1972, April). *Changes in intrinsic motivation as a function of negative feedback and threats.* Presented at the meeting of the Eastern Psychological Association, Boston.

Deci, E. L., Eghrari, H., Patrick, B. C., & Leone, D. R. (1994). Facilitating internalization: The self-determination theory perspective. *Journal of Personality, 62,* 119–142.

Deci, E. L., Koestner, R., & Ryan, R. M. (1998). *Extrinsic rewards and intrinsic motivation: Clear and reliable effects.* Unpublished manuscript, University of Rochester.

Deci, E. L., Nezlek, J., & Scheinman, L. (1981). Characteristics of the rewarder and intrinsic motivation of the rewardee. *Journal of Personality and Social Psychology, 40,* 1–10.

Deci, E. L., & Ryan, R. M. (1985). *Intrinsic motivation and self-determination in human behavior.* New York: Plenum.

Grolnick, W. S., Deci, E. L., & Ryan, R. M. (1997). Internalization within the family: The self-determination perspective. In J. E. Grusec & L. Kuczynski (Eds.), *Parenting and children's internalization of values: A handbook of contemporary theory* (pp. 135–161). New York: Wiley.

Grolnick, W. S., & Ryan, R. M. (1987). Autonomy in children's learning: An experimental and individual difference investigation. *Journal of Personality and Social Psychology, 52,* 890–898.

Harackiewicz, J. (1979). The effects of reward contingency and performance feedback on intrinsic motivation. *Journal of Personality and Social Psychology, 37,* 1352–1363.

Harter, S. (1981). A new self-report scale of intrinsic versus extrinsic orientation in the classroom: Motivational and informational components. *Developmental Psychology, 17,* 300–312.

Hayamizu, T. (1997). Between intrinsic and extrinsic motivation: Examination of reasons for academic study based on the theory of internalization. *Japanese Psychological Research, 39,* 98–108.

Hull, C. L. (1943). *Principles of behavior.* New York: Appleton–Century–Crofts.

Koestner, R., Ryan, R. M., Bernieri, F., & Holt, K. (1984). Setting limits on children's behavior: The differential effects of controlling versus informational styles on intrinsic motivation and creativity. *Journal of Personality, 52,* 233–248.

Lepper, M. R., Greene, D., & Nisbett, R. E. (1973). Undermining children's intrinsic interest with extrinsic rewards: A test of the "overjustification" hypothesis. *Journal of Personality and Social Psychology, 28,* 129–137.

Miserandino, M. (1996). Children who do well in school: Individual differences in perceived competence and autonomy in above-average children. *Journal of Educational Psychology, 88,* 203–214.

Nicholls, J. G. (1984). Achievement motivation: Conceptions of ability, subjective experience, task choice, and performance. *Psychological Review, 91,* 328–346.

Reeve, J., & Deci, E. L. (1996). Elements of the competitive situation that affect intrinsic motivation. *Personality and Social Psychology Bulletin, 22,* 24–33.

Ryan, R. M. (1982). Control and information in the intrapersonal sphere: An extension of cognitive evaluation theory. *Journal of Personality and Social Psychology, 43,* 450–461.

Ryan, R. M. (1995). Psychological needs and the facilitation of integrative processes. *Journal of Personality, 63,* 397–427.

Ryan, R. M., & Connell, J. P. (1989). Perceived locus of causality and internalization: Examining reasons for acting in two domains. *Journal of Personality and Social Psychology, 57,* 749–761.

Ryan, R. M., & Grolnick, W. S. (1986). Origins and pawns in the classroom: Self-report and projective assessments of individual differences in children's perceptions. *Journal of Personality and Social Psychology, 50,* 550–558.

Ryan, R. M., Kuhl, J., & Deci, E. L. (1997). Nature and autonomy: Organizational view of social and neurobiological aspects of self-regulation in behavior and development. *Development and Psychopathology, 9,* 701–728.

Ryan, R. M., & Stiller, J. (1991). The social contexts of internalization: Parent and teacher influences on autonomy, motivation and learning. In P. R. Pintrich & M. L. Maehr (Eds.), *Advances in motivation and achievement* (Vol. 7, pp. 115–149). Greenwich, CT: JAI Press.

Ryan, R. M., Stiller, J., & Lynch, J. H. (1994). Representations of relationships to teachers, parents, and friends as predictors of academic motivation and self-esteem. *Journal of Early Adolescence, 14,* 226–249.

Seligman, M. (1975). *Helplessness: On depression, development, and death.* San Francisco: W. H. Freeman.

Sheldon, K. M., & Kasser, T. (1995). Coherence and congruence: Two aspects of personality integration. *Journal of Personality and Social Psychology, 68,* 531–543.

Skinner, B. F. (1953). *Science and human behavior.* New York: Macmillan.

Vallerand, R. J., & Bissonnette, R. (1992). Intrinsic, extrinsic, and amotivational styles as predictors of behavior: A prospective study. *Journal of Personality, 60,* 599–620.

Vallerand, R. J., & Reid, G. (1984). On the causal effects of perceived competence on intrinsic motivation: A test of cognitive evaluation theory. *Journal of Sport Psychology, 6,* 94–102.

White, R. W. (1959). Motivation reconsidered. *Psychological Review, 66,* 297–333.

Williams, G. C., & Deci, E. L. (1996). Internalization of biopsychosocial values by medical students: A test of self-determination theory. *Journal of Personality and Social Psychology, 70,* 767–779.

Zuckerman, M., Porac, J., Lathin, D., Smith, R., & Deci, E. L. (1978). On the importance of self-determination for intrinsically motivated behavior. *Personality and Social Psychology Bulletin, 4,* 443–446.

Address correspondence and reprint requests to Richard Ryan, University of Rochester, Meliora 492, Rochester, NY 14627.

Self-Efficacy: An Essential Motive to Learn

During the past two decades, self-efficacy has emerged as a highly effective predictor of students' motivation and learning. As a performance-based measure of perceived capability, self-efficacy differs conceptually and psychometrically from related motivational constructs, such as outcome expectations, self-concept, or locus of control. Researchers have succeeded in verifying its discriminant validity as well as convergent validity in predicting common motivational outcomes, such as students' activity choices, effort, persistence, and emotional reactions. Self-efficacy beliefs have been found to be sensitive to subtle changes in students' performance context, to interact with self-regulated learning processes, and to mediate students' academic achievement. © 2000 Academic Press

Barry J. Zimmerman

Graduate School and University Center of City University of New York

Educators have long recognized that students' beliefs about their academic capabilities play an essential role in their motivation to achieve, but self-conceptions regarding academic performance initially proved difficult to measure in a scientifically valid way. Initial efforts to study students' self-beliefs gave little attention to the role of environmental influences, such as specific features of performance contexts or domains of academic functioning. In the late 1970s, a number of researchers began to assess self-beliefs in a more task-specific way, and one of the most important of these efforts focused on self-efficacy. In 1977(a) Bandura proposed a theory of the origins, mediating mechanisms, and diverse effects of beliefs of personal efficacy, and he provided guidelines for measurement of self-efficacy beliefs for different domains of functioning. In the present article, I define self-efficacy and distinguish it from related conceptions in the literature, describe its role in academic motivation and learning (with special attention to students' capabilities to regulate their own learning activities), and discuss its susceptibility to instruction and other social-cultural influences. Because of space limitations, I cite only key studies and do not consider other issues such as theoretical controversies or gender differences in self-efficacy. For comprehensive reviews of research on academic self-efficacy, I recommend Bandura (1997), Pajares (1996b, 1997), Schunk (1989), and Zimmerman (1995).

SELF-EFFICACY AND ITS DIMENSIONS

Before Bandura (1977a) introduced self-efficacy as a key component in social cognitive theory, he discussed human motivation primarily in terms of outcome expectations. However, during the treatment of phobic individuals with mastery modeling techniques, individual differences in generalization were found regardless of the fact that all subjects could successfully interact with the target of their fear (e.g., touch a snake or dog) without adverse consequences at the end of therapy. Although the subjects developed a strong outcome expectancy that proper techniques (e.g., for handling a snake or dog) would protect them from adverse consequences (such as biting), they still differed in their perceived capabilities to use the techniques outside the therapeutic setting. Bandura labeled this individual difference *self-efficacy* and sought to measure it using task-specific scales. Although self-efficacy and outcome expectations were both hypothesized to affect motivation, he suggested that self-efficacy would play a larger role because "the types of outcomes people anticipate depend largely on their judgments of how well they will be able to perform in given situations" (Bandura, 1986, p. 392).

Bandura (1977a, 1997) formally defined perceived self-efficacy as personal judgments of one's capabilities to organize and execute courses of action to attain designated goals, and he sought to assess its level, generality, and strength across activities and contexts. The *level* of self-efficacy refers to its dependence on the difficulty of a particular task, such as spelling words of increasing difficulty; *generality* pertains to the transferability of self-efficacy beliefs across activities, such as from algebra to statistics; *strength* of perceived efficacy is measured by the amount of one's certainty about performing a given task. These properties of self-efficacy judgments are measured using questionnaire items that are task specific, vary in difficulty, and capture degrees of confidence (e.g., from 0 to 100%).

From *Contemporary Educational Psychology,* Volume 25, January 2000, pp. 82-91. © 2000 by Academic Press. Reprinted by permission of the publisher.

With regard to their content, self-efficacy measures focus on *performance capabilities* rather than on personal qualities, such as one's physical or psychological characteristics. Respondents judge their capabilities to fulfill given task demands, such as solving fraction problems in arithmetic, not who they are personally or how they feel about themselves in general. Self-efficacy beliefs are not a single disposition but rather are *multidimensional* in form and differ on the basis of the domain of functioning. For example, efficacy beliefs about performing on a history test may differ from beliefs about a biology examination. Self-efficacy measures are also designed to be sensitive to variations in performance *context,* such as learning in a noisy lounge compared to the quietude of the library. In addition, perceptions of efficacy depend on a *mastery criterion* of performance rather than on normative or other criteria. For example, students rate their certainty about solving a crossword puzzle of a particular difficulty level, not how well they expect to do on the puzzle in comparison to other students. Finally, self-efficacy judgments specifically refer to *future* functioning and are assessed before students perform the relevant activities. This antecedent property positions self-efficacy judgments to play a causal role in academic motivation.

SELF-EFFICACY AND RELATED BELIEFS

Self-efficacy beliefs differ conceptually and psychometrically from closely related constructs, such as outcome expectations, self-concept, and perceived control. The conceptual distinction that Bandura (1986) drew between academic self-efficacy and *outcome expectancies* was studied psychometrically in research on reading and writing achievement. Shell, Murphy, and Bruning (1989) measured self-efficacy in terms of perceived capability to perform various reading and writing activities, and they assessed outcome expectancies regarding the value of these activities in attaining various outcomes in employment, social pursuits, family life, education, and citizenship. Efficacy beliefs and outcome expectancies jointly predicted 32% of the variance in reading achievement, with perceived efficacy accounting for virtually all the variance. Only perceived self-efficacy was a significant predictor of writing achievement. These results not only show the discriminant validity of self-efficacy measures, they support Bandura's contention that self-efficacy plays a larger role than outcome expectancies in motivation.

One of the closest constructs to self-efficacy is *self-concept.* The latter belief is a more general self-descriptive construct that incorporates many forms of self-knowledge and self-evaluative feelings (Marsh & Shavelson, 1985). Historically, self-concept was defined by phenomenologists (e.g., Rogers, 1951) as a global perception of oneself and one's self-esteem reactions to that self-perception, but this global measure of self-belief was not found to be related consistently to students' academic performance (Hattie, 1992; Wylie, 1968). Perhaps as a result, a number of theorists (e.g., Harter, 1978; Marsh & Shavelson, 1985) reconceptualized self-concept as a hierarchical construct, with a global self-concept at the apex of a self-hierarchy but added subcategories such as academic self-concept in the middle of the hierarchy and academic do-

main-specific self-concepts at the bottom. The latter self-concept measures emphasize *self-esteem reactions* by posing self-evaluative questions, such as "How good are you in English?" By contrast, self-efficacy items focus exclusively on task-specific *performance expectations,* such as "How certain are you that you can diagram this sentence?" Although prior task reactions and future performance expectations are often correlated, Bandura (1997) notes it is possible conceptually to have high self-efficacy about a capability that one does not particularly esteem as well as the reverse.

There is growing evidence that, although self-efficacy measures offer predictive advantages when a task is familiar and can be specified precisely. For example, Pajares and Miller (1994) used path analysis procedures to examine the predictive and mediational roles of these two constructs in mathematical problem solving by college students. Math self-efficacy was more predictive of problem solving than was math self-concept or, for that matter, perceived usefulness of mathematics, prior experience with mathematics, or gender. The effect of prior math experiences on math problem solving was mediated primarily by self-efficacy beliefs, but self-concept played a small but significant role. Thus, when self-concept and self-efficacy beliefs are both included in regression equations, self-efficacy beliefs display discriminant validity by independently predicting future academic achievement. Although self-efficacy questionnaire items should be adapted to specific tasks, the scope of these tasks can vary on the basis of the user's intended purpose, ranging from proficiency in an academic domain (e.g., writing or mathematics) to proficiency in a subskill (e.g., grammar or fractions). This second criterion for developing self-efficacy measures involves their *correspondence* to the performance capability in question. Pajares (1996a) demonstrated that the predictiveness of self-efficacy measures increases as a function of both their specificity and correspondence to a skill. Thus, self-efficacy differs from self-concept in both its specificity and correspondence to varying performance tasks and contexts.

Another closely associated construct to self-efficacy is *perceived control,* which emerged from research on locus of control (Rotter, 1966). Perceived control refers to general expectancies about whether outcomes are controlled by one's behavior or by external forces, and it is theorized that an internal locus of control should support self-directed courses of action, whereas an external locus of control should discourage them. Locus-of-control scales are neither task nor domain specific in their item content but rather refer to general beliefs about the internality or externality of causality. Bandura (1986) has questioned the value of general control beliefs because students may feel anxious about controlling one type of subject matter or performance setting (e.g., solving mathematical problems in a limited time period) but not others. In support of this contention, Smith (1989) found that locus of control measures did not predict improvements in academic performance or reductions in anxiety in highly self-anxious students who underwent an intensive coping skills training program, but self-efficacy scales did predict such improvements.

In summary, measures of self-efficacy are not only conceptually distinctive from closely associated constructs such as outcome expectancies, self-concept, and perceived control, they have discriminant validity in predicting a variety of academic outcomes.

ROLE OF SELF-EFFICACY IN ACADEMIC MOTIVATION

Self-efficacy beliefs have also shown convergent validity in influencing such key indices of academic motivation as choice of activities, level of effort, persistence, and emotional reactions. There is evidence (Bandura, 1997) that self-efficacious students participate more readily, work harder, persist longer, and have fewer adverse emotional reactions when they encounter difficulties than do those who doubt their capabilities.

In terms of *choice of activities,* self-efficacious students undertake difficult and challenging tasks more readily than do inefficacious students. Bandura and Schunk (1981) found that students' mathematical self-efficacy beliefs were predictive of their choice of engaging in subtraction problems rather than in a different type of task: The higher the children's sense of efficacy, the greater their choice of the arithmetic activity. Zimmerman and Kitsantas (1997; 1999) also found self-efficacy to be highly correlated with students' rated intrinsic interest in a motoric learning task as well as in a writing revision task. Furthermore, measures of self-efficacy correlate significantly with students' choice of majors in college, success in course work, and perseverance (Hackett & Betz, 1989; Lent, Brown, & Larkin, 1984).

Self-efficacy beliefs are predictive of two measures of students' *effort:* rate of performance and expenditure of energy. For example, Schunk and colleagues found that perceived self-efficacy for learning correlates positively with students' rate of solution of arithmetic problems (Schunk & Hanson, 1985; Schunk, Hanson, & Cox, 1987). Salomon (1984) has found that self-efficacy is positively related to self-rated mental effort and achievement during students' learning from text material that was perceived as difficult. Regarding the effects of perceived self-efficacy on *persistence,* path analyses have shown that it influences students' skill acquisition both directly and indirectly by increasing their persistence (Schunk, 1981). The direct effect indicates that perceived self-efficacy influences students' methods of learning as well as their motivational processes. These results validate the mediational role that self-efficacy plays in motivating persistence and academic achievement. In a meta-analytic review of nearly 70 studies of persistence and rate measures of motivation, Multon, Brown, and Lent (1991) found a significant positive effect size of students' self-efficacy beliefs.

Student's beliefs about their efficacy to manage academic task demands can also influence them *emotionally* by decreasing their stress, anxiety, and depression (Bandura, 1997). For example, Pajares and Kranzler (1995) have studied the relationship between self-efficacy and students' anxiety reactions regarding mathematics. Although the two measures were nega-

tively correlated, only self-efficacy was predictive of mathematics performance when compared in a joint path analysis. There is also evidence that students' performance in academically threatening situations depends more on efficacy beliefs than on anxiety arousal. Siegel, Galassi, and Ware (1985) found that self-efficacy beliefs are more predictive of math performance than is math anxiety. The strength of efficacy beliefs accounted for more than 13% of the variance in their final math grades, whereas math anxiety did not prove to be a significant predictor. These studies provide clear evidence of the discriminant and predictive validity of self-efficacy measures, and they suggest particular benefit if educators focus on fostering a positive sense of personal efficacy rather than merely diminishing scholastic anxiety.

SELF-EFFICACY AND SELF-REGULATION OF LEARNING

Self-efficacy beliefs also provide students with a sense of agency to motivate their learning through use of such self-regulatory processes as goal setting, self-monitoring, self-evaluation, and strategy use. For example, there is evidence (Zimmerman, Bandura, & Martinez-Pons, 1992) that the more capable students judge themselves to be, the more challenging the *goals* they embrace. When self-efficacy and personal goal setting from the beginning of a school term were used jointly to predict final course grades in high school social studies, they increased prediction by 31% over a measure of prior grades in social studies. Similarly, when self-efficacy and personal goal setting were compared with the verbal subscale of the Scholastic Aptitude Test, there was an increase of 35% in predicting college students' final grades in a writing course (Zimmerman & Bandura, 1994). Although prior course grades and general measures of ability are considered exemplary predictors of achievement, these studies demonstrated that self-efficacy beliefs and goal setting add significantly to the predictiveness of these measures.

The effects of efficacy beliefs on students' *self-monitoring* was studied during concept learning (Bouffard-Bouchard, Parent, & Larivee, 1991). Efficacious students were better at monitoring their working time, more persistent, less likely to reject correct hypotheses prematurely, and better at solving conceptual problems than inefficacious students of equal ability. Self-efficacy beliefs also affect the *self-evaluation* standards students use to judge the outcomes of their self-monitoring. In a path analytic study (Zimmerman & Bandura, 1994), self-efficacy for writing beliefs significantly predicted college students' personal standards for the quality of writing considered self-satisfying as well as their goal setting and writing proficiency. Self-efficacy beliefs also motivate students' use of *learning strategies.* With fifth, eighth, and eleventh grade students, there were developmental increases in perceived verbal and mathematical efficacy as well as strategy use, and there was a substantial relation (16 to 18% shared variance) between efficacy beliefs and strategy use across the three grade levels of schooling (Zimmerman & Martinez-Pons, 1990).

The greater motivation and self-regulation of learning of self-efficacious students produces higher *academic achievement* according to a range of measures. Multon, Brown, and Lent (1991) found an overall effect size of .38, indicating that self-efficacy accounted for approximately 14% of the variance in students' academic performance across a variety of student samples, experimental designs, and criterion measures. This represents further evidence of the convergent validity of self-efficacy beliefs.

INSTRUCTIONAL AND SOCIAL INFLUENCES ON SELF-EFFICACY BELIEFS

In contrast to trait measures of self-perceptions, self-efficacy indices focus on cognitive beliefs that are readily influenced by four types of experience: enactive attainment, vicarious experience, verbal persuasion, and physiological states. *Enactive* experiences are the most influential source of efficacy belief because they are predicated on the outcomes of personal experiences, whereas *vicarious* influences depend on an observer's self-comparison with as well as outcomes attained by a model. If a model is viewed as more able or talented, observers will discount the relevance of the model's performance outcomes for themselves. *Verbal persuasion* has an even more limited impact on students' self-efficacy because outcomes are described, not directly witnessed, and thus depend on the credibility of the persuader. Finally, students base their self-efficacy judgments on their perceived *physiological reactions,* such as fatigue, stress, and other emotions that are often interpreted as indicators of physical incapability. Unlike self-beliefs assumed to have trait-like stability across time and setting, self-efficacy is assumed to be responsive to changes in personal context and outcomes, whether experienced directly, vicariously, verbally, or physiologically. As a result of this sensitivity, self-efficacy beliefs are studied as indicators of change during instructional interventions as well as indicators of initial individual differences.

To facilitate improvements in perceived efficacy, researchers have trained students with learning and motivational deficiencies by modeling specific self-regulatory techniques, describing their form, and providing enactive feedback regarding their impact. For example, youngsters who observed an adult model the use [of] a cognitive strategy had significantly higher levels of perceived efficacy and academic skills than youngsters who received didactic instruction (Schunk, 1981). Asking students to set proximal goals enhanced self-efficacy and skill development more effectively than asking them to set distal goals because the proximal attainments provide evidence of growing capability (Bandura & Schunk, 1981). Verbally encouraging students to set their own goals improved not only their efficacy beliefs and achievement but also their commitment to attaining the goals (Schunk, 1985). The frequency and immediacy of enactive feedback also created higher perceptions of personal efficacy (Schunk, 1983). When students were taught to attribute their enactive feedback to effort, they perceived greater progress, maintained higher motivation, and reported greater efficacy for further learning (Schunk, 1987). In these investigations, Schunk and his colleagues not only demonstrated the sensitivity of efficacy beliefs to instructional interventions, but also the mediational role of these beliefs in explaining changes in learners' self-regulation and achievement outcomes (Berry, 1987; Schunk, 1981). Self-efficacy beliefs increased prediction of academic outcomes as much as 25% of the variance above instructional influences. Clearly, students' self-efficacy beliefs are responsive to changes in instructional experience and play a causal role in students' development and use of academic competencies.

CONCLUSION

Students' self-perceptions of efficacy are distinctive from related motivational constructs because of their specificity and close correspondence to performance tasks. These cognitive beliefs differ conceptually and psychometrically from trait self-belief measures due to their sensitivity to variations in experience and task and situational context. Two decades of research have clearly established the validity of self-efficacy as a predictor of students' motivation and learning. Although self-efficacy correlates with other related constructs, it has also shown discriminant validity by its unique predictiveness of these outcomes when included in multiple regression analyses. It has shown convergent validity in predicting diverse forms of motivation, such as students' activity choices, effort, persistence, and emotional reactions. Finally, when studied as a mediating variable in training studies, self-efficacy has proven to be responsive to improvements in students' methods of learning (especially those involving greater self-regulation) and predictive of achievement outcomes. This empirical evidence of its role as a potent mediator of students' learning and motivation confirms the historic wisdom of educators that students' self-beliefs about academic capabilities do play an essential role in their motivation to achieve.

I express my gratitude to Frank Pajares and Manuel Martinez-Pons for their helpful comments on an earlier draft of this article.

Address correspondence and reprint requests to Barry J. Zimmerman, Educational Psychology Program, CUNY Graduate School, 365 Fifth Ave., New York, NY 10016–4309.

I Think I Can, I Think I Can: Understanding and Encouraging Mastery Motivation in Young Children

Penny Hauser-Cram

"She works very hard when she's trying to build a block construction." "He is so curious about how gadgets work." These are comments often made by parents and teachers in their conversations about young children. Children's motivation to solve and complete tasks they set out to do is a central part of the way teachers and parents view children. Is such motivation intrinsic? Are children with developmental disabilities as motivated as other children? How is motivation influenced by caregivers? Does motivation vary in different contexts, such as the classroom and the home? What do we know about motivation, and how can preschool teachers encourage it?

Perspectives on motivation

Based largely on Piaget's (1952) writings, developmental theorists (White 1959; Hunt 1965) have proposed that children's motivation to explore the world around them is the foundation upon which learning occurs. Such motivation is considered to be intrinsic, universal, and an integral part of development. All children are born with curiosity and a desire to learn about the world.

White (1959) contended that children have a need to produce an effect on their environment and that they achieve this through exploration and play. He proposed that children have "an urge toward competence," and he defined this urge as effectance or competence motivation.

Harter (1975) further defined effective motivation as a "desire to solve cognitively challenging problems for gratification inherent in discovering the solution" (p. 370). She highlighted several key components: curiosity, preference for challenge, internal criteria of success, and working for one's own satisfaction.

In studying motivation in school-age children, Dweck (1986) described some children as "mastery-oriented" (i.e., challenge seeking and persistent in attempting to solve difficult problems) and others as "helpless" (i.e., challenge avoidant and low in persistence). She maintained that some children exhibit "learned helplessness" because they believe, based on past experiences, that they have little control over the events that affect them. Children who exhibit patterns of learned helplessness attribute their successes to external factors, such as luck, and their failures to internal factors, such as ability (Dweck & Elliott 1983). Researchers suggest that teachers can promote mastery-oriented, rather than helpless, behavior by providing tasks in which the goal is learning (i.e., developing different strategies) rather than performance (i.e., focusing on correct or incorrect responses) (Stipek 1996).

Studies on toddlers and preschool-age children have focused on mastery motivation, which is assumed to be a precursor to later development of motivation to achieve academically. *Mastery motivation* is defined as a "psychological force that stimulates an individual to attempt independently, in a focused and persistent manner, to solve a problem or master a skill or task which is at least moderately challenging for him or her" (Morgan, Harmon, & Maslin-Cole 1990, 319). Key components of this definition include (1) attempts to master a task independent of adult direction; (2) persistence in mastering a task even when difficulties arise; and (3) selection of a task that is neither extremely easy nor extremely difficult. Researchers have stressed the importance of individually determined moderate challenge as children persist less with tasks that they find too easy or too difficult (Redding, Morgan & Harmon 1988). Thus, by identifying the kinds of tasks individual children engage in and persist with, teachers can provide opportunities that will offer optimal challenges.

Regardless of their theoretical background, intelligent, sensitive adults who closely observe children discover the same things—because that's the way children are—there are a number of "universals."

How does mastery motivation change during early childhood?

Most developmental psychologists contend that children begin life as motivated beings. Children strive to understand the world and to affect it. Developmentally, children progress through several shifts in motivation, so the motivated child behaves differently at different phases of life. The motivated infant, younger than six months of age, explores objects through reaching, mouthing, and visual exploration. Around nine months infants begin to understand simple notions of cause-and-effect, and the motivated infant of this age begins to engage in goal-directed activity with unfamiliar tasks (Jennings 1993). Another transition occurs around 18 months of age when children begin to be able to compare their behavior with that of a standard (Jennings 1993). The motivated toddler attempts to approximate the standard. During the preschool years motivated children begin to self-select challenging tasks and prefer tasks that "make them think" to those that are easy for them to accomplish (Stipek 1996).

How does motivation relate to cognition?

Motivation and cognition are conceptually different, but researchers have found that the two constructs are intertwined during infancy (Yarrow et al. 1982; Yarrow et al. 1983). Infant mastery motivation measures have been found to be better predictors of preschool measures of cognition than are standardized infant developmental quotients (Messer et al. 1986). Measures of mastery motivation may be good indicators of the way in which children approach learning about objects. Infants and toddlers who appear more motivated may take full advantage of a range of spontaneous learning opportunities and ultimately demonstrate more advanced cognitive performance.

During the preschool period, correlations between measures of motivation and those of intelligence are only modestly related (Morgan, MacTurk, & Hrncir 1995). While the motivated preschooler is one who persists at difficult tasks, and thus creates and engages in cognition enriching activities, cognitively advanced preschoolers are not necessarily highly motivated. The low correlation between intelligence and motivation indicates that aspects of children's lives other than cognition, such as the actions of important adults, may explain differences in mastery motivation.

How do caregivers affect mastery motivation?

Motivation is often assumed to be intrinsic, but it also appears to be affected by the transactions between children and their parents and other caregivers. The role played by caregivers, however, varies with the age of the child (Busch-Rossnagal, Knauf-Jensen, & DesRosiers 1995). For example, Yarrow and his colleagues (Yarrow et al. 1984) reported that parents who provided more sensory stimulation for their young infants had infants who were more persistent in their exploration of objects. After children begin engaging in cause-and-effect actions with objects, during the latter part of the first year of life, caregivers' role in providing stimulation becomes more complex. Parents who interfere in children's attempts to engage in autonomous activity diminish children's motivated behavior (Frodi, Bridges, & Grolnick 1985; Wachs 1987; Hauser-Cram 1993). Researchers (e.g., Morgan et al. 1991) contend that parents who are highly directive may encourage children to be efficient responders but not effective initiators. In contrast, parents who provide a range of challenges and support children's autonomy have children who display high levels of mastery motivation.

What do we know about motivation in children with developmental or physical disabilities?

Although less research has been conducted on motivation in children with disabilities, a picture of motivated behavior has begun to emerge. Researchers

© Elisabeth Nichols

Eriksonians emphasize the industriousness of children in this age range. They have a strong, innate urge to become competent. During the preschool years, motivated children begin to self-select challenging tasks and prefer tasks that "make them think" to those that are easy for them to accomplish. Motivation is intrinsic, but it also is affected by transactions between children and the important adults in their lives.

studying children with physical disabilities and mental retardation (MacTurk et al. 1985; Hauser-Cram 1996) have reported that levels of persistence on challenging tasks are similar for children with and without disabilities during the infant and toddler years. Discrepancies in mastery motivation of children with and without disabilities begin to emerge during the preschool and early school-age years (Harter & Zigler 1974; Jennings, Connors, & Stegman 1988).

Although the cause of the decline in motivated behavior of children with disabilities has not been determined, home and classroom factors may provide a clue. Studies of parent-child interaction in the home indicate that many parents of children with developmental disabilities and delays are highly directive in their play (Mahoney, Fors, & Wood 1990). Preschool classroom observation studies indicate that teachers, too, often highly direct children with disabilities (Hauser-Cram, Bronson, & Upshur 1993; Bronson, Hauser-Cram, & Warfield 1997). In both settings children with disabilities may have little opportunity for executing autonomy and independence in attempts to master tasks.

Can parents and teachers accurately assess mastery motivation?

Although the preponderance of studies on mastery motivation have been based on behavioral assess-

ments, an increasing number are incorporating parents' or teachers' ratings of children's motivated behavior. Ratings are quicker and easier to gather, and they have been found to correlate significantly with behavioral assessments (Morgan et al. 1993). Furthermore, ratings can take advantage of parents' and teachers' knowledge of children in multiple settings and with a wide range of tasks.

The Dimensions of Mastery Questionnaire (DMQ) has been found to be a reliable and valid source of ratings of children's persistence on object-oriented tasks, social-symbolic activities, and gross-motor play (Morgan et al. 1993). In studies in which parents and teachers have been asked to use the DMQ to rate the same child's mastery motivation, parents usually provide more positive ratings.

This trend was reported in a recent study of three-year-old children with developmental disabilities (Hauser-Cram et al. 1997). Results of this study also indicated that parents' ratings of mastery motivation were more predictive of children's later performance than were teachers' ratings. Therefore, parents' perceptions of children's motivated behavior offer unique and valuable information to teachers.

What can teachers do to encourage mastery motivation?

Research on mastery motivation does not have a long history, but much of the research has been undertaken with a view toward application and intervention. Several

© Elisabeth Nichols

important suggestions emerge from the studies conducted so far.

1. Provide a moderate choice of activities. Choosing activities promotes autonomy and offers children some control over their own learning. Research indicates that a modest number of choices, rather than no choice or a large number of choices, is optimal in enhancing intrinsic motivation (Stipek 1996).

2. Provide children with activities that offer opportunities to learn rather than opportunities only to be correct or incorrect. For example, provide problem-posing tasks, games, or other activities in which there are several possible ways to solve the problems posed.

3. Support children's activities in ways that do not interfere with autonomy. Sometimes this requires adults to wait rather than anticipate a child's needs when she encounters difficulty with a task. If the child is getting very frustrated, a well-timed suggestion (e.g., "Maybe if you turn that piece around . . .") rather than a direct command (e.g., "That piece fits here") may support her attempts to persist.

4. Ask parents about their perspectives on their child's motivation. Parents know what children enjoy doing and what challenges provide them with pride in accomplishment.

What future research is needed on children's mastery motivation?

Current work on mastery motivation is somewhat limited by a focus on the individual child's independent activities, yet preschool classrooms are social organizations where children play and learn together. Future work on mastery motivation will benefit by considering the influence of the social context in which children learn. To what extent do peers challenge each other as they persist together on a joint enterprise? To what extent do the social dynamics of a classroom offer a range of challenges appropriate for each child? To what extent do children develop a sense of shared agency in making a difference in their preschool classroom? Many questions will undoubtedly emerge as we extend the construct of mastery motivation to include the collective intricacies of the social settings in which children engage in learning. Adults, siblings, and peers are all potential partners in children's motivation, and future research can help us understand these partnerships and the ways in which all can contribute to optimizing mastery-oriented behavior in young children.

References

Bronson, M. B., P. Hauser-Cram, & M. E. Warfield. 1997. Classrooms matter: Relations between the classroom environment and the social and mastery behavior of five-year-old children with disabilities. *Applied Developmental Psychology* 18: 331–48.

Busch-Rossnagel, N. A., D. E. Knauf-Jensen, & F. S. DesRosiers. 1995. Mothers and others: The role of the socializing environment in the development of mastery motivation. In *Mastery motivation: Origins, conceptualizations, and applications*, eds. R. H. MacTurk & G. A. Morgan, 117–45. Norwood, NJ: Ablex.

Dweck, C., & E. S. Elliot. 1993. Achievement motivation. In *Handbook of child psychology, Vol. 4: Socialization, personality, and social development*. 4th ed., series ed. P. H. Mussen, vol. ed. E. M. Hetherington, 643–91. New York: Wiley.

Dweck, C. S. 1986. Motivational processes affecting learning. *American Psychologist* 41: 1040–48.

Frodi, A., L. Bridges, & W. Grolnick. 1985. Correlates of mastery-related behavior: A short-term longitudinal study of infants in their second year. *Child Development* 56: 1291–98.

Harter, S. 1975. Developmental differences in the manifestations of mastery motivation on problem-solving tasks. *Child Development* 46: 370–78.

Harter, S., & E. Zigler. 1974. The assessment of effectance motivation in normal and retarded children. *Developmental Psychology* 45:661–69.

Hauser-Cram, P. 1993. Mastery motivation in three-year-old children with Down syndrome. In *Mastery motivation in early childhood: Development, measurement, and social processes*, ed. D. J. Messer, 230–50. London: Routledge.

Hauser-Cram, P. 1996. Mastery motivation in toddler with developmental disabilities. *Child Development* 67: 236–48.

Hauser-Cram, P., M. B. Bronson, & C. C. Upshur. 1993. The effects of the classroom environment on classroom behaviors of young children with disabilities. *Early Childhood Research Quarterly* 8: 479–97.

Hauser-Cram, P., M. W. Krauss, M. E. Warfield, & A. Steele. 1997. Congruence and predictive power of mothers' and teachers' ratings of mastery motivation in children with mental retardation. *Mental Retardation* 35: 355–63.

Hunt, J. McV. 1965. Intrinsic motivation and its role in psychological development. In *Nebraska symposium on motivation*, ed. D. Levine, 189–282. Lincoln: University of Nebraska Press.

Jennings, K. D. 1993. Mastery motivation and the formation of self-concept from infancy through early childhood. In *Mastery motivation in early childhood: Development, measurement, and social processes*, ed. D. J. Messer, 36–54. London: Routledge.

Jennings, K. D., R. E. Connors, & C. E. Stegman. 1988. Does a physical handicap alter the development of mastery motivation during the preschool years? *Journal of the American Academy of Child and Adolescent Psychiatry* 27: 312–17.

MacTurk, R., P. M. Vietze, M. E. McCarthy, S. McQuiston, & L. J. Yarrow. 1985. The organization of exploratory behavior in Down syndrome and nondelayed infants. *Child Development* 56: 573–81.

Mahoney, G., S. Fors, & S. Wood. 1990. Maternal directive behavior revisited. *American Journal on Mental Retardation* 94: 398–406.

Messer, D. J., M. E. McCarthy, S. McQuiston, R. H. MacTurk, L. J. Yarrow, & P. M. Vietze. 1986. Relations between mastery motivation in infancy and competence in early childhood. *Developmental Psychology* 22: 336–72.

Morgan, G. A., R. J. Harmon, & C. A. Maslin-Cole. 1990. Mastery motivation: Definition and measurement. *Early Education and Development* 1: 318–39.

Morgan, G. A., R. H. MacTurk, & E. J. Hrncir. 1995. Mastery motivation: Overview, definitions, and conceptual issues. In *Mastery motivation: Origins, conceptualizations, and applications*, eds. R. H. MacTurk & G. A. Morgan. Norwood, NJ: Ablex.

Morgan, G. A., C. A. Maslin-Cole, Z. Biringer, & R. J. Harmon. 1991. Play assessment of mastery motivation in infants and young children. In *Play diagnosis and assessment*, eds. C. E. Schaefer, K. Gitlin, & A. Sandgrund, 65–86. New York: Wiley.

Morgan, G. A., C. Maslin-Cole, R. J. Harmon, N. A. Busch-Rossnagel, K. Jennings, P. Hauser-Cram, & L. Brockman. 1993. Parent and teacher perceptions of young children's mastery motivation: Assessment and review of research. In *Mastery motivation in early childhood: Development, measurement, and social processes*, ed. D. Messer, 109–31. London: Routledge.

Piaget, J. 1952. *The origins of intelligence in children*. New York: International Universities Press.

Redding, R. E., G. A. Morgan, & R. J. Harmon. 1988. Mastery motivation in infants and toddlers: Is it greatest when tasks are moderately challenging? *Infant Behavior and Development* 11: 419–30.

Stipek, D. J. 1996. Motivation and instruction. In *Handbook of educational psychology*, eds. D. Berliner & R. Calfee, 85–113. New York: Macmillan.

Wachs, T. D. 1987. Specificity of environmental action as manifest in environmental correlates of infant's mastery motivation. *Developmental Psychology* 23: 782–90.

White, R. W. 1959. Motivation reconsidered: The concept of competence. *Psychological Review* 66: 297–333.

Yarrow, L., R. H. MacTurk, P. M. Vietze, M. E. McCarthy, R. P. Klein, & S. McQuiston. 1984. Developmental course of parental stimulation and its relationship to mastery motivation during infancy. *Developmental Psychology* 20: 492–503.

Yarrow, L., S. McQuiston, R. MacTurk, M. McCarthy, R. Klein, & P. Vietze. 1983. Assessment of mastery motivation during the first year of life: Contemporaneous and cross-age relationships. *Developmental Psychology* 19: 159–71.

Yarrow, L., G. Morgan, K. Jennings, & R. Harmon. 1982. Infants' persistence at tasks: Relationships to cognitive functioning and early experience. *Infant Behavior and Development* 5: 131–41.

*E*ditor's note: As Penny Hauser-Cram tells us, developmental psychologists have focused mainly on mastery motivation in individual children and are now beginning to consider the influence of the social context in which children learn.

The latter is one of the areas of expertise of excellent early childhood educators. They have learned much through their work, which is with groups, about the group dynamics, interpersonal relations, cooperative behaviors, and peer example that power or impede children as they strive to create a project, conquer a difficulty, or solve a problem they've encountered.

We will all benefit when specialists in these two related areas—developmental psychology and early childhood education—pool their knowledge and move on to learn more.

Penny Hauser-Cram, Ed.D., is an associate professor of developmental and educational psychology at the School of Education at Boston College. Penny's research focuses on the development of children with disabilities.

This is one of a regular series of Research in Review columns. The column in this issue was invited by Research in Review Editor **Martha B. Bronson,** Ph.D., professor at Boston College, Chestnut Hill, Massachusetts.

Moving beyond Management as Sheer Compliance:
Helping Students to Develop Goal Coordination Strategies

Specific classroom situations require individualized management techniques, not a "rubber-stamp" approach. A cohesive relationship between teaching style and behavior management style is essential.

by Mary McCaslin and Thomas L. Good

Historically classroom management has been seen largely as controlling students—getting them to respond quickly to teacher demands, needs, and goals. Although for some educators this conception is beginning to change, much emphasis remains on behavioral control.[1] This is especially the case in "packaged" prescriptive management programs.[2] When control strategies fail, students' noncompliance is met with an arsenal of punishment and removal strategies.[3]

We begin by noting that there are distinctly different ways to conceptualize management goals and, within a particular management goal, there are many competing views of how to think about management. We will argue that teachers can and should promote the goal for students to develop their capacity for self-regulation. Although there are no foolproof prescriptions for successful management, teachers can help students to achieve more capacity for self-direction by encouraging them to conceptualize problem-solving behaviors vis-à-vis their

Reprinted with permission from *Educational Horizons,* Summer 1998, pp. 169–176. © 1998 by Phi Lambda Theta, Inc., international honor society and professional association in education, Bloomington, IN 47404-6626.

When control strategies fail, students' noncompliance is met with an arsenal of punishment and removal strategies.

own academic and social goals (much as one teaches curriculum content in a problem-solving fashion). Helping students to develop strategies for coordinating their goals is one important aspect of facilitating student capacity for adaptive self-regulation of their learning, motivation, and behavior.

Discipline Goals

It is possible to distinguish among three discipline goals: compliance, identification, and internalization.[4] Compliance is achieved when an individual behaves simply to get a reward or to avoid a punishment. Identification occurs when an individual acts "appropriately" when a valued model is salient (especially when they are present in a situation). Internalization is inferred when an individual's behavior is stable across a variety of settings in the absence of external inducements. In our opinion, these three discipline goals differ in terms of students' commitment to a standard of action (compliance = I'll stop or start when you tell (consequate) me to do it; identification = I'll start because I know you would want me to; internalization = I act this way because I have accepted your value as my own). Sheer compliance is a sufficient goal for many classroom tasks (e.g., raise your hand for recognition in school whether or not you value hand raising or sanctioned recognition). For other tasks, however, compliance is at best a starting point.

We write this paper for educators who want to achieve more than sheer compliance. However, make no bones about it, compliance is a major goal of classroom management (students must be safe, bullies cannot harass, students must be on time, individuals cannot continuously monopolize classroom discussion). Whether or not a student prefers or values aggression, it cannot be tolerated. Similarly, a student who complies by accepting peer conflict resolution rather than fighting after school represents a favorable

discipline outcome (whether or not the student values conflict resolution).

We prefer goals that include internalization rather than only sheer compliance for three basic reasons. First, the success of a compliance model depends upon constant monitoring (if the teacher turns her or his back, students misbehave; if the electricity in the fence goes off, the cattle flee). Second, if compliance obtained through the judicious use of rewards (and to a lesser extent punishment) is the only controlling mechanism, appropriate behavior and dispositions will not transfer from one setting to another (students may not steal in school, but may do so in the mall; students may try to do their best when the popcorn party is this week, but not take their work seriously the week after the party). In short, compliance with rules and acceptable standards of behavior is, of course, always one goal, but sheer compliance is less durable and transferable than compliance that occurs because of identification (with sports stars who don't smoke or fight—i.e., the "squash it" campaign) or internalization (fighting and smoking are detrimental and things I will not do). A third reason to promote more than compliance is that some complex forms of instruction simply cannot occur if students operate at only a sheer compliance level. For example, if small-group instruction is to work effectively, it is necessary that students value and support cooperative and divergent exchanges. Additionally, students' behavior in small groups often is unsupervised; thus, group management will vary widely as a function of students' commitment to a standard of action and valuing of diversity.

Representations of Management

There are multiple ways to conceptualize management issues in school settings. Indeed, how a teacher or administrator frames a management problem is a critical determinant of how he or she responds to a specific classroom issue. For example, different beliefs about why a student misbehaves influences specific strategies that teachers use in attending to particular classroom events. As can be seen in Table 1, students may misbehave for different reasons and, of course, some of these reasons occur simultaneously.

> ### Table 1: Reasons Why Students Misbehave
>
> 1. Lonely or scared
> 2. Out of control or hostile
> 3. Face-saving or don't know what to do
> 4. Have failed to learn, bored or frustrated
> 5. Physiological need (pain, sleep deprivation, withdrawal) or satiation
> 6. Distracted by peers, events, or memories

A student who is bored because the work is inappropriately difficult is different from the student who is bored because he or she is satiated and needs a change of activity. Similarly, students who misbehave because they do not know what to do require a different response than students who misbehave because they are distracted by peers. The possible reasons for misbehavior are countless but Table 1 helps to make the point—students misbehave because of cognitive, emotional, and physiological reasons. This analysis also helps to explain why prescriptive programs with regimented responses for student misbehavior often miss the mark. If teachers have management goals other than sheer compliance, then it is important to determine *why* students misbehave. And, even if sheer compliance is the goal, knowing why students misbehave prevents inefficient and potentially counterproductive use of discipline strategies (offering help to a student bored with unchallenging work).

It also is possible to discuss management in terms of *when* students misbehave as somewhat independent from *why* they misbehave (see Table 2).

> ### Table 2: When Misbehavior Occurs
>
> 1. Before the lesson starts
> 2. In the initial stages of a lesson
> 3. Transition from one lesson activity to another
> 4. Transition from teacher-directed to student-directed control of the lesson
> 5. Conclusion of a lesson

Data illustrate that the times listed in Table 2 are when misbehavior most often occurs—especially when whole-class instructional models are being used. The literature on classroom management provides strategies for how to proactively circumvent these "time-based" problems.[5] Further, it's important to understand that these timing problems typically occur because of teachers' instructional or managerial errors. Informed teachers recognize that sometimes students misbehave for reasons that are primarily due to teacher behavior.

Another conceptualization of management is problem ownership. Table 3 defines five types of problem ownership: teacher-owned, student-owned, shared between teacher and student, class-owned, and school-owned problems.[6] If a teacher is angry (as in teacher-owned problem situations) the teacher must recognize the anger to deal capably with student misbehavior (i.e., do more than punish).

Educators who conceptualize management from the perspective of problem ownership have provided rich strategies for dealing with different types of problem students (e.g., shy, hostile, hyperactive) as a

Table 3: Problem Ownership Definitions	
Ownership	**Problem**
Teacher-owned	Student behavior prevents teacher need satisfaction (makes teacher angry)
Student-owned	Student need satisfaction is stymied by someone other than teacher
Shared	Teacher and student partially prevent one another's need satisfaction
Class-owned	Classroom structure prevents students' and teachers' need satisfaction
School-owned	School policies keep students and teachers from achieving needs

function of problem ownership.[7] Most classification systems for dealing with problem ownership have dealt only with the first three types of problems that are caused by other persons. However, it is also possible to conceptualize problems that are classroom-based or school-based due to official *policies*, not only the individuals who enforce them. Some schools, for example, have allowed businesses (McDonald's, Pizza Hut) to advertise in schools and sponsor school programs. Channel One monitors the news that students watch and advertises products along with news broadcasts.[8] One critic of such practices illustrates how a school-level function (allowing tennis shoes to be advertised) may create classroom-level problems (fighting over tennis shoes). Alex Molnar puts it this way, "At a time when poor children have been killed for their shoes, they are forced to watch advertising messages for high-priced sneakers. At a time when American children are increasingly overweight and at risk of coronary disease, they have been taught how the heart functions from a poster advertising junk food and then served high-fat meals by the fast food concessionaires that run their school cafeterias. At a time when too many children abuse alcohol, they are taught history by a brewery."[9]

Yet another way to conceptualize management is the possible interaction between the roles that teachers and students may adopt. Here, the number of comparisons is almost infinite; however, for discussion purposes, some examples are provided in Table 4. As is the case in most representations, this conception interacts with others. For example, an authoritarian teacher typically has a lower threshold for "seeing" a management problem in the first place (especially defiance) than does a laissez-faire teacher.

Table 4 has been organized to show how a particular teacher role may exacerbate certain types of problems students have and how certain student roles may highlight vulnerabilities in certain types of teachers. For example, teachers differ in the amount of control they exert in the classroom. Laissez-faire teachers tend to be relatively tolerant of a range of student behavior (e.g., noise, movement), choosing not to intervene unless required to do so. These teachers' management "plan" is more about reaction and remediation than proactive prevention. In these classrooms students who do not provoke teacher attention do not receive teacher attention. Thus, in such classrooms, the shy or passive student is likely to receive too little structure, demands, or guidance to become more actively engaged and self-regulating. In contrast, the authoritarian teacher who runs a "tight ship" is apt to be over-controlling and thereby triggers the defiant student who likes to test boundaries. Similarly, teachers differ in their relative emphasis of academic or social goal orientation in their classroom. Teachers who value academic goals relatively more than social ones may well find themselves "locking horns" with the underachiever who has grown comfortable with the "gentleman's C." Teachers who attend to social development as a primary goal will likely confront the "I'm the best, I'm the king/queen of the

---

Table 4: Management as a Function of Teacher Role and Student Role

Teacher Role	Student Role
1. Laissez-faire Control	Passive student
2. Authoritarian Control	Defiant student
3. Academic Focus	Underachieving student
4. Social Focus	Self-aggrandizing student

Table 5: Five Personality Factors

1. Agreeableness, Altruism, Affection vs. Hostility
2. Extroversion, Energy, Enthusiasm vs. Introversion
3. Conscientiousness, Control, Constraint vs. Impulsiveness
4. Neuroticism, Negativism, Nervousness vs. Emotional Stability
5. Intellectual Openness, Originality, Flexibility vs. Narrowness, Simplicity, Shallowness

This table has been condensed from Richard Snow, Lyn Corno, and Doug Jackson, III, "Individual Differences in Affective and Conative Functions," in D. Berliner and R. Calfee, eds., Handbook of Educational Psychology (New York: Macmillan, 1996), 243-310.

---

world" student as a major challenge to their instructional goals. Table 4 presents two anchors of teacher behavior on each of two dimensions. Consider the likely management issues that arise when, for example, a laissez-faire teacher with an academic focus implements project-based science. What types of behavior would you predict from each of the student roles listed? What if they were members of the same group?

Researchers who have examined the extensive literature on individual differences have noted that five major personality factors describing dispositions teachers and students bring to the classroom can be derived from the research (see Table 5).[10] As suggested by Table 5, a teacher with one personality orientation necessarily must deal with many students whose personalities may differ in major ways from one another and from the teacher. An introverted teacher who prefers to be low-key in the classroom, for example, can (and sometimes must) project enthusiasm, firmness, or assertiveness as the educational context affords or demands.

Table 5 indicates the complexity of potential interactions. For example, each factor (e.g., agreeable vs. hostile) is associated with multiple characteristics (affectionate, unselfish, trusting, etc.); however, even the most agreeable person will be cold and unfriendly in some situations. Basic personality dispositions (e.g., honesty) are more likely to be exhibited in some situations but not others (e.g., Joan would never cheat on an exam but would copy off another student's homework). Given such complexity it simply is not possible to understand student disposition, behavior, and needs without *listening* to them.[11]

As seen through the representations we have introduced, classroom management is complex: what constitutes a good management strategy depends (at least) upon the teacher's role, personality, goals, and strategies; characteristics of the management "problem"; and the role, personality, developmental level, and goals of the students. Again, we emphasize a key premise of this article—if teachers want to influence students and want them to respond for reasons other than sheer compliance, teachers cannot let packaged, prescriptive programs do their thinking for them.

Teach for Understanding; Manage for Compliance: Any Questions?

Ironically, and unfortunately, many who write about classroom management answer "no" to the above question. We contend that to teach for understanding while managing for compliance is self-defeating. Too many classroom-management writers ignore the important link

It seems highly unlikely that students will profit from the incongruous messages we send when we manage for obedience and teach for exploration and risk taking.

between the need for more advanced management approaches (i.e., moving beyond sheer compliance) if certain types of instructional processes and goals are to be achieved. It is not uncommon to find educational writers who strongly advocate a thinking or problem-solving curriculum while directly, or indirectly, arguing for behavioral control of students. For example, Carolyn Evertson and her colleagues note that Walter Doyle incorrectly " . . . suggests that classrooms with complex organization will require more direct management and control than simpler settings."[12] In marked contrast to Doyle's position, Evertson and colleagues note that classroom researchers contend that "instead of more teacher control, these settings will need a different *kind* of teacher control."[13] They argue that when complex instructional goals are required, it is more efficacious for the teacher to delegate authority to students or groups of students, rather than attempting to supervise directly the multitude of overlapping activities, claiming that "direct supervision is more appropriate to [and, we would add, theoretically consistent with] simpler routine tasks."[14] Simply put, if the teacher is trying to create a trusting, cooperative learning environment for students, then the management system must also promote these same dispositions, behaviors, and skills—in part through opportunities for thinking and problem solving in the academic *and* social spheres.

Goal Coordination: Moving beyond Compliance

We have presented several representations of management and each one provides a legitimate lens for thinking about how to conceptualize and implement classroom management goals and strategies. Now we want to introduce another representation; one that we feel is especially relevant for contemporary classrooms. Elsewhere, we have suggested that in many classrooms there is a fundamental mismatch in the promotion of a problem-solving curriculum while using a behavioral control approach to management.[15] It seems highly unlikely that students will profit from the incongruous messages we send when we manage for obedience and teach for exploration and risk taking. We put our argument this way:

Educators have created an oxymoron: a curriculum that urges problem solving and critical thinking and a management system that requires compliance and narrow obedience. The management system at least dilutes, if not obstructs, the potential power of the curriculum for many of our students. Students are asked to think and understand, but in too many classrooms they are asked to think noiselessly, without peer communication or social exchange. And the problems they are asked to think about must be solved, neatly, within (at most) forty-five-minute intervals. In the problem-solving curriculum, in too many cases, the teacher sets the performance goals, identifies relevant resources, establishes criteria for evaluation, and eventually announces winners and losers. Students generally gain recognition and approval by paying close attention to recommended procedures and by taking few academic risks (e.g., reading and extensively footnoting fifteen secondary sources rather than venturing their own informed opinions).[16]

If we want students to develop thoughtful work habits it seems necessary to help them think about how they acquire, elaborate, and integrate academic knowledge; consider the relations among their knowledge, beliefs, and identity; and locate those processes and persons who support them in complicated learning. Simply put, if we want students to understand (i.e., not memorize) academic content, value the process of academic learning, and internalize their education, then we need to help students understand their own behavior in school settings and develop a capacity for managing and regulating themselves and others in a way that supports their learning goals.

Multiple Goals

Teachers can help students become more adept at self-management, or "self-regulation," by helping them learn to coordinate their social and academic lives. This involves identifying goals and their interrelationships and strategically coordinating among them. Students (like teachers) pursue multiple goals simultaneously (with more and less success). Often students must choose between competing goals (asking the teacher a question about the trig assignment at the end of class or catching up with a friend who won't be seen the rest of the school day to ask about substituting that afternoon at McDonald's). Further, as we note in *Listening in Classrooms,* students often pursue a goal for multiple reasons (e.g., strategic use of study time as a way both to learn and ensure weekend privileges), and strategies and goals can be *multi-functional* (e.g., "obvious" effort may promote achievement and it is also an effective impression-management strategy).[17] Also, relations among goals are multidimensional. When multiple goals are pursued at the same time and do not overlap, time pressure can make it difficult to establish priorities and then pursue goals sequentially. In addition, goal coordination becomes more complex when multiple goals are difficult (i.e., they take time, attention, and energy to achieve). Third, personal goals often clash with others' needs and interests. Conflict with others makes goal pursuit and coordination more difficult and costly. Teachers sometimes inadvertently create goal conflict and thwart learning goal coordination. For example, teachers typically give deadline extensions when performance events occur midweek. Students who receive extensions do not learn how to prioritize and follow through; instead, they learn that the teacher devalues school work. Peers without extensions may learn to prioritize; however, they also may learn that their multiple goals and time constraints are not noteworthy. Both groups of students have had another piece added to their friendship task.

Dealing with multiple goals is a part of life and people who can do so successfully are apt to be more productive and satisfied than those who cannot. Single-mindedness—all the eggs in one basket—is not a healthy

Teachers can help students become more adept at self-management, or "self-regulation," by helping them learn to coordinate their social and academic lives.

Table 6: Goal-coordination Strategies

1. *A single, integrative strategy:* Although this is the most efficient and inclusive strategy, the goals obviously need to be compatible. One example is the high-ability, highly focused student who is involved in the school yearbook and student government, has a part-time job at the local Quick Print, and hopes to attend college to study journalism. This student's achievement, belongingness, power, independence, and present and future career needs are met with a single broad, integrative strategy.

2. *Multiple, simultaneous strategies:* Simultaneous strategies require goals to be compatible with or independent of each other and for some to be less difficult so that the student can do more than one thing at a time. Academically more-capable students are often able to meet the demands of the task, follow procedures, and catch up on the "chit-chat" with their group members. Thus, they follow the routines like "good" students, successfully complete the task like "smart" students, and maintain friendly banter like "popular" students.

3. *Deferment strategies:* Deferment strategies result when the student realizes that she or he can't "have it all" and prioritizes. Nonpriority goals are put on the back burner, not abandoned. As compared with the integrative and simultaneous strategies, deferment means less gets done because less can get done. We suspect this is the initial reasoning as students begin to restrict their hobbies: piano is deferred for now to allow more time for flute and the school band; soccer takes priority over track, etc.

4. *Modification strategies:* Goals or the criteria for their successful attainment are modified to make goals more compatible. Students may decide that each and every paper in English does not have to be their best; it is important that some of their time be spent on science class, too. Learning to modify goals is a particularly important skill that teachers can help students to develop. Adolescents as well as first-graders can easily lose a sense of proportion in the goals they set and their abilities to meet them.

5. *Goal substitution:* One goal replaces the original goal. Although goal substitution need not have a negative connotation, it is often offered as an explanation for student gang membership and general theories of "negative identity." That is, students who are unable to achieve belongingness in family or sense of place and recognition in school substitute membership and status in gangs to fulfill unmet needs. All of us have had "goal-substitution" experiences, however, and they typically are positive, involving more realistic aspirations. Consider the student who wants to be part of the school play; although stage fright and basic lack of talent may prohibit being cast in an acting role, scenery always needs painting.

6. *Goal abandonment.* By goal abandonment we mean to simply give up on a goal without deferring, modifying, or substituting another. In the specific instance, goal abandonment may be appropriate. For example, simply giving up and going home to regroup may help a student cope with temporary embarrassment. Giving up the goal to always be the best at whatever one does is probably a good idea—as long as it does not translate into giving up trying or giving up altogether.

This table has been adopted (slightly condensed) from McCaslin and Good, Listening in Classrooms.

---

life strategy. Students must learn to identify individual goals, assess their relative importance, and their relationship. Teachers also need to understand the goal coordination task that they impose on students when they assign multiple, simultaneous, and difficult requirements. Teachers who are mindful of students' goal coordination tasks can co-regulate students' learning how to strategically organize and achieve them. Teachers can help students accomplish personal goals by teaching (a) goal-compatibility features and (b) goal-coordination strategies.

Goal Compatibility

Educational researchers have argued that goals can be *compatible* in three ways.[18]

First, they may be compensatory as effort (to some extent) can compensate for ability. Second, compatible goals can be complementary as, for example, cooperative behavior complements cooperative learning. Third, compatible goals can be instrumental—studying now makes it easier to be admitted to college later. Goals (like many classroom goals) can be largely *independent* of each other. For example, wanting to be on time to sit with friends at lunch is usually independent of wanting to do well on a chemistry test. Finally, goals can be *incompatible* by interfering or negating one another. Goal interference can occur when teachers inadvertently place students, especially preadolescents, in a conflict between the goal of being a good student and the goal of being a good friend. For example, often teachers

ask one student to explain to another (who has been unable to answer) how a process works or why an answer is incorrect. Students may solve the goal-conflict by feigning ignorance—friendship matters more than being right and a "good" student. Incompatible goals also might negate one another. A student who strives to improve her game, meet the no-pass-play academic criterion, and "party hearty" risks failure of academic and athletic goals. And, if "caught," she neither plays, nor remains in school, nor is allowed to go out with friends. Prioritizing and choosing among independent and incompatible goals is essential if students are to meet any of them. Think of how much energy, time, and emotion is spent futilely because an individual does not realize that he cannot have his cake and eat it too, and as a result, achieves neither experience.

Goal-Coordination Strategies

In addition to helping students recognize the degree of compatibility (or lack thereof) among goals, teachers can also help students develop strategies to coordinate among them. In Table 6 we describe four strategies that Dodge and colleagues argue promote goal coordination.[19] We add two strategies (points 5, 6) to their list and place the strategies on a continuum of inclusiveness from greater inclusiveness to less.

School-Wide Co-regulation

If teachers are to be notably effective in helping students to develop goal-coordination strategies and, more broadly, to increase their capacity for self-regulation, teachers will need to work with colleagues at earlier and later grade levels. Elsewhere it has been argued that often first- and second-grade

Students should be allowed, taught, and expected to assume more responsibility for their goals and behavior as they progress through school.

students have more opportunity for self-direction, self-evaluation, and choice than do sixth-grade or twelfth-grade students.[20] Unfortunately, the progress that one teacher makes in helping students to develop their capacity for self-regulation in a given year can be dissipated the following year when the next teacher imposes a more controlling (and therefore regressive) system.[21] As we have noted previously, it is time to examine the connectedness of classroom management systems. Educators need to become more sensitive to building better bridges between grades.[22] Students should be allowed, taught, and expected to assume more responsibility for their own goals and behavior as they progress through school.

In this article, we have argued that there are many ways to conceptualize classroom management and we have recommended that teachers can benefit from using multiple perspectives. We argue that successful management has to be conceptualized as fluid and transitional: that is, teachers must continue to adjust their management systems to changes in context, including students' expanding needs and abilities.

1. See Mary McCaslin and Thomas L. Good, *Listening in Classrooms* (New York: Harper Collins, 1996); Mary McCaslin and Tom Good, "Compliant Cognition: the Misalliance of Management and Instructional Goals in Current School Reform," *Educational Researcher* 21 (1992): 4–17; Carolyn Evertson and Catherine Randolph, "Perspectives on Classroom Management for Learner-centered Classrooms," in H. Waxman and H. Walberg, eds., *New Directions for Research on Teaching* (Berkeley, Calif.: McCutchan, in press); and Alfie Kohn, *Beyond Discipline: From Compliance to Community* (Alexandria, Va.: Association for Supervision and Curriculum Development, 1996).

2. For an example of one type of the packaged management programs that we find self-defeating, see Lee Canter and Marlene Canter, *Assertive Discipline: Positive Behavior Management for Today's Classroom* (Santa Monica, Calif.: Lee Canter and Associates, 1992).

3. Some of the school-level control strategies in popular use are blatantly contradictory. For example, some schools that have zero-tolerance programs for drugs (i.e., students are kicked out of school for any violation and placed on the street where they can acquire drugs among other things) have tough policies on student truancy that are imposed by state law (e.g., prosecute parents of heavy-truancy students). Apparently it is okay for the school to allow students not to go to school, but the same option does not exist for parents!

4. Herbert C. Kelman, "Compliance, Identification, and Internalization: Three Processes of Attitude Change," *Journal of Conflict Resolution,* vol. 2 (1958): 51–60; and Herbert C. Kelman, "Processes of Opinion Change," *Public Opinion Quarterly* 25 (1961): 57–78.

5. See Thomas L. Good and Jere Brophy, *Looking in Classrooms,* 7th ed. (New York: Harper Collins, 1997).

6. Thomas Gordon, *Teacher Effectiveness Training* (New York: Wyden, 1974); and Jere Brophy and Mary McCaslin, "Teachers' Reports of How They Perceive and Cope with Problem Students," *Elementary School Journal* 93, no. 1 (1992): 3–68.

7. Ibid, Brophy and McCaslin, "Teachers' Reports."

8. Bradley Greenberg and Jeffrey Brand, "Channel 1: But What about the Advertising?" *Educational Leadership* 51 (1994): 56–58.

9. See Alex Molnar, *Giving Kids the Business: The Commercialization of American Schools* (New York: Westview Press, 1996), 49.

10. See Richard Snow, Lyn Corno, and Doug Jackson III, "Individual Differences in Affective and Conative Functions," in D. Berliner and R. Calfee, eds., *Handbook of Educational Psychology* (New York; Macmillan, 1996), 243–310.

11. Mary McCaslin and Thomas L. Good, *Listening in Classrooms* (New York: Harper Collins, 1996).

12. See Carolyn Evertson, K. Weeks, and C. Randolph, *Creating Learning-centered Classrooms: Implications for Classroom Management* (Nashville, Tenn.: Vanderbilt University, March 1997, mimeo); Walter Doyle, "Classroom Organization and Management," in M. Wittrock, Ed., *Handbook of Research on Teaching,* 3rd ed. (New York: MacMillan, 1986), 392–431.

13. See Hermine Marshall, "Beyond the Workplace Metaphor: Toward Conceptualizing the Classroom as a Learning Setting," *Theory into Practice* 29 (1990): 94–101; and Alfie Kohn and Lotan, "Teachers as Supervisors of Core Technology," *Theory into Practice* 29 (1990): 78–84.

14. Ibid, Marshall, "Beyond the Workplace."

15. See Mary McCaslin and Thomas L. Good, "Compliant Cognition: the misalliance of Management and Instructional Goals in Current School Reform," *Educational Researcher* 21 (1992): 4–17.

16. Ibid.

17. See McCaslin and Good, *Listening in Classrooms,* 65, 66.

18. See Kenneth Dodge, Steven Asher, and Jennifer Parkhust,"Social Life as a Goal-Coordination Task," in C. Ames and R. Ames, eds., *Research on Motivation and Education: Volume 3: Goals and Cognition* (New York; Academic Press, 1989), 107–135.

19. Ibid.

20. Thomas L. Good, "What Is Learned in Elementary Schools," in Tommy Tomlinson and Herbert Walberg, eds., *Academic Work and Educational Excellence* (Berkeley, Calif.: McCutchan, 1986), 87–114.

21. Nedra Fetterman, *The Meaning of Success and Failure: A Look at Social Instructional Environments of Four Elementary School Classrooms,* unpublished doctoral dissertations. Bryn Mawr College, Bryn Mawr, Pa.

22. Mary McCaslin and Thomas L. Good, "Classroom Management and Motivated Student Learning," in Tommy Tomlinson, ed., *Motivating Students to Learn; Overcoming Barriers to High Achievement* (Berkeley, Calif.: McCutchan, 1993), 245–261.

Mary McCaslin and Thomas L. Good are associate professor and professor, respectively, of educational psychology in the College of Education at the University of Arizona, Tucson.

Teaching Students to Regulate Their Own Behavior

During the 1994–95 school year, 43% of all students with disabilities were served in general education classrooms (18th Annual Report, 1997).

Children and Adults with Attention Deficit Disorders (CHADD) estimates that there are 3.5 million children with ADHD (CHADD, 1993).

Of the 5.4 million children nationwide with disabilities, 8.7% are identified as emotionally disturbed/behavior disordered, and 80% of these children are co-diagnosed with ADHD (Mathes & Bender, 1997).

Lewis R. Johnson   •   Christine F. Johnson

Before general education teachers refer a child to special education services, the teachers must implement program modifications and strategies and document that the modifications were insufficient to remedy the student's problem. For these reasons, general educators and special education teachers/consultants need methods to successfully include students with disabilities in general education programs.

A Question of Generalization

Sometimes, consultants and classroom teachers collaboratively develop prereferral interventions or behavior management plans that require the teacher to monitor, record, and issue contingent reinforcers. This type of behavior management program is time-consuming; and if more than one student in the class is "on a plan," it can be overwhelming.

In 1973 Glynn, Thomas, and Shee described an effective procedure for general education teachers to employ so students can self-monitor and improve their on-task behavior. Although recent research has focused on the use of self-regulation techniques for students with disabilities in special education settings, it is peculiar that the technique is not used more in general education classrooms as prereferral interventions and to facilitate inclusion of students with disabilities.

Self-regulation techniques can be used with students from preschool age through postsecondary age when educators adapt the level of sophistication to the age group. One limitation of self-regulation training conducted by special education teachers in the special education setting is the lack of generalization of the behavior change in the general education setting.

One way to facilitate generalization of skills is to provide the training in the setting in which you want the generalization to occur (Guevremont, Osnes, & Stokes, 1988). In this article we present a description of self-regulation and the specific procedures for teaching students to employ self-regulation of classroom work-study behavior.

Components of Self-Regulation

Self-regulation requires students to stop, think about what they are doing, compare their behavior to a criterion, record the results of their comparison, and receive reinforcement for their behavior if it meets the criterion (Webber, Scheuermann, McCall, & Coleman, 1993). Self-monitoring involves all the steps in self-regulation, except the issuing of reinforcement.

When you begin the program, first teach students to ask the monitoring question aloud. Then, as the program becomes more

> **Self-regulation requires students to stop, think about what they are doing, compare their behavior to a criterion, record the results of their comparison, and receive reinforcement for their behavior if it meets the criterion.**

routine, students ask the monitoring question in a whisper. In the initial stages of self-regulation, use a tone sounded in the classroom at random intervals to cue the students to ask the question. Cued monitoring is much more effective than uncued monitoring. When you must conduct a training session outside the general classroom, the use

From *Teaching Exceptional Children*, March/April 1999, pp. 6-10. © 1999 by The Council for Exceptional Children. Reprinted by permission.

of the same tone aids in maintaining the skills across settings.

The Steps of Self-Regulation

Students use the following sequence of steps to use self-regulation:

1. Self-observation—looking at one's own behavior given a predetermined criterion.
2. Self-assessment—deciding if the behavior has occurred, through some self-questioning activity.
3. Self-recording—recording the decision made during self-assessment on a private recording form.
4. Self-determination of reinforcement—setting a criterion for success, and selecting a reinforcer from a menu of reinforcers.
5. Self-administration of reinforcement—administering a reinforcer to oneself (Glynn et al., 1973).

According to Barkley (1990), 3%–5% of all school-age children may have attention deficit hyperactivity disorder (ADHD).

Target Behavior

Self-regulation is most widely used during independent seatwork; however, you may apply the technique to a variety of classroom activities. Here are kinds of behavior commonly targeted by self-regulation:

- Staying on task.
- Assignment completion (productivity).
- Appropriate classroom behavior (such as staying in one's seat).
- Accuracy of completed work (percent correct).

The student should focus on positive behavior. The choice of a target behavior for self-regulation is important and may be individually selected, depending on student needs.

Initially, you may want to select a single target behavior for the entire class group. Then, after the students learn the technique, you may want to select different kinds of behavior to target to meet the needs of individual students. Although teachers most frequently select on-task behavior, improvement in on-task behavior may not promote improved academic outcomes. Researchers have found that a *combination* of types of target behavior, including both work-study and accuracy of assignment completion, seems to work best (Rooney, Polloway, &

Hallahan, 1985). Young students respond to task completion as a criterion, whereas older students respond best to completion of tasks with an accuracy criteria (Maag, Reid, & Di-Ganni, 1993).

Procedure

Before you begin a self-regulatory program, collect program data to determine the students' current level of performance regarding the behavior problem. The special education teacher/consultant or a classroom assistant can collect preintervention "on-task" data using an interval observation method on several students over several visits.

For interval observation, the observer records "+" or "−" every 10 seconds to indicate if the student was on/off task during that interval. The observer then divides the number of intervals marked "+" by the total number of intervals in the observation to get a percentage of time on task (see Figure 1). Then the teacher begins the procedure for teaching the students to self-regulate their behavior, as follows:

1. Model the procedure, using a suitable behavior. Model being cued to engage in self-observation/recording by a tone provided by an audiotape (available from ADD Warehouse; see box, "Internet Sites").
2. Students observe you modeling the procedure.
3. The students practice self-observation/recording on a single behavior.

Internet Sites for ADHD

Children and Adults with Attention Deficit Disorders

http://www.chadd.org

Teaching Children with ADHD

http://www.kidsource.com/kidsource/content2/add.html

A.D.D. Warehouse (catalog)

http://www.addwarehouse.com

ADD Treatment Information

http://www.mediconsult.com/add/shareware/decad_brain/cope.html

1. Self-observation.
2. Self-assessment.
3. Self-recording.
4. Self-determination of reinforcement.
5. Self-administration of reinforcement.

4. Students employ the procedure daily.
5. The students graph their own observation data, in a manner appropriate to the age and ability of students.
6. Introduce self-reinforcement, such as "I did a good job staying on task," to the students. Better grades and teacher praise are effective reinforcers of accurate and honest self-recording.
7. Collect posttraining data over several observation sessions.
8. Suggest that some students self-observe and record a different behavior, based on individual student need.
9. With each student, review the weekly self-recording data. Introduce the concept of self-determination of a goal and self-reinforcement.

To teach students to use the self-regulation procedure, use the following direct instruction approaches—modeling and guided practice.

Format for Training Grade 2 Students: Modeling

1. "Class, I am concerned that when a student correctly responds to a question, I have not been providing praise as regularly as I should have. I need to find a way to improve how I respond to students who answer my questions."
2. *Thinking aloud,* say: "I will use this tape, which makes a sound every so often to remind me to ask myself, 'Did I offer praise for correct student answers?' If I did offer praise since the last tone, I will put a mark in the *yes*

Figure 1. Classroom Observation of "On-Task" Student Behavior

Student	1	2	3	4	5	6	7	8	9	10	11	12	13	14	15	16	17	18	19	20	%

column on my record sheet if I said something like 'thank you' or 'that's correct.' " (See Figure 2 for the recording sheet.)

3. "Class, what am I going to ask myself?" Group response—

4. "Class, if I said something like 'thank you' or 'that's correct' to a student, what will I mark?" Group response—

You should then begin the tape, which has several tones at intervals of 2–4 minutes, and then begin a short group lesson that lends itself to individual student responding. At the sound of each tone, the teacher will ask in a volume so all students can hear, "Did I offer praise?" Each time, record on the chalkboard or on an overhead a mark in the "Yes" or "No" column.

Self-regulation techniques can be used with students from preschool age through postsecondary age. Self-regulation is most widely used during independent seatwork.

After the short lesson is done, "think aloud," making comments about the number of marks in each column and how the students responded to the lesson. This think-aloud action is necessary to demonstrate to the students the relationship between the data collection and an evaluation of the outcome—the lesson.

After you have fully modeled the self-regulation procedure with the "think alouds," begin training the class using the single target behavior, such as on-task behavior.

Format for Training Group 2 Students: Guided Practice

1. Distribute a "Check Yourself" recording form to each student, and make a "Yes/No" box on the chalkboard. Say, "Class, when you hear the tone, ask yourself, 'Am I working?' " Provide examples of what is considered working and not working. This aspect of training is important so students will be able to make a quick decision and record it without asking you about a common task-related behavior. (Figures 3 and 4 show variations on the "Check Yourself" student form.)

2. Begin the tape of the tones and continue talking: "When you hear the tone, ask yourself in your quiet voice, 'Am I working?' Put a check mark in the 'Yes' box or the 'No' box. Are you always going to be working or listening to the lessons? No, sometimes you won't. That's OK. This strategy will help you become a better student. It is not possible to always be working on an assignment."

3. Continue teaching the group lesson started during the modeling phase and the tape of the recorded tones. When the class hears the first tone, the students (with your assistance) ask out loud, "Am I working?" You answer "Yes" and record a check in the "Yes" box on the chalkboard. Each student will record the response on his or her record sheet. The procedure continues with tones at random intervals, which are frequent enough to allow four or five recordings within a 10–15-minute time period.

4. At the conclusion of the lesson, say, "You did a good job asking the 'Am I working?' question and recording your answer. We will practice this again later."

Graphing and Record Keeping

Graphing the self-recording data can be an excellent activity for upper elementary age students to help them keep a long-term record of their performance and begin to set behavior goals. Older students can compute and record the percentage of "Yes" responses. Younger students may need to count total number of checks, "Yes" and "No," and record that total on a graph. Then they will count just the "Yes" checks and record that total on the graph. The goal is to make the distance be-

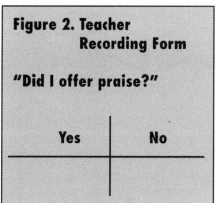

Figure 2. Teacher Recording Form

"Did I offer praise?"

Yes	No

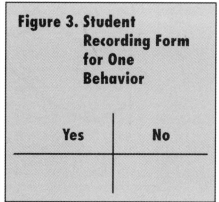

Figure 3. Student Recording Form for One Behavior

Yes	No

Figure 4. Student Recording Form for Several Types of Behavior

	Yes	No
"Am I working?"		
"Did I stay in my seat?"		
"Did I do my work?"		

tween the total number of checks and number of "Yes" checks as small as possible. (See Figure 5 for an example of student data and a sample graph.)

Benefits and Potential

The strengths of the self-regulatory program include the following:

- Reduced teacher time for monitoring and responding to student behavior.
- The ability to vary the target behavior from simple on-task behavior to the complex self-monitoring of strategy usage.

- The ability to individualize target behavior to accommodate a variety of student ability levels.

The teaching of self-regulation has the potential of providing students with a skill that will have an ongoing benefit as students become self-directed, lifelong learners.

References

18th Annual Report affirms CEC's policy on inclusive settings. (1997). *CEC Today, 3*(7), 1.

Barkley, R. A. (1990). *Attention-deficit hyperactivity disorder: A handbook for the diagnosis and treatment.* New York: Guilford.*

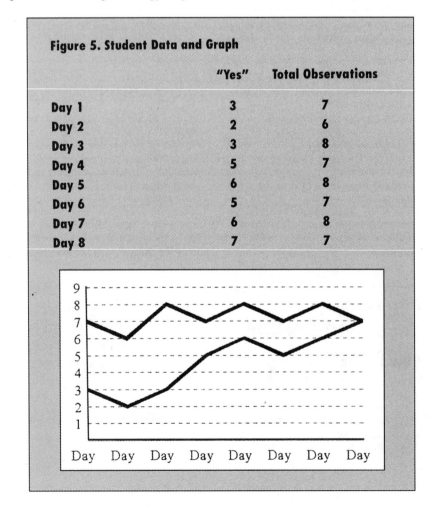

Figure 5. Student Data and Graph

	"Yes"	Total Observations
Day 1	3	7
Day 2	2	6
Day 3	3	8
Day 4	5	7
Day 5	6	8
Day 6	5	7
Day 7	6	8
Day 8	7	7

> **Researchers have found that a *combination* of types of target behavior, including both work-study and accuracy of assignment completion, seems to work best.**

Children and Adults with Attention Deficit Disorders. (1993). *CHADD facts 8: The national organization working for children and adults with attention deficit disorders.* Washington, DC: Author.*

Glynn, E. L., Thomas, J. D., & Shee, S. M. (1973). Behavioral self-control of on-task behavior in an elementary classroom. *Journal of Applied Behavior Analysis, 6*(1), 105–113.

Guevremont, D. C., Osnes, P. G., & Stokes, T. P. (1988). The functional role of preschoolers' verbalizations in the generalization of self-instructional training. *Journal of Applied Behavior Analysis, 21*(1), 45–55.

Maag, J. W., Reid, R., & DiGanni, S. A., (1993). Differential effects of self-monitoring attention, accuracy, and productivity. *Journal of Applied Behavior Analysis, 26*(3), 329–344.

Mathes, M. Y., & Bender, W. N. (1997). The effects of self-monitoring on children with attention-deficit/hyperactivity disorder who are receiving pharmacological interventions. *Remedial and Special Education, 18*(2), 121–128.

Rooney, K. J., Polloway, E. A., & Hallahan, D. P. (1985). The use of self-monitoring procedures with low IQ learning disabled students. *Journal of Learning Disabilities, 18,* 384–389.

Webber, J., Scheuermann, B., McCall, C., & Coleman, M. (1993). Research on self-monitoring as a behavior management technique in special education classrooms: A descriptive review. *Remedial and Special Education, 14*(2), 38–56.

BooksNow

To order books marked by an asterisk (*), please call 24 hrs/365 days: 1–800–BOOKS–NOW (266–5766) or (801) 261–1187, or visit them on the Web at http://www.BooksNow.com/TeachingExceptional.htm. Use VISA, M/C, or AMEX or send check or money order + $4.95 S&H ($2.50 each add'l item) to: Books Now, Suite 125, 448 East 6400 South, Salt Lake City, UT 84107.

Lewis R. Johnson (CEC Chapter #345), Assistant Professor, Department of Special Education; **Christine E. Johnson,** Graduate Student, Department of Speech Pathology, Arkansas State University, State University.

Address correspondence to Lewis R. Johnson, P.O. Box 1450, Arkansas State University, State University, AR 72467 (e-mail: Ljohnson@kiowa.astate.edu).

Using Classroom Rules to Construct Behavior

I've come to a frightening conclusion that I am the decisive element in the classroom. It's my approach that creates the climate. It's my daily mood that makes the weather. As a teacher, I possess a tremendous power to make a child's life miserable or joyous. I can be a tool of torture or an instrument of inspiration. I can humiliate or humor, hurt or heal. In all situations, it is my response that decides whether a crisis will be escalated or de-escalated and a child humanized or dehumanized. (Haim Ginott, *The Teacher*, January 2000)

David F. Bicard

In many middle school classrooms, teachers attempt to influence the behavior of students through the use of rules. However, rules alone exert little effect on student behavior. Teachers may sometimes be unaware of the effects their actions have on the behavior of their students. Two classic studies may help to illustrate the effects of teacher-made rules and teacher behavior on the activity of their students. Madsen, Becker, and Thomas (1968) found that when a teacher provided rules alone to her students, the students' appropriate and inappropriate behavior remained at relatively the same level as when she provided no rules. Major decreases in inappropriate conduct and increases in appropriate conduct occurred when the teacher showed approval for appropriate behavior in combination with ignoring some inappropriate behavior. Similarly, Thomas, Becker, and Armstrong (1968) found that teachers could produce or eliminate appropriate and inappropriate behavior by varying approval and disapproval statements. When the teachers delivered positive statements to their students

regarding their classroom behavior, the students maintained appropriate conduct; and when the teachers withdrew positive statements and delivered frequent disapproval statements, inappropriate behavior increased.

While rules by themselves may not be effective, they do provide structure, communicate teacher expectations, provide a foundation for learning, and help maintain a well-run and organized classroom. Positive rules, along with consistent action by the teacher, set the stage for praising student achievement that benefits the teacher as much as the students. Good classrooms where students are highly involved do not just happen. They exist because effective teachers have constructed the types of classroom conditions and student interactions necessary for a positive learning environment (Emmer, Evertson, Clements, & Worsham, 1994). In *Middle School Journal,* Mills (1997) described how one effective teacher named Suzan constructed her classroom to ensure successful learning. Suzan "modeled a way of teaching, learning, and behaving that she shared, both explicitly and implic-

From *Middle School Journal,* May 2000, pp. 37-45. © 2000 by the National Middle School Association. Reprinted by permission.

Figure 1

Examples of Positive, Negative, and Vague Rules		
Positive	**Negative**	**Vague**
Raise your hand when you want to talk.	Don't interrupt others.	Respect others.
Keep your eyes on the teacher.	Don't look around the room.	Listen to the teacher.
Bring a pencil to class every day.	Don't come to class without a pencil.	Come to class prepared.
Before you leave make sure your desk is clean.	You are not ready to leave until your desk is clean.	Keep the classroom neat.
Be in your seat when the bell rings.	Don't be out of your seat when the bell rings.	Be on time for class.

itly, with her students. . . . [Her approach] held expectations for student responsibility, for a caring atmosphere, and for student success" . . . . Throughout this article we will return to Suzan's classroom to demonstrate how effective teachers can use words and actions to construct positive rules for their students.

Rules are one of the most cost effective forms of classroom management available to teachers (Catania, 1998). However, not all teachers recognize the benefits of teaching rules. In *Setting Limits in the Classroom*, Mackenzie (1996) noted 10 common misconceptions held by teachers about the use of rules, among them, "teaching rules is the parents' job," "students should know what I expect," "I can't afford to take precious time away from instruction," and "explaining my rules to students should be enough." The reality is that in the classroom, teaching rules is one of the teacher's jobs, with parents' help. In addition, students need time to learn the rules and expectations of their teachers. Rules need to be taught with words as well as actions; the time invested up front will pay huge dividends in the end.

Ginott (2000) suggested that teachers are the decisive element in the classroom. In that role, they should take the responsibility for constructing and implementing positive rules as a management system to build academic success. This article describes the characteristics of positive rules, offers suggestions for developing and implementing the rules, and provides guidelines for what to do when students break the rules.

Characteristics of Positive Rules

The first part of this section will describe the differences between some common rules that exist in many middle school classrooms. The second part discusses an often overlooked, yet extremely important, component of effective rules. These small differences in the way teachers construct rules may have a big influence on the way students behave in the classroom.

Positive rules specify appropriate student behavior in observable terms

Rules come in three basic varieties: positive rules that communicate how to behave, negative rules that communicate how not to behave, and vague rules that communicate neither how nor how not to behave (Figure 1). A common rule about completing assigned work can be worded positively ("Answer each problem until you are done"), negatively ("Don't stop unless you are done"), or vaguely ("Stay on task"). Small differences in wording make a substantial difference in the way students will respond and how teachers will focus their attention. The positive version of the rule lets the student know how to behave so that teachers can provide approval when students follow the rule. Conversely, in the negative and vague examples, nothing has been said on how to respond; the student is left with only how not to respond. More important, in the negative and vague examples, teachers are more likely to recognize students only when they do not follow the rule. When rules state what the student *can do* in specific and observable terms, both teachers and students can easily recognize whether a rule is being followed. Teachers are more likely to notice appropriate behavior and celebrate student success. Positive rules tell students what to do instead of what not to do and are thus more instructive (Paine, Radicchi, Rosellini, Deutchman, & Darch, 1983).

When rules state only what the student *cannot do* or are *vague*, teacher attention will likely be on punishment for inappropriate behavior (Zirpoli & Melloy, 1993). When teacher attention is focused on punishment, the classroom becomes coercive, authoritarian, and punitive. It becomes a teacher's job to investigate violations, determine guilt, and mete out sentences. Less time is left for teaching. Frequent disapproval may also deter student learning in other ways. Greer (1981) found that the use of disapproval statements by teachers resulted in the students avoiding what was taught during free time. For example, if when teaching reading a teacher delivers frequent disapproval statements to his or her students, the students will be less likely to read books when they have leisure time. As Sulzer-Azaroff and Mayer (1986) noted, "One more critical disadvantage to resorting to punishment too frequently is that the practice inadvertently may teach others to use it as well" (p. 146).

A key component of effective rules is that the rules specify observable student behavior. In this respect *observable* means something a teacher can count, for example raising a hand. When a teacher can count behaviors, students become accountable for those behaviors. Vague rules such as "respect others" or "stay on task" may be as difficult for students to follow as they are for teachers to enforce because behaviors are extremely difficult to count. A teacher who can observe specific instances of appropriate student conduct is prepared to celebrate students' successes.

When attention is focused on appropriate behavior through the use of positive rules, teachers promote a sense of personal efficacy in students that communicates the trust, competence, responsibility, affiliation, and awareness so important in middle level curriculum (Stevenson, 1998). In short, teachers should be in the business of constructing behaviors not eliminating them (W. L. Heward, personal communication, February 12, 1998).

Suzan "told her students what she expected and wanted.... She reminded the students of proper lab behavior before each lab activity.... She gave examples of acceptable comments that focused on their learning and encouraged students" (Mills, 1997, pp. 33–34). Yet simply stating positive rules is only the first step of effective classroom management.

Positive rules specify observable consequences

Another important, though often overlooked, component of effective rules is a statement of consequences. Consequences are the *quid pro quo* of rules, letting students know what they get in return. Classroom studies conducted by Braam and Malott (1990) and Mistr and Glenn (1992) have shown that rules specifying only response requirements did not reliably guide student behavior; conversely when rules specified observable behavior *and* consequences, they were effective in maintaining appropriate behavior. Consequences are important because they teach responsibility and accountability to the teacher as well as the student. Providing clear consequences will help to break the cycle of limit-testing so common with middle school students. In the example, "Raise your hand when you want to talk," the students are left to discover what will happen next; they may raise their hands and then begin to talk. If the teacher provides a consequence, for example, "and I will call on you when it's your turn," the students will not have to guess. This is especially significant when we look at negative rules, such as "Don't talk until called upon." When a consequence is provided, "or your name will be written on the board," the focus of attention will necessarily be on elimination of behavior. It is also important that students be aware of the consequences for not following the rules. For example, during science experiments Mills' (1997) expert teacher "reminded the students of the cost of activities and suggested the principal, 'won't give me money for labs if you're not mature enough to handle them well' " (p. 34).

Developing Positive Rules

Three strategies help develop effective rules. The first strategy helps teachers to conceptualize a basic framework for identifying situations in which rules should be specified. The next two strategies are specific processes teachers can use to develop successful classroom rules.

Figure 2

Keys to Developing and Implementing Positive Rules in Classrooms

Characteristics of Positive Rules
- Positive rules specify appropriate student behavior in observable terms
- Positive rules specify observable consequences

Developing Positive Rules
- Develop a framework before the school year begins
- Include students in the decision-making process
- Get agreement by students, teachers, and parents

Using Positive Rules Effectively
- Teach the rules
- Catch students following the rules
- Monitor your behavior
- Include students as monitors

What To Do When Students Break the Rules
- Use the least intrusive procedures first
- Praise other students for following the rules
- Give verbal redirection
- Remain unemotional yet firm when intervening

Develop a framework before the school year

All rules must follow the policies and procedures of the school; however, these are typically general guidelines that can easily be incorporated into a set of classroom rules. Once teachers, or a team of teachers, have information about school policy and procedures, they can begin to plan rules for their classrooms and team

Rules are one of the most cost effective forms of classroom management available to teachers.

areas. Paine and associates (1983) maintained that the best time to develop rules is *before* the school year begins. Teachers should decide what kinds of situations to cover and what kinds of rules to write for those situations. For example, a science teacher may have one set of rules during experiments and another during whole-class time. This basic framework will help teachers to guide students toward a formalized version of the rules.

Include students in the decision-making process

Once the guidelines are in place, the next step is involving students in deciding the specific rules. Student participation in rule setting has been demonstrated to be effective for increased compliance (Dickerson & Creedon, 1981), lower numbers of violations (Felixbrod & O'Leary, 1974), and academic success (Lovitt & Curtis, 1969). Emmer, Evertson, Clements, and Worsham (1994) noted that involving students in rule setting helps to promote student ownership and responsibility. Incorporating students in the process communicates respect and concern, lets students know they are important elements in the classroom, and serves to promote student acceptance.

There are a number of techniques teachers can use. For example, the first day of class can begin with a discussion of the role of rules in society and their application to the classroom. A teacher could ask the students to describe model behavior, then use this as a basis for discussing what types of rules are appropriate in the classroom. Specifying student behaviors in observable terms provides the foundation for the rules, and identifying teacher behavior provides the foundation for the consequences. The teacher may need to guide the students in providing positive examples, as middle school students tend to focus on violations (Emmer et al., 1994). Suzan had students "brainstorm appropriate comments and role-play supportive situations" (Mills, 1997, p. 35). It is important to note that student-made rules are sometimes too stringent, so again, it is a good idea to have a basic framework in mind prior to discussing rules with the students.

Try to keep the rules to a minimum: It is recommended that teachers use no more than three or four rules for each situation. To help students remember the rules and help teachers make praise statements within the wording of the rules, keep the wording as simple as possible. When the rules are established consequences must also be established. A simple method for achieving positive rules and consequences is to ask students to list possible consequences for following classroom rules. These can be favorite classroom activities, free time, or a note to parents. Students should also list consequences for not following the rules—for example, a "three strikes policy," then loss of free time, then a note to parents. An example of a positive rule might be when a student completes assigned work before the end of class, the teacher will give him or her five minutes of free time. Teachers can decide on whole class and individual contingencies based on the list each student completes. This process will allow flexibility in classroom management.

Create a contract for the students, teachers, and parents

Once the rules are in place have each student write the rules on a piece of paper, sign it, take it home for the parents or guardians to sign, and bring it back to school the next day. Jones and Jones (1990) recommended including a statement about classroom philosophy regarding management and instruction: "This lets you present the issues of rules in a positive manner that indicates

their relationship to effective instruction and student learning." The contingency contract provides a number of useful advantages: students cannot say they were unaware of the rules; parents know the expectations of the teachers and have agreed, fostering a home-school partnership; and there is a record on file for future reference. (For more information regarding contingency contracts see Cooper, Heron, & Heward, 1987, pp. 466–485.)

Using Rules Effectively

Now that the rules have been specified and the consequences set forth, teachers are ready to begin using the rules to guide student learning. It is worth mentioning again that, without reliable enforcement by teachers, rules have very little effect on student conduct.

When rules specified observable behavior and consequences, they were effective in maintaining appropriate behavior.

Teach the rules

A crucial component of positive classroom management is how teachers implement the rules. The first step in teaching the rules is to post them prominently in the classroom. Suzan, "at the beginning of the year displayed a life-size female adolescent labeled 'scientist,' a smaller poster of rules near a frog saying 'hop to it'" (Mills, 1997, p. 33). An effective strategy is to designate a student from each class to make a poster listing the rules and consequences, or, if teachers decide on one set of rules for all their classes, a competition can be held and prizes awarded for the three best posters. For the first two or three days after the rules are in place, devote five minutes of class time to teaching the rules through examples. Doing this at the beginning of each class is an excellent way to keep the students engaged while taking attendance or gathering materials. Teachers can guide this discussion or designate a student to lead the class. It is important to have all the students state the rules, then have students role-play acceptable and unacceptable behavior. This is a perfect time to begin to catch students following the rules and praise them. Teachers can continue teaching the rules in this fashion each Monday for the first month of the school year and again the first Monday after long breaks. Whenever students need a "booster shot" during the school year, teachers can go back to this activity. Although this procedure may seem somewhat elementary, it is useful to teach rule following just as one would teach any other subject.

Catch students following the rules

Teaching positive rules does not end in the first five minutes of class or in the first week of school; it continues throughout the school year. Suzan "provided numerous opportunities for students to experience success. Her students experienced frequent success and received teacher praise for their efforts" (Mills, 1997, p. 35). Praise should be immediate, consistent, and contingent upon "catching the students being good." Consistent means a teacher reliably recognizes student behavior as it occurs. Contingent specifies a relationship between praise and the student's behavior. When students are behaving appropriately, follow the "if, then rule"—if students have done something appropriate, *then* praise them (Paine et al., 1983). An example from Mills (1997) illustrates this point. "Suzan once shared the compliments that a substitute teacher had made about the students and thanked them for their good behavior.... 'When I saw the work you had done in groups [while I was gone] I knew you had been wonderful' " (p. 35).

When praising always identify the rule, the behavior, and the student or students by name, "I like the way Jennifer put things away when the bell rang because that shows she is ready to learn. Nice job Jennifer." Public praise can occur in several situations: while teaching, when near a student, or in the presence of other teachers. This may be especially helpful for some students who are having difficulty in other classrooms. Sometimes public praise might be a problem with middle school students, so teachers may want to praise some students only when nearby or in private. Teachers can write a note on a student's paper or praise the student during individual seat work. Sometimes a call home to parents or even to a student is a good technique. For Suzan, "quiet, supportive exchanges with individual students took place literally during every occasion" (Mills, 1997, p. 34).

Monitor teacher behavior

An effective way to achieve success using positive rules is for teachers to monitor their own behavior. Initially, teachers can count the number of approval and disapproval statements. It is not as difficult as one would think. Generally, middle level teachers are excellent time managers. Begin counting, and when five minutes have passed, note the number of approval and disapproval statements. This then becomes a measure per unit of time. Teachers may be surprised and somewhat shocked at how little praise has been given. A good rule of thumb is to have a 3:1 ratio of approval to disapproval statements (Englemann & Carnine, 1991).

One technique for helping to pinpoint specific approval statements is a variation of "the timer game" (Lovitt, 1995, p. 322). Identify the behaviors to "catch," for example, students active at work stations making entries in their notebooks. Set a goal such as five praise statements in five minutes. The next and easiest step is for teachers to identify a reward for themselves, maybe a chocolate bar at lunch. Once these are in place, teachers can set a timer for five minutes and begin teaching. During teaching simply make a mark on a spare piece of paper for every praise statement. When the timer goes off, students will probably be very interested in what is going on. This is a good time to let them in on the secret. Take a few minutes to discuss this practice and why it is being used. The students may be willing to assist in counting. It also has the added benefit of notifying students of what behaviors are being monitored and may help to promote appropriate classroom conduct.

Student participation in rule setting has been demonstrated to be effective for increased compliance.

Another useful strategy is to place "reminders" in the classroom such as a sign in the back of the room to prompt the teacher. Mills (1997) reported that in Suzan's classroom, "virtually every week, new student work was displayed.... Before class started, Suzan would call my attention to the students' work, call students over to show me their efforts or explain the concept, and tell me loudly how proud she was of their efforts" (pp. 35–36). Monitoring teacher behavior helps to promote a positive classroom environment. In the classroom it is the teacher who sets the standards. By modeling appropriate behavior teachers communicate with words and actions that they value a supportive, responsible, and respectful classroom.

Include students as monitors

Students play an active role in controlling peer behavior (Lovitt, 1995). Middle school teachers are well aware of the effects of peer attention on student behavior. Unfortunately, this has usually been correlated with inappropriate behavior. The results of a study by Carden-Smith and Fowler (1984) suggested that peers can serve to increase and maintain appropriate classroom behavior, provided they are given proper instruction and feedback from a teacher. Here is how Suzan involved students as monitors, "One particular day, the students had given oral reports and presented visuals on different animals; following each report the students asked for questions and comments. All students received praise from classmates about some aspect of their reports or drawings" (Mills, 1997, p. 35). Suzan "reminded her students during lab activities to 'check with your buddy' or 'help your partner' " (Mills, 1997, p. 34). Encouraging students to praise their peers has many benefits. In the above example, a mutually reinforcing relationship is established that will increase the probability of more praise statements to follow. Another example shows how involving students frees the teacher to take on other responsibilities:

> During the first observation, a group of students who finished their assignments early were designated by Suzan as "wizards." Suzan explained the next assignment to the wizards, and they were to provide and explain the worksheet to other students as they completed their work. All students were to seek help from the wizards before they asked questions of Suzan. (Mills, 1997, p. 35)

A useful and highly effective strategy for involving students as peer monitors is a variation of "the good behavior game" (Barrish, Saunders, & Wolf, 1969). This strategy is appropriate for whole groups or individual students. The technique requires teachers to model appropriate behaviors and then designate a student or group of students to identify instances of appropriate behavior by other students. In this game all students can win if they simply engage in appropriate behavior. Each team or individual can choose rewards the students and teacher have selected prior to the game. Successfully including peers as monitors may take some time and creativity on the part of a teacher, but the benefits of a cohesive, nurturing classroom are well worth the investment.

What to Do When Students Break the Rules

There will be times when students behave in unacceptable ways. This is as true for the best students as it is for the worst. The decisions teachers make during these times can escalate or de-escalate an already unfavorable situation. Heward has noted that teachers can maintain and increase deviant behavioral patterns even though they are trying to help their students. This process

> begins with a teacher request that the student ignores and follows a predictable and escalating sequence of teacher pleas and threats that the student counters with excuses, arguments, and eventually a full-blown tantrum. The aggression and tantrumming is so aversive to the teacher that she withdraws the request (thereby reinforcing and strengthening the student's disruptive behavior) so the student will stop the tormenting (thereby reinforcing the teacher for withdrawing the request). (Heward, 2000)

This increasing escalation of disruptive behavior is called *coercive pain control* (Rhode, Jensen, & Reavis, 1998) because the student learns to use painful behavior to escape or avoid the teacher's requests. It is best to try to anticipate these times by preparing a plan of action before the situation occurs. The following five proven strategies can be used separately or in combination to assist teachers when students behave unacceptably in the classroom.

Use the least intrusive procedures first

The first technique to use is simply to arrange seating patterns so teachers can reach every part of their classrooms. Second, certain objects may be removed from the classroom if they prove to be distracting. However, keep in mind that having interesting objects in the classroom provides a great teaching opportunity since the student's attention is naturally directed toward the object. Another useful, unobtrusive technique is known as "planned ignoring" (Walker & Shea, 1995). Before attempting to use this technique, first try to determine why the student is engaging in unacceptable behavior. If it is determined he or she is doing this to get attention, then any response

Teaching positive rules does not end in the first five minutes of class or in the first week of school; it continues throughout the school year.

(positive or negative) will increase the probability of this behavior re-occurring in the future. With planned ignoring the teacher does not make any contact with the student. This technique works especially well in combination with praising other students. When a teacher uses this technique, at first unacceptable behavior may increase in intensity or duration. This should not be cause for alarm because it is an indication that the technique is working. It is important to resist the temptation to react. Once the student stops the unacceptable behavior the teacher can catch some appropriate behavior and praise it. If the teacher determines the unacceptable behavior is maintained by other students or is dangerous, then planned ignoring will not work and should not be attempted. At this point a teacher may want to intervene directly.

Praise other students for following the rules

Praising other students for following the rules serves as a reminder to a student that he or she is not behaving appropriately. This reminder encourages the student to adjust his or her own behavior (Sulzer-Azaroff & Mayer, 1986). For example, if James is staring out the window when most of the other students are working diligently on math problems, the teacher may call a student by name and praise him—"I like the way DeMarco is working; one bonus point for DeMarco." More often than not, James will then begin to work on his math. After a few seconds, praise James to encourage him to keep working.

This strategy is effective and has the benefit of notifying the student who is acting inappropriately without having to single him out. At the same time, it recognizes a student who is behaving appropriately.

Use proximity control and signal interference

Proximity control and signal interference are two less obtrusive techniques that are frequently used in conjunction with one another (Walker & Shea, 1995). When teachers move around the classroom their presence often serves as a cue to students, who stop behaving unacceptably. When a student is misbehaving, casually move in the direction of the student and attempt to make eye contact. Sometimes simply making eye contact is enough, other times nonverbal cues such as facial expressions, toe taps, or body language may be necessary. These nonverbal signals may alert a student that a behavior is disruptive. Walker and Shea noted, "In addition, proximity can have a positive effect on students experiencing anxiety and frustration. The physical presence of a teacher or parent available to assist has a calming effect on troubled children" (p. 228). Often nonverbal signals help the student to "save face" with his peers and promote a sense of respect on the part of the teacher. This technique is also appropriate for reinforcing acceptable behavior. After making eye contact, the teacher can simply smile or give a thumbs-up sign (Walker & Shea, 1995).

Peers can serve to increase and maintain appropriate classroom behavior, provided they are given proper instruction and feedback from a teacher.

Give verbal redirection

Occasionally students engage in minor disruptions during daily classroom routines such as attendance, returning homework, or when listening to daily messages over the intercom. This is a good time to channel their energy toward acceptable behavior. For example Lynn passes a note to Juan through Chuck. Ask Lynn to assist in passing out homework. Ask Juan a question about an upcoming activity and tell Chuck to read today's assignment off the blackboard. Verbal redirection can be an extremely effective technique, but caution should be used if the student is engaging in the behavior to get the teacher's attention.

Remain unemotional yet firm when intervening

It is best to remain unemotional yet firm when dealing with rule violations. As classroom leaders, teachers set the tone when things do not go as planned. The most effective strategy teachers can use is to handle minor disruptions before they become worse. Jones and Jones (1990) noted, "An inappropriately angry teacher's response creates tension and increases disobedience and disruptive behavior. When a teacher reacts calmly and quickly to a student's disruptive behavior, other students respond by improving their own behavior" (p. 295). The first step when intervening is to make contact with the student. Never assume the student is aware he or she is breaking a classroom rule; let the student know what is acceptable: "Carlos, the rule is, raise your hand when you want to speak, and I will call on you as soon as possible." As soon as Carlos raises his hand, the teacher should call on him and praise him for behaving responsibly. Teachers can intervene publicly as a message to the entire class; however, it is best to deliver reprimands in private. When teachers show respect for students, they will be more likely to comply with the teacher's instructions, and the teacher has averted turning a minor disruption into a major catastrophe.

Conclusion

Following this four-part framework for constructing behaviors can result in positive approaches to middle level classroom management. Figure 2 provides an outline of this approach for reference. The goal of setting positive rules and procedures is to maintain a healthy and respectful classroom. As the decisive element, teachers can create a supportive, caring community of learners through the words they choose and the actions they take. Mills (1997) captured this approach this way: "Suzan communicated to her students a pervasive caring by helping them feel a sense of belonging; learn acceptable, supportive behaviors; experience frequent success; and assume they have a promising future" (p. 34).

Author's Note: Support for this article was provided by a Leadership Training Grant (#H3253980018) from the Office of Special Education and Rehabilitation Services, U.S. Department of Education. I thank David A. and Barbara Bicard for being the decisive elements in my life. I also thank William L. Heward for his constructive comments.

References

Barrish, H. H., Saunders, M., & Wolf, M. M. (1969). Good behavior game: Effects of individual contingencies for group consequences on disruptive behavior in a classroom. *Journal of Applied Behavior Analysis, 2,* 119–124.

Braam, C., & Malott, R. M. (1990). "I'll do it when the snow melts": The effects of deadlines and delayed outcomes on rule-governed behavior in preschool children. *The Analysis of Verbal Behavior, 8,* 67–76.

Carden-Smith, L. K., & Fowler, S. A. (1984). Positive peer pressure: The effects of peer monitoring on children's disruptive behavior. *Journal of Applied Behavior Analysis, 17,* 213–227.

Catania, A. C. (1998). *Learning* (4th ed.). Upper Saddle River, NJ: Prentice Hall.

Cooper, J. O., Heron, T. E., & Heward, W. L. (1987). *Applied behavior analysis.* Upper Saddle River, NJ: Prentice Hall/Merrill.

Dickerson, E. A., & Creedon, C. F. (1981). Self-selection of standards by children: The relative effectiveness of pupil-selected and teacher-selected standards of performance. *Journal of Applied Behavior Analysis, 14,* 425–433.

Englemann, D., & Carnine, D. (1991). *Theory of instruction* (rev. ed.). Eugene, OR: ADI Press.

Emmer, E. T., Evertson, C. M., Clements, B. S., & Worsham, M. E. (1994). *Classroom management for secondary teachers* (3rd ed.). Needham, MA: Allyn and Bacon.

Felixbrod, J., & O'Leary, K. (1974). Self-determination of academic standards by children: Toward freedom from external control. *Journal of Educational Psychology, 66,* 845–850.

Ginott, H. (2000). *The teacher.* Retrieved January 6, 2000 from the World Wide Web: http://www.geocities.com/Heartland/Plains/3565/haimginott.htm

Greer, R. D. (1981). An operant approach to motivation and affect: Ten years of research in music learning. In Documentary report of the Ann Arbor symposium: *Application of psychology to the teaching and learning of music.* Washington, DC: Music Educators National Conference.

Heward, W. L. (2000). *Exceptional children: An introduction to special education* (6th ed.). Upper Saddle River, NJ: Prentice Hall.

Jones, V. F., & Jones, L. S. (1990). *Comprehensive classroom management.* Needham Heights, MA: Allyn and Bacon.

Lovitt, T. C. (1995). *Tactics for teaching* (2nd ed.). Upper Saddle River, NJ: Prentice Hall.

Lovitt, T. C., & Curtis, K. (1969). Academic response rate as a function of teacher- and self-imposed contingencies. *Journal of Applied Behavior Analysis, 2,* 49–53.

Madsen, C. H., Becker, W. C., & Thomas, D. R. (1968). Rules, praise, and ignoring: Elements of elementary classroom control. *Journal of Applied Behavior Analysis, 1,* 139–150.

Mackenzie, R. J. (1996). *Setting limits in the classroom.* Rocklin, CA: Prima Publishing.

Mills, R. A. (1997). Expert teaching and successful learning at the middle level: One teacher's story. *Middle School Journal, 29*(1), 30–38.

Mistr, K. N., & Glenn, S. S. (1992). Evocative and function-altering effects of contingency-specifying stimuli. *The Analysis of Verbal Behavior, 10,* 11–21.

Paine, S. C., Radicchi, J., Rosellini, L. C., Deutchman, L., & Darch, C. B. (1983). *Structuring your classroom for academic success.* Champaign, IL: Research Press.

Rhode, G., Jensen, W. R., & Reavis, H. K. (1998). *The tough kid book: Practical classroom management strategies.* Longmont, CO: Sopris West.

Stevenson, C. (1998). Finding our priorities for middle level curriculum. *Middle School Journal, 29*(4), 53–57.

Sulzer-Azaroff, B., & Mayer, G. R. (1986). *Achieving educational excellence using behavioral strategies.* New York: CBS College Publishing.

Thomas, D. R., Becker, W. C., & Armstrong, M. (1968). Production and elimination of disruptive classroom behavior by systematically varying teachers' behavior. *Journal of Applied Behavior Analysis, 1,* 35–45.

Walker, J., & Shea, T. M. (1995). *Behavior management: A practical approach for educators.* Englewood Cliffs, NJ: Prentice Hall.

Zirpoli, T. J., & Melloy, K. J. (1993). *Behavior management: Applications for teachers and parents.* Don Mills, Ontario: Macmillan Publishing.

David F. Bicard is a doctoral student in special education at The Ohio State University, Columbus.

HOW TO DEFUSE DEFIANCE, THREATS, CHALLENGES

CONFRONTATIONS...

The T-Shirt attention getter...
Prohibited cookies on the bus...
Profanity in class...
Outright refusal to do classwork...
Chair-throwing...

A comprehensive system of behavior management has three critical components: prevention, defusion, and follow-up.

Geoff Colvin
David Ainge
Ron Nelson

■

Do some of your students engage in confrontational behavior like this? Here's a litany of such behavior: attention-getting, defiance, challenges, disrespect, limit testing, verbal abuse, blatant rule violations, threats, and intimidation. Some students test the patience of teachers who have what they thought was an effective behavior-management system. This article presents teacher-tested ways to *defuse* such behavior and allow the students to learn and participate in positive ways.

Special education teachers have always had the task of managing students who display seriously disturbing behavior. More recently, these teachers are expected to provide support and consultation to general education teachers who need assistance on managing the behavior of all students in inclusive classrooms. Special education teachers can assist other educators in a comprehensive system of behavior management composed of three critical components: prevention, defusion, and follow-up (see box, "Three Approaches to Behavior Management").

We focus here particularly on *defusion,* an approach that is helpful with students who are continually confrontational. Such behavior not only leads to class disruption, but also can readily escalate to more serious behavior—and threats to the safety of both staff and students. Let's look at some examples of confrontational behavior and then explore how we can deal with it.

Three Confrontational Students

- Joe steps onto the school bus holding a monster cookie in his hand. Above his head is a large sign that reads, "No food on the bus." Joe looks at the driver, takes a huge bite of the cookie, and takes another step on the bus. The bus driver points to the sign and says quite emphatically, "Look, no food on the bus. You'll have to give me that cookie." Joe says equally emphatically, "No," and takes another bite. The driver looks him right in the eye and says, "If you don't give me the cookie, you will not ride the bus." Joe says, "So," takes another bite of the cookie, and begins to move toward his seat. The driver calls transportation to have the student removed from the bus.
- Sarah walks into the classroom wearing a T-shirt displaying a toilet bowl with an arrow coming up out of the bowl and a written statement underneath, "Up your AZ." Some students giggle, and another asks, "Where did you get that?" The teacher comes over and says, "Sarah, that shirt is not acceptable in a public school. You had better go to the restroom and turn it inside out." Sarah looks at the teacher and says, "I'm not gonna do that. My dad gave it to me and you can't make me turn it inside out." The teacher says that if she does not cooperate, she

will be sent to the office. Sarah throws her book down and heads to the back of the room.

- Jamie is sitting at his desk, arms folded, shoulders rounded, feet firmly planted on the floor, and staring at the floor with a scowl on his face, while the rest of the class is working on an independent math assignment. The teacher eventually approaches Jamie and prompts him to start on his math. He scowls and says in a harsh tone that he can't do it. So the teacher offers to help him. He says he still can't do it. The teacher provides more detail with the explanation and directs him to make a start. He says he hates math. The teacher tells him that he needs to start or he will have to do his math during the break. He utters a profanity and storms out of the room.

What Happened?

In each case, the supervising staff person reacts to a problem behavior in a direct manner. There is a high likelihood that the student *expects* a response. In fact, the student not only expects a response, but he or she expects a *particular* response.

For all practical purposes, the staff person is *already set up for confrontation.* In other words, the student displays engaging behavior that is highly likely to elicit a predictable response from staff that includes a clear direction. The student refuses to follow the direction, which engages staff further, leading to ultimatums and additional problem behavior.

Moreover, if the staff person becomes confrontational at this point, there is a strong likelihood that the student will react with more serious behavior. In effect, we can see a pattern—a cycle—of successive interactions beginning with problem behavior leading to more serious behavior, such as throwing a book (Sarah), continuing to disregard requests (Joe), or profanity (Jamie). These vignettes have five common features:

1. The student displays defiant, challenging, or inappropriate behavior.
2. The supervising staff person reacts to the problem behavior and provides a direction in opposition to the student's behavior.
3. The student challenges the direction by not complying and by displaying other inappropriate behavior.
4. The staff person reacts to the non-compliance and presents an ultimatum.
5. The student takes up the challenge of the ultimatum with further defiance and exhibits hostile and explosive behavior.

What Strategies Can Help?

When students exhibit confrontational behavior, you need approaches that are likely to defuse the problem behavior, rather than lead to more serious behavior. Defusing strategies minimize the likelihood that interactions between you and the student will escalate the confrontation. We have found five defusing strategies that work—in order of least intrusive student behavior to more serious confrontational behavior. These strategies range from ignoring the behavior to delaying a response and allowing the student to calm down.

Focus on the Task to Defuse Minor Attention-Getting Behavior

Students often display minor problem behavior to secure attention: talking out in class, moving out of their seats, starting work slowly, and pencil tapping. Once you respond to such behavior, the student may exhibit more attention-getting behavior. The basic approach for managing this level of problem behavior is to use a *continuum* of steps based on the level of attention you provide:

• Attend to the students exhibiting expected behavior, and ignore the students displaying the problem behavior.

• Redirect the student to the task at hand. Do not respond to or draw attention to the problem behavior.
• Present a choice between the expected behavior and a small negative consequence (such as a loss of privilege).

For example, Michael is out of his seat wandering around the room while other students are seated and engaged in a class activity. The teacher moves among the students who are on task, acknowledges their good work and ignores Michael. Michael continues to move around the class. The teacher approaches him and says privately, "Michael, listen, it's math time. Let's go," and points to his seat. Michael still does not return to his seat. The teacher secures his attention and says calmly and firmly, "Michael, you have been asked to sit down and start work or you will have to do the work in recess. You decide." The teacher follows through on whatever Michael chooses to do.

Present Options Privately in the Context of a Rule Violation

Sometimes students will break a rule to challenge you. They know you will react and give a direction. The student will then refuse to follow the direction. In this way, a confrontation scene is established. For example, in the cases of Joe and Sarah, the staff member gave the students a direction that the students refused to follow—the cookie was not turned in to the driver, the T-shirt was not turned inside out. Here are steps to follow in such cases:

• State the rule or expectation.
• Request explicitly for the student to "take care of the problem."
• Present options for the student on how to take care of the problem.

In this way, you lessen the chance of confrontation when you present options and focus [on] how the student might decide to take care of the problem, rather than whether the student follows a specific direction.

For example, the bus driver might have quietly said something like this to Joe: "Look, there is no food on the bus, thank you. You had better take care of that. You can eat it before you get on or leave it here and collect it later." Note the options the bus driver might have provided.

Or, to deal with Sarah's offensive T-shirt, the teacher might take Sarah aside and say, "Sarah, that shirt is not OK in a public school. It has a rude message. You can turn it inside out, get a shirt from the gym, or wear a jacket."

Reduce Agitation in a Demand Situation

Sometimes students are already agitated when they enter a situation. When you or

other people place demands on them, their behavior will likely escalate.

For example, Jamie's body posture and tone of voice suggest he is upset. When the teacher tries to prompt him to work, even in a very reasonable manner, his behavior escalates to storming out of the room. Here, the teacher might have used agitation-reduction techniques.

First, communicate concern to the student. Then allow the student time and space. Give the student some choices or options.

Signs of Agitation. Students show agitation by either increasing distracting behavior or decreasing active, engaged behavior (Colvin, 1992). Here are common signs of increases in *distracting behavior:*

• Darting eyes
• Nonconversational language
• Busy hands
• Moving in and out of groups
• Frequent off-task and on-task behavior
• Starting and stopping activities
• Moving around the room

Paradoxically, sometimes agitation doesn't seem to live up to its name. Some students can be agitated and not show it. Watch for the following *decreases in behavior* and a lack of engagement in class activities:

• Staring into space
• Subdued language
• Contained hands
• Lack of interaction and involvement in activities
• Withdrawal from groups and activities
• Lack of responding in general
• Avoidance of eye contact

Techniques for Reducing Agitation. Once you recognize that the student's behavior is agitated, your primary goal is to use strategies to calm the student down and assist him or her to become engaged in the present classroom activity. Because these strategies are supportive in nature, you need to use them *before* the behavior becomes serious; otherwise, you risk reinforcing the seemingly endless chain of inappropriate behavior. The critical issue is *timing.* Use the following techniques at the *earliest* indications of agitation:

Teacher support: Communicate concern to the student.

The most important thing to remember is that your responses can change things.

Space: Provide the student with an opportunity to have some isolation from the rest of the class.

Choices: Give the student some choices or options.

Preferred activities: Allow the student to engage in a preferred activity for a short period of time to help regain focus.

Teacher proximity: Move near or stand near the student.

Independent activities: Engage the student in independent activities to provide isolation.

Movement activities: Use activities and tasks that require movement, such as errands, cleaning the chalkboard, and distributing papers.

Involvement of the student: Where possible, involve the student in the plan. In this way, there is more chance of ownership and generalization to other settings.

Relaxation activities: Use audiotapes, drawing activities, breathing and relaxation techniques.

Now let's replay Jamie's situation. This time, the teacher determines that Jamie seems to be agitated—he shows a *decrease* in behavior. The teacher says, as privately as possible, "Jamie, it's time for math. Are you doing OK? Do you need some time before you start?" In this way, the teacher is recognizing the agitation, communicating concern to Jamie, and giving him time to regain his focus.

Preteach and Present Choices to Establish Limits and Defuse Noncompliance

Use this strategy to establish limits and to defuse sustained noncompliance. Essentially, the student is refusing to follow the teacher's directions.

For example, suppose that Scott has been off task and distracting other students for several minutes. The teacher has tried to provide assistance, redirect him, and give a formal direction to begin work. Scott refuses to cooperate. At this point, the teacher wants to communicate to him that "enough is enough," and to establish some classroom limits. When the teacher tries to establish limits, however, Scott may become more hostile and aggressive.

The following steps in the preteaching strategy can establish limits without escalating the behavior. Role-playing these steps can help students learn how to use self-control.

Preteach the procedures: Carefully rehearse the procedures with the student, give

explanations, model the steps, and describe the consequences. Do preteaching at a neutral time when the student is relatively calm and cooperative.

Deliver the information to the students without being confrontational:

1. Present the expected behavior and the negative consequence as a decision; place responsibility on the student.
2. Allow a few seconds for the student to decide. This small amount of time helps the student calm down, enables face saving in front of peers, enables you to pull away from the conflict, and leaves the student with the decision.
3. Withdraw from the student and attend to other students. You thus help the student focus on the decision, not attend to you.

Follow through: If the student chooses the expected behavior, briefly acknowledge the choice and continue with the lesson or activity. If the student has not chosen the expected behavior, deliver the negative consequence. Debrief with the student and problem solve.

For example, if Sarah refused to take care of the T-shirt problem, the teacher could say, "Sarah, you have been asked to take care of the shirt (expected behavior), or I will have to make an office referral (negative consequence). You have a few seconds to decide." The teacher moves away from Sarah and addresses some other students or tasks. The teacher follows through on the choice made by the student.

Disengage and Delay Responding in the Presence of Serious Threatening Behavior

Students may escalate to a point of serious confrontational behavior involving threats or intimidation. For example, the teacher may have presented options, given the student time, and provided a consequence: "Eric, you are asked to start work or you will have to stay after school. You have a few seconds to decide." Eric walks over to the teacher and says, "I know where you live."

Suppose a more serious situation occurs, such as this real incident: An administrator told a student to go to the in-school suspension area or he would call his probation of-

Defusing strategies minimizes the likelihood that interactions between you and the student will escalate the confrontation.

Three Approaches to Behavior Management

Prevention. The teacher places a strong focus on teaching desirable behavior and orchestrating effective learning activities. These proactive strategies are designed to establish a positive classroom structure and climate for students to engage in productive, prosocial behavior.

Defusion. Teachers use strategies designed to address problem behavior after the behavior has commenced. The goal here is to arrest the behavior before it escalates to more serious behavior and to assist the student to resume class activities in an appropriate manner.

Follow-up. A teacher or an administrator may provide consequences for the problem behavior and endeavors to assist the student to terminate the problem behavior and to engage in appropriate behavior in the future.

The goal of these approaches is to provide information to the student on the limits of behavior and to use problem-solving strategies to enable the student to exhibit alternative appropriate behavior in subsequent events (Biggs & Moore, 1993; Colvin & Lazar, 1997; Kameenui & Darch, 1995; Myers & Myers, 1993; Sprick, Sprick & Garrison, 1993; Sugai & Tindal, 1993; Walker, Colvin, & Ramsey, 1995).

ficer. The student picked up a cup of coffee from the secretary's desk, moved to the administrator, held the coffee in his face, and said, "You call my P.O. and I will throw this in your f_____ face."

In each of these cases, there is a direct threat to a staff member and the danger that the student's behavior may escalate. Whether the student's behavior becomes more serious *depends on the staff member's initial response to the threat.* The primary intent of this strategy is to avoid responding directly to the student's behavior and to disengage momentarily and then to redirect the student.

We are *not* suggesting that this strategy is all you need to do. Rather, the primary purpose of this strategy is to defuse a crisis situation. Once the crisis has been avoided, you should follow up and address the previous threatening behavior so that such behavior does not arise again. Here are steps to use in disengaging and delaying:

Break the cycle of successive interactions by delaying responding: This pattern consists of successive hostile or inflammatory interactions between you and the student—the student challenges you to respond. The first step is to *delay responding*, because the student is expecting an immediate response. To delay responding, very briefly look at the student, look at the floor, look detached, and pause.

Prevent explosive behavior by making a disengaging response: Do not leave the student waiting too long; otherwise, an "extinction burst" may occur. That is, if events do not go the way the student expects them to, he or she may exhibit explosive behavior, such as throwing a chair at the wall (or staff, or another student), or throwing the coffee cup. To prevent this burst, disengage swiftly and engage in something neutral or unrelated (Lerman & Iwata, 1995). For example, say to the student, "Just a minute," and move and pick up something on your desk.

Return to the student, redirect, and withdraw: If the student has not exhibited further problem behavior and is waiting, simply return to the student and present the original choice.

For example, approach the student and say, "You still have a moment or two to decide what you wish to do," and withdraw. If the student engages in more serious behavior, implement emergency procedures and policies established by the school or district.

Follow through: If the student chooses the expected behavior, acknowledge the choice briefly and debrief later. If the student does not choose the expected behavior, deliver consequences and debrief later.

Debrief: The debriefing activity is designed to help the student problem solve by reviewing the incident and events leading up to the incident, identifying the triggers, and examining alternatives. The debriefing finishes with a focus or agreement on what the student will try to do next time that would

*S*ometimes students will break a rule to chal - lenge you; others are already agitated when you try to correct them.

be an appropriate response to the situation (Sugai & Colvin, in press).

Now Let's Debrief

How many Sarahs and Jamies and Erics do you know? Are you tired of throwing up your hands and sending these students to the office, or facing hostility and muttered challenges—or even threats to your own safety? Are you equally concerned that these students (and other students in your class) may be missing out on learning opportunities?

The most important thing to remember is that *your responses can change things.* Go back to the section on "Disengage and Delay Responding" and memorize it. Then follow the steps in "Preteaching," and you are on your way to helping students control their own behavior and create a better environment for learning.

References

Biggs, J. B., & Moore, P. J. (1993). *The process of learning.* New York: Prentice Hall.

Colvin, G. (1992). *Video program: Managing acting-out behavior.* Eugene, OR: Behavior Associates.

Colvin, G., & Lazar, M. (1997). *The effective elementary classroom: Managing for success.* Longmont, CO: Sopris West.

Kameenui, E. J., & Darch, C. B. (1995). *Instructional classroom management: A proactive approach to behavior management.* White Plains, NY: Longman.

Lerman, D., & Iwata, B. (1995). Prevalence of the extinction burst and its attenuation during treatment. *Journal of Applied Behavior Analysis, 28,* 93–94.

Myers, C. B., & Myers, L. K. (1993). *An introduction to teaching and schools.* Fort Worth, TX: Rinehart and Winston.

Sprick, R., Sprick, M., & Garrison, M. (1993). *Interventions: Collaborative planning for students at risk.* Longmont, CO: Sopris West.

Sugai, G., & Colvin, G. (in press). Debriefing: A proactive addition to negative consequences for problem behavior. *Education and Treatment of Children.*

Sugai, G., & Tindal, G. (1993). *Effective school consultation: An interactive approach.* Pacific Grove, CA: Brooks/Cole.

Walker, H., Colvin, G., & Ramsey, E. (1995). *Antisocial behavior in school: Strategies and best practices.* Pacific Grove, CA: Brooks/Cole.

Geoff Colvin *(Oregon Federation), Research Associate, Special Education and Community Resources, University of Oregon, Eugene.* **David Ainge,** *Senior Lecturer, Special Education Department, James Cook University, Queensland, Australia.* **Ron Nelson** *(CEC Chapter #374), Associate Professor, Applied Psychology Department, Eastern Washington University, Spokane.*

Address correspondence to Geoff Colvin, Special Education and Community Resources, University of Oregon, Eugene, OR 97405 (e-mail: geoff_colvin@ccmail. uoregon.edu).

Salinas, California:
Peace Breaks Out

Teaching K–8 pays a visit to a K–6 school, where every day is a good day to discourage violence

IAN ELLIOT

We were still a block away from the Jesse G. Sanchez School in Salinas, California, when we got our first taste of the PeaceBuilders™ program in action. A sharp-eyed member of the *Teaching K–8* team, drawing on her many years of experience as a classroom teacher, spotted it right away.

"See those boys over there?" she said, indicating several groups of students on their way to school. "They're not grabbing bookbags or running into each other. They're just walking peacefully."

Nothing earthshaking about that, of course; nevertheless, it's typical of what's been going on in Salinas for the past two years. No, Salinas is not one big, ever-so-peaceful community, but it's getting there, thanks to PeaceBuilders.

Background. *Teaching K–8* was in Salinas recently to find out more about PeaceBuilders and how it works in a K–6 school. Our first stop was the central office of the Alisal Union School District, where we spoke with Roberta Emmerson, the district's curriculum director. Since Roberta plays a leading role in implementing the program in the district's seven elementary schools (with a total of over 6,000 students), she was able to provide us with some much-needed background.

Sanchez School, she told us, is located in a low socio-economic area. The student body is about 96 percent Spanish-speaking with about 80 percent of the students classified as "limited English-speaking."

This means they speak almost no English when they enter school.

To make matters even more challenging for Sanchez educators, many of the students are chil-

CLAY PETERSON

A large *billboard (above)* in front of the school has a message in English and Spanish. Left above: These buttons are worn by many faculty members.

dren of migrant workers. The youngsters leave town (and school) with their families when crops need to be harvested elsewhere, and are gone for many weeks at a time.

It's a serious problem if ever there was one, but it's not the school district's *only* serious problem. There's also the problem of violence around the schools.

"In this area of Salinas," Roberta said, "we've had a lot of problems with rival gangs—the North gangs and the South gangs—who wear clothing and certain colors that identify them. We've had a lot of shootings and a lot of school violence.

Want to Learn More?

For more information about the PeaceBuilders program, contact Heartsprings, Inc., P.O. Box 12158, Tucson, AZ 85732; 520–322–9977; fax, 520–322–9983; e-mail, mik@heartsprings.org

"The community knew it had to do something about the problem and so it worked hard to clean up a dangerous part of town, and to get neighbors to know each other and combat violence.

"PeaceBuilders got the schools involved. We recognized that we had to intervene early. It's too late to wait until middle school and junior high, and so PeaceBuilders was put into effect in all seven elementary schools during the 1995–96 school year."

Successful? No doubt about it. On the community level, negative behavior (including violence) is down significantly all across the board. Other communities plagued by the same problem now regard Salinas and PeaceBuilders as helpful models. And in 1996, President Clinton visited Salinas to praise the community's efforts of "fighting crime and rescuing children."

PeaceBuilders has been no less successful in the district's elementary schools. A survey taken at the end of the program's first year showed the following reductions in negative behavior: disciplinary actions by 49%; serious violence episodes by 59%; tardiness by 20%; absences by 31%; vandalism incidents by 61%; and vandalism costs by 61%.

Getting started. The PeaceBuilders program was created by Dr. Dennis Embry of Tucson, Arizona, who played a major role in getting the Salinas program off the ground by conducting inservice sessions for all teachers and non-teaching staff in the district.

Four basic principles are at the heart of the program: 1) Praise people; 2) Give up putdowns; 3) Notice hurts and right wrongs; and 4) Seek wise people.

"They're very simple principles," Roberta pointed out. "The program is not so much a curriculum as a way of life. If it's going to be successful in the schools—or anywhere, for that matter—it has to be modeled by adults. It's not going to work in the classroom if the teacher doesn't buy into it. Actually, most of our teachers have been really comfortable with it."

Judging from the decor in all of the classrooms at Sanchez school, "comfortable" may be the understatement of the year. PeaceBuilders posters in English and in Spanish, were on every classroom wall—and that's just the start of it. Here are a few more reminders that PeaceBuilders is alive and well at Sanchez:

• Teaching a peace pledge in sign language.

Nora Bustos, who teaches grades 3 and 4, English only, goes over a PeaceBuilders book with Principal Ruben Pulido.

• PeaceBuilders boards, where children can write peace notes to one another.
• PeaceBuilders buttons and T-shirts.
• Monday morning assemblies, where the school acknowledges PeaceBuilders of the Week in front of the student body. Example: A student on his way to school noticed that a driver was pushing his car at a busy intersection. The boy put his books down on the corner and helped push the car out of the intersection. (Salinas police officers also recognize the program by issuing citations when they see students doing something helpful; the citations can be exchanged for a free video at the video store.)

Pauline Torres' third and fourth grade classroom is blinigual–
and shows it in the books and posters on display.

today?' I use it in physical education, too. There
may be a conflict when we go outside and the kids
have to right some wrongs.

"We're always praising. I try to be a role model
with other teachers in front of my students. I've
noticed a big plus. I have minor discipline problems, like talking in class, but I don't have major
ones. I've never sent a child to the office. If we have
a problem, we settle it right there, not at the end
of the day."

Successful Model

According to Assistant Principal Donna Kiernan, the J. M.
Smuckers Company in Salinas has been a successful
model for the entire community.

"They've joined the school as PeaceBuilders to enhance
the education of children and the self-esteem of their workers," she said.

"They've held reading and writing contests (for which
they gave students gift certificates and book bags), supported our choir and soccer teams, sent readers once a
month to classrooms, donated turkeys to our families at
Christmas and provided awards for the Students of the
Month."

No matter how you look at it–front or back–this is
definitely a PeaceBuilders tee-shirt.

Two views. How do classroom teachers view the
PeaceBuilders program? Here's what two of them
have to say.

Morey Fugate, *1st and 2nd grades:* "I think Peace-
Builders is a way of life, something that we instill
in children when they're young. We give them skills
they'll carry with them for the rest of their lives.
This carries over to the work they're doing. There's
definitely an increase in academic skills."

Barbara Mazzuca Mahaffey, *6th grade:* "I integrate PeaceBuilders all day long, from the time I
come in until the time I leave. I use it in writer's
workshop. I tell students to go home and write a
two-page essay on 'How Were You a PeaceBuilders

Community program. What with all the emphasis on
PeaceBuilders in the classroom, it's easy to forget that
this is a community program, not just a school program. In addition to the Alisal Union School District,
Salinas' business community, youth agencies,
churches, law enforcement agencies, doctors, health
care providers, libraries, service clubs and parents are
all active, enthusiastic supporters of the program.

Principal Ruben Pulido gave *Teaching K–8* an indication of just how enthusiastic the community
can be when it comes to supporting PeaceBuilders.

"Our kickoff for PeaceBuilders the last two years
has been a march that promoted non-violence," he
said. "We had a host of community people coming
out to join us. They were so enthusiastic, because
we were marching to promote safety and security.

"As we were walking around the community, parents and others were coming out of their homes to
join us—not just the families of migrant workers, but
second and third generation families, too. We started
out with a student body of about 960 and came back
to school with at least 1,300 participants."

Feeling safer. Assistant Principal Donna Kiernan
was equally enthusiastic about the community's ac-
tivism. "I'm amazed at the community's support and
at how people want to get together to help out.

Sanchez Principal Ruben Pulido and Assistant Principal Donna Kiernan.

Reciting the PeaceBuilders pledge is a daily ritual for these primary graders.

The PeaceBuilders pledge adorns a classroom wall.

A patch for a quilt links "forever" Jesse G. Sanchez School and the PeaceBuilders program.

Colorful skirts aswirl, Sanchez girls rehearse a dance for cinco de mayo, a Mexican holiday. The girls are taught by Dana Mills-Helman,

About Jesse G. Sanchez School

No. of students: Approx. 855 students without children of migrant workers; approx. 940 with these children.

No. of teachers: 31, plus resource teachers.

No. of classrooms: 31 (4 or 5 per grade level); 1 multi-age classroom and many combination classrooms.

Class size: Aprox. 30 students per classroom, except for 1st grade, which has approx. 20 students per classroom.

Types of classroom (based on English proficiency): Spanish, pre-transitional, transitional, post-transitional, English only.

School organization: Divided into 3 mini-schools, primarily to make school more approachable for parents.

After-school programs: Title V Extended Day, coordinated by Devorah Duncan. The Title V collaborative, the largest after-school program, has been

Pauline Torres leads her first graders in reciting the PeaceBuilders pledge.

Children study plant growth and native plants in this greenhouse.

Students came up with a wide variety of colors and designs for patches for a PeaceBuilders quilt.

Jesse G. Sanchez School is located in a spacious park-like setting. with plenty of room for sports or just running around.

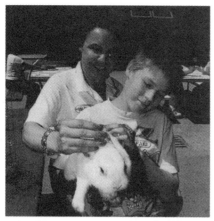 

Top Left: Sixth grade teacher Barbara Mazzuca Mahaffey, one of her students and a classroom pet. *Top Right:* Roberta Emmerson of the Alisal Union School District gets into the swing of things as she and class recite the PeaceBuilders pledge. *Bottom Left:* This fanciful, student-made illustration features both happy and sad faces and even yin and yang. *Bottom Right:* More reminders of the basic principles of the PeaceBuilders program.

"It doesn't matter what position a person holds. We've had the Mayor, a Councilman and a Congressman here. Salinas knows there's a problem and is doing something about it, but there's still a lot of work to be done.

"I think that basically, the children feel safer. They feel that when they come to school, they're secure. We're certainly not having the problems at school we used to have. It's been a great success because of teamwork and collaboration."

In the future. What next in the Alisal Union School District? Well, as you read this, there's an ongoing effort to provide more in-depth training of faculty and staff, along with an effort to involve more people in the home environments by bringing them into the schools. The City of Salinas is in high gear, too, and is implementing the PeaceBuilders program in the city's middle schools.

There will certainly be more ahead. A lot more. Sanchez and the other district schools have helped cut violence in half in a little over two years—but that's just the beginning. Recently, the school held another march and had a turnout of about 1,200. With those kind of numbers, it's obvious that someone must be doing something right.

Unit 6

Unit Selections

Key Points to Consider

❖ What are some important principles for using standardized tests scores to improve instruction? What are some limitations of standardized tests?

❖ What are some examples of performance assessment? What are the strengths and limitations of these assessments?

❖ Many educators believe that schools should identify the brightest, most capable students. What are the assessment implications of this philosophy? How would low-achieving students be affected?

❖ What principles of assessment should teachers adopt for their own classroom testing? Is it necessary or feasible to develop a table of specifications for each test? How do we know if the test scores teachers use are reliable and if valid inferences are drawn from the scores?

❖ How can teachers grade thinking skills such as analysis, application, and reasoning? How should objectives for student learning and grading be integrated? What are some grading practices to avoid? Why?

 **Links**

www.dushkin.com/online/

These sites are annotated on pages 4 and 5.

In which reading group does Jon belong? How do I construct tests? How do I know when my students have mastered the course objectives? How can I explain test results to Mary's parents? Teachers answer these questions, and many more, by applying principles of assessment. Assessment refers to procedures for measuring and recording student performance and constructing grades that communicate to others levels of proficiency or relative standing. Assessment principles constitute a set of concepts that are integral to the teaching-learning process. Indeed, a significant amount of teacher time is spent in assessment activities, and with more accountability has come a greater emphasis on assessment.

Assessment provides a foundation for making sound evaluative judgments about students' learning and achievement. Teachers need to use fair and unbiased criteria in order to assess student learning objectively and accurately and make appropriate decisions about student placement. For example, in assigning Jon to a reading group, the teacher will use his test scores as an indication of his skill level. Are the inferences from the test results valid for the school's reading program? Are his test scores consistent over several months or years? Are they consistent with his performance in class? The teacher should ask and then answer these questions so that he or she can make intelligent decisions about Jon. On the other hand, will knowledge of the test scores affect the teacher's perception of classroom

performance and create a self-fulfilling prophecy? Teachers also evaluate students in order to assign grades, and the challenge is to balance "objective" test scores with more subjective, informally gathered information. Both kinds of evaluative information are necessary, but both can be inaccurate and are frequently misused.

The first article in this unit examines assessment principles in the context of large-scale standardized testing, which is being used with increased frequency for evaluating student and school performance. The next two articles discuss what has become called "alternative" assessment. Performance-based assessment is promoted by Judy Arter in second article. This form of assessment has great potential to integrate measurement procedures with instructional methods more effectively and to focus student learning on the application of thinking and problem-solving skills in real-life contexts. Arter demonstrates this through a thorough review of all aspects of performance assessment, including scoring criteria, rubrics, and principles of grading. She also shows how performance assessment, in comparison to other kinds of assessment, is based on constructivistic learning theory. A related form of assessment, using portfolios, is described in "Lessons Learned About Student Portfolios."

In the last article, Gregory Cizek examines grading practices and makes suggestions for how to assign grades so that the results provide accurate and helpful information as well as motivate students.

Why Standardized Tests Don't Measure
Educational Quality

Educators are experiencing almost relentless pressure to show their effectiveness. Unfortunately, the chief indicator by which most communities judge a school staff's success is student performance on standardized achievement tests.

W. James Popham

These days, if a school's standardized test scores are high, people think the school's staff is effective. If a school's standardized test scores are low, they see the school's staff as ineffective. In either case, because educational quality is being measured by the wrong yardstick, those evaluations are apt to be in error.

One of the chief reasons that students' standardized test scores continue to be the most important factor in evaluating a school is deceptively simple. Most educators do not really understand why a standardized test provides a misleading estimate of a school staff's effectiveness. They should.

What's in a Name?

A standardized test is any examination that's administered and scored in a predetermined, standard manner. There are two major kinds of standardized tests: aptitude tests and achievement tests.

Standardized *aptitude* tests predict how well students are likely to perform in some subsequent educational setting. The most common examples are the SAT-I and the ACT both of which attempt to forecast how well high school students will perform in college.

But standardized *achievement*-test scores are what citizens and school board members rely on when they evaluate a school's effectiveness. Nationally, five such tests are in use: California Achievement Tests, Comprehensive Tests of Basic Skills, Iowa Tests of Basic Skills, Metropolitan Achievement Tests, and Stanford Achievement Tests.

A Standardized Test's Assessment Mission

The folks who create standardized achievement tests are terrifically talented. What they are trying to do is to create assessment tools that permit someone to make a valid inference about the knowledge and/or skills that a given student possesses in a particular content area. More precisely, that inference is to be norm-referenced so that a student's relative knowledge and/or skills can be compared with those possessed by a national sample of students of the same age or grade level.

Such relative inferences about a student's status with respect to the mastery of knowledge and/or skills in a particular subject area can be quite informative to parents and educators. For example, think about the parents who discover that their 4th grade child is performing really well in language arts (94th percentile) and mathematics (89th percentile), but rather poorly in science (39th percentile) and social studies (26th percentile). Such information, because it illuminates a child's strengths and weaknesses, can be helpful not only in dealing with their child's teacher, but also in determining at-home assistance. Similarly, if teachers know how their students compare with other students nationwide, they can use this information to devise appropriate classroom instruction.

But there's an enormous amount of knowledge and/or skills that children at any grade level are likely to know. The substantial size of the content domain that a standardized achievement test is supposed to represent poses genuine difficulties for the developers of such tests. If a test actually covered all the knowledge and skills in the domain, it would be far too long.

So standardized achievement tests often need to accomplish their measurement mission with a much smaller collection of test items than might otherwise be employed if testing time were not an issue. The way out of this assessment bind is for standardized achievement tests to sample the knowledge and/or skills in the content domain. Frequently, such tests try to do their assessment job with only 40 to 50 items in a subject field—sometimes fewer.

Accurate Differentiation As a Deity

The task for those developing standardized achievement tests is to create an assessment instrument that, with a handful of items, yields valid norm-referenced interpretations of a student's status regarding a substantial chunk of content. Items that do the best job of discriminating among students are those answered correctly by roughly half the students. Developers avoid items that are answered correctly by too many or by too few students.

As a consequence of carefully sampling content and concentrating on items that discriminate optimally among students, these test creators have produced assessment tools that do a great job of providing relative comparisons of a student's content mastery with that of students nation-wide. Assuming that the national norm group is genuinely representative of the nation at large, then educators and parents can make useful inferences about students.

One of the most useful of those inferences typically deals with students' relative strengths and weaknesses across subject areas, such as when parents find that their daughter sparkles in mathematics but sinks in science. It's also possible to identify students' relative strengths and weaknesses within a given subject area if there are enough test items to do so. For instance, if a 45-item standardized test in mathematics allocates 15 items to basic computation, 15 items to geometry, and 15 items to algebra, it might be possible to get a rough idea of a student's relative strengths and weaknesses in those three realms of mathematics. More often than not, however, these tests contain too few items to allow meaningful within-subject comparisons of students' strengths and weaknesses.

A second kind of useful inference that can be based on standardized achievement tests involves a student's growth over time in different subject areas. For example, let's say that a child is given a standardized achievement test every third year. We see that the child's percentile performances in most subjects are relatively similar at each testing, but that the child's percentiles in mathematics appear to drop dramatically at each subsequent testing. That's useful information.

Unfortunately, both parents and educators often ascribe far too much precision and accuracy to students' scores on standardized achievement tests. Several factors might cause scores to flop about. Merely because these test scores are reported in numbers (sometimes even with decimals!) should not incline anyone to attribute unwarranted precision to them. Standardized achievement test scores should be regarded as rough approximations of a student's status with respect to the content domain represented by the test.

> **Parents and educators often ascribe far too much precision and accuracy to students' scores on standardized achievement tests.**

To sum up, standardized achievement tests do a wonderful job of supplying the evidence needed to make norm-referenced interpretations of students' knowledge and/or skills in relationship to those of students nationally. The educational usefulness of those interpretations is considerable. Given the size of the content domains to be represented and the limited number of items that the test developers have at their disposal, standardized achievement tests are really quite remarkable. They do what they are supposed to do.

But standardized achievement tests should not be used to evaluate the quality of education. That's not what they are supposed to do.

Measuring Temperature with a Tablespoon

For several important reasons, standardized achievement tests should not be used to judge the quality of education. The overarching reason that students' scores on these tests do not provide an accurate index of educational effectiveness is that any inference about educational quality made on the basis of students' standardized achievement test performances is apt to be invalid.

Employing standardized achievement tests to ascertain educational quality is like measuring temperature with a tablespoon. Tablespoons have a different measurement mission than indicating how hot or cold something is. Standardized achievement tests have a different measurement mission than indicating how good or bad a school is. Standardized achievement tests should be used to make the comparative interpretations that they were intended to provide. They should not be used to judge educational quality. Let's look at three significant reasons that it is thoroughly invalid to base inferences about the caliber of education on standardized achievement test scores.

Testing-Teaching Mismatches

The companies that create and sell standardized achievement tests are all owned by large corporations. Like all for-profit businesses, these corporations attempt to produce revenue for their shareholders.

Recognizing the substantial pressure to sell standardized achievement tests, those who market such tests encounter a difficult dilemma that arises from the considerable curricular diversity in the United States. Because different states often choose somewhat different educational objectives (or, to be fashionable, different content standards), the need exists to build standardized achievement tests that are properly aligned with educators' meaningfully different curricular preferences. The problem becomes even more exacerbated in states where different counties or school districts can exercise more localized curricular decision making.

At a very general level, the goals that educators pursue in different settings are reasonably similar. For instance, you can be sure that all schools will give attention to language arts, mathematics, and so on. But that's at a general level. At the level where it really makes a difference to instruction—in the classroom—there are significant differences in the educational objectives being sought. And that presents a problem to those who must sell standardized achievement tests.

In view of the nation's substantial curricular diversity, test developers are obliged to create a series of one-size-fits-all assessments. But, as most of us know from attempting to wear one-size-fits-all garments, sometimes one size really can't fit all.

The designers of these tests do the best job they can in selecting test items that are likely to measure all of a content area's knowledge and skills that the nation's educators regard as important. But the test developers can't really pull it off. Thus, standardized achievement tests will always contain many items that are not aligned with what's emphasized instructionally in a particular setting.

To illustrate the seriousness of the mismatch that can occur between what's taught locally and what's tested through standardized achievement tests, educators ought to know about an important study at Michigan State University reported in 1983 by Freeman and his colleagues. These researchers selected five nationally standardized achievement tests in mathematics and studied their content for grades 4–6. Then, operating on the very reasonable assumption that what goes on instructionally in classrooms is often influenced by what's contained in the textbooks that children use, they also studied four widely used textbooks for grades 4-6.

Employing rigorous review procedures, the researchers identified the items in the standardized achievement test that had not received meaningful instructional attention in the textbooks. They concluded that between 50 and 80 percent of what was measured on the tests was not suitably addressed in the textbooks. As the Michigan State researchers put it, "The proportion of topics presented on a standardized test that received more than cursory treatment in each textbook was never higher than 50 percent" (p. 509).

Well, if the content of standardized tests is not satisfactorily addressed in widely used textbooks, isn't it likely that in a particular educational setting, topics will be covered on the test that aren't addressed instructionally in that setting? Unfortunately, because most educators are not genuinely familiar with the ingredients of standardized achievement tests, they often assume that if a standardized achievement test asserts that it is assessing "children's reading comprehension capabilities," then it's likely that the test meshes with the way reading is being taught locally. More often than not, the assumed match between what's tested and what's taught is not warranted.

If you spend much time with the descriptive materials presented in the manuals accompanying standardized achievement tests, you'll find that the descriptors for what's tested are often fairly general. Those descriptors need to be general to make the tests acceptable to a nation of educators whose curricular preferences vary. But such general descriptions of what's tested often permit assumptions of teaching-testing alignments that are way off the mark. And such mismatches, recognized or not, will often lead to spurious conclusions about the effectiveness of education in a given setting if students' scores on standardized achievement tests are used as the indicator of educational effectiveness. And that's the first reason that standardized achievement tests should not be used to determine the effectiveness of a state, a district, a school, or a teacher. There's almost certain to be a significant mismatch between what's taught and what's tested.

A Psychometric Tendency to Eliminate Important Test Items

A second reason that standardized achievement tests should not be used to evaluate educational quality arises directly from the requirement that these tests permit meaningful comparisons among students from only a small collection of items.

A test item that does the best job in spreading out students' total-test scores is a test item that's answered correctly by about half the students. Items that are answered correctly by 40 to 60 percent of the students do a solid job in spreading out the total scores of test-takers.

Items that are answered correctly by very large numbers of students, in contrast, do not make a suitable contribution to spreading out students' test scores. A test item answered correctly by 90 percent of the test-takers is, from the perspective of a test's efficiency in providing comparative interpretations, being answered correctly by too many students.

Test items answered correctly by 80 percent or more of the test takers, therefore, usually don't make it past the final cut when a standardized

FIGURE 1

A 3rd grade standardized achievement test item in mathematics

Sally had 14 pears. Then she gave away 6. Which of the number sentences below can you use to find out how many pears Sally has left?

A. $14 + 6 = \_$

B. $6 + 14 = \_$

C. $\_ - 6 = 14$

D. $14 - 6 = \_$

achievement test is first developed, and such items will most likely be jettisoned when the test is revised. As a result, the vast majority of the items on standardized achievement tests are "middle difficulty" items.

As a consequence of the quest for score variance in a standardized achievement test, items on which students perform well are often excluded. However, items on which students perform well often cover the content that, because of its importance, teachers stress. Thus, the better the job that teachers do in teaching important knowledge and/or skills, the less likely it is that there will be items on a standardized achievement test measuring such knowledge and/or skills. To evaluate teachers' instructional effectiveness by using assessment tools that deliberately avoid important content is fundamentally foolish.

Confounded Causation

The third reason that students' performances on these tests should not be used to evaluate educational quality is the most compelling. Because student performances on standardized achievement tests are heavily influenced by three causative factors, only one of which is linked to instructional quality, asserting that low or high test scores are caused by the quality of instruction is illogical.

> The better the job that teachers do in teaching important knowledge and/or skills, the less likely it is that there will be items on a standardized achievement test measuring such knowledge and/or skills.

To understand this confounded-causation problem clearly, let's look at the kinds of test items that appear on standardized achievement tests. Remember, students' test scores are based on how well students do on the test's items. To get a really solid idea of what's in standardized tests, you need to grub around with the items themselves.

The three illustrative items presented here are mildly massaged versions of actual test items in current standardized achievement tests. I've modified the items' content slightly, without altering the essence of what the items are trying to measure.

The problem of confounded causation involves three factors that contribute to students' scores on standardized achievement tests: (1) what's taught in school, (2) a student's native intellectual ability, and (3) a student's out-of-school learning.

What's taught in school. Some of the items in standardized achievement tests measure the knowledge or skills that students learn in school. In certain subject areas, such as mathematics, children learn in school most of what they know about a subject. Few parents spend much time teaching their children about the intricacies of algebra or how to prove a theorem.

So, if you look over the items in any standardized achievement test, you'll find a fair number similar to

the mathematics item presented in Figure 1, which is a mildly modified version of an item appearing in a standardized achievement test intended for 3rd grade children.

This mathematics item would help teachers arrive at a valid inference about 3rd graders' abilities to choose number sentences that coincide with verbal representations of subtraction problems. Or, along with other similar items dealing with addition, multiplication, and division, this item would contribute to a valid inference about a student's ability to choose appropriate number sentences for a variety of basic computation problems presented in verbal form.

If the items in standardized achievement tests measured only what actually had been taught in school, I wouldn't be so negative about using these tests to determine educational quality. As you'll soon see, however, other kinds of items are hiding in standardized achievement tests.

A student's native intellectual ability. I wish I believed that all children were born with identical intellectual abilities, but I don't. Some kids were luckier at gene-pool time. Some children, from birth, will find it easier to mess around with mathematics than will others. Some kids, from birth, will have an easier time with verbal matters than will others. If children came into the world having inherited identical intellectual abilities, teachers' pedagogical problems would be far more simple.

Recent thinking among many leading educators suggests that there are various forms of intelligence, not just one (Gardner, 1994). A child who is born with less aptitude for dealing with quantitative or verbal tasks, therefore, might possess greater "interpersonal" or "intrapersonal" intelligence, but these latter abilities are not tested by these tests. For the kinds of items that are most commonly found on standardized achievement tests, children differ in their innate abilities to respond correctly. And some items on standardized achievement tests are aimed directly at measuring such intellectual ability.

Consider, for example, the item in Figure 2. This item attempts to measure a child's ability "to figure out" what the right answer is. I don't think that the item measures what's taught in school. The item measures what students come to school with, not what they learn there.

In Figure 2's social studies item for 6th graders, look carefully at the four answer options. Read each option and see if it might be correct. A "smart" student, I contend, can figure out that choices A, B, and D really would not "conserve resources" all that well; hence choice C is the winning option. Brighter kids will have a better time with this item than their less bright classmates.

But why, you might be thinking, do developers of standardized tests include such items on their tests? The answer is all too simple. These sorts of items, because they tap innate intellectual skills that are not readily modifiable in school, do a wonderful job in spreading out test-takers' scores. The quest for score variance, coupled with the limitation of having few items to use in assessing students, makes such items appealing to those who construct standardized achievement tests.

But items that primarily measure differences in students' in-born intellectual abilities obviously do not contribute to valid inferences about "how well children have been taught." Would we like all children to do well on such "native-smarts" items? Of course we would. But to use such items to arrive at a judgment about educational effectiveness is simply unsound.

Out-of-school learning. The most troubling items on standardized achievement tests assess what students have learned outside of school. Unfortunately, you'll find more of these items on standardized achievement tests than you'd suspect. If children come from advantaged families and stimulus-rich environments, then they are more apt to succeed on items in standardized achievement test items than will other children whose environments don't mesh as well with

---

F I G U R E 3

A 6th grade standardized achievement test item in science

A plant's fruit always contains seeds. Which of the items below is not a fruit?

A. orange

B. pumpkin

C. apple

D. celery

---

what the tests measure. The item in Figure 3 makes clear what's actually being assessed by a number of items on standardized achievement tests.

This 6th grade science item first tells students what an attribute of a fruit is (namely, that it contains seeds). Then the student must identify what "is not a fruit" by selecting the option without seeds. As any child who has encountered celery knows, celery is a seed-free plant. The right answer, then, for those who have coped with celery's strings but never its seeds, is clearly choice D.

But what if when you were a youngster, your folks didn't have the money to buy celery at the store? What if your circumstances simply did not give you the chance to have meaningful interactions with celery stalks by the time you hit the 6th grade? How well do you think you'd do in correctly answering the item in Figure 3? And how well would you do if you didn't know that pumpkins were seed-carrying spheres? Clearly, if children know about pumpkins and celery, they'll do better on this item than will those children who know only about apples and oranges. That's how children's socioeconomic status gets mixed up with children's performances on standardized achievement tests. The higher your family's socioeconomic status is, the more likely you are to do well on a number of the test items you'll encounter in such a test.

Suppose you're a principal of a school in which most students come from genuinely low socioeconomic situations. How are your students likely to perform on standardized achievement tests if a substantial number of the test's items really measure the stimulus-richness of your students' backgrounds? That's right, your students are not likely to earn very high scores. Does that mean your school's teachers are doing a poor instructional job? Of course not.

Conversely, let's imagine you're a principal in an affluent school whose students tend to have upper-class, well-educated parents. Each spring, your students' scores on standardized achievement tests are dazzlingly high. Does this mean your school's teachers are doing a super instructional job? Of course not.

One of the chief reasons that children's socioeconomic status is so highly correlated with standardized test scores is that many items on standardized achievement tests really focus on assessing knowledge and/or skills learned outside of school—knowledge and/or skills more likely to be learned in some socioeconomic settings than in others. Again, you might ask why on earth would standardized achievement test developers place such items on their tests? As usual, the answer is consistent with the dominant measurement mission of those tests, namely, to spread out students' test scores so that accurate and fine-grained norm-referenced interpretations can be made. Because there is substantial variation in children's socioeconomic situations, items that reflect such variations are efficient in producing among-student variations in test scores.

You've just considered three important factors that can influence students' scores on standardized achievement tests. One of these factors was directly linked to educational quality. But two factors weren't.

What's an Educator to Do?

I've described a situation that, from the perspective of an educator, looks pretty bleak. What, if anything, can be done? I suggest a three-pronged attack on the problem. First, I think that you need to learn more about the viscera of standardized achievement tests. Second, I think that you need to carry out an effective educational campaign so that your educational colleagues, parents of children in school, and educational policymakers understand what the evaluative shortcomings of standardized achievement tests really are. Finally, I think that you need to arrange a more appropriate form of assessment-based evidence.

Learning about standardized achievement tests. Far too many educators haven't really studied the items on standardized achievement tests since the time that they were, as students, obliged to respond to those items. But the inferences made on the basis of students' test performances rest on nothing more than an aggregated sum of students' item-by-item responses. What educators need to do is to spend some quality time with standardized achievement tests—scrutinizing the test's items one at a time to see what they are really measuring.

Spreading the word. Most educators, and almost all parents and school board members, think that schools should be rated on the basis of their students' scores on standardized achievement tests. Those people need to be educated. It is the responsibility of all educators to do that educating.

If you do try to explain to the public, to parents, or to policymakers why standardized test scores will probably provide a misleading picture of educational quality, be sure to indicate that you're not running away from the need to be held accountable. No, you must be willing to identify other, more credible evidence of student achievement.

Coming up with other evidence. If you're going to argue against standardized achievement tests as a source of educational evidence for determining school quality, and you still are willing to be held educationally accountable, then you'll need to ante up some other form of evidence to show the world that you really are doing a good educational job.

I recommend that you attempt to assess students' mastery of genuinely significant cognitive skills, such as their ability to write effective compositions, their ability to use lessons from history to make cogent analyses of current problems, and their ability to solve high-level mathematical problems.

If the skills selected measure really important cognitive outcomes, are seen by parents and policymakers to be genuinely significant, and can be addressed instructionally by competent teachers, then the assembly of a set of pre-test-to-post-test evidence showing substantial student growth in such skills can be truly persuasive.

What teachers need are assessment instruments that measure worthwhile skills or significant bodies of knowledge. Then teachers need to show the world that they can instruct children so that those children make striking pre-instruction to post-instruction progress.

The fundamental point is this: If educators accept the position that standardized achievement test scores should not be used to measure the quality of schooling, then they must provide other, credible evidence that can be used to ascertain the quality of schooling. Carefully collected, nonpartisan evidence regarding teachers' pre-test-to-post-test promotion of undeniably important skills or knowledge just might do the trick.

Right Task, Wrong Tools

Educators should definitely be held accountable. The teaching of a nation's children is too important to be left unmonitored. But to evaluate educational quality by using the wrong assessment instruments is a subversion of good sense. Although educators need to produce valid evidence regarding their effectiveness, standardized achievement tests are the wrong tools for the task.

References

Freeman, D. J., Kuhs, T. M., Porter, A. C., Floden, R. E., Schmidt, W. H., & Schwille, J. R. (1983). Do textbooks and tests define a natural curriculum in elementary school mathematics? *Elementary School Journal*, 83(5), 501–513.

Gardner, H. (1994). Multiple intelligences: The theory in practice. *Teacher's College Record*, 95(4), 576–583.

Author's note: A longer version of this article will appear in the final chapter of W. James Popham's book *Modern Educational Measurement: Practical Guidelines for Educational Leaders,* 3rd ed., (forthcoming); Needham Heights, MA: Allyn & Bacon.

W. James Popham is a UCLA Emeritus Professor. He may be reached at IOX Assessment Associates, 5301 Beethoven St., Ste. 190, Los Angeles, CA 90066 (e-mail: wpopham@ucla.edu).

Teaching About Performance Assessment

How should we teach prospective teachers about performance assessment? What are the issues and concerns that new teachers will encounter as they begin their teaching careers? How can assessment and instruction be better integrated in classrooms?

Judy Arter

Northwest Regional Educational Laboratory

If there is anything definite about performance assessment, it is that experts cannot agree on a definition. Because of this, it is prudent to let readers know the definition used in the current article: Performance assessment is assessment based on observation and judgment (Airasian, 1991, p. 252; Stiggins, 1997, p. 175). One observes a performance or a product and then judges its quality. Examples abound, everything from the driver's test and Olympic judging to the multitude of formal and informal observations teachers make in the classroom: skill levels on such things as oral presentations and wrestling, quality of products such as essays and laboratory reports, and affective orientation, including level of effort and desire to learn. Although fairly broad, this definition is not intended to include *all* constructed-response-type items (especially short answer and fill in the blank), but, admittedly, the line between constructed response and performance assessment is thin. (This is probably why there are so many attempts at definition.)

Performance assessment is not new. Teachers have always observed student performances and products and made judgments about them. However, there are recent developments that highlight the current importance of teaching teachers to do performance assessment well (Herman, 1997). Although undoubtedly familiar to readers, I mention them briefly because they set up major themes for the text that follows.

1. Teachers are being asked to assist students to acquire more complex skills than ever before. Witness the content standards being developed by many states and professional organizations. Students are to read with comprehension, write well, be critical thinkers, be lifelong learners, be collaborative workers, be able to communicate their mathematical understanding, and so

From *Educational Measurement: Issues and Practices,* Summer 1999, pp. 30-44. © 2000 by the National Council on Measurement in Education. Reprinted by permission of the publisher.

forth. Such complex learning targets for students require complex assessments, including performance assessments.

2. Teachers are being asked to use formal performance assessments on a daily basis, and for purposes other than grading. It is not enough to wait until the year-end, large-scale assessment to see what percentage of students meet "mastery." Continuous classroom monitoring of student progress toward important, and frequently complex, learning targets is the essence of standards-based instruction and education.

3. Since performance assessments are increasingly being used for additional purposes, some of which are high stakes, there have been many efforts to make this essentially subjective form of assessment as objective as possible. Familiar examples are standardization of tasks and criteria, careful training of those judging work, and technical work on thorny issues such as sampling and generalizability. Although the focus for this work is generally large-scale assessment, the resulting refinement of performance assessment methods has implications for improving classroom practice as well.

4. There is tantalizing preliminary evidence that performance assessments can be used for more than simply providing information about students for decision making (as important as this is). Developing and using performance assessments can have positive impacts on instruction and student attitudes and learning, even to the point that performance assessment materials and methods can be used to help students acquire the very skills being assessed (e.g., Arter, Spandel, Cuiham, & Pollard, 1994; Borko et al., 1997; Clarke & Stephens, 1996; Khattri, 1995; Office of Educational Research and Improvement, 1997).

Because of these trends and findings, teachers need to know how to do performance assessment well (i.e., prudently, efficiently, validly, and with positive consequences for students). Yet, studies continue to show that K–12 teachers lack skill in assessing their students (Hills, 1991; Impara, Plake, & Fager, 1993; Plake, Impara, & Fager, 1993) and that they feel unprepared and uncomfortable in terms of their knowledge of assessment practices (Shafer, 1993; Wise, Lukin, & Roos, 1991; Zhang, 1997). Additionally a recent study (Fager, Plake, & Impara, 1997) found that even in those institutions where preservice course work is required or offered, there is a certain amount of feeling that it does not cover what teachers will really need to know and be able to do and that the courses are not taught by those most familiar with assessment issues and developments. Given the importance of effective assessment, we must all continue to think about and discuss what teachers need to know and be able to do with respect to classroom assessment, the best ways to assist them in learning it, and how we will know when they are competent.

Based on the experience of the Northwest Regional Educational Laboratory (NWREL) in conducting thousands of workshops for teachers on assessment and the fruitful ideas of other preservice and in-service instructors (such as Airasian, 1991; Marzano & Kendall, 1996; McTighe, 1996; and Stiggins, 1997), this article describes seven topics that should be included in a course on performance assessment and provides some ideas for teaching them. The focus is on performance assessment as practiced in the classroom; because teachers also need to know about large-scale assessments, however, this topic is discussed as well.

The following is a series of questions to consider: Do you believe that good classroom assessment can improve student achievement? Do you believe that assessing students well will make teachers' lives easier? Do you believe that it is possible to use assessment as a tool that can directly influence student learning as well as a tool for making educational decisions about students? Do you believe that assessment and instruction can be integrated? If we believe these things, then we have to be ready to demonstrate them to teachers or they will not engage in the process of learning to do classroom assessment differently. I propose that we can demonstrate all of these things with performance assessment if we approach it correctly. Not that these things cannot be demonstrated with other forms of assessment. Rather, performance assessment especially lends itself to these ideas, can draw teachers into the topic of assessment in general, and is the focus of this article.

What Teachers Need to Know and Be Able to Do With Respect to Performance Assessment

The *Standards for Teacher Competence in Educational Assessment of Students* (American Federation of Teachers, National Council on Measurement in Education, and National Education Association, 1990) provide a good starting place for describing what teachers need to know and be able to do with respect to performance assessment. The *Standards* specify that teachers be competent in seven areas:

1. Choosing assessment methods appropriate for instructional decisions.
2. Developing assessment methods appropriate for instructional decisions.
3. Administering, scoring, and interpreting results of assessments.
4. Using assessment results when making decisions.
5. Developing valid pupil grading procedures.
6. Communicating assessment results to students and others.
7. Recognizing unethical, illegal, and inappropriate assessment methods and uses.

The *Standards* are a good place to start and provide a wealth of detail on the specific knowledge and skills teachers should have in these areas, but they do not adequately cover several important topics, those especially relevant to performance assessment.

First, the document does not mention the central necessity of having a clear conception of what is to be assessed and being sure that these targets are the best ones to shoot for. How can one assess (or teach) something if it is not clear exactly what knowledge or skills a student is to possess? Having clear targets means more than merely stating that a learning goal for students is "writing" or "problem solving." Rather, *clarity* of targets requires knowing, for example, what good writing looks like, how students develop toward this target, and what adequate (and weak) writing looks like at various grade levels.

In my work with teachers, I am becoming more and more convinced (along with others, such as Stiggins, 1997, chap. 3, and Marzano & Kendall, 1996, p. 27) that improving classroom assessment has less to do with the actual mechanism of developing assessments than with being clearer on what is to be assessed. As one reviewer of an earlier version of this article stated, "If you can hammer away on exactly what it is the teacher wants the student to be able to do, sometimes the assessment sort of pops out of the discussion." For example, in writing teachers need to grapple with the balance between assessing enabling skills for writing well (e.g., spelling, grammar, good sentence structure, developing a main idea with details, different ways to organize ideas) and determining whether students can use these skills in concert to actually write. Both probably need to be addressed, but exactly which skills and in what balance?

Table 1

Summary of Performance Assessment Knowledge and Skills

General topic	Specific subtopics	Relationship to standards	Relationship to 3 additional topics
What performance assessment is and why we should care	Definitions Two mandatory parts to a performance assessment: tasks and criteria	Standards 1, 2	Clear targets Use a tool for learning
When to use performance assessment	Which student learning targets are best assessed with a performance assessment and which with another method Balance—performance assessment not always the answer Balance—ideal against practical	Standards 1, 2	Target-method match Use as a tool for learning
Design options	Design options for tasks Design options for criteria	Standard 2	
The nature of quality and why we should care	Quality in tasks and when to use various design options Quality in performance criteria and when to use various designs Consistency in scoring Sampling Avoiding possible sources of bias and distortion Building in features that result in positive consequences for teachers, instruction, and students	Standards 1–4, 7	Clear targets Target-method match Use as a tool for learning
How to develop tasks and criteria	Practice developing tasks and criteria	Standard 2	Clear targets
Use as an instructional methodology	How to use criteria to assist students to self-assess, and features of criteria that maximize this use How to teach criteria to students The role of performance criteria in standards-based education		Clear targets Use as a tool for learning

The second topic, not emphasized strongly enough in the *Standards,* is "target-method match." The *Standards* stress matching purposes with methods (see Standards 1 and 2) but not choosing the assessment method that best matches the skills and knowledge to be assessed. The third topic not covered well in the *Standards* is the use of assessment as a tool for learning.

Keeping all of this in mind, Table 1 presents a summary of what classroom teachers need to know and be able to do with respect to performance assessment. The first column lists general topics for instruction, the second column provides subtopics, the third column cross references the topics to the *Standards for Teacher Competence,* and the final column cross references topics to the three additional areas described earlier: clear and appropriate targets, target-method match, and using assessment as a tool for learning.

Table 1 provides an outline for the remainder of the article. It is impossible in a short article to completely describe such a unit on performance assessment, including ideas on how to teach each topic. Therefore, I try here to (a) hit the high points and major things that seem to confuse teachers, (b) provide some ideas on where to begin so that the order is not only logical but immediately engaging to the adult learner, (c) describe how topics interrelate, and (d) provide references to other documents I have found to be particularly useful. I also emphasize the classroom instructional uses of performance assessment, since that topic has been less well developed by others. To avoid confusion, I refer to child learners as "students" and preservice or in-service teachers as "teachers" or "adult learners."

What Performance Assessment Is and Why We Should Care

Performance Assessment "Kick Off" Readings

Three papers useful for beginning a unit on performance assessment are those of Rudner and Boston (1994), Wiggins (1992), and Stayter and Johnston (1990). The Rudner and Boston article is a balanced overview of the rationale for performance assessment, what various groups are doing with respect to performance assessment, and current issues. (Much of this is still relevant, although descriptions of activities in specific states have changed somewhat since 1994.) The basic message of the Wiggins article is that quality matters. The point of the Stayter and Johnston chapter is that assessment affects kids; if we want it to have a positive effect, we need to pay close attention to design issues. Teachers find these articles accessible, informative, and provocative. As they read, teachers can make notes on what ideas they like, find problematic, and want to know more about. This "kick-off' activates prior knowledge, sets the tone that learning will be cooperative, provides the instructor with infor-

mation about adult learners' prior knowledge and attitudes, and emphasizes the major themes of the unit.

Using Performance Assessment Definitions to Emphasize Why We Should Care

A useful way to proceed is to familiarize teachers with the definition of performance assessment and ask them to cite examples in daily life and the classroom. This provides an excellent opportunity to point out that performance assessment is not fundamentally new, to outline changes in performance assessment (as outlined in the introduction), and to emphasize the need for balance in assessment (performance assessment is simply one tool, not a cure-all). Regardless of the specific definition of performance assessment one uses, it is important to emphasize early on that there are two parts to a performance assessment: tasks and criteria. It is not assessment if it does not include both.

The Importance of Criteria. One consistently encounters "performance assessments" from supposedly reputable organizations that are simply tasks. For example, a recent Association for Supervision and Curriculum Development (ASCD) publication (Checkley, 1997) extolled the virtues of the following geography "authentic assessment." The teacher asked his students to research the name of their town. The students found other towns all across the United States with the same name. The students wrote to each of these towns and prepared a research paper and a museum display. This process purportedly assessed research skills, geographic knowledge, and communication skills. However, there were no criteria for judging the quality of student performance on any of these skills in the context of this task. So, why is this assessment? Granted, this might be a rich, "authentic," engaging task for students in which they might actually learn something about research skills, geography, and communication. But there is no way to know what, in fact, they learn.

Teachers tend to be better at developing rich, interesting tasks in which to engage students than they are at developing the criteria that describe quality performance on the task. This point is made repeatedly by those assisting teachers in developing performance assessments:

> Respondents claim that an important purpose of portfolios is valid assessment of student progress and growth, yet nowhere in the packets have we found a clear account of how achievement is to be measured. None of the portfolio guide books . . . [provide] help in analysis, scoring, or grading. (Calfee & Perfumo, 1993, p. 534)

> Teachers [frequently] ask the wrong question first. . . "What do we do?"—putting the focus immediately on designing tasks—when they need to ask, "What do we want kids to know and be able to do? How well? What does quality look like?" [We] need to ask these questions very clearly first. (Hibbard, 1996, p. 5)

In my work with teachers, it is the skill of "rubric writing" which is most elusive. Perhaps it's because we're used to assigning single grades for complex assignments, knowing what an "A" looks like in our heads, but rarely "putting it to paper" so that our students can see it as well. Perhaps the difficulty in writing scoring criteria also lies in the challenge of describing just what it really looks like to perform well, or better yet, to perform at a variety of levels of competency. Nevertheless, it is the use of rubrics as an indispensable part of the instructional process which completes the vital link between assessment and instruction. Until we invest the time discerning for ourselves what excellence in writing, or speaking, or dancing, or singing, or whatever looks like, we are unable to fully "teach" our students to achieve at these levels. (Mendel, undated)

High-quality performance criteria are essential for providing consistency between raters and for use with students as a learning tool. Good ways to illustrate the importance of criteria for these two uses are provided in the next two sections.

Using Performance Criteria to Provide Consistency Between Raters. Give adult learners a performance to assess; for example, show them a student giving an oral presentation. Ask them to evaluate the quality of performance on that task without providing them any criteria. Have them discuss their frustrations, ideas, and solutions in small groups. Then provide illustrations of good-quality performance criteria for oral presentations (Massachusetts State Department of Education, 1983; Usrey, 1998) and ask the adult learners to again evaluate performance on the task. Have them discuss the differences that good criteria make.

This activity points to the first need for criteria: to provide consistency between raters and within the same rater over time and across tasks. This activity can also lead to a good discussion of the desirability of standard criteria for use by all teachers in a grade, building, district, or department. Furthermore, it can result in a useful discussion about how high-quality criteria define complex learning targets; in fact, high-quality criteria are the final definition of complex learning targets. Teachers can then discuss how having such clear definitions might decrease their anxiety level by helping them to see desired student learning targets more clearly. Finally, the activity of scoring performance both with and without criteria can lead to a fruitful examination of the need to include the correct indicators in the criteria; the criteria must describe what we mean by quality performance. If they do not, teachers will teach to the wrong targets.

Using Performance Criteria to Improve Student Achievement. Discuss the criteria used on a driver's test. Actually contact the Department of Motor Vehicles and ask what the criteria are. (If an individual is to obtain a driver's license in the state of Washington, for example, the examiner must ultimately decide that the individual has adequate skill, has not caused congestion, and has not caused a danger.) Ask the adult learners whether it would be important for students to "know" these criteria in advance and, if so, why. The answer is typically a resounding "yes," because criteria help students know what counts so that they can practice. This decreases student anxiety levels.

Then ask the adult learners what it means to "know" criteria. Is it enough simply to hand the criteria to prospective drivers as they begin their test? (Teachers always say "no.") If students are to *know* criteria, they must be discussed beginning on the first day of class, practiced with feedback, be illustrated with examples of good and poor performance on each important trait or dimension, modeled by the teacher, used by the students to assess their own work and that of others, and used to guide the revision of performance.

This activity points to the second major use for performance criteria: helping students understand the nature of the skills they are to master and providing a standard of comparison against which students can measure their progress. In short, performance criteria can be a tool to help students acquire the very skills assessed.

These two activities—"scoring with and without performance criteria" and "the driver's test"—begin right away to emphasize the use of performance criteria (a) to clarify the targets of instruction, (b) to track student progress toward these targets, and (c) as an instructional tool in the classroom, as noted in Table 1.

The Importance of Tasks. The other half of the performance assessment equation involves the tasks assigned to students. Tasks elicit a product or performance that can then be assessed with the criteria. Much has been written about developing rich, engaging, real-life tasks, tasks that are capable of eliciting the desired complex performances on the part of the student (e.g., McTighe, 1996). One point about performance tasks that is frequently confusing to teachers is that the task can be *any* activity during the course of which the quality of performance will be observed; it does not necessarily have to be something that occurs separately at the end of instruction. There is a place for these summative, separate assessments, but much "observation and judgment" will occur during the course of regular instruction; for example, how well is a student reading today, or how effective is group collaboration on a particular activity? The key to having daily observation be sound assessment is to have high-quality criteria that teachers have internalized to the extent that they can consistently judge performances, regardless of the context. The presence of criteria makes daily "anecdotal records" actually mean something.

When to Use Performance Assessment

Good assessment means balanced assessment: having a clear idea of what one wants to assess and then choosing the best way to assess it (target-method match; see Table

Table 2

Matching Learning Targets to Assessment Methods

	Selected response	Essay	Performance assessment	Personal communication
Knowledge mastery	X	X		X
Reasoning proficiency	O	X	X	X
Skills			X	X
Ability to create products			X	
Dispositions	X	O	O	X

1). A rule of thumb is that simple learning targets involve simple assessment and complex learning targets involve complex assessment. For example, knowledge and simple skills (e.g., long division) can be assessed well via multiple-choice, matching, true-false, and short answer formats. However, a performance assessment is probably needed to assess writing, mathematical problem solving, science process skills, critical thinking, oral presentations, and group collaboration skills.

Good treatments of matching methods to targets can be found in Stiggins (1997, p. 81) and Marzano and Kendall (1996, p. 311). Stiggins, for example, matches methods to targets as shown in Table 2. An X denotes a good match. An O denotes a partial match. A complete treatment of the reasons for the Xs and Os is outside the scope of this article (and has already been done very well in the sources just cited). However, it is useful to note here that the best way to think of "good" matches is as follows: prudent, efficient, valid, and having positive consequences. Thus, although one could use performance assessment to assess all student outcomes, one probably should not because it would not be very efficient or prudent or necessarily have positive outcomes for instruction and students. It is best to save the power of performance assessment for the outcomes most needing it, especially those situations in which having written criteria for complex skills and products will help students understand the nature of the targets they are to reach.

It is useful to show adult learners examples of attempts to assess targets such as reasoning or reading comprehension in a multiple-choice format. Then show them performance assessments aimed at the same target and discuss what each format is—and is not—capable of assessing. Fixed response assessments, even when done well, tend to address decontextualized skills in isolation, while performance assessments, if done well, require students to select skills to use in concert to produce a product or perform an act. Both are useful, depending on what it is one wants to assess. It always goes back to being clear enough about the target to be assessed.

Three examples of thinking skills assessments that involve different methods and could be compared in the manner described above are: the Cornell Critical Thinking Test (multiple choice; Ennis, Millman, & Tomko, 1985), the Test on Appraising Observations (choose an answer and then justify one's choice; Norris, 1990), and performance criteria for judging the "intellectual quality" of student work (Newmann, Secada, & Wehlage, 1995).

Design Options

The tasks and performance criteria used in performance assessments vary widely. The following are the major ways in which I have seen tasks vary. (I include variations in both stimulus and response because both represent task demands on the student; examples of these types are detailed in Regional Educational Laboratories, 1998, chap. 3.)

- A single correct answer or multiple, equally good answers
- Group work, individual work, or a combination of both
- All written versus manipulatives and equipment
- Amount of choice on how to respond (written, picture, oral, etc.)
- Format/length/complexity (on demand, project, portfolio)
- Amount of scaffolding: steps and processes spelled out or left to the student
- Student choice of which task to perform

The major ways in which performance criteria appear to vary include the following:

- Task-specific or general. Task-specific performance criteria spell out separately what responses should look like on each task; there is a separate scoring guide for each task (e.g., the open-ended math items on the Constructed Response Supplement to the Iowa Tests, 1997). In general performance criteria, the same rubric is used across similar tasks (e.g., the six-trait model for writing; see the Appendix).

- Holistic or analytic trait. In holistic performance criteria, there is one score for the overall product or performance (e.g., the math rubrics on the Constructed Response Supplement to the Iowa Tests, 1997). In analytical trait performance criteria, there are multiple scores for a single performance or product, one for each important dimension or trait (e.g., the reading rubrics used in the Oregon state assessment or the six-trait model in the Appendix).
- Number of score points. Generally there are from three (e.g., several items on the Washington Assessment of Student Learning [Washington Commission on Student Learning, 1998]) to six (e.g., Oregon state assessments [Oregon Department of Education, 1997]).
- Amount of detail used to describe each score point. Some performance criteria are extremely skimpy (e.g., Washington state's writing rubric [Washington Commission on Student Learning, 1998]), while others attempt to be extremely descriptive (e.g., the six-trait model for assessing writing; see the Appendix).
- Type of detail used to describe each score point. There are some rubrics (e.g., early attempts in Vermont [Vermont Mathematics Portfolio Project, 1991]) for which the only distinctions between score point levels are words such as *inappropriate, appropriate, workable,* and *efficient* or *rarely, sometimes, frequently,* and *extensively*. It is difficult for performance raters to know when "extensively" has occurred, which can result in low rater consistency. It is also difficult for students to understand how to improve a performance or product if they are told only that their work "rarely exhibits a sense of personal expression." Other rubrics (e.g., the six-trait model) use extensive detail to describe the specific features of work that are indicators of quality. This helps in making meaning clearer, both to raters of performance and to students trying to learn the nature of quality. (In all fairness to Vermont, the Department of Education has supplied many samples of student work to demonstrate the levels and has, through the years, worked to define the levels more thoroughly.)
- Quantitative versus qualitative descriptions of score points. A quantitative score point description might be as follows: "to get an excellent, the paper must have 10 references" (for an example, see Baker, Aschbacher, Niemi, & Sato, 1992, pp. 73—74). Although amount might sometimes be a good indicator of quality, I generally dislike this type of rubric because 3 really good references might be better than 10 bad ones.
- Presence or absence of preset performance standard. On some performance criteria, the score points represent performance standards by definition (4 = "ex-

ceeds expectations," 3 = "meets expectations," 2 = "partially meets expectations," 1 = "expectations are not met"; e.g., North Dakota Fourth Grade Writing Assessment [North Dakota Department of Public Instruction, 1998]). Developers define 3 as "meeting standards" and then go about defining characteristics of such work and finding samples to illustrate what they mean. A contrasting procedure is to first develop a scale that defines the range of quality products or performances (I have seen scales ranging from 3 to 6 points) and then go back and decide where on this scale performance is good enough to meet various performance standards. This is the approach taken by the Oregon Department of Education (1998). Oregon developed a 6-point scale to define the range of quality and then went back to determine where the performance standards would be. In writing, for example, performance standards range from "3" to "4" depending on grade level.

Before teachers can discuss why assessment developers make the choices they do, they need to be able to recognize variations. An instructor may ask teachers to do a type of "scavenger hunt" activity in which they look for as many examples of each variation as possible. After adult learners are able to distinguish the options, the questions to be addressed are as follows: Why do developers make these choices? What are the advantages and disadvantages of each? Choices are usually made by balancing an ideal choice (for users, uses, and learning targets) against practical considerations and throwing in technical concerns for good measure. The next two sections elaborate considerations when making choices.

The Nature of Quality and Why We Should Care

Teaching the Characteristics of Quality Performance Assessment

Many thorough lists of quality considerations for performance assessments exist (Table 3 summarizes what others have said; another good source is Herman, 1996). Note that such lists include the need for clear and appropriate learning targets, matching performance assessment choices to targets, and use as a tool for learning (see Table 1, "The nature of quality" col. 4).

Coming up with a list of quality features of performance assessment is the easy part. Teaching adult learners the nature of quality and why they should care is the tricky part. A strategy that does not seem to be effective is that of showing teachers the list of quality considerations and lecturing one's way from beginning to end. What seems to work better is to engage adult learners

Table 3

Criteria for Performance Assessments

Dimension	Yes	Somewhat	No
1. Content/skill coverage and correct method The assessment: Clearly states skills and content to be covered Correctly uses performance assessment to measure these skills and content Avoids irrelevant and/or unimportant content Deals with enduring themes or significant knowledge Matches statements of coverage to task content and performance criteria	3	2	1
2. Performance criteria Include everything of importance and omit irrelevant features of performance State criteria clearly and provide samples of student work to illustrate them Are stated generally, especially if the intent is used as an instructional tool Are analytical trait, especially if the intent is use as an instructional tool	3	2	1
3. Performance tasks General Elicit the desired performances or work Recreate an "authentic" context for performance Exemplify good instruction Are reviewd by others (students, peers, experts) Sampling/representativeness/generalizability Cover the content or skill area well; results can be generalized Sample performance in a way that is representative of what a student can do Bias and distortion Avoid factors that might get in the way of students' ability to demonstrate what they know and can do	3	2	1
4. Fairness and rater bias Performance tasks Have content and context that are equally familiar, acceptable, and appropriate for students in all groups Tap knowledge and skills all students have had adequate time to acquire in class Are as free as possible of cultural, ethnic, or gender stereotypes Are as free as possible of language barriers Performance criteria and rater training Ensure that irrelevant features of performance do not influence how other, supposedly independent features are judged Ensure that knowledge of the type of student does not influence judgments about performance quality Ensure that knowledge of individual students does not affect judgements about performance quality	3	2	1
5. Consequences The assessment: Communicates appropriate messages Results in acceptable effects on students, teachers, and others Is worth the instructional time devoted to it; students learn something from doing the assessment and/or using the performance criteria Provides information relevant to the decisions being made Is perceived by students and teachers as valid	3	2	1
6. Cost and efficiency The assessment: Is cost efficient—the results are worth the investment Is practical	3	2	1

Note. Copyright 1998 by Northwest Regional Educational Laboratory. Adapted with permission.]

in a bad performance assessment and let *them* articulate what the problems are.

One example of this is a learning activity written for use by teacher trainers and instructors (Regional Educational Laboratories, 1998, Activity 1.5: Clapping Hands): In this fishbowl activity four or five teachers are the "assessees" and three to five teachers are the "assessors." Assessees are asked to perform a simple task, but each is treated differently via providing them with more information and help as the activity progresses. Likewise, assessors are given more information as the activity progresses. At the end, each participant describes what he or she was thinking and feeling as the activity progressed, and the entire group is invited to comment and provide examples from their own experience of occasions when they were in the position of one of the volunteers. Finally the group generates a list of what it takes to avoid the problems demonstrated in the activity: characteristics of quality tasks, performance criteria, preparation of raters, preparation of students, and reporting. Special attention is given to potential sources of bias and distortion that could lead one to draw an inappropriate conclusion about a student's achievement. These teacher-generated lists are essentially "criteria" for quality performance assessments.

A teacher more readily understands sampling, bias, unclear tasks, and unclear performance criteria when he or she personally experiences their effects. Table 4 shows a list of quality characteristics (criteria) for performance assessments generated by several teacher groups. Teachers can compare their list of criteria with that experts use for guiding the quality development of performance assessments (e.g., the list of criteria included in Table 3). In this way teachers can relate what they already know to a larger conceptual scheme.

After teachers have described for themselves what constitutes sound performance assessment, it is important for them to practice applying their criteria for quality performance assessments to actual sample assessments. It is useful to find performance assessments that are weak and strong on each dimension (trait) that is to be emphasized (e.g., tasks, criteria) and ask the teachers to critique each as a group. Then ask the adult learners what advice they would give the author of the assessment to make the assessment better on a particular trait and have them work in groups to improve the assessment using their own suggestions. It is important to focus on only a few features at a time so that teachers do not become overwhelmed with having to notice and fix everything all at once.

When the adult learners have had experience with this, have them develop their own tasks and criteria and work in peer review groups to improve their efforts. Learners could even keep a portfolio on their efforts and reflect on how their ability to develop and critique assessments has improved with time.

The interesting part of the process of (a) developing criteria for performance assessments, (b) critiquing and revising examples of anonymous performance assessments, (c) developing one's own performance assessments with peer input, and (d) keeping a portfolio is that this is exactly the same way to teach any criteria to any group of adults or students. Thus, in essence, this process models, for prospective or active teachers, what they should do with their own students in the future.

The Need to Consider Use When Determining Quality

An added complexity in discussions of quality is that use must be taken into account. Performance assessments that are adequate for one use might not be appropriate for another. For example, the features most desirable in tasks or criteria used for a large-scale, high stakes assessment might not be those most desirable in a classroom assessment that will also be used instructionally Thus, learners will need to critique sample assessments with a specific use in mind.

As an example of how use affects assessment design, consider the various design options for performance criteria described earlier. Many large-scale performance assessment developers use task-specific, holistic criteria because (a) raters can be trained more quickly (b) scores can be computed more quickly and (c) it is believed that such criteria will result in higher agreement rates among raters. More useful in the classroom, however, are generalized, analytical trait criteria, which help teachers and students articulate the features of solid work that can be generalized from task to task. The value of generalized criteria for instruction has been noted in recent studies by Arter et. al (1994) and the Office of Educational Research and Improvement (1997, p. *xx*).

Consider another example of how use affects the design of performance criteria. If the purpose of the assessment is to make overall judgments about student competence, the criteria only need to be detailed enough to ensure consistent rating. If, however, the assessment is to be used to diagnose student strengths and learning needs or for instruction, all essential aspects of performance must be present, and descriptive detail is essential. Descriptive detail is important because the criteria are being used to communicate with students about the features that contribute most to the quality of a product or performance. What is left out of the criteria will be left out of the performance or product. Furthermore, this descriptive detail must be in language that students can understand, so there should be "student-friendly" versions.

An example of performance criteria that are instructionally useful (analytical trait, general, detailed, and having student-friendly versions) can be found in the six-trait model for assessing writing (NWREL, 1990, 1997; Spandel & Culham, 1998; Spandel & Stiggins, 1997). The adult version of the six-trait model is included in the Appendix.

Table 4

Performance Assessment: The Meaning of Quality (Typical Teacher Responses)

Area	Responses
Designing tasks	Be careful of public performances; treat all students equitably; put the performance into a realistic context; be specific on insturctions; open-ended; meaningful to students; consider how to handle diversity and differences (e.g., special education,, cultures, gender, learning styles); the task itself is a learning experience; nonthreatening; matched to valued outcomes; equity; enough time; proper resources and equipment; can be approached by the student in a variety of ways; responses can be given in a variety of ways
Designing performance criteria	Matched to valued outcomes; clearly stated; elaboration on how to assign points; agreement on what the criteria should be; models/examples; rater buy-in; match performance criteria to task; define range of score points; covers only the important stuff; provides a "picture" of what performance would look like; has many descriptors of quality
Preparing raters	Practice; discuss differences of opinion; have models/examples of different score points; have the raters do the assessment themselves; have raters explain their ratings; calibrate the raters; check consistency over time
Preparing students	Share criteria well ahead; give students the opportunity to add to criteria; train students on what the criteria mean and how it looks when performance is good or poor; use models; do formative assessments with feedback; make the assessment purpose clear; students must have prerequisite skills; students need to trust the raters; self-assessment using the criteria
Reporting results	Make sure the scores have meaning; treat students equitably; be specific and descriptive; provide evidence; allow time for discussion; emphasize what students can do, not what they can't do; nonthreatening; meaningful to students or parents
Overall	Avoid potential sources of bias and distortion: bias in tasks, criteria, or administration; criteria that don't cover the right "stuff"; poor training of raters; poor student preparation; tasks that don't elicit the right performance; sampling inadequacy; student personality; embarrassment with regard to being compared with others; changing criteria; scheduling the assessment at bad times; fatigue of raters or students; poor student or rater motivation; lack of teacher, student, or rater buy-in; rater bias; developmentally inappropriate tasks or criteria; the tendency for raters to score toward the center of the scale; examinee manipulation of the situation or raters; testwiseness; students not knowing the criteria for success; student anxiety; too much teacher help; negative teacher attitude toward the assessment; readability of assessment materials; distractions during assessment; cultural inappropriateness of tasks

Note. Copyright 1998 by Northwest Regional Educational Laboratory. Adapted with permission.

How to Develop Performance Tasks and Criteria

A good source for assisting teachers to develop performance tasks and a variety of associated rubric types is Jay McTighe's work with the Maryland Assessment Consortium (McTighe, 1996). Here I concentrate on three ways to develop the generalized, analytical trait, detailed performance criteria that are most useful for instruction.

First, given sufficient expertise on the skills for which criteria are being developed, a person can sometimes just sit down and write out the criteria. This process can be illustrated with many common everyday situations. For example, most adults have fun developing criteria for effective whining, room cleaning, or restaurants. In education, most of us are familiar enough with oral presentations that we stand a chance of articulating and writing out decent criteria. And measurement experts usually can write out the criteria for a good-quality performance assessment.

These "off the top of my head" criteria, however, need to be subjected to a reality test. After the criteria have been written down, it is always a good idea to gather samples of the performance under consideration and try to rate them according to one's criteria. This process helps one notice important aspects of performance one has forgotten, borderline cases that need to be clarified through refined statements in the criteria, the need to more clearly specify levels of performance with indicators of quality and so forth. (Note that the criteria for a high-quality performance assessment included in Table 3 do not have levels defined.)

The second way to develop general performance criteria is to simply start with the student work, and this is actually where most teachers begin. Obtain sets of student work that illustrate various levels of quality on the skill in question: writing, communicating mathematical understanding, critical thinking, and so forth. Ask adult learners to sort the work into three performance stacks: strong, medium, and weak. Then have them describe the differences among the stacks (this method is illustrated in detail in Regional Educational Laboratories, 1998, Activity 2.1: Sorting Student Work).

The main problem teachers run into when sorting and describing is using descriptors that are too general. For example, when generating criteria for math problem solving, teachers want to say that one feature of a strong student response is that it is "logical." The challenge is to dig beneath the general descriptor to find the specific characteristics of the work that make one believe it is logical. I usually ask teachers to find a piece they think is logical and point out the aspects that made them think so. They usually mention things such as the following: The student chose the correct information to use, went through from beginning to end without any sidesteps, chose a procedure that would lead to a correct solution, used a problem representation (visual or mathematical) that helped clarify the problem's meaning, restated the problem accurately in his or her own words, seemed to know which representations were right for the problem, and knew when and where to make connections with other knowledge in order to proceed. If such statements can then be connected to actual samples of student work, it provides a powerful instructional tool for teachers and a powerful learning tool for students.

If adult learners have trouble sorting work, they might not have enough of an idea of the construct in question to have formed even intuitive criteria. This leads to the third approach for helping adult learners define performance criteria: They need to read the literature in the content area in question. This frequently occurs, for example, when teachers are attempting to develop criteria for criti-

cal thinking. Defining the construct and collecting relevant samples of student work to sort provides a way to profitably interact with preservice content area courses.

Even though developing criteria is a good exercise, it is fortunate that teachers do not always have to start from scratch. There are many good sources of criteria and rubrics. One of my favorites is Perlman (1994). The 70 or so rubrics in this collection provide a good opportunity for adult learners to practice distinguishing good criteria from weak ones and to practice distinguishing criteria that might work for large-scale assessment from those that might be most useful in the classroom.

Use of Criteria as an Instructional Methodology

There are two steps involved in making performance criteria work as tools for learning in the classroom: having a clear notion in one's own mind of what the criteria are and then teaching them to students. The first step was described in the previous section on developing performance criteria. The second step in making performance criteria work as instructional tools in the classroom is to teach them to students. My colleagues have developed seven strategies for teaching criteria to students (Spandel & Culham, 1998; Spandel & Stiggins, 1997). These strategies were developed in the context of writing, but several of them transfer easily to other performances and products.

The first strategy is to *teach students the vocabulary they need to think and speak like writers, communicators, and problem solvers.* Help students understand the nature of quality through engaging them in the kinds of sorting and descriptive activities described earlier. In other words, engage students in developing criteria for quality. Students need to have versions of criteria written in language they can understand (i.e., "student-friendly" rubrics). For example, the six-trait model has student-friendly versions available for primary elementary and secondary students (Regional Educational Laboratories, 1998). I have also seen student-friendly versions of mathematics problem-solving rubrics produced by the Oregon Department of Education and Washington State's Central Kitsap District (1997).

The second strategy is to *read, discuss, and score anonymous samples of student work.* Once criteria are in place, students need to practice using them, noting what is strong and weak in work. They need to not only judge the quality of work but articulate the reasons for their judgment; there is no such thing as a "correct" score, only a justifiable score. To justify their scores, students are asked to find the words in the rubric that describe the work under consideration.

The third strategy is to *practice focused revision.* In addition to being able to notice what is strong or weak in work, students need to know how to fix that which is weak. One procedure is to ask students to give advice to the author and then work in groups to improve the sample performance using the advice given. For example, when working on ideas in writing, students might note that the paper is weak because it is unfocused, emphasizes irrelevant details, or does not include enough descriptive detail to make a point (all descriptors in the trait of "ideas" in the Appendix). The students might advise the author to narrow the topic by selecting one potentially interesting point and elaborating on it using relevant details and anecdotes. Students would then revise the writing using their own advice.

The fourth strategy is to *use reallife samples to illustrate criteria*. In terms of writing, this can be done with various published items (stories, picture books, manuals, instructions, etc.). In helping students learn, for example, the concept of "voice" in writing, one might ask them to match text to authors (Mark Twain, Nathaniel Hawthorne, etc.). Or one could have students compare different writing styles.

The fifth strategy is to *have students help the teacher revise the teacher's products or performances using the criteria for quality*. For example, you could ask your adult learners to critique the performance assessments you use in your class, give you advice on how to improve them, and help you revise them. In K–12, a teacher could ask students to help revise his or her own writing. Sometimes students are amazed to see that writing does not simply emerge full blown from the pen during the first draft.

The sixth strategy is to *allow students opportunities to articulate their emerging notion of quality*. In writing, for example, students could write letters to authors describing why, using the language of the performance criteria, they like the work, or students could describe their progress to parents using the language of the performance criteria.

The final strategy is to *teach minilessons*. For writing, this means organizing regular instructional lessons by trait: ideas, organization, voice, word choice, sentence fluency and conventions. If the criteria really do describe what we mean by quality, why not teach directly to them? Teachers already teach the traits of good writing. What is often lacking is the conscious link between what is being taught and the standards being developed.

Two papers that articulate well the power of using general performance criteria to help students learn are those of Spandel (1996) and Arter (1996).

I have begun asking participants in my workshops (teachers, administrators, and others) to state the most salient characteristics of "standards-based instruction" as they currently understand it. Admittedly an unscientific sample, here is the essence of what they have said.

- There are clearly stated long-term learning targets for students (content standards): what we want students to know and be able to do when they leave K–12 education.
- There are benchmarks along the way so that we know whether we are on track in terms of guiding students to the ultimate level of competency.
- These learning targets are connected to the real world.
- Instruction and assessment are aimed at these important targets and aligned across grade levels to reduce duplication and make it clear how the skills and understandings developed one year will be built upon the next year.
- Standards-referenced descriptions of student learning are used rather than norm-referenced or self-referenced; we define the nature of quality and match student achievement to it in order to judge achievement.
- Everybody—students, teachers, parents, community members — is aware of the nature of excellence and what it takes to succeed. Students can see where they are. Teachers can tell parents at any time how their children are progressing toward "proficiency."

The performance criteria associated with performance assessments can be a prime example of such standards-based instruction.

- Performance criteria help define standards; they are the final definition.
- Developing performance criteria is more than assessment; it helps instruction.
- Performance criteria make standards clear to students (and teachers).
- Teaching criteria to students improves the very skills being assessed.

Grading and Reporting

Grading and reporting is the final topic in Table 1 that should be covered in a course on performance assessment. This topic is covered more thoroughly in the article by Susan Brookhart and so is not discussed at length here. Let me mention, however, that the most frequent question from teachers relating to performance assessment and grading is "How do I convert rubric scores to grades?" Any instruction on performance assessment would be incomplete without helping teachers think about this question. This question is tricky because the purpose of using rubrics to begin with (to help students learn) can be at odds with the purpose of grading (to report student progress or to discipline or reward students), and frequently rubric scores need to be combined with scores from other types of assessment to arrive at a final grade. As pointed out by many authors (e.g., Association for Supervision and Curriculum Development,

1996; Kohn, 1994), teachers need to first think about the purposes for grading: Who are the users? What are the uses? What is grading supposed to accomplish? From this reflection, a method for combining rubric scores with other measures of student achievement to arrive at a "grade" sometimes emerges. One way to involve teachers in this discussion is provided in Activities 4.2 (Putting Grading and Reporting Questions in Perspective) and 4.6 (How to Convert Rubric Scores to Grades) in Regional Educational Laboratories (1998).

Conclusion

Teachers need to know how to construct, administer, score, and use the results from good-quality performance assessments. They need to know these things not just to grade or satisfy some external mandate (although the current climate demands this), but because expertise in performance assessment can make instruction faster, easier, and better. To help teachers see this, instruction on performance assessment must include building the vision of performance assessment as a tool for learning as well as a tool for tracking student progress. There is also a certain immediacy to teachers' need to know about assessment; they literally need information they can use on Monday morning. If we, as preservice and in-service instructors, cannot capture teachers' attention right away and give them something to use immediately, learning to be good assessors will take a back seat to other topics that vie for teacher attention.

What features of performance assessments make them most useful in the classroom as instructional tools? What is the impact on student achievement of using performance assessment in this manner? What approaches to teaching assessment motivate teachers to want to learn more? These are profitable areas for continuing inquiry and research.

Appendix
The Six-Trait Model for Assessing Student Writing

Note. Copyright 1998 by Northwest Regional Educational Laboratory. Adapted with permission.

Ideas and Content (Development)

Level 5: *This paper is clear and focused. It holds the reader's attention. Relevant anecdotes and details enrich the central theme.*

a. The topic is narrow and manageable.
b. Relevant, telling, quality details give the reader important information that goes beyond the obvious or predictable.
c. Reasonably accurate details are present to support the main ideas.

d. The writer seems to be writing from knowledge or experience; the ideas are fresh and original.
e. The reader's questions are anticipated and answered.
f. Insight—an understanding of life and a knack for picking out what is significant—is an indicator of high-level performance, though not required.

Level 3: *The writer is beginning to define the topic, even though development is still basic or general.*

a. The topic is fairly broad; however, you can see where the writer is headed.
b. Support is attempted but doesn't go far enough yet in fleshing out the key issues or story line.
c. Ideas are reasonably clear, though they may not be detailed, personalized, accurate, or expanded enough to show in-depth understanding or a strong sense of purpose.
d. The writer seems to be drawing on knowledge or experience but has difficulty going from general observations to specifics.
e. The reader is left with questions. More information is needed to "fill in the blanks."
f. The writer generally stays on the topic but does not develop a clear theme. The writer has not yet focused the topic past the obvious.

Level 1: *As yet, the paper has no clear sense of purpose or central theme. To extract meaning from the text, the reader must make inferences based on sketchy or missing details. The writing reflects more than one of these problems:*

a. The writer is still in search of a topic, brainstorming, or has not yet decided what the main idea of the piece will be.
b. Information is limited or unclear or the length is not adequate for development.
c. The idea is a simple restatement of the topic or an answer to the question with little or no attention to detail.
d. The writer has not begun to define the topic in a meaningful, personal way.
e. Everything seems as important as everything else; the reader has a hard time sifting out what is important.
f. The text may be repetitious, or may read like a collection of disconnected, random thoughts with no discernible point.

Organization

Level 5: *The organization enhances and showcases the central idea or theme. The order, structure, or presentation of information is compelling and moves the reader through the text.*

a. An inviting introduction draws the reader in; a satisfying conclusion leaves the reader with a sense of closure and resolution.

b. Thoughtful transitions clearly show how ideas connect.

c. Details seem to fit where they're placed; sequencing is logical and effective.

d. Pacing is well controlled; the writer knows when to slow down and elaborate and when to pick up the pace and move on.

e. The title, if desired, is original and captures the central theme of the piece.

f. Organization flows so smoothly the reader hardly thinks about it; the choice of structure matches the purpose and audience.

Level 3: *The organizational structure is strong enough to move the reader through the text without too much confusion.*

a. The paper has a recoguizable introduction and conclusion. The introduction may not create a strong sense of anticipation; the conclusion may not tie up all loose ends.

b. Transitions often work well; at other times, connections between ideas are fuzzy.

c. Sequencing shows some logic, but not under control enough that it consistently supports the ideas. In fact, sometimes it is so predictable and rehearsed that the structure takes attention away from the content.

d. Pacing is fairly well controlled, though the writer sometimes lunges ahead too quickly or spends too much time on details that do not matter.

e. A title (if desired) is present, although it may be uninspired or an obvious restatement of the prompt or topic.

f. The organization sometimes supports the main point or story line; at other times, the reader feels an urge to slip in a transition or move things around.

Level 1: *The writing lacks a clear sense of direction. Ideas, details, or events seem strung together in a loose or random fashion; there is no identifiable internal structure. The writing reflects more than one of these problems:*

a. There is no real lead to set up what follows, no real conclusion to wrap things up.

b. Connections between ideas are confusing or not even present.

c. Sequencing needs lots and lots of work.

d. Pacing feels awkward; the writer slows to a crawl when the reader wants to get on with it, and vice versa.

e. No title is present (if requested), or if present, does not match well with the content.

f. Problems with organization make it hard for the reader to get a grip on the main point or story line.

Voice

Level 5: *The writer speaks directly to the reader in a way that is individual, compelling, and engaging. The writer "aches with caring," yet is aware and respectful of the audience and the purpose for writing.*

a. The reader feels a strong interaction with the writer, sensing the person behind the words.

b. The writer takes a risk by revealing who he/she is and what he/she thinks.

c. The tone and voice give flavor and texture to the message and are appropriate for the purpose and audience.

d. Narrative writing seems honest, personal, and written from the heart. Expository or persuasive writing reflects a strong commitment to the topic by showing why the reader needs to know this and why they should care.

e. This piece screams to be read aloud, shared, and talked about. The writing makes you think about and react to the author's point of view.

Level 3: *The writer seems sincere, but not fully engaged or involved. The result is pleasant or even personable, but not compelling.*

a. The writing communicates in an earnest, pleasing manner.

b. Only one or two moments here or there surprise, delight, or move the reader.

c. The writer seems aware of an audience but weighs ideas carefully and discards personal insights in favor of safe generalities.

d. Narrative writing seems sincere, but not passionate; expository or persuasive writing lacks consistent engagement with the topic to build credibility.

e. The writer's willinguess to share his/her point of view may emerge strongly at some places, but is often obscured behind vague generalities.

Level 1: *The writer seems indifferent, uninvolved, or distanced from the topic and/or the audience. As a result, the paper reflects more than one of the following problems:*

a. The writer speaks in a kind of monotone that flattens all potential highs or lows of the message.

b. The writing is humdrum and "risk free."

c. The writer is not concerned with the audience, or the writer's style is a complete mismatch for the intended reader.

d. The writing is lifeless or mechanical; depending on the topic, it may be overly technical or jargonistic.

e. No point of view is reflected in the writing.

Word Choice

Level 5: *Words convey the intended message in a precise, interesting, and natural way. The words are powerful and engaging.*

a. Words are specific and accurate; it is easy to understand just what the writer means.

b. The words and phrases create pictures and linger in your mind.

c. The language is natural and never overdone; both words and phrases are individual and effective.

d. Striking words and phrases often catch the reader's eye— and linger in the reader's mind. (You can recall a handful as you reflect on the paper.)

e. Lively verbs energize the writing. Precise nouns and modifiers add depth and specificity

f. Precision is obvious. The writer has taken care to put just the right word or phrase in just the right spot.

Level 3: *The language is functional, even if it lacks much energy. It is easy to figure out the writer's meaning on a general level.*

a. Words are adequate and correct in a general sense; they simply lack much flair and originality.

b. Familiar words and phrases communicate, but rarely capture the reader's imagination. Still, the paper may have one or two fine moments.

c. Attempts at colorful language show a willinguess to stretch and grow, but sometimes it goes too far (thesaurus overload!).

d. The writing is marked by passive verbs, everyday nouns and adjectives, and lack of interesting adverbs.

e. The words are only occasionally refined; it's more often "the first thing that popped into my mind."

f. The words and phrases are functional—with only a moment or two of sparkle.

Level 1: *The writer struggles with a limited vocabulary, searching for words to convey meaning. The writing reflects more than one of these problems:*

a. Language is so vague that only a limited message comes through.

b. "Blah, blah, blah" is all that the reader reads and hears.

c. Words are used incorrectly, making the message secondary to the misfires with the words.

d. Limited vocabulary and/or frequent misuse of parts of speech impair understanding.

e. Jargon or cliches distract or mislead. Persistent redundancy distracts the reader.

f. Problems with language leave the reader wondering what the writer is trying to say. The words just don't work in this piece.

Sentence Fluency

Level 5: *The writing has an easy flow, rhythm, and cadence. Sentences are well built, with strong and varied structure that invites expressive oral reading.*

a. Sentences are constructed in a way that underscores and enhances the meaning.

b. Sentences vary in length as well as structure. Fragments, if used, add style. Dialogue, if present, sounds natural.

c. Purposeful and varied sentence beginnings add variety and energy.

d. The use of creative and appropriate connectives between sentences and thoughts shows how each relates to and builds upon the one before it.

e. The writing has cadence; the writer has thought about the sound of the words as well as the meaning. The first time you read it aloud is a breeze.

Level 3: *The text hums along with a steady beat, but tends to be more pleasant or businesslike than musical, more mechanical than fluid.*

a. Although sentences may not seem artfully crafted or musical, they get the job done in a routine fashion.

b. Sentences are usually constructed correctly; they hang together; they are sound.

c. Sentence beginnings are not all alike; some variety is attempted.

d. The reader sometimes has to hunt for clues (e.g., connecting words and phrases like *however, therefore, naturally, after a while, on the other hand, to be specific, for example, next, first of all, later, but as it turned out, although,* etc.) that show how sentences interrelate.

e. Parts of the text invite expressive oral reading; others may be stiff, awkward, choppy or gangly.

Level 1: *The reader has to practice quite a bit in order to give this paper a fair interpretive reading. The writing reflects more than one of the following problems:*

a. Sentences are choppy, incomplete, rambling, or awkward; they need work. Phrasing does not sound natural. The patterns may create a sing-song rhythm or a chop-chop cadence that lulls the reader to sleep.

b. There is little or no "sentence sense" present. Even if this piece were flawlessly edited, the sentences would not hang together.

c. Many sentences begin the same way—and may follow the same patterns (e.g., *subject-verb-object*).

d. Endless connectives (*and, and so, but then, because, and then,* etc.) or a complete lack of connectives create a massive jumble of language.

e. The text does not invite expressive oral reading.

Conventions

Level 5: *The writer demonstrates a good grasp of standard writing conventions (e.g., spelling, punctuation, capitalization, grammar, usage, paragraphing) and uses conventions effectively to enhance readability. Errors tend to be so few that just minor touch-ups would get this piece ready to publish.*

a. Spelling is generally correct, even on more difficult words.

b. The punctuation is accurate, even creative, and guides the reader through the text.

c. A thorough understanding and consistent application of capitalization skills are present.

d. Grammar and usage are correct and contribute to clarity and style.

e. Paragraphing tends to be sound and reinforces the organizational structure.

f. The writer may manipulate conventions for stylistic effect—and it works! The piece is very close to being ready to publish.

Note: Grades 7 and up only—The writing is sufficiently complex to allow the writer to show skill in using a wide range of conventions. For writers at younger ages, the writing shows control over those conventions that are grade/age appropriate.

Level 3: *The writer shows reasonable control over a limited range of standard writing conventions. Conventions are sometimes handled well and enhance readability; at other times, errors are distracting and impair readability.*

a. Spelling is usually correct or reasonably phonetic on common words, but more difficult words are problematic.

b. End punctuation is usually correct; internal punctuation (*commas, apostrophes, semicolons, dashes, colons, parentheses*) is sometimes missing/wrong.

c. Most words are capitalized correctly; control over more sophisticated capitalization skills may be spotty.

d. Paragraphing is attempted but may run together or begin in the wrong places.

e. Problems with grammar or usage are not serious enough to distort meaning but may not be correct or accurately applied all of the time.

f. Moderate (a little of this, a little of that) editing would be required to polish the text for publication.

Level 1: *Errors in spelling, punctuation, capitalization, usage and grammar, and/or paragraphing repeatedly distract the reader and make the text difficult to read. The writing reflects more than one of these problems:*

a. Spelling errors are frequent, even on common words.

b. Punctuation (including terminal punctuation) is often missing or incorrect.

c. Capitalization is random, and only the easiest rules show awareness of correct use.

d. Errors in grammar or usage are very noticeable, frequent, and affect meaning.

e. Paragraphing is missing, irregular, or so frequent (every sentence) that it has no relationship to the organizational structure of the text.

f. The reader must read once to decode, then again for meaning. Extensive editing (virtually every line) would be required to polish the text for publication.

References

Airasian, P. W. (1991). *Classroom assessment.* New York: McGraw-Hill.

American Federation of Teachers, National Council on Measurement in Education, and National Education Association. (1990). *Standards for teacher competence in educational assessments of students.* Washington, DC: Authors.

Arter, J. (1996). Using assessment as a tool for learning. In R. Blum & J. Arter (Eds.), *Student performance assessment in an era of restructuring.* Alexandria, VA: Association for Supervision and Curriculum Development.

Arter, J., Spandel, V., Culham, R., & Pollard, J. (1994). *The impact of training students to be self-assessors of writing.* Paper presented at the annual meeting of the American Educational Research Association, New Orleans, LA.

Association for Supervision and Curriculum Development. (1996). *Communicating student learning* (T. Guskey, Ed.). Alexandria, VA: Author.

Baker, E. L., Aschbacher, P. R., Niemi, D., & Sato, E. (1992). *CRESST performance assessment models: Assessing content area explanations.* Los Angeles: CRESST.

Borko, H., Mayfield, V., Marion, S., et al. (1997). Teachers' developing ideas and practices about mathematics performance assessment: Successes, stumbling blocks, and implications for professional development. *Teaching and Teacher Education, 13,* 259–278.

Calfee, R., & Perfumo, P. (1993). Student portfolios: Opportunities for a revolution in assessment. *Journal of Reading, 36,* 534.

Central Kitsap School District. (1997). *The student friendly guide to mathematics problem solving.* Silverdale, WA: Author.

Checkley, K. (1997). Assessment that serves instruction. *Education Update, 39*(4), 1.

Clarke, D., & Stephens, M. (1996). The ripple effect: The instructional impact of the systemic introduction of performance assessment in mathematics. In M. Birenbaum & F. Dochy (Eds.), *Alternatives in assessment of achievements, learning processes and prior knowledge.* Norwell, MA: Kluwer Academic.

Constructed Response Supplement to the Iowa Tests. (1997). Itaska, IL: Riverside.

Ennis, R. H., Millman, J., & Tomko, T. (1985). *Cornell Critical Thinking Tests* (3rd ed.). Pacific Grove, CA: Midwest.

Fager, J. J., Plake, B. S., & Impara, J. C. (1997). *Examining teacher educators' knowledge of classroom assessment: A pilot study.* Paper presented at the NCME national conference, Chicago, IL.

Herman, J. (1996). Technical quality matters. In R. Blum & J. Arter (Eds.), *Student performance assessment in an era of restructuring.* Alexandria, VA: Association for Supervision and Curriculum Development.

Herman, J. (1997). *Assessing new assessments: How do they measure up?* Los Angeles: Graduate School of Education and Information Studies, University of California, Los Angeles.

Hibbard, M. (1996). *Education Update, 38*(4), p. 5.

Hills, J. R. (1991). Apathy concerning grading and testing. *Phi Delta Kappan, 72,* 540–545.

Impara, J. C., Plake, B. S., & Fager, J. J. (1993). Teachers' assessment background and attitudes toward testing. *Theory into Practice, 32,* 113–117.

Khattri, N. (1995). *Performance assessments: Observed impacts on teaching and learning.* Washington, DC: Pelavin Associates.

Kohn, A. (1994, October). Grading: The issue is not how but why. *Educational Leadership,* pp. 38–41.

Marzano, R. J., & Kendall, J. S. (1996). *Designing standards-based districts, schools and classrooms.* Aurora, CO: Mid-Continent Regional Educational Laboratory.

Massachusetts State Department of Education. (1983). *Development of the state speaking assessment instrument: Reliability and feasibility.* Malden, MA: Author.

McTighe, J. (1996). Performance-based assessment in the classroom: A planning framework. In R. Blum & J. Arter (Eds.), *Student performance assessment in an era of restructuring.* Alexandria, VA: Association for Supervision and Curriculum Development.

Mendel, S. (undated). *Creating portraits of performance.* Aurora, CO: Peakview Elementary School.

Newmann, F., Secada, W., & Weblage, G. (1995). *A guide to authentic instruction and assessment.* Madison: School of Education, University of Wisconsin.

Norris, S. P (1990). *Test on Appraising Observations.* St. John's, Newfoundland: Memorial University of Newfoundland.

North Dakota Department of Public Instruction. (1998). *North Dakota fourth grade writing calibration packet.* Bismarck, ND: Author. Northwest Regional Educational Laboratory. (1990). Writing assessment: Training in analytical scoring [video]. Los Angeles: lOX.

Northwest Regional Educational Laboratory. (1997). *Seeing with new eyes* [video]. Los Angeles: lOX.

Office of Educational Research and Improvement. (1997). *Studies of education reform: Assessment of student performance.* Washington, DC: Author.

Oregon Department of Education. (1997). *Read Informative and Literary Texts—Official scoring guides.* Salem, OR: Author.

Oregon Department of Education. (1998). *Performance standards.* Available: http://www.open.k12.or.us/jitt/standards/perform.htm

Perlman, C. (1994). *The CPS performance assessment idea book.* Chicago: Chicago Public Schools.

Plake, B. S., Impara, J. C., & Fager, J. J. (1993). Assessment competencies of teachers: A national survey. *Educational Measurement: Issues and Practice, 12*(4), 10–12, 39.

Regional Educational Laboratories. (1998). *Improving classroom assessment: A toolkit for professional developers* (2nd ed.). Portland, OR: Northwest Regional Educational Laboratory.

Rudner, L., & Boston, C. (1994). Performance assessment. *ERIC Review, 3*(1), 2–12.

Shafer, W. D. (1993). Assessment in teacher education. *Theory into Practice, 32*, 118–126.

Spandel, V. (1996, January). Criteria: The power behind revision. *Writing Teacher,* pp. 9–25.

Spandel, V., & Culham, R. (1998). *Writing workshop materials.* Portland, OR: Northwest Regional Educational Laboratory.

Spandel, V., & Stiggins, R. J. (1997). *Creating writers: Linking writing assessment and instruction.* New York: Longman.

Stayter, F., & Johnston, P. (1990). Evaluating the teaching and learning of literacy. In T. Shanahan (Ed.), *Reading and writing together: New perspectives for the classroom.* Norwood, MA: Christopher-Gordon.

Stiggins, R. J. (1997). *Student-centered classroom assessment* (2nd ed.). Columbus, OH: Merrill.

Usrey, P (1998). *The traits of a competent oral communicator.* Portland, OR: Northwest Regional Educational Laboratory.

Vermont Mathematics Portfolio Project. (1991). *Resource book.* Montpelier: Vermont Department of Education.

Washington Commission on Student Learning. (1998). *Assessment sampler Grade 7.* Olympia, WA: Author.

Wiggins, G. (1992, May). Creating tests worth taking. *Educational Leadership,* pp. 26–33.

Wise, S. L., Lukin, L. E., & Roos, L. L. (1991). Teacher beliefs about training in testing and measurement. *Journal of Teacher Education, 42*, 37–42.

Zhang, Z. (1997). *Assessment Practices Inventory: A multivariate analysis of teachers' perceived assessment competency.* Paper presented at the NCME national conference, Chicago, IL.

Judy Arter is Assessment Unit Manager, Northwest Regional Educational Laboratory, 101 SW Main Street, Suite 500, Portland, OR 97204. Her specializations are classroom assessment and performance assessment.

Lessons Learned About Student Portfolios

CLASSROOM PRACTICE

The idea of going beyond test scores to collect more substantive evidence of a school's curriculum and teaching initiatives seemed innovative to faculty members at Crow Island School a decade ago, Ms. Hebert notes. What they didn't know then was that the process of selecting samples of work and assembling them into a portfolio is profoundly important to children.

By Elizabeth A. Hebert

Illustration by John Berry

A DECADE ago we began a project with student portfolios at Crow Island School in Winnetka, Illinois. Influenced by Howard Gardner's theory of multiple intelligences, our faculty explored the many learning experiences of our students and decided to encourage the children to gather their work over time so that they themselves could see evidence of their learning. During the past 10 years we have learned so much more than we imagined. We now know quite a bit about what a portfolio is and probably more about what a portfolio is not. But what continues to energize our thinking after all this time is what a portfolio can be.

When we started this project, we didn't fully understand the possibilities that portfolios could offer. The notion that there could be some child-centered, qualitative supplement to the single-number characterizations of learning emphasized by our testing culture seemed reason enough to organize our efforts and those of our students. The idea of collecting more substantive evidence of our curriculum and teaching initiatives to counteract narrowly defined test scores seemed innovative at the time. What we didn't know then was that the process of selecting samples of one's own work and assembling them into a portfolio is profoundly important to children. We also learned that all children have a natural ability and desire to tell their story through the contents of the portfolio. Even now, we remain excited

From *Phi Delta Kappan,* April 1998, pp. 583–585. © 1998 by Phi Delta Kappa, Inc. Reported by permission.

about capturing the individual voices of our students through portfolio collections.

Over the past 10 years we've discussed and rethought many aspects of our understanding of portfolios. Here are some of the lessons we've taken to heart:

• *Don't get too focused on delineating the contents of the portfolio.* In the early years of our work, we were far too concerned about the specific contents of the portfolios. Looking back, I believe that discussing this matter is a natural way to explore the purposes of portfolios; however, it's important not to become rigid about what goes into a portfolio. I'm always reminded of the wonderful definition offered by staff developers Pearl Paulsen and Leon Paulsen: "Portfolios tell a story. . . . Put in anything that helps to tell the story." The real contents of a portfolio are the child's thoughts and his or her reasons for selecting a particular entry. That selection process reflects the interests and metacognitive maturity of the child and the inspiration and influence offered by the teachers.

When teachers first get involved with portfolios, they tend to have different ideas and suggestions about what to put on the portfolio "must list." Fortunately, we never committed ourselves to making such a list, and I suspect that is why, in part, we are still so fascinated with this topic. After 10 years we realize that there is no best notion of what goes into a portfolio; rather, portfolios serve as a metaphor for our continued belief in the idea that children can play a major role in the assessment of their own learning. This perspective, rather than a predetermined list of curriculum samples, should be the guideline for placing particular items into a portfolio.

• *The "container" issue.* Initially, most teachers gathered children's work in a wide variety of containers. Hanging file folders became a popular organizing tool. The issue of what work was sent home and what work stayed in the classroom was important in the early years. It took time to establish the expectation that most of the children's work would stay at school. Faculty members spent many hours discussing details: the type and color of containers, the location and labeling of the intermediate gathering folders, the importance of dating all student work, and the directions we would give to the students about selections. Some tensions and anxieties surfaced in response to our open conversations, and there were some disagreements about the contents and purposes of portfolios.

Thus the security of knowing we would definitely be using red, yellow, blue, and green legal-sized folders in grades 1–4 and black binders in grade 5 was a source of great comfort. Issues of giving tangible form to the often unwieldy openness of student-centered portfolios need to be addressed but must be secondary to the larger and more fundamental discussions about what a portfolio can represent about a child's learning.

• *Whose portfolio is it?* Because our initial understanding was that portfolios might counterbalance the narrowness of test scores with concrete examples of our students' interests and abilities, we assumed the role of portfolio managers. The notion that children could or should participate in the selection of the contents of the portfolios was intriguing to us, but we didn't have a clear plan to implement that idea.

How does the child know what to choose? What if a child doesn't select balanced evidence of the teacher's curriculum for his or her portfolio? Is it appropriate for a child to present a portfolio that excludes a major content area? These questions continue to be a part of our ongoing discussions as we discover the ever-growing metacognitive voices of our children—voices that we train to become competent and thoughtful tellers of the stories of their learning.

We now believe that the selection of the contents of the portfolio is an evolving process shared by child and teacher. When children are just beginning to understand what a portfolio is, they require clear scaffolding. We advise students about including certain pieces of work that we feel will be valued—if not now, at a later time. We have discovered that the conversations that take place as portfolios are being compiled give the children the security to suggest additional entries that are more personal or unique to their own school experience. One message about child ownership is very clear: we do not assign a letter grade or evaluation to the portfolio. We honor the child's world that is represented by the portfolio. We want to learn more about that world so that we can more sensitively help each child grow.

• *An archive adds a sense of history to the portfolio.* As children's work was gathered, we were uncertain what to do with it at the close of the school year. Our faculty discussions emphasized how important it was for the children to have access to their work over time so that they could develop a better understanding of their histories

as students. We decided to use the term *portfolio* when referring to a single year's selection of works and *archive* for the total collection, which could span up to six years (K–5). Establishing the physical space to house an archive (in our school, the library/resource center) was an important step: It signaled to all children that each of them was an important part of the history of our school.

• *Defining an audience is crucial.* The notion of gathering work to "tell your story" is far too abstract for young students unless they know who is listening to that story. The question of the contents of a portfolio becomes much clearer once an audience is defined. For our students; the parents were the most natural audience. Other audiences could be siblings, other students from the same or different grade levels, prior teachers in the school, or senior citizens in the community.

• *Attaching meaning to the contents of the portfolio contributes to the child's metacognitive growth.* The collecting of student work was initially overwhelming. Some students saved everything, and others were reluctant to make a decision about what to select for their portfolios. We needed a mechanism to assist students—and ourselves—in managing the size of an individual portfolio and, more important, to inject more thoughtfulness into the selection process. The idea of "reflection tags" quickly worked its way around the building. The basic idea is to consider reasons for including a piece of work in the portfolio, to record these statements of value on a tag of paper, and to attach the tag to the sample of student work. This idea is usually presented in a rug-time discussion with students.

In the early grades, conversations with children focus on the purposes of maintaining a portfolio. In first grade, students are reminded of the baby books that their parents have put together. This example introduces the concepts of purposeful selection, life history, and evidence of change over time. "Now that you're in first grade, you will select some of your first-grade work, and we'll keep it in a portfolio." The first-graders love the sound of this grown-up word and remember that their kindergarten teachers introduced this idea to them last spring. Often fifth-grade student buddies assist the children in sorting through their work and selecting items for their portfolios.

In second grade, children may be asked, "Why would you put something in your portfolio?" "Because it's my best work" is usually the first response. With patience, the teacher elicits further value statements from the students. "Because I'm proud of it." "Because I didn't think I could do this." "Because I worked very hard on it." The teacher records these thoughts on tags of paper and asks the children to affix them to particular entries in their portfolios. "Do you have any blank tags?" asks another student, demonstrating that further ideas have occurred about why one keeps artifacts in a portfolio and indicating that the transfer of ownership from teacher to child has begun. The use of individual reflection tags (or some other open-ended written reflection) about the contents of a portfolio is an important element in portfolio construction. The physical act of attaching meaning to a specific piece of work contributes significantly to the child's metacognitive growth.

• *A celebratory event brings child, portfolio, and audience together.* Trying to balance the micro and macro issues surrounding our portfolio project was no small task. Discussions about contents, containers, file folders, and the location of the archive, together with the philosophical issues of portfolio ownership, the role of portfolios in assessment, and educating parents about the use of portfolios, had us going in many directions at once. What we needed was a unifying experience that would consolidate all our discussions and concerns and that would clearly communicate to both students and parents the value we assigned to portfolios.

Learning is worth celebrating, and children can be competent participants in that celebration. Gradually we have developed structures to express that belief as part of our school culture. By far, the most powerful celebration of student competence has been the Portfolio Evening, an opportunity for children to present their portfolios to their own parents. At one of our regularly scheduled conferences with parents, the children are given the responsibility to present their portfolios individually to their parents and to explain to them the process by which the materials were generated, the self-reflections involved in the selection of the materials, the conversations with the teacher that spurred particular choices, and any other aspects of their "learning stories" they want to share.

To prepare for this event, the children spend several weeks talking about their portfolios and archives with their teachers, with peers, and often with older students. Specific lessons are focused on how to organize selections of work; how to place them in chronological order; how to think about work as evidence of competence in more than one subject area; how to compare earlier work with present work, showing the acquisition of more advanced skills; and, most important, how to reflect on the portfolio as a whole. Students complete portfolio means called "Ask me about" sheets. On these organizing sheets the students highlight the contents of their portfolios and emphasize learning experiences that are important to their portfolio story.

Another aspect of the Portfolio Evening is the production of a classroom videotape of approximately 15 to 20 minutes in length. The video is intended to portray a day in the life of this particular group of students, including the learning that takes place in special subject areas of art, music, physical education, Spanish, and computers. In addition, many videotapes include recess activities and selected field trips. The project of organizing, scripting, and filming these videotapes is one that the children look forward to with great enthusiasm. Of greater value, however, is the fact that the production of this brief videotape provides an important metacognitive task for each group of children as they reflect on and develop descriptive language for each segment of the school day—as they understand it.

The dates of the Portfolio Evenings appear on the annual school calendar, and parents are also invited by letter. The event takes place over two nights, with half of the class and their parents attending each night for approximately 90 minutes. In the days just prior to the event, the children add final touches to their presentations and select an area of the classroom where they can hold a private conversation with their parents.

• *Parent education is required.* Another lesson we have learned is that we need to deliberately teach the parents about the value of student portfolios—what they mean to us, how we use them as a part of our curriculum, their immeasurable value to the children, and how they fit into an assessment program for our school. It's important to emphasize that portfolios do not replace more standardized measures. Standardized tests address the question "Which child knows more?" whereas portfolios address the question. "What does this child know?" One question is not better than the other; posing both questions will provide a more comprehensive perspective of a child's work in school.

For the past three years a panel of eight faculty members representing grades K–5 have presented an informational program for our parents. At this evening meeting, the teachers speak briefly about their understanding of the value and purposes of portfolios for the particular age group they teach. From our years of conversations and direct experience, we are able to provide the scaffolding that enables parents to better understand their children's portfolio presentations and gain a more in-depth view of their children as learners.

These are some of the lessons we've learned about portfolios over the past 10 years. When the adoption of portfolios is first being considered, it's important to begin with a discussion of beliefs about children and learning and the connection between them. And then, of course, there's the question "What is our role in all of this?" More than any book we've read or speaker we've listened to, our own ongoing discussions about portfolios—what they can do and represent—provide direction for our own professional growth. It is important for us to continue to take the time we need to pursue this topic in depth, and we continue to share with one another any new activities and suggestions that might be helpful.

The involvement, the sense of connectedness, and the self-discovery that children demonstrate in compiling their portfolios have taught us that our work over these 10 years has to a large extent fulfilled many of the promises that we though portfolios held. Of course, we know that there are many more lessons to be learned as we listen intently to the children during this process and learn more about the meaning and value they assign to the development of their portfolios.

ELIZABETH A. HERBERT is the principal of Crow Island School, Winnetka, Ill.

Grades: The Final Frontier in Assessment Reform

The task of reforming educational assessment has just begun. New forms of assessment cannot provide clearer or more complete information about student achievement unless the ways in which achievement is communicated are refined. The real challenge for assessment reform will be to bring assessment and grading practices into the fold.

By Gregory J. Cizek

Assessment reform has become a centerpiece of efforts to improve U.S. education (Stiggins, 1988; Wolf, LeMahieu, and Eresh, 1992). The list of innovations is familiar: Students are preparing portfolios of their work to demonstrate complex characteristics like employability skills. Teachers are gathering and synthesizing more information about students involving a greater diversity of valuable educational outcomes. Administrators are evaluating the use of new forms of assessment. Districts are rethinking promotion and retention policies and the measures used to inform those decisions. Professional associations are promulgating new standards for both content and assessment. Test publishers are incorporating a wider variety of alternative assessment formats into their products. Nationally, the importance of assessment can be seen in the Goals 2000 legislation and other federal initiatives.

One might conclude that assessment reform efforts are making great strides toward a common goal: improving the range and quality of information about educational performance available to students, teachers, parents, administrators, and the public. But, maybe not.

How Performance Is Communicated

Despite all the other changes, a student's educational performance is still primarily reported using grades. Actually, the older term "marks" might be more accurate than grades, because the way achievement is reported does not always involve the use of grades. Instead, the marks *might* be in the form of letters (A, B, C, D, F); numbers (percent correct); symbols (S = Satisfactory, N = Needs Improvement, U = Unsatisfactory); descriptors (Emerging, Developing, Maturing); or other systems.

Regardless of the kinds of marks, however, at the local level, where an individual student's performance matters most to the student, parents, teachers, and others intimately involved in the student's education, grades continue to be relied upon to communicate important information about performance and progress. But they probably don't.

What's Wrong with Grades?

Grades in whatever form are primitive tools for doing the job they are asked to accomplish. As communication devices, they are more like two tin cans and a length of string

Despite all the other changes, a student's educational performance is still primarily reported using grades.

than a cellular phone. It's an interesting contrast: As bubble sheets whiz through a scanner in a district testing office, a teacher mulls a pile of papers with stickers and happy faces on them, concluding that this student's work merits an A for the marking period.

In a recent study, teachers from midwestern schools were asked about their assessment and grading practices. The findings revealed great differences in what teachers do, and great uncertainty about what they

should do. For example, teachers were asked to indicate what factors they consider when assigning marks to assignments and tests. A clear majority (83 percent) indicated they considered the percent or number correct on the assignment; from one-third to one-half the teachers, however, also said they considered the difficulty of the assignment, how the class performed overall, the individual students' ability levels, and the effort a student put into the work.

It appears that nearly *everything* is considered when assigning a mark. There are probably two reasons for this. First, educators want to consider all relevant aspects of a student's classroom experience when assigning a mark. At the same time, there is apparently no clear consensus about which factors *are* relevant to assigning a grade.

What about final grades? To this question, teachers responded that they combined the marks they had assigned to individual assignments and tests—that uncertain mix described above—with three other kinds of information:

- Formal achievement-related measures (attendance, class participation)
- Informal achievement-related measures (answers in class, one-on-one discussions)
- Other informal information (impressions of effort, conduct, teamwork, leadership, and so on).

Unfortunately, this mix of factors is difficult to disentangle. In an attempt to clear things up, teachers were asked to explain how they combine these diverse factors into a single mark. The interviews led to other revealing perspectives on classroom assessment practice.

Deciding on a Grade

Many teachers expressed a clear preference for non-cognitive outcomes. As one elementary teacher said, "Getting the child through the level with a positive attitude and good memories is more important than a raw number grade.... Shaping the kids' minds through group interaction, effort, and participation is more important than averaging tests and quiz scores."

Another teacher reported that "assignments, quizzes, and tests are not crucial in [her] grading policies." This teacher "stresses group interaction and uses several other subjective methods combined with intuition to formulate a final grade." Attendance and participation were also highly valued by the teachers in the study, and these factors were also considered in assigning a final grade.

It was particularly interesting to learn how teachers reported combining the divergent sources of information into the final grade. Although many teachers did not provide much detail regarding how the composite was formed, one teacher said she "considers attendance, participation, effort, conduct,

and teamwork, and adds to this things such as tests and quizzes."

Another teacher was more specific about details. She designs the test she uses herself, and uses "an average of 16–20 grades during the grading period in calculating the final grade. However, the lower grades are not factored into the average." To this mix, she adds her "overall impressions of effort and how the class performed."

Attendance and participation were also highly valued by the teachers in the study, and these factors were also considered in assigning a final grade.

The practice described by this teacher is apparently not uncommon. Several teachers reported similar practices, throwing out the worst quiz score for each student, considering class performance as a whole, and considering impressions of a student's effort and ability.

The practice of "throwing out" one or more poor scores on formal assessments is apparently quite widespread. Ostensibly, teachers use the practice so that a single low score does not inappropriately affect a student's grade. No teacher, however, reported throwing out a single high score that might inappropriately inflate a student's final grade.

Finally, several teachers made specific mention of taking "extra credit" into account when assigning the final grade.

What Do These Practices Tell Us?

Taken together, these practices point to what might be called a *success orientation* in assigning marks. While educators consider a variety of factors in assigning a final grade, they combine the information in idiosyncratic ways: Not only do different teachers use different factors, they also combine the elements in different proportions within classrooms. The factors considered in arriving at a final grade are weighted in ways that are most advantageous for each student.

In math class, for example, a student who has not mastered fractions may still be awarded a B+ for maintaining a positive attitude, regularly participating in class discussions, and trying hard. On the other hand, an A student who has mastered fractions would usually not be downgraded for being pessimistic, silent during discussions, and "coasting."

Teachers seem to follow the advice our parents gave us: "If you can't say something nice about someone, don't say anything at all." In most cases, they are able to find something good to say.

Although our parents may be happy that we are following their advice, the parents of the students may not be so happy. They assume grades indicate achievement or content mastery. Students themselves are unlikely to be sophisticated enough to understand that their grades are complex composites. Instead, they probably assume—as nearly everyone else does—that their A's and B's mean they have successfully mastered rigorous academic work.

Perhaps the innovations accompanying assessment reform have prompted teachers to gather a more diverse array of information about student performance. The new problems, though, are "What should be done with all this information?" or "How should grades be assigned?" Unfortunately, these are questions that educators are currently not well-prepared to answer. Today many teachers are simply not comfortable with the task of assigning grades.

At least two factors contribute to the problem:

First, little training in educational assessment is available at undergraduate and graduate levels of teacher training, and competence in assessment is not always a prerequisite to licensure.[1]

The research paints an even grimmer picture about the training and experience of administrators with respect to assessment. A recent study sponsored by the National Association of Elementary School Principals (NAESP), the American Association of School Administrators (AASA), and the National Association of Secondary School Principals (NASSP) illustrates the need for educational leaders to become more "assessment literate" (Stiggins, 1991; Impara, 1993).

Second, many educators simply lack an interest in testing and grading (Hills, 1991).

Grades and Report Cards: What Can Be Done?

The lack of knowledge and interest in grading translates into a serious information breakdown in education. A recent study of how the content of report cards facilitates or hinders parents' understanding of the information they provide was not optimistic. The authors concluded that report cards are not successfully transmitting teachers' intended meaning to parents (Waltman and Frisbie, 1994).

The reform of classroom assessment and grading practices must become a top priority if educational improvement is to be effective. New forms of assessment are welcome, but there will be no educational advantage if the meaning of these measures remains murky. Assessment reforms have introduced a wealth of information to teachers, parents, and students. Our ability to *use* this information, however, has remained essentially unchanged.

The lack of knowledge and interest in grading translates into a serious information breakdown in education.

At least eight initiatives are warranted; the effort should include all who are interested in reform.

1. All educators must make a commitment to professional development.

Professional development in assessment should become a top priority. There may be different focuses for these efforts: Teachers may be more interested in classroom assessment issues and administrators may be more in need of developing a vision for integrated, planned assessment systems.

2. Training in assessment must be relevant to classrooms.

Even when teachers and administrators receive formal training in assessment, university coursework often focuses on aspects of testing and grading that may not be applicable to those who actually *do* these things. College coursework should be redesigned to provide more relevant training.

3. Professional organizations must promote sound assessment practice.

Professional organizations have become active in this area,[2] although more work is necessary to highlight the need for assessment competence and the benefits of sound assessment practices for both teachers and students.

4. Educational leaders must develop an "assessment vision."

Considering the increasing attention to assessment and all the diverse purposes it serves, it is fair to say the big picture in educational assessment is sometimes chaotic, and is perhaps the most neglected issue in assessment reform. Educational leaders should promote a clear, coordinated conception about the varieties of assessment in classrooms and the purposes and uses they serve.[3] To be effective in promoting reforms, this vision must be

communicated to teachers, parents, community members, and students.

5. Grading policies must be developed and applied consistently.

Administrators, parents, and teachers must work together to develop, disseminate, and maintain consistent grading policies. To maximize the utility of grades, developmental efforts should work to build consensus on the policies, listening closely to the information needs of parents, students, employers, and universities. A beginning effort might include discussions about what current policies reveal about the need for assessment reform: for example, many policies simply list percentage ranges for A's, B's, C's, D's, and F's and give teachers little additional guidance about sound evaluation practices.

6. End isolation.

Poor assessment practices flourish in schools where teachers are isolated and do not benefit from interaction about difficult assessment issues. Teachers must take the initiative to collaborate and cooperate on testing and grading practices. Administrators must facilitate collaboration and encourage consistency in grading practices.

7. Students must be initiated into a new grading culture.

Students often see grades and learning as separate, or value grades more than education. A significant educational reform will help students see the link between mastery of knowledge, skills, and abilities, and the grades they receive. We should teach students to value real learning.

8. Assessment experts must lend a hand.

New methods of assessment promise more and better information about student performance, but proliferation of innovative assessment formats has outstripped the development of ways to interpret and report this information. Experts in testing should explore new ways of synthesizing and communicating the information provided by alternative assessments to take full advantage of the innovations.

As the list of challenges implies, the task of assessment reform has just begun. New forms of assessment such as portfolios or performance assessments cannot provide clearer or more complete information about student achievement unless the ways achievement is communicated are refined. The real challenge for assessment will be to make assessment and grading practices part of the reform effort.

Notes

1. These problems have been well-documented for several years. See, for example, Ward (1980), Gullickson (1986), Schafer and Lissitz (1987), O'Sullivan and Chalnick (1991), and Wise, Lukin, and Roos (1991).
2. For one example, see the Standards for Teacher Competence in Educational Assessment of Students, developed by the Ameri-

can Federation of Teachers, National Council on Measurement in Education, and National Education Association, Washington, D.C., 1990.

3. See Cizek and Rachor (1994) for a more detailed description about what such a vision might entail—what the authors refer to as "planned assessment systems."

References

American Federation of Teachers, National Council on Measurement in Education, National Education Association. *Standards for Teacher Competence in Educational Assessment of Students.* Washington, D.C.: National Council on Measurement in Education, 1990.

Cizek, G. J., and Rachor, R. E. "The Real Testing Bias: The Role of Values in Educational Assessment." *NASSP Bulletin,* March 1994.

Gullickson, A. R. "Teacher Education and Teacher-Perceived Needs in Educational Measurement and Evaluation." *Journal of Educational Measurement* 23(1986): 347–54.

Hills, J. R. "Apathy Concerning Testing and Grading." *Phi Delta Kappan* 72(1991): 540–45.

Impara, J. C. "Joint Committee on Competency Standards in Student Assessment for Educational Administrators Update: Assessment Survey Results." Presented at the Annual Meeting of the National Council on Measurement, New Orleans, La., April 1993.

O'Sullivan, R. G., and Chalnick, M. K. "Measurement-Related Course Work Requirements for Teacher Certification and Recertification." *Educational Measurement: Issues and Practice* 10(1991): 17–19, 23.

Schafer, W. D., and Lissitz, R. W. "Measurement Training for School Personnel: Recommendations and Reality." *Journal of Teacher Education* 38(1987): 57–63.

Stiggins, R. J. "Assessment Literacy." *Phi Delta Kappan* 72(1991): 534–39.

_____. "Revitalizing Classroom Assessment: The Highest Instructional Priority." *Phi Delta Kappan* 69(1988): 363–68.

Waltman, K. K., and Frisbie, D. A. "Parents' Understanding of Their Children's Report Card Grades." *Applied Measurement in Education* 7(1994): 223–40.

Ward, J. G. "Teachers and Testing: A Survey of Knowledge and Attitudes." In *Testing in Our Schools,* edited by L. M. Rudner. Washington, D.C.: National Institute of Education, 1980.

Wise, S. L.; Lukin, L. E.; and Roos, L. L. "Teacher Beliefs About Training in Testing and Measurement." *Journal of Teacher Education* 42(1991): 37–42.

Wolf, D. P.; LeMahieu, P. G.; and Eresh, J. "Good Measure: Assessment as a Tool for Educational Reform." *Educational Leadership* 49(1992): 8–13.

Acknowledgment: The author is grateful for the support of this work provided by the University of Toledo College of Education and Allied Professions.

Gregory J. Cizek is associate professor of educational research and measurement, University of Toledo, Ohio; readers may continue the dialogue on the Internet at **gcizek@utnet.utoledo.edu.**

Test Your Knowledge Form

We encourage you to photocopy and use this page as a tool to assess how the articles in **Annual Editions** expand on the information in your textbook. By reflecting on the articles you will gain enhanced text information. You can also access this useful form on a product's book support Web site at **http://www.dushkin.com/online/.**

NAME: DATE:

TITLE AND NUMBER OF ARTICLE:

BRIEFLY STATE THE MAIN IDEA OF THIS ARTICLE:

LIST THREE IMPORTANT FACTS THAT THE AUTHOR USES TO SUPPORT THE MAIN IDEA:

WHAT INFORMATION OR IDEAS DISCUSSED IN THIS ARTICLE ARE ALSO DISCUSSED IN YOUR TEXTBOOK OR OTHER READINGS THAT YOU HAVE DONE? LIST THE TEXTBOOK CHAPTERS AND PAGE NUMBERS:

LIST ANY EXAMPLES OF BIAS OR FAULTY REASONING THAT YOU FOUND IN THE ARTICLE:

LIST ANY NEW TERMS/CONCEPTS THAT WERE DISCUSSED IN THE ARTICLE, AND WRITE A SHORT DEFINITION:

ANNUAL EDITIONS revisions depend on two major opinion sources: one is our Advisory Board, listed in the front of this volume, which works with us in scanning the thousands of articles published in the public press each year; the other is you—the person actually using the book. Please help us and the users of the next edition by completing the prepaid article rating form on this page and returning it to us. Thank you for your help!

ANNUAL EDITIONS: Educational Psychology 01/02

ARTICLE RATING FORM

Here is an opportunity for you to have direct input into the next revision of this volume. We would like you to rate each of the 42 articles listed below, using the following scale:

1. Excellent: should definitely be retained
2. Above average: should probably be retained
3. Below average: should probably be deleted
4. Poor: should definitely be deleted

Your ratings will play a vital part in the next revision. So please mail this prepaid form to us just as soon as you complete it. Thanks for your help!

RATING

ARTICLE

1. The Year That I Really Learned How to Teach
2. Reflection Is at the Heart of Practice
3. Schools and Curricula for the 21st Century: Predictions, Visions, and Anticipations
4. The Standards Juggernaut
5. What Do We Know From Brain Research?
6. Play an Endangered Species
7. Re-Evaluating Significance of Baby's Bond With Mother
8. Self-Esteem and Beyond
9. How Well Do You Know Your Kid?
10. The Truth About High School
11. Does My Child Need Ritalin? Stimulants Are Still the Most Effective Treatment for ADHD. The Challenge Is to Use Them Wisely
12. Good Questions to Ask: When a Child With a Developmental Delay Joins Your Class
13. Meeting the Needs of Gifted Learners in the Early Childhood Classroom
14. Gifted Students Need an Education, Too
15. The Goals and Track Record of Multicultural Education
16. Celebrate Diversity!
17. Cultural and Language Diversity in the Middle Grades
18. Voices and Voces: Cultural and Linguistic Dimensions of Giftedness
19. Brain Basics: Cognitive Psychology and Its Implications for Education
20. In Search of . . . Brain-Based Education
21. Educators Need to Know About the Human Brain

RATING

ARTICLE

22. Ability and Expertise: It's Time to Replace the Current Model of Intelligence
23. Caution—Praise Can Be Dangerous
24. Constructivist Theory in the Classroom: Internalizing Concepts Through Inquiry Learning
25. The Challenges of Sustaining a Constructivist Classroom Culture
26. Keeping in Character: A Time-Tested Solution
27. Improving Student Thinking
28. Mapping a Route Toward Differentiated Instruction
29. Reconcilable Differences? Standards-Based Teaching and Differentiation
30. Educating the Net Generation
31. Intrinsic and Extrinsic Motivations: Classic Definitions and New Directions
32. Self-Efficacy: An Essential Motive to Learn
33. I Think I Can, I Think I Can: Understanding and Encouraging Mastery Motivation in Young Children
34. Moving Beyond Management as Sheer Compliance: Helping Students to Develop Goal Coordination Strategies
35. Teaching Students to Regulate Their Own Behavior
36. Using Classroom Rules to Construct Behavior
37. How to Defuse Defiance, Threats, Challenges, Confrontations . . .
38. Salinas, California: Peace Breaks Out
39. Why Standardized Tests Don't Measure Educational Quality
40. Teaching About Performance Assessment
41. Lessons Learned About Student Portfolios
42. Grades: The Final Frontier in Assessment Reform

(Continued on next page)

We Want Your Advice

ANNUAL EDITIONS: EDUCATIONAL PSYCHOLOGY 01/02

BUSINESS REPLY MAIL
FIRST-CLASS MAIL PERMIT NO. 84 GUILFORD CT

POSTAGE WILL BE PAID BY ADDRESSEE

McGraw-Hill/Dushkin
530 Old Whitfield Street
Guilford, CT 06437-9989

Ill...Il...I.I.I.Il.IlI.I.IlI.I.I.I.I.I.I.I.I.I.I.I.I.I

ABOUT YOU

Name   Date
_____   _____

Are you a teacher? ☐ A student? ☐
Your school's name
_____

Department
_____

Address   City   State   Zip
_____

School telephone #
_____

YOUR COMMENTS ARE IMPORTANT TO US !

Please fill in the following information:
For which course did you use this book?
_____

Did you use a text with this *ANNUAL EDITION*? ☐ yes ☐ no
What was the title of the text?
_____

What are your general reactions to the *Annual Editions* concept?
_____

Have you read any particular articles recently that you think should be included in the next edition?
_____

Are there any articles you feel should be replaced in the next edition? Why?
_____

Are there any World Wide Web sites you feel should be included in the next edition? Please annotate.
_____

May we contact you for editorial input? ☐ yes ☐ no
May we quote your comments? ☐ yes ☐ no